CHOCTAW OF MISSISSIPPI INDIAN CENSUS 1929 - 1932
WITH
BIRTHS AND DEATHS 1924 - 1931

VOLUME I

TRANSCRIBED BY

JEFF BOWEN

NATIVE STUDY
Gallipolis, Ohio
USA

Copyright © 2022
by Jeff Bowen

ALL RIGHTS RESERVED
No part of this publication may be reproduced,
distributed, or transmitted in any form or by any means,
without the prior written permission of the publisher.

Originally published:
Signal Mountain, Tennessee
1997

Santa Maria, California
2020

Reprinted by:

Native Study LLC
Gallipolis, Ohio
www.nativestudy.com

Library of Congress Control Number: 2022905968

ISBN: 978-1-64968-157-7

Title Page Image:
Moshulatubbee (He-who-puts-out-and-kills)
by Geo. Catlin, 1834

Made in the United States of America.

This series is dedicated to the
people within these pages and
their ancestors.

Other Books and Series by Jeff Bowen

Compilation of History of the Cherokee Indians and Early History of the Cherokees by Emmet Starr with Combined Full Name Index
(Hardbound & Softbound)

1901-1907 Native American Census Seneca, Eastern Shawnee, Miami, Modoc, Ottawa, Peoria, Quapaw, and Wyandotte Indians (Under Seneca School, Indian Territory)

1932 Census of The Standing Rock Sioux Reservation with Births And Deaths 1924-1932

Census of The Blackfeet, Montana, 1897- 1901 Expanded Edition

Eastern Cherokee by Blood, 1906-1910, Volumes I thru XIII

Choctaw of Mississippi Indian Census 1929-1932 with Births and Deaths 1924-1931 Volume I
Choctaw of Mississippi Indian Census 1933, 1934 & 1937, Supplemental Rolls to 1934 & 1935 with Births and Deaths 1932-1938, and Marriages 1936-1938 Volume II

Eastern Cherokee Census Cherokee, North Carolina 1930-1939 Census 1930-1931 with Births And Deaths 1924-1931 Taken By Agent L. W. Page Volume I
Eastern Cherokee Census Cherokee, North Carolina 1930-1939 Census 1932-1933 with Births And Deaths 1930-1932 Taken By Agent R. L. Spalsbury Volume II
Eastern Cherokee Census Cherokee, North Carolina 1930-1939 Census 1934-1937 with Births and Deaths 1925-1938 and Marriages 1936 & 1938 Taken by Agents R. L. Spalsbury And Harold W. Foght Volume III

Seminole of Florida Indian Census, 1930-1940 with Birth and Death Records, 1930-1938

Texas Cherokees 1820-1839 A Document For Litigation 1921

Starr Roll 1894 (Cherokee Payment Rolls) Districts: Canadian, Cooweescoowee, and Delaware Volume One
Starr Roll 1894 (Cherokee Payment Rolls) Districts: Flint, Going Snake, and Illinois Volume Two
Starr Roll 1894 (Cherokee Payment Rolls) Districts: Saline, Sequoyah, and Tahlequah; Including Orphan Roll Volume Three

Cherokee Intruder Cases Dockets of Hearings 1901-1909 Volumes I & II

Indian Wills, 1911-1921 Records of the Bureau of Indian Affairs Books One thru Seven

Other Books and Series by Jeff Bowen

Native American Wills & Probate Records 1911-1921

Turtle Mountain Reservation Chippewa Indians 1932 Census with Births & Deaths, 1924-1932

Chickasaw By Blood Enrollment Cards 1898-1914 Volume I thru V

Cherokee Descendants East An Index to the Guion Miller Applications Volume I
Cherokee Descendants West An Index to the Guion Miller Applications Volume II (A-M)
Cherokee Descendants West An Index to the Guion Miller Applications Volume III (N-Z)

Applications for Enrollment of Seminole Newborn Freedmen, Act of 1905

Eastern Cherokee Census, Cherokee, North Carolina, 1915-1922, Taken by Agent James E. Henderson
    Volume I (1915-1916)
    Volume II (1917-1918)
    Volume III (1919-1920)
    Volume IV (1921-1922)

Complete Delaware Roll of 1898

Eastern Cherokee Census, Cherokee, North Carolina, 1923-1929, Taken by Agent James E. Henderson
    Volume I (1923-1924)
    Volume II (1925-1926)
    Volume III (1927-1929)

Applications for Enrollment of Seminole Newborn Act of 1905 Volumes I & II

North Carolina Eastern Cherokee Indian Census 1898-1899, 1904, 1906, 1909-1912, 1914 Revised and Expanded Edition

1932 Hopi and Navajo Native American Census with Birth & Death Rolls (1925-1931) Volume 1 - Hopi
1932 Hopi and Navajo Native American Census with Birth & Death Rolls (1930-1932) Volume 2 - Navajo

Western Navajo Reservation Navajo, Hopi and Paiute 1933 Census with Birth & Death Rolls 1925-1933

Cherokee Citizenship Commission Dockets 1880-1884 and 1887-1889 Volumes I thru V

Applications for Enrollment of Chickasaw Newborn Act of 1905 Volumes I thru VII

Other Books and Series by Jeff Bowen

Cherokee Intermarried White 1906 Volume I thru X

Applications for Enrollment of Creek Newborn Act of 1905 Volumes I thru XIV

Applications for Enrollment of Choctaw Newborn Act of 1905 Volumes I thru XX

Choctaw By Blood Enrollment Cards 1898-1914 Volumes I thru XX

Oglala Sioux Indians Pine Ridge Reservation 1932 Census Book I
Oglala Sioux Indians Pine Ridge Reservation Birth and Death Rolls 1924-1932 Book II

Census of the Sioux and Cheyenne Indians of Pine Ridge Agency 1896 - 1897 Book I
Census of the Sioux and Cheyenne Indians of Pine Ridge Agency 1898 - 1899 Book II

Northern Cheyenne Tongue River, Montana 1904 - 1932 Census 1904-1916 Volume I
Northern Cheyenne Tongue River, Montana 1904 - 1932 Census 1917-1926 Volume II

Identified Mississippi Choctaw Enrollment Cards 1902-1909 Volumes I, II & III

Sac & Fox - Shawnee Estates 1885-1910 (Under Sac & Fox Agency) Volumes I-VIII
Sac & Fox - Shawnee Estates 1920-1924 (Under The Sac & Fox Agency, Oklahoma) & Wills 1889-1924 Volume IX
Sac & Fox - Shawnee Deaths, Cemetery, Births, & Marriage Cards (Under The Sac & Fox Agency, Oklahoma) 1853-1933 Volume X
Sac & Fox - Shawnee Marriages, Divorces, Estates Log Books Volumes 1 & 2, Log Book Births & Deaths (Under Sac & Fox Agency, Oklahoma)1846-1924 Volume XI
Sac & Fox - Shawnee Guardianships Part 1 (Under Sac & Fox Agency, Oklahoma) 1892-1909 Volume XII
Sac & Fox - Shawnee Guardianships, Part 2 (Under The Sac & Fox Agency, Oklahoma) 1902-1910 Volume XIII
Sac & Fox - Shawnee Guardianships, Part 3 (Under The Sac & Fox Agency, Oklahoma) 1906-1914 Volume XIV

Visit our website at **www.nativestudy.com** to learn more about these and other books and series by Jeff Bowen

Choctaw Chief
Pushmataha
(c. 1764 - December 24, 1824)

The reason both sets of Instructions that came with these records are included with this text is because the persons dealing with the records involved did not always follow their own set of rules. These Instructions, in most situations, hopefully will bring you an understanding in reading the text. As the transcriber finds so many times the rules change according to the agent or assistants at the time. As mentioned before in different volumes involving different tribes it is only hoped that the person researching will find their ancestors and personally fill in a piece of their puzzle.

INSTRUCTIONS

(*A*) A separate roll is to be made of each reservation; also, of each *rancheria* or reserve, and a separate roll of Indians allotted on the public domain or homesteading. The roll is to be based on enrollment and not on residence.

(*B*) Persons are to be listed by families alphabetically; that is, not only by the first letter of the surname, but also by the second and subsequent letters when the first letter or letters are the same. For example: A*b*alon, A*b*bott, A*b*con, A*b*end, A*b*ict; B*a*ll, B*e*ll, B*i*ll, B*o*ll, B*u*ll; ...etc. Families having the same surname are also to be listed in this way, e.g.; Brown, *A*nson; Brown, *B*ill; Brown, *C*harles; Brown, *D*avid. In the case of English translations of Indian names, such as John *Flying-Elk*, Flying-Elk is the surname and is to be listed under F. In such cases the first word of the translated Indian name determines the alphabetical position. The best way to accomplish this will be to write the names of each family group on a separate card; then, arrange the cards alphabetically and type the names therefrom onto the census roll.

Members of a family are to be listed in the following order: Head, first; wife, second; then children, whether sons or daughters, *in the order of their ages*; and lastly, all other relatives and persons living with the family who do not constitute another family group.

Annuity and per capita payment rolls are also to be prepared in the same manner.

(*C*) A family is composed of the following members:
1. Both parents and their unmarried children, if any, living with them; all other relatives and persons living with the family who do not constitute another family group.
2. Either parent and the unmarried children, if the other parent is dead; all other relatives and persons living with the family who do not constitute another family group.
3. A single person over 21 years of age, not living with a relative.

(*D*) For each person the following information is to be furnished:
1. NUMBER. – A number is to be assigned in serial order. Thus, the first person listed is to be numbered as "1," the second, as "2," and so on until the census is completed.
2. NAME. – If there are both an Indian and an English name, the allotment or annuity roll name is to be given. First, the last or surname;

then, the given name in full. Ditto marks are to be used under the surname of the head for the surnames of the other members of one family.
3. SEX. – "M" for male; "F" for female.
4. AGE AT LAST BIRTHDAY. – Age in completed years at last birthday is to be shown. For infants under 1 year, age in completed months, expressed as twelfths of a year. Thus, 3 months as 3/12 yr.
5. TRIBE. – Care is to be taken that tribe, not band or local name, is given. Thus, Ute tribe, not Pahvant, which is a band of Ute. Likewise, Hupa tribe, not Bear River, which is a local name for the members of the Hupa tribe living near Bear River.
6. DEGREE OF BLOOD. – "F" for full blood; "1/4+" for one-fourth or more Indian blood; "-1/4" for less than one fourth Indian blood.
7. MARITAL STATUS. – "S" for a single or unmarried person; "M" for a married person; and "Wd" for widowed of either sex.
8. RELATIONSHIP TO HEAD OF FAMILY. – The head, whether husband or father, widow or unmarried person of either sex, is to be designated as such. For the other members, the appropriate term which designates the particular relationship the person bears to the head is to be used.
9. RESIDENCE. –
   (*a*) At *jurisdiction* where enrolled: Yes or no. The term jurisdiction includes all reservations and public domain allotments under the agency.
   (*b*) *Or* at another jurisdiction. The name of the jurisdiction is to be given.
   (*c*) *Or* elsewhere:
      1. Post office: Both the proper name of the post office and the class by which it is known (city, town, village, etc.) are to be given. Thus, Lewiston, city.
      2. County.
      3. State.
10. WARD. – Yes or no. Wardship depends primarily upon the ownership of individual property held in trust or upon membership in a tribe living on a Federal reservation.
11. ALLOTMENT, ANNUITY, AND IDENTIFICATION NUMBERS. —"Al", for allotment; "An", for annuity; and "Id", for identification, before the appropriate number or numbers. All numbers are to be shown.

(*E*) Rolls not prepared in strict conformity with the above instructions will be returned for correction.

INSTRUCTIONS FOR COMPLETION

Names are to be listed by families alphabetically. Members of each family, in the following order:
First, head; second, wife; then children, whether sons or daughters, in order of their age; and lastly, all other relatives and persons living with them, who do not constitute another family group.

1. A family is composed of the following members:
    (*a*) Both parents and their unmarried children, if any, living with them. In the case of plural wives, the oldest with her unmarried children is to be listed first; the others, in order of their ages.
    (*b*) Either parent and the unmarried children, if the other is dead or permanently residing elsewhere.
    (*c*) A single person over 18 years of age, not living with any relatives.

2. For each person the following information is to be furnished:
    (*a*) Census numbers, both present and last.
    (*b*) Name, Indian and English, if any. First the surname, then the given. Care is to be exercised in their spelling and ditto marks are to be used when the surname is the same as that of the person in the preceding line.
    (*c*) Allotment, annuity, and identification numbers. Write "Al" for allotment, "An" for annuity, and "Id" for identification, before the appropriate number or numbers.
    (*d*) Date of birth by month, day, and year.
    (*e*) Degree of blood. If full blood use "F", if mixed, "M."
    (*f*) Marital condition. "S" for a single or unmarried person of whatever age, "M" for married, and "Wd" for widowed of either sex.
    (*g*) Relation to head of family. The head, whether husband or wife or unmarried person of either six, is to be designated by the word, "head." For the other members of the family use wife, son, daughter, etc., according to the peculiar relationship which the person bears to the head.

"...General Andrew Jackson and General Thomas Hinds, with free liquor to bribe and soften the Choctaw hearts, had, first by honeyed inveigling, difficult for even the most sophisticated to contest, them by threats and at the last by fits of vociferous anger, frightened the beleaguered Choctaws into giving up five million acres. Jackson had called the expanse 'that useless little slip of land,' but within two weeks the Port Gibson "Correspondent" described it as 'fine as any in the United States,...exhibiting at once the most pleasing variety of hill and dale, prairie and grove, and furnishing a variety of soil, and a salubrity of air, not surpassed by any other region.' The thirteen million acres in the West the Choctaws were promised could not even be identified until a new treaty was held five years later in Washington. It was the treaty, Luther Cashdollar had told Jesse Furver, that cost the Choctaws the lives of their most notable chiefs. The great Pushmataha died in Washington before the treaty was signed. Puckshunubbee died in route."

> Will D. Campbell, *Providence*, p. 250-251, para. 6

"Of the 370 Indian Treaties the U.S. Senate has ratified, provisions in every single one have been violated. Since 1849 the Department of Interior has been a party to each broken one."

> Will D. Campbell, *Providence*, p. 252, para 1

Table of Contents

Introduction	xiii
Treaty of Dancing Rabbit Creek	
(Original)	xxiii
(Transcription)	xlix
1929 Census	3
1930 Census	67
1931 Census	139
1932 Census	211
Supplement No. I	283
Births	287
Deaths	305
Limited Index	315

Introduction

An introduction for the Choctaw couldn't be written without mentioning the famed Choctaw Chief Pushmataha on the front of this book by Charles Bird King in 1824. This is a man that actually tried to help Andrew Jackson like the Cherokee during the uprising of the Creek Indians in the early 1800's; only to later receive from Jackson a decisive blow to what would finish the Choctaw's lives as they knew them. The Treaty of Dancing Rabbit Creek would be that tool of destruction like a Communist taking what you worked for your whole life and giving it to their elitist friends. Even though Pushmataha during a time of hardship for General Jackson needing an army to defeat the Creeks he was there for a young Republic. It was said, "His personal bravery in battle proved his leadership for both Choctaws and whites. He led Choctaw troops under Andrew Jackson in the War of 1812 and the Creek War. He was welcomed at Fort Madison in 1813, wearing the full military regalia of the U.S. army--dress uniform, gold braid and epaulets, and silver medal. He joined the evening promenade of officers with his wife on his arm. Pushmataha personifies the forces acting on the full-blood Choctaws of his time. He fought with the valor of a traditional Choctaw warrior, but on the side of the white leader, Andrew Jackson, against the Creek tribe."[1] Interestingly Pushmataha wasn't at home with his family on Christmas Eve of 1824 but was in Washington trying to negotiate with the powers that be in a government that would eventually take the land of his people. Not knowing that six years later through a treaty only to eventually be broken as so many others, that evening Pushmataha not willingly, died of what has been thought of as pneumonia. His final resting place surely not of his choice, buried in a strange place, the Congressional Cemetery. "Laid among thieves", he would likely say.

The so called civilized probably thought these are Indians. But the commentary spoken of them when approached by the whites wasn't what most would think, "As farmers the Choctaws had few peers. After clearing the land around their villages, by burning the underbrush and girdling the trees, they planted maize (their staple crop), beans, pumpkins, and melons. William Bartram, the English botanist who visited the Gulf Coast of Mississippi in 1777, said they were the 'most ingenious

---

[1] Kidwell, Choctaws and Missionaries in Mississippi 1818-1919, p. 18, para.2

Introduction

and industrious husbandmen, having large plantations, or country farms, where they employ much of their time in agricultural improvements, . . . by which means their territories are more generally cultivated, and better inhabited, than any other Indian republic that we know of."[2]

The Choctaw were a self-sustaining people not just as crop farmers but as producers of beef cattle. Whatever corn they didn't use as their daily staple they used in feeding their beef. They were so capable in their livestock skills that they were able to finance their endeavors through the sales of newly bred cattle. Most whites when approaching the Choctaw found an uncommon vision before them unlike most Native tribes they had seen. They said, "Their homes were permanent type structures, log and stucco houses grouped together near their farm land in concentrations so large that the early white explorers and settlers who made contact with the Choctaws spoke of the settlements as towns. The settlements were normally located around the edge of the district as a protective barrier against potential enemies; inland, the district was sparsely settled and resembled extensive plantations with cabins or homes "a gunshot distant from each other."[3]

One hundred years prior to this census, the Choctaw of Mississippi were being betrayed and driven from a home they had known their whole lives. Not many realize that the Choctaw Tribe of Mississippi was one of the largest tribes east of the river ranging possibly from 18,000 to 21,000 people. Also they were one of the first to be forcibly removed in the early time period of 1831-1833 previous to others who were considered the Five Civilized Tribes. This removal unfortunately brought forth a perilous pattern for the rest of the decade, causing the irrational deaths of thousands of Native Americans from numerous tribes. The loss of the Choctaw homeland and a civilized people as large and deadly as it turned out to be was only a portion of unspeakable crimes that would be thrust upon the Native American during our nation's early history. In the years surrounding the early 1800's or even to this day as we stand enamored looking up at a man's face in marble thinking he must have been a

---

[2] DeRosier, The Removal of the Choctaw Indians, p. 9-10, para. 4

Introduction

marvelous creature. But you have to think again when reading his own words, and learning about his dark under lying motives. Suddenly opinions change, the statue we are staring at proudly suddenly breaks your heart. Thinking of him as humane while we stand at the base of this National monument we have no idea of who he really was and what he did until reading Native American history. As firmly stated, "The reason must be that he never actually intended to allow his wiser and more humane policies to prevail. Evidence of this hypothesis is found in the letters he wrote to Indian agents and influential frontier leaders, advocating Indian agriculture strictly as a means of confining the Indians to a small plot of land so that the government could buy up the large surplus and sell it cheaply to frontier settlers. His motives can also be interpreted from a letter he wrote to Andrew Jackson on February 16, 1803, in which he asserted that the basic reason for keeping agents among the Indians was to obtain their land. 'Toward effecting this object, we consider leading the Indian to agriculture . . . .When they shall cultivate small spots of earth, and see how useless their extensive forests are, they will sell . . . .' Each Indian agent 'shall be estimated by us in proportion to the benefits he can obtain for us,' Jefferson said, and he ended his letter with the demand that his views 'be pursued unremittingly.' During that same year Jefferson also wrote Willian Henry Harrison that he was not interested in the particular method used to secure large holdings of Indian lands, but rather that he was solely concerned with the end result."[4] History like this makes a person weary.

Mentioned previously in this Introduction and the years surrounding the early 1800's, what could be called the first removal of the Choctaw they were being convinced that they needed to sign a treaty that was supposed to be to their advantage. Only to be broken before the ink was even dry. They were called negotiations only really they were threats from politicians of the day like Harrison, Monroe, Jefferson and Jackson to name a few or even to this day we find stories for example; in a book called, *Providence*, how it points out that things never change. The author tells of a place in Mississippi called Providence Farm or Section 13 that once belonged to the

---

[3] DeRosier, The Removal of the Choctaw Indians, p. 11, para.2
[4] DeRosier, The Removal of the Choctaw Indians, p. 25-26, para.4

Introduction

Choctaw. The author Will D. Campbell tells of how he met two men in 1955 and listened to their story or dilemma of how 32 years later their land and broken dreams devastates them with what he calls the second removal. They are trying to decide what to do with the property all these years later. Their board for Providence was having to decide what to do with this beloved land, likely a painful experience that had gone on for years. But finally a suggestion had been given with a possible answer being money was never a factor because of a few people and their dedication in a purpose to help others they decided to give the land back to the Choctaws. They brought this idea to the Choctaw Chief at the time, 1987. Only to receive a letter, "Two weeks after my visit and conversation with Chief Martin, the Providence board received a letter from the U.S. Department of Interior. They wanted 540 acres of Providence land for a game management program. They offered almost three hundred thousand dollars for it."[5] A few lines after Campbell states, "It was incredulous news. Why now? After all these years? The Department of Interior, the agency that dogged not only the Choctaw but every other native tribe and nation since it took over their management in 1849. Of the 370 Indian treaties the U.S. Senate has ratified, provisions in every single one have been violated. Since 1849 the Department of Interior has been a party to each one broken."[6]

Reading can be a curse but shouldn't be left to a dusty shelf. It only creates ignorance and a future of hopelessness or victimization. As Mr. Campbell so aptly quotes Arthur DeRosier, Jr., "Jefferson had encouraged the Choctaws to run deeply in debt at the trading posts because, he said, they were then willing to lop off the debts with cessions of land. He openly called it bribery and said bribery was preferable to war. No doubt it was, but in addition to his advocacy of extortion, he later said if that policy did not work he was prepared to push a constitutional amendment to remove the Indians by force to the West."[7]

---

[5] Campbell, Providence, p. 251, para. 5
[6] Campbell, Providence, p. 251-252, para. 6-7
[7] Campbell, Providence, p. 29, para. 2

Introduction

People might think that 186 years ago the Choctaw didn't have far to travel for their removal but they did. They were being marched out on foot, their children with them. They weren't getting in their cars and taking a couple hours' drive. They were being torn from their homes. They were leaving almost everything in their world behind. The homes they had built the land they had cleared and planted their whole lives, gone. Their cattle and other animals, gone. They had to walk for the most part to a land filled with forests, brush, brambles, and swampy land having to cross unknown water during treacherous times. This is a description of what they faced and when. Think of how we complain about a little inconvenience and what these people put up with let alone burying their loved ones along the way in strange ground by the side of some dirt path if that. The Choctaws' history says, "The main removals took place during 1831, 1832, and 1833. The sufferings of the emigrants were almost beyond belief. It was a difficult journey at best--350 miles through a wild unsettled country of vast swamps, dense forests, impenetrable canebrakes, and swollen rivers. Added to this was a great deal of blundering and inefficiency on the part of the War Department. Additional suffering and loss of life was caused by one of the worst blizzards in the history of that region, which broke upon the emigrants who were removed during the Winter of 1831-32; and the cholera epidemic, which swept down the Mississippi and caught those who were crossing the following Summer. The population of the tribe was permanently decreased by the losses sustained during this terrible experience. White Americans, with their more mobile habits, have never been able to appreciate the hopeless grief of this despoiled people when they abandoned their ancient homes, and in a strictly literal sense, the bones of their beloved dead."[8]

It is always a goal to give a little history in each introduction so you'll have a chance to understand what your ancestors went through and possibly where. Hopefully to understand who you are and where to look while conducting your genealogical hunt for those sometime elusive family members. It's always good to understand who your tribal family is today and below you can read about them in today's world. As previously mentioned the book *Providence*, would be worth

---

[8] Debo, The Rise and Fall of the Choctaw Republic, p. 56, para. 1-2

Introduction

reading with an amazing story let alone great references to read in searching Choctaw history. The Mississippi Band of Choctaw Indians current location is Mississippi with approximately 28,402 acres and a tribal enrollment of 9,483 members. "The Choctaw Reservation encompasses nine communities: Pearl River, Bogue Chitto, Tucker, Red Water, Standing Pine, Conehatta, Crystal Ridge, Bogue Homa, and Ocean Springs. Choctaw people lived throughout the Mississippi and Alabama region, hunting game and farming the area's rich soil for subsistence. The Choctaw's name is an anglicized version of Chahta, the name of a chief. At least 90 percent of the Mississippi Band of Choctaw Indians' tribal members continue to speak the indigenous Muscogean language, while English serves as the second language. Tribal members continue to practice traditional cultural elements. The Choctaw's first interaction with European explorers occurred in 1540 when the de Soto Expedition marched northwest across the continent--an encounter that resulted in the deaths of 1,500 to 3,000 Choctaw people. In 1786, the Choctaws signed the Treaty of Hopewell, which bestowed federal recognition of their sovereignty, but white settlers continued to settle on Choctaw land. The historic Treaty of Dancing Rabbit Creek, signed in 1830, deemed removal voluntary and provided land grants and citizenship for those who chose to remain in Mississippi. Approximately 5,000 Choctaws decided to stay in Mississippi. Seven communities, which coincide with the reservation's current community centers, grew from where they congregated. The band's initial isolation largely accounts for the persistent use of their native language. Since 1979, the Choctaw have experienced phenomenal economic growth, largely due to lucrative gaming operations. In 2002, the Mississippi Choctaw Tribe was the second largest employer in the state and the single largest employer in Neshoba County."[9]

"The Mississippi Band of Choctaw Indians is one of three federally recognized tribes of Choctaw Native Americans, and the only one in this state. On April 20, 1945, this band organized under the Indian Reorganization Act of 1934. Also in 1945 the Choctaw Indian Reservation was created in Mississippi by the

---

[9] Indian Nations of North America, p. 92-96, para. 1-5

Introduction

federal government by acquisition of lands in Neshoba, Leake, Newton, Scott, Jones, Attala, Kemper, and Winston counties. Other federally recognized tribes are the Choctaw Nation of Oklahoma, the largest, and the Jena Band of Choctaw Indians, a small group located in Louisiana.

By a deed dated August 18, 2008, the state returned *Nanih Waiya* in Mississippi to the Choctaw. This ancient earthwork mound and site, built ca. 1-300 CE, has been venerated by the Choctaw since the 17th century as a sacred place of origin of their ancestors. The Mississippi Band of Choctaw have made August 18 a tribal holiday to celebrate their regaining control of the sacred site.

The historic Choctaw had emerged as a tribe and occupied substantial territory in what is now considered the state of Mississippi. In the early nineteenth century, they were under increasing pressure by European Americans, who wanted to acquire their land for agricultural development. President Andrew Jackson gained congressional passage of the Indian Removal Act in 1830 to accomplish this and extinguish Native American land claims in the Southeast.

The chiefs signed the Treaty of Dancing Rabbit Creek with the United States, which was ratified by the U.S. Senate on February 25, 1831. President Jackson was anxious to make the Choctaw removal a model for other tribes to be taken out of the Southeast to territory well west of the Mississippi River. After ceding close to 11 million acres (45,000 km^2), the Choctaw were to emigrate in three stages; the first in the fall of 1831, the second in 1832, and the last in 1833. Although the removals continued into the early 20th century, some Choctaw remained in Mississippi. They continued to live in their ancient homeland. According to the terms of removal, the nearly 5000 Choctaw who remained in Mississippi became citizens of the state and United States.

For the next ten years, they were subject to increasing legal conflict, harassment, and intimidation by white settlers. Racism against them was rampant. The Choctaw described their situation in 1849, we have had our habitations torn down and burned, our fences destroyed, cattle turned into our fields and we ourselves have been scourged, manacled, fettered and otherwise personally abused, until by such treatment some of our best men have died.

Introduction

In 2002, the United States Congress formally recognized the entire Choctaw Nation in 25 U.S.C. 1779, including those Choctaw in Mobile and Washington counties, Alabama. They were described as Full-Blooded Choctaw equally and in the same Mississippi Choctaw Jurisdictional Act of 1934, by which the Mississippi Band of Choctaw reorganized.

After nearly two hundred years, the Mississippi Band of Choctaw have retaken control of the ancient site of *Nanih Waiya*, an earthwork mound built about 300-600CE. They have traditionally venerated this site as their place of origin and the home of their ancestors. For years the state protected the site as a Mississippi state park. It returned *Nanih Waiya* to the Choctaw in 2006, under Mississippi Legislature State Bill 2803.

The deed was signed on August 18, 2008, which the Choctaw have made a tribal holiday. They have celebrated the day since, and made it an occasion for telling stories of their origin and history, serving traditional foods, and conducting related dances.

Old Choctaw country included dozens of towns, such as Lukfata, Koweh Chito, Oka Hullo, Pante, Osapa Chito, Oka Cooply, and Yanni Achukma, located in and around Neshoba and Kemper counties.

The Choctaw regularly traveled hundreds of miles from their homes for long periods of time, moving to seasonal hunting grounds in the winter. They set out early in the fall and returned to their reserved lands at the opening of spring to plant their gardens. At that time they visited the Europeans at Columbus, Mississippi; Macon, Brooksville, and Crawford, and the region where Yazoo City now is located.

Presently, the Mississippi Choctaw Indian Reservation has eight communities.

- Bogue Chitto or "Bok Cito", Mississippi
- Bogue Homa [20]
- Conehatta
- Crystal Ridge
- Henning, Tennessee
- Pearl River

Introduction

Red Water

Tucker

Standing Pine

These communities are located in parts of nine counties throughout the state. The largest concentration of land is in Neshoba County, at 32°48'56"N 89°14'46"W32.81556°N 89.24611°W, which comprises more than two-thirds of the reservation's land area and holds more than 62 percent of its population, as of the 2000 census. The total land area is 84.282 km² (32.541 sq mi), and its official total resident population was 5,190 persons. The nine counties are Neshoba, Newton, Leake, Kemper, Jones, Winston, Attala, Jackson, and Scott counties."[10]

This work was originally published in 1997 and has been expanded upon through careful study by reading many sources. Also while going through the film it was made sure that nothing was left out and every piece of information placed within these pages is in the same order it was found. Other than stating everyone is human and makes mistakes the best care possible was taken to make sure you'll find what you are looking for. You will find after this introduction a copy of the Treaty of Dancing Rabbit Creek both in original form and transcribed by the author so you will be able to read it without having to work so hard while trying to understand what it says. The information contained within this two book series was obtained from National Archival Microfilm rolls M-595 Rolls 41 and 42, NATIVE AMERICAN CENSUS ROLLS 1885-1940; Volume I; Choctaw of Mississippi; 1929-1932; with Birth and Death Rolls, 1924-1932. Then in Volume II you will find numerous categories or classifications titled the Choctaw Censuses of 1933 and 1934, Supplemental Rolls for 1934-35, Addition Rolls 1934-35, Addition Roll Unreported Births 1935, Deduction Rolls 1934-35, Birth Rolls 1934, Unreported Births 1934, Death Rolls 1934-36, Supplemental Census Roll 1935 (Header 1936), Marriages 1936, Census Roll 1937, Births Roll 1, (2 missing), and 3 as of 1936 Unreported Births. Births January 1 to December 31, 1936, then the same for 1934-33 and 1932. Then Death Rolls 1936, Unreported Deaths 1935-36 through 1932 (All reported backwards in years).

---

[10] Wikipedia, Mississippi Band of Choctaw Indians

Introduction

Supplemental Roll 1938 (Live Births 1937), All Other Additions 1937, Unreported Births 1937. Marriages 1937, Deaths 1937, Births 1938, Unreported Births 1938, Omissions 1938 and Marriages 1939 (No Marriages listed within material for 1938). Deaths 1938, Deaths Not Reported prior to 1938 (Occurring between 1933-37), 1938 Transfer or Adjustment Roll (Corrections in sex 1-1-1939), Added Females on account of error in sex, and finally Indians returning to jurisdiction where enrolled as of 1-1-1939. The table of contents hopefully will bring a little order to these pages but it was felt that you should know what course this material took while transcribing, since it was felt that the recorders failed in many instances to understand the term chronological order.

This piece was a mass of difficult record keeping while having to roam through each page and wonder what were the recorders thinking, while listing people's names under every circumstance. These people just wanted respect and order in their lives, they just wanted to keep their traditions and culture alive and be remembered by their people. They just wanted to take care of their loved ones. From studies made by this author it seems as though they have done a wonderful job to this point in time. This transcription is dedicated to those within these pages and their descendants.

Jeff Bowen
Gallipolis, Ohio
NativeStudy.com

[Copy of the Original]

Treaty of Dancing Rabbit Creek

1830
~~1831~~

Treaty with the Choctaws Sep. 27, 1830
And 28th Sepr 1830
Ratified Feby 24th 1831.

A treaty of perpetual friendship, cession and limits entered into by John H Eaton and John Coffee for and in behalf of the Government of the United States and the Mingoes Chiefs Captains and Warriors of the Choctaw Nation begun and held at Dancing Rabbit Creek on the 15th of September in the year 1830.

Whereas the General Assembly of the State of Mississippi has extended the laws of said State to persons and property within the Chartered limits of the same and the President of the United States has said that he cannot protect the Choctaw people from the operation of these laws; Now therefore that the Choctaw may live under their own laws in peace with the United States and the State of Mississippi they have determined to sell their lands east of the Mississippi & have accordingly agreed to the following articles of treaty

Article 1st

Perpetual peace and friendship is pledged and agreed upon by and between the United States and the Mingoes, Chiefs, & Warriors of the Choctaw Nation of Red People; and that this may be considered the treaty existing between the parties all other treaties heretofore existing & inconsistent with the provisions of this are hereby declared null and void.

Article 2nd

The United States under a grant specially to be made by the President of the U.S. shall cause to be conveyed to the Choctaw Nation a tract of Country west of the Mississippi River, in fee simple to them & their descendants, to ensure to them while they shall exist as a nation & live on it, beginning near Fort Smith where the Arkansas boundary crosses the Arkansas River, Running thence west to the source of the Canadian fork; if in the limits of the United States, or to those limits; thence due South to Red River, and down Red River to the West boundary of the Territory of Arkansas; thence North along that line to the beginning.

the boundary of the same to be agreable to the treaty made and concluded at Washington City in the year 1825. The grant to be executed so soon as the present Treaty shall be ratified.— Article 3rd.

In consideration of the provisions contained in the several articles of this Treaty, the Choctaw Nation of Indians consent, and hereby cede to the United States, the entire Country they own and possess, East of the Mississippi River; and they agree to remove beyond the Mississippi River, early as practicable, and will so arrange thier removal, that as many as possible of thier people not exceeding one half of the whole number, shall depart during the falls of 1831 and 1832; the residue to follow during the succeeding fall of 1833; a better opportunity in this manner will be afforded the Government, to extend to them the facilities and comforts which it is desireable should be extended in conveying them to thier new Homes.— Article 4th.

The Government and people of the United States are hereby obliged to secure to the said Choctaw Nation of Red People the Jurisdiction and Government, of all the Persons & Property that may be within thier limits West, so that no Territory or State shall ever have a right to pass laws for the Government of the Choctaw Nation of Red People & thier Descendants; and that no part of the land granted them shall ever be embraced in any Territory or State; but the U.S. shall forever secure said Choctaw Nation from, & against, all laws except such as from time to time may be enacted in thier own National Councils, not inconsistent with the Constitution, Treaties, and laws of the United States; & except such as may, & which have been enacted by Congress, to the extent that Congress under the Constitution are required to excerscise a legislation over Indian affairs. But the Choctaws, should this treaty be ratified, express a wish that Congress may grant to the Choctaws the right of punishing by their own laws, any white man who shall come into their Nation, & infringe any of their National regulations

Article 5th

The United States are obliged to protect the Choctaws from domestic strife & from foreign enemies on the same principles that the Citizens of the United States are protected, so that whatever would be a legal demand upon the U.S. for defence or for wrongs committed by an Enemy, on a Citizen of the U.S, shall be equally binding on ~~it favour~~ of the Choctaws, & in all cases where the Choctaws shall be called upon by a legal authorized Officer of the U.S. to fight an Enemy, such Choctaw shall receive the pay & other emoluments, which Citizens of the U.S. receive in such cases, provided, no war shall be undertaken or prosecuted by said Choctaw Nation but by declaration made in full Council, & to be approved by the U.S. unless it be in self defence against an open rebellion or against an enemy marching into their Country, in which cases they shall defend, until the U.S. are advised thereof.

Article 6th

Should a Choctaw or any party of Choctaws commit acts of violence upon the person or property of a Citizen of the U.S, or join any war party against any neighbouring tribe of Indians, without the authority in the preceding article; & except to oppose an actual or threatened invasion or rebellion, such person so offending shall be delivered up to an Officer of the U.S. if in the power of the Choctaw Nation, that such offender may be punished as may be provided in such cases, by the laws of the U.S.; but if such offender is not within the control of the Choctaw Nation, then said Choctaw Nation shall not be held responsible for the injury done by said Offender.

Article 7th

All acts of violence committed upon persons and property of the people of the Choctaw Nation, either by Citizens of the U.S. or neighbouring tribes of Red people, shall be referred to some authorized agent, by him to be referred to the President of the U.S. Who shall examine into such cases and see that every possible degree of justice is done to said Indian party of the Choctaw Nation —

Article 8th

Offenders against the laws of the U.S. or any individual State shall be apprehended & delivered to any duly authorized person where such Offender may be found in the Choctaw Country, having fled from any part of U.S. but in all such cases application must be made to the Agent or Chiefs & the expense of his apprehension and delivery provided for & paid by the U States

Article 9th

Any Citizen of the U.S. who may be Ordered from the Nation by the Agent & Constituted authorities of the Nation and refusing to obey or return into the Nation without the Consent of the aforesaid persons, shall be subject to such pains and penalties as may be provided by the laws of the U.S. in such cases. Citizens of the U.S. travelling peaceably under the authority of the laws of the U.S. shall be under the care & protection of the Nation

Article 10th

No person shall expose goods or other article for sale as a trader, without a written permit from the Constituted authorities of the Nation, or authority of the laws of the Congress of the U.S. under penalty of forfeiting the Articles, & the Constituted authorities of the Nation shall grant no license except to such persons as reside in the Nation and are answerable to the laws of the Nation. The U.S. shall be particularly obliged to assist in preventing ardent spirits from being introduced into the Nation

Article 11th

Navigable streams shall be free to the Choctaws who shall pay no higher toll or duty than Citizens of the U.S. It is agreed further that the U.S. shall establish one or more Post Offices in said Nation, & may establish such Military post roads, and posts, as they may consider necessary

Article 12th

All intruders shall be removed from the Choctaw Nation and kept without it. Private property to be always respected & on no occasion taken for public purposes without just compensation being made therefor to the rightfull owner. If an Indian unlawfully take or steal any property from a White Man a citizen of the U.S. the offender shall be punished. And if a white Man unlawfully take or steal any thing from an Indian, the property shall be restored & the offender punished. It is further agreed that when a Choctaw shall be given up to be tried for any offence against the laws of the U.S. if unable to employ Counsel to defend him, the U.S. will do it, that his trial may be fair and impartial

Article 13th

It is consented that a qualified Agent shall be appointed for the Choctaws every four Years, unless sooner removed by the President; and he shall be removed on petition of the Constituted Authorities of the Nation the President, being satisfied there is sufficient cause shown. The Agent shall fix his residence convenient to the great body of the people; & in the selection of an Agent immediately after the ratification of this Treaty, the wishes of the Choctaw Nation on the subject shall be entitled to great respect

Article 14th.

Each Choctaw head of a family being desirous to remain & become a Citizen of the States, shall be permitted to do so, by signifying his intention to the Agent within Six Months from the ratification of this Treaty. He shall thereupon be entitled to a reservation of one Section of Six Hundred and forty Acres of Land, to be bounded by sectional lines of survey; in like manner shall be entitled to one half that quantity for each unmarried child which is living with him over Ten Years of Age, & a quarter section to such child as may be under 10 years of age, to adjoin the location of the Parent. If they reside upon said lands intending to become Citizens of the States for five Years after the ratification of this Treaty in that case a grant in fee simple shall issue; said reservation shall include the present improvements of the head of the family, or a portion of it. Persons who claim under this Article shall not loose the priviledge of a Choctaw Citizen, but if they ever remove are not to be entitled to any portion of the Choctaw Annuity.

Article 15th

To each of the Chiefs in the Choctaw Nation (to wit) Greenwood Laflore, Nutackachie, and Mushulatubbe there is granted a reservation of four Sections of land, two of which shall include and adjoin their present improvements, & the other two located where they please but on unoccupied unimproved lands, such sections shall be bounded by sectional lines, & with the consent of the President they may sell the same. Also to the three principal Chiefs & their successors in office there shall be paid Two Hundred and fifty Dollars annually, while they shall continue in thier respective offices, except to Mushulatubbe who as he has an annuity of One Hundred & fifty Dollars for life under a former treaty, shall receive only the addional sum of One Hundred Dollars, while he shall continue in office as Chief; & if in addition to this the Nation shall think propper to elect an additional principal Chief of the whole to superintend and govern upon republican principles he shall receive annually for his services Five Hundred Dollars, which allowance to the Chiefs and thier Successors in office, shall continue for Twenty Years, At any time when in Military service, & while in service by authority of the U.S. the district Chiefs under and by selection of the President shale be entitled to the pay of Majors; the other Chief under the same Circumstances shall have the pay of a Lieutenant Colonel. The speakers of the three districts, shall receive Twenty five Dollars a Year for four Years, & the three Secretaries one to each of the Chiefs, fifty Dollars each for four years. Each Captain of the Nation, the number not to exceed ninety nine, thirty three from each District shall be furnished upon removing to the West, with each a good suit of clothes & a broad sword as an outfit; & for four years commencing with the first of thier removal, shall each receive Fifty Dollars a Year, for the trouble of keeping thier people in order in settling; & whenever they shall be in military service by authority of the U.S. shall receive the pay of a captain

Article 14th

In waggons, & with Steam Boats as may be found necessary The U.S. agree to remove the Indians to thier new Homes at thier expense and under the care of discreet and carefull persons, who will be kind & brotherly to them. They agree to furnish them with ample corn and beef, or pork for themselves & families for Twelve months after reaching thier new homes.

It is agreed further that the U.S. will take all their cattle, at the valuation of some discreet person to be appointed by the President, & the same shall be paid for in Money after their arrival at their new homes; or in other cattle such as may be desired shall be furnished them, notice being given through their Agent of their wishes upon this subject before their removal that time to supply the demand may be afforded.

Article 17th

The several Annuities and sums secured under former Treaties to the Choctaw Nation and People shall continue as tho' this Treaty had never been made. And it is further agreed that the U.S. in addition will pay the sum of Twenty thousand Dollars for Twenty Years, commencing after their removal to the West, of which, in the first year after their removal, Ten thousand Dollars shall be divided and arranged to such as may not receive reservations under this Treaty.

Article 18th

The U.S. shall cause the lands hereby ceded to be surveyed, & surveyors may enter the Choctaw Country for that purpose, conducting themselves properly & disturbing or interrupting none of the Choctaw people. But no person is to be permitted to settle within the Nation, or the lands to be sold before the Choctaws shall remove. And for the payment of the several amounts secured in this Treaty, the lands hereby ceded are to remain a fund pledged to that purpose, until the debt shall be provided for and arranged. And further it is agreed, that in the construction of this Treaty wherever well founded doubt shall arise, it shall be construed most favourably towards the Choctaws.

Article 19th

The following reservations of land are hereby admitted. To Col. David Folsom Four Sections of which Two shall include his present improvements, & two may be located elsewhere, on unoccupied, unimproved land.

To J. Garland, Col. Robert Cole, Tuppanahomer, John Pytchlyn, Charles Juzan, Toh Ke betubbe, Cray cha hobia, Ofe homa two sections each, to include their improvements, and to be bounded by sectional lines, & the same may be disposed of and sold with the consent of the President. And that others not provided for, may be provided for, there shall be reserved as follows.

First, One Section to each head of a family not exceeding Forty in number, who during the present year, may have had in actual cultivation, with a dwelling House thereon Fifty Acres or more. Secondly, three quarter sections after the manner aforesaid to each head of a family not exceeding Four Hundred and Sixty, as shall have cultivated Thirty Acres and less than Fifty, to be bounded by quarter section lines of survey, & to be contiguous & adjoining.

Third, One half section as aforesaid to those who shall have cultivated from Twenty to Thirty Acres the number not to exceed Four Hundred. Fourth, a quarter section as aforesaid to such as shall have cultivated from twelve to twenty Acres, the number not to exceed three hundred and fifty, and one half that quantity to such as shall have cultivated from two to twelve acres, the number also not to exceed three hundred and fifty persons. Each of said class of cases shall be subject to the limitations contained in the first class, & shall be so located as to include that part of the improvements which contains the dwelling House. If a greater number shall be found to be entitled to reservations under the several classes of this article, than is stipulated for under the limitation prescribed, then & in that case the Chiefs separately or together shall determine the persons who shall be excluded in the respective districts. Fifth; Any Captain the number not to exceed ninety persons, who under the provisions of this article shall receive less than a section, he shall be entitled, to an additional quantity of half a section adjoining to his other reservation. The several reservations secured under this Article, may be sold with the consent of the President, of the U.S. but should any prefer it, or omit to take a reservation for the quantity he may be entitled to the U.S. will on his removing pay fifty cents an acre, after reaching their new homes, provided that before the first of January next they shall adduce to the Agent or some other authorized person to be appointed, proof of his claim & the quantity of it. Sixth; likewise children of Choctaw Indians residing in the Nation, who have neither father nor mother a list of which, with satisfactory proof of Parentage and Orphanage being filed with Agent in Six months to be forwarded to the War Department, shall be entitled to a quarter section of Land, to be located under the direction of the President & with his consent the same May be sold and the proceeds applied to some beneficial purpose for the benefit of said Orphans —

Article 20th.

The U.S. agree & stipulate as follows, that for the benefit and advantage of the Choctaw people, & to improve their condition, there shall be educated under the direction of the President & at the expense of the U.S. forty Choctaw Youths for Twenty years. This number shall be kept at school, & as they finish their education others to supply their places shall be received for the period stated. The U.S. agree also to erect a Council House for the Nation at some convenient central point, after their people shall be settled, & a House for each Chief, also a church for each of the three Districts, to be used also as school

Houses, until the Nation may conclude to build others; & for these purposes Ten thousand Dollars shall be appropriated; Also Fifty thousand Dollars (Viz) Twenty five Hundred Dollars annually shall be given for the support of three Teachers of schools for Twenty Years. Likewise there shall be furnished to the Nation, three Blacksmiths one for each Distrix for Sixteen Years, & a qualified Mill wright for five years; Also there shall be furnished the following articles, Twenty One Hundred Blankets, To each warrior in the emigrating a rifle, Moulds, Wipers and ammunition. One thousand axes, Ploughs, Hoes, Wheels and Cards each; and four Hundred looms. There shall also be furnished One Ton of Iron & two hundred weight of Steel annually to each Distrix for Sixteen years.

Article 21st.

A few Choctaw Warriors yet survive who marched and fought in the Army with General Wayne the whole number stated not to exceed Twenty. These it is agreed shall hereafter while they live receive Twenty Five dollars a year; a list of them to be early as practicable, & within six months made out, and presented to the Agent to be forwarded to the War Department. —

Article 22d.

The Chiefs of the Choctaws have suggested that their people are in a state of rapid advancement in education and refinements and have expressed a solicitude that they might have the priviledge of a Delegate on the floor of the House of Representatives extended to them. The Commissioners do not feel, that they can under a treaty stipulation accede to the request, but at their desires, present it in the Treaty, that Congress may consider of and decide the application.

Done and signed and executed by the Commissioners of the United States and the Chiefs Captains and Head Men of the Choctaw Nation at Dancing Rabbit Creek this 27th day of September Eighteen Hundred and Thirty.

his mark

In Presence of

E. Breathitt Secty
to the Comms —
William Ward
for Choctaws.
John Pitchlynn
U.S. Intr.
M Mackey
U.S. Intr.
Geo S Gaines
of Alabama
R. Jervin
Sike Howard
Sam S. Worcester
Jno N Byrn
John Bell
Jno Garland

W H Eaton (seal)
Jno Coffee (seal)
Greenwood Leflore (seal)
Cullus hola tubbee (seal) X
Nittuckachee (seal) X
Eyarhouttubbee (seal) X
Iyacher hopia (seal) X
Offa hoomah (seal) X
Archatatey (seal)
Onnee hubbee (seal)
Holarten hoomah (seal) X
Hopiauncha hubbee (seal) X
Ishomingo (seal) X
Captain thacko (seal) X
James Shield (seal) X
Pistonubbee (seal) X
Tobatgauncha hubbee (seal) X
Hou bbee (seal)
Robert Cole (seal)
Moke lar char hopia (seal) X
Lewis Perry (seal) X
Artonamastubbee (seal) X
Hopiaytubbee (seal)
Hosha hoomah (seal) X
Chuacsa hoomah (seal) X
Joseph Kincaide (seal)
Artook lubbee tubby (seal) X
Atte tubbee (seal) X
Arsarkatubbee (seal) X
Issater hoomah

Name		Mark
Chohtahmatahah	Seal	X
Tummuppashubbee	Seal	X
Okecharyer	Seal	X
Hoshhopia	Seal	X
Warsharthahopia	Seal	X
Moashunchahubbee	Seal	X
Mishaiyubbee	Seal	X
Daniel McCurtain	Seal	X
Tushkerharcho	Seal	X
Hoktoontubbee	Seal	X
Nuknaavehookmanhubbee	Seal	X
Mingo hoomah	Seal	X
Pisinhocuttubbee	Seal	X
Tullarhachen	Seal	X
Little hader	Seal	X
Moanhutter	Seal	X
Cowe hoomah	Seal	X
Fillamoer	Seal	X
Immillacha	Seal	X
Antopulachubbee	Seal	X
Shulphen unchahubbee	Seal	X
Nitter hoomah	Seal	X
Oaklarzubbee	Seal	X
Pukumma	Seal	X
Arpalar	Seal	X
Hosher	Seal	X
Hoparmingo	Seal	X
Ispayhoomah	Seal	X
Lieberhoomah	Seal	X
Toshoholarter	Seal	X
Alahayarchubber	Seal	X
Arlarter	Seal	X
Nittahubbee	Seal	X
Tishonowan	Seal	X
Warsharchahooma	Seal	X

Isaac James
Hopiaintuhken X
Aryahkarnes X
Shemotar X
a Hopiaisketina X
  Thomas LeFlore X
Arnkeohatutteu X
Shokperlukna X
Posherhoomah X
  Robert Johow X
Arharyotuttee X
Kukonolarten X
James Vaughan X
James Karnes X
Tishohakubbee X
Narfenalar X
  Perinashoe X
Inhargarken X
Mututtee X
Narharyutteu X
Ishmaryutteu X
~~Camiintor~~ James deKing X
Lewis Wilson X
Istonarkerharcho X
Hoshinchamartarker X
Kummeashottu X
Oyarturstuttee X
Saml Garland
Thomas Wall
Saml Worcester
Jacob Folsom
William ~~F~~oster
Ontionharcho X
Hughes Foster
Prince Juzan

Mr. Pitchlynn Jr.   Seal
David Folsom   Seal
Sholohammastube   Seal ×
Tisho   Seal ×
Lawechatee   Seal ×
Hashehomma   Seal ×
Ofenowa   Seal ×
Ahekoche   Seal ×
Kaloshaube   Seal ×
Atoko   Seal ×
Ishtonoleche   Seal ×
Smttotahabe   Seal ×
Piles D. Fisher   Seal
Isaac Folsom   Seal ×
He Ratube   Seal ×
Hakseche   Seal ×
Jerry Carney   Seal ×
John Washington   Seal ×
Phiplip   Seal ×
Meshamuye   Seal ×
Ishtelika   Seal ×
Heshohomma   Seal
John McKelberry   Seal ×
Benjn. James   Seal
Ishbachahombe   Seal ×
Aholiktube   Seal
Wacking Wolf   Seal ×
John Waicle   Seal ×
Big Ace   Seal ×
Bob   Seal ×
Tush Kochaubbe   Seal ×
It ta be   Seal ×
Tishowa Karye   Seal

Holifommra   Seal ×
John Garland   Seal ×
Kvahona   Seal ×
Ishteyuhomube   Seal ×
Oklanowa   Seal ×
Neta   Seal ×
James Fletcher   Seal ×
Giles D Pitchlynn Seal
Mr William Trahern Seal
Josh Kahemmitta   Seal ×
Tethataye   Seal ×
Emoklashahopie   Seal ×
Ishoimita   Seal ×
Thomas I Foster   Seal
Badoc Brashears

Levi Perkins
Isaac Perry
Ishtonocka Hoomah
Hiram King
Ogla Enlih
Nukelahtubbee
Iuska Hollattah
Panshatubbee

P P Pitchlynn
    Iul Hail
Sofia Stonakey
Fischoomma
William Wade
Pansh Stick ubbee
Ho lit tauh chah ubbee
Ka hlauh chah abbee

Eyarpulubbee
Okentahubbee
Living War Club
John Jones
Charles Jones
Isaac Jones
Hooklucha
Muscogee
Edan Nelson

In the Senate of the United States
February 21st: 1831.

Resolved, (two thirds of the Senators present concurring) That the Senate do advise and consent to the ratification of the Treaty, between the United States of America and the Mingoes, Chiefs, Captains and Warriors of the Choctaw Nation, concluded at Dancing Rabbit Creek on the 15th of September 1830, together with the supplement thereto, concluded at the same place the 28th of September 1830; with the exception of the preamble.

Attest, Walter Lowrie

Andrew Jackson,
President of the United States of America,
To all and singular to whom these presents shall come, Greeting:

Whereas a Treaty between the United States of America, and the Mingoes, Chiefs, Captains and Warriors of the Choctaw Nation was entered into at Dancing Rabbit Creek, on the twenty-seventh day of September in the Year of our Lord one thousand eight hundred and thirty, and of the Independence of the United States, the fifty-fifth, by John H. Eaton and John Coffee, Commissioners on the part of the United

States, and the Chiefs, Captains and Head-Men of the Choctaw Nation, on the part of said Nation;— which Treaty, together with the Supplemental article thereto, is in the words following, To wit:

A Treaty

Various Choctaw persons have been presented by the chiefs of the Nation with a desire that they might be provided for, Being particularly deserving, an earnestness has been manifested that provision might be made for them. It is therefore by the undersigned Commissioners here assented to with the understanding that they are to have no interest in the reservations which are devoted and provided for under the general Treaty to which this is a Supplement.

As evidence of the liberal and kind feelings of the President and Government of the United States the Commissioners agree to the request as follows (to wit) Pierre Suzan, Peter Pitchlynn, G. W. Harkins, Jack Pitchlynn, Israel Fulson, Louis Laflore, Benjamin James, Joel H. Nail, Hopoyurahubbee, Onokhubbee, Benjamin Laflore, Michael Laflore, Allen Yates, & wife shall be entitled to a reservation of two sections of land each to include their improvement where they at present reside, with the exception of the three first named persons & Benj. Letleve who are authorized to locate one of their sections on any other unimproved and unoccupied land, within their respective districts.

Article 2d

And to each of the following persons there is allowed a reservation of a section and a half of land, James L. McDonald, Robert Jones, Noah Wall, James Campbell, G. Nelson, and Vaughn Brasheans, R. Harris, Little Leader, S. Foster, J. Vaughn, L. Durant, Samuel Long, J. Magagha, Thos. Everg, Giles Thompson, Garland, John Bond, William Laflore, and Turner Brasheans; the two first named persons, may locate one section each, and one section jointly on any unimproved and unoccupied land, these not residing in the Nation. The others are to include their present residence and improvement.

Also one Section is allowed to the following persons (to wit) Middleton Mackey, Wesley Train, Cheehoma, Moses Foster, D. McWall, Charles Scott

Molly Nail, Susan Colbert, who was formerly Susan James, Saml Garland, Silas Fisher, D. McCartain, Oaklahoma, & Polly Fillecathey, to be located in entire sections to include their present residence and improvement, with the exception of Molly Nail & Susan Colberts, who are authorized to locate theirs on any unimproved unoccupied land.

John Pitchlynn has long and faithfully served the Nation in character of U. States interpreter, he has acted as such for forty years, in consideration it is agreed, in addition to what has been done for him there shall be granted to two of his Children, (to wit.) Silas Pitchlynn, & Thomas Pitchlynn one section of land each to adjoin the location of their father. likewise to James Madison and Peter Sons of Mushulatubbe one section of land each to include the old House and improvement of where their father formerly lived on the old Military road, adjoining a large Prerarie.

And to Henry Graves Son of the Chief Nattiacche there is one section of land given to adjoin his fathers land.

And to each of the following persons Half a section of land is granted on any unoccupied and unimproved lands in the Districts where they respectively live (to wit) Willis Harkins, James D. Hamilton, William Jozan, Tobias Loffin Jo Doake, Jacob Fulsom, P. Hays, Saml. Worcester, Geo. Hunter, William Trair and Robert Nail and Alexander McKee.

And there is given a quarter section of land each to Delila and her five fatherless Children, She being a Choctaw woman residing out of the Nation, also the same quantity to Peggy Trihaw another Indian Woman residing out of the Nation & her two fatherless Children; & to the widows of Pushmitahaw, & Puckshenubbee, who were formerly distinguished Chiefs of the nation and for their Children four Sections of land, each in trust for themselves & their Children

All of said last mentioned reservations are to be located under and by direction of the President of the U States.

Article 3

The Choctaw people now that they have ceded their lands are solicitous to get to their new homes early as possible & accordingly they wish that a party may be permitted to proceed this fall to ascertain whereabouts will be most advantageous for their people to be located.

It is therefore agreed that three or four persons (from each of the three districts) under the guidance of some discreet and well qualified person or persons may proceed during this fall to the West upon an examination of the Country.

For their time and expenses the U States agree to allow the said Twelve persons Two Dollars a day each, not to exceed One Hundred days, which is deemed to be ample time to make an examination.

If necessary Pilots acquainted with the Country will be furnished when they arrive in the West

Article 4th

John Donly of Alabama who has several Choctaw Grandchildren; and who for Twenty years has carried the mail through the Choctaw Nation, a desire by the Chiefs is expressed that he may have a Section of land; it is accordingly granted, to be located in one entire Section, on any unimproved & unoccupied land.

Allen Glover and George S Gaines licensed Traders in the Choctaw Nation, have accounts amounting to upwards of Nine thousand Dollars against the Indians who are unable to pay their said debts without distressing their families, a desire is expressed by the Chiefs that Two sections of land be set apart to be sold and the proceeds thereof to be applied toward the payment of the aforesaid debts. It is agreed that two sections of any unimproved and unoccupied land be granted to George S Gaines who will sell the same for the best price he can obtain and apply the proceeds thereof to the credit of the Indians on their accounts due to the before mentioned Glover and Gaines; & shall make the application to the present Indian Agent

At the earnest and particular request of the Chief Greenwood Leflore there is granted to David Haley One half Section of land to be located in a half section on any unoccupied and unimproved land as a compensation for a journey to Washington City with despatches to the Government and returning others to the Choctaw Nation

The foregoing is entered into, as supplemental to the treaty concluded yesterday.—

Done at Dancing Rabbit Creek the 28th day of September 1830

Jno H Eaton

In presence of
E. Breathitt Secty to Com:
W. Ward Agt for Choctaws
M. Mackey U.S. Intr.

John Pitchlynn
U.S. Intr.
[signatures]
Jno Pitchlynn
Geo S Gaines

The following words on this supplement were interlined before being signed "John Pitchlerte" & "Allen Yates to wife" also "By Leflore" "or nearly Iron" "Choolehoma" "person or persons"

In presence of
E. Breathitt Secly to Com:

Jno Coffee Comr
Greenwood Leflore
Nittuackee his X mark
Mushulatubbee his X mark
Ofahooma his X mark
Eyarhocuttubbee his X mark
Ishacher Hopia his X mark
Holubbee his X mark
Onarhubbee his X mark
Robert Cole his X mark
Hopiaunchahubbee his X mark
David Folsom
John Garland his X mark
Hopiahoma his X mark
Captain Thotka his X mark
Pierre Juzan
Immartatartar his X mark
Hokimahomartartar his X mark

Now, therefore, be it known, that I, Andrew Jackson, President of the United States of America, having seen and considered said Treaty, do, in pursuance of the advice and consent of the Senate, as expressed by their Resolution of the twenty first day of February, one thousand eight hundred and thirty-one, accept, ratify and confirm the same, and every clause and article thereof, with the exception of the Preamble.

In Testimony whereof, I have caused the seal of the United States to be hereunto affixed, having signed the same with my hand.

Done at the City of Washington, this twenty fourth day of February, in the Year of our Lord one thousand eight hundred and thirty-one, and of the Independence of the United States, the fifty-fifth.

Andrew Jackson

By the President,
M. Van Buren,
Secy of State

Treaty of Dancing Rabbit Creek

[Transcription of Original]

Treaty of Dancing Rabbit Creek

1830

~~1831~~

Treaty

with the

Choctaws

Sep. ~~15~~ 27, 1830

And 28th Sep[r] 1930

Ratified Feb[r] 24th 1831

A treaty of perpetual friendship, cession and limits entered into by John H. Eaton and John Coffee for and in behalf of the Government of the United States and the Mingoes Chiefs Captains and Warriors of the Choctaw Nation begun and held at Dancing Rabbit Creek on the 15th of September in the year 1830.

  WHEREAS the General Assembly of the State of Mississippi has extended the laws of said State to persons and property within the chartered limits of the same and the President of the United States has said that he cannot protect the Choctaw people from the operation of these laws; Now therefore that the Choctaw may live under their own laws in peace with the United States and the State of Mississippi they have determined to sell their lands east of the Mississippi & have - accordingly agreed to the following articles of treaty ─────

Article 1st

  Perpetual peace and friendship is pledged and agreed on by and between United States and the Mingoes, Chiefs, & Warriors of the Choctaw Nation of Red People; and that this may be considered the ~~only~~ treaty existing between the parties all other treaties heretofore existing and inconsistent with the provisions of this are hereby declared null and void. ─────

Article 2nd

  The United States under a grant specially to be made by the President of the U. S. shall cause to be conveyed to the Choctaw Nation a tract of country west of the Mississippi River in fee simple to them & their descendants, to insure to them while they shall, exist as a nation and live on it beginning near Fort Smith where the

Treaty of Dancing Rabbit Creek

Arkansas boundary crosses the Arkansas River, Running thence ~~with~~ to the scource[sic] of the Canadian fork; if in the limits of the United States, or to those limits; thence due South to Red River, and down Red River to the West boundary of the Territory of Arkansas; thence North along that line to the beginning. The boundary of the same to be agreably[sic] to the treaty made and concluded at Washington City in the year 1825 The grant to be executed so soon as the present Treaty shall be ratified ——

Article 3$\underline{d}$

In consideration of the provisions contained in the several articles of this Treaty, the Choctaw Nation of Indians consent and hereby cede to the United States, the entire country they own and possess, East of the Mississippi River; and they agree to remove beyond the Mississippi River, early as practicable, and will so arrange their removal, that as many as possible of thier[sic] people not exceeding one half of the whole number, shall depart during the falls of 1831 and 1832; the residue to follow during the succeeding fall of 1833; a better opportunity in this manner will be afforded the Government, to extend to them the facilities and comforts which it is desirable should be extended in conveying them to thier new Homes. ——

Article 4$\underline{th}$

The Government and people of the United States are hereby obliged to secure to the said Choctaw Nation of Red People the Jurisdiction and Government of all the Persons and Property that may be within thier limits West, so that no territory or State shall ever have a right to pass laws for the Government of the Choctaw Nation of Red People and thier Descendants; and that no part of the land granted them shall ever be embraced in any territory or State; but the U. S. shall forever secure said Choctaw Nation from, & against, all laws except such as from time to time may be enacted in their own National Councils, not inconsistent with the Constitution, Treaties, and laws of the United States; & except such as may, & which have been enacted by Congress, to the extent that Congress under the Constitution are required to exerscise[sic] a legislation over Indian Affairs. But the Choctaws, should this treaty be ratified, express a wish that Congress may grant to the Choctaws the right of punishing by thier own laws, any white man who shall come into thier Nation, & infringe any of their National regulations.

Article 5$\underline{th}$

The United States are obliged to protect the Choctaws from domestic strife & from foreign enemies on the same principles that the citizens of the United States are protected, so that whatever would be a legal demand upon the U. S. for defence[sic] or for wrongs committed by an Enemy, on a Citizen of the U. S, shall be equally binding

Treaty of Dancing Rabbit Creek

in favour[sic] of the Choctaws, & in all cases where the Choctaws shall be called upon by a legally authorized officer of the U. S. to fight an Enemy, such Choctaw shall receive the pay & other emoluments, which citizens of the U. S. receive in such cases, provided, no war shall be undertaken or prosecuted by said Choctaw Nation but by declaration made in full Council, & to be approved by the U. S. unless it be in self defence against an open rebellion or against an enemy marching into thier country, in which cases they shall defend, until the U. S. are advised thereof.

Article 6th

Should a Choctaw or any party of Choctaws commit acts of violence upon the person or property of a citizen of the U. S, or join any war party against any neighbouring[sic] tribe of Indians, without the authority in the preceding article; & except to oppose an actual or threatened invasion or rebellion, such person so offending shall be delivered up to an Officer of the U. S. if in the power of the Choctaw Nation, that such offender may be punished as may be provided in such cases, by the laws of the U. S.; but if such Offender is not within the control of the Choctaw Nation, then said Choctaw Nation shall not be held responsible for the injury done by said offender.

Article 7th

All acts of violence committed upon persons and property of the ~~Cho~~ people of the Choctaw Nation either by Citizens of the U. S. or neighbouring[sic] tribes of Red people, shall be referred to some authorized agent by him to be referred to the ~~U.S.~~ President of the U. S, who shall examine into such cases and see that every possible degree of justice is done to said Indian party of the Choctaw Nation.

Article 8th

Offenders against the laws of the U. S. or any individual State shall be apprehended & delivered to any duly authorized person where such offender may be found in the Choctaw Country, having fled from any part of U. S. but in all such cases application must be made to the Agent or Chiefs & the expense of his apprehension and delivery provided for & paid by the U States.

Article 9th

Any citizen of the U. S. who may be ordered from the Nation by the Agent & constituted authorities of the Nation and refusing to obey or return into the Nation without the consent of the aforesaid persons, shall be subject to such pains and penalties as may provided by the laws of the U. S. in such cases. Citizens of the U. S.

Treaty of Dancing Rabbit Creek

travelling peaceably under the authority of the laws of the U. S. shall be under the care and protection of the Nation.

Article 10th

No person shall expose goods or other article for sale as a trader, without a written permit from the constituted authorities of the Nation, or authority of the laws of the Congress of the U. S. under penalty of forfeiting the articles, & the constituted authorities of the Nation shall grant no license except to such persons as reside in the Nation and are answerable to the laws of the Nation. The U. S. shall be particularly obliged to assist to prevent ardent spirits from being introduced into the Nation.

Article 11th

Navigable streams shall be free to the Choctaws who shall pay no higher toll or duty than Citizens of the U. S. It is agreed further that the U. S. shall establish one or more Post Offices in said Nation, & may establish such military post roads, and posts, as they may consider necessary.

Article 12th

All intruders shall be removed from the Choctaw Nation and kept without it. Private property to be always respected & on no occasion taken for public purposes without just compensation being made therefor to the rightful owner. If an Indian unlawfully take or steal any property from a white man a citizen of the U. S. the offender shall be punished. And if a white man unlawfully take or steal any thing from an Indian, the property shall be restored & the offender punished. It is further agreed that when a Choctaw shall be given up to be tried for any offence against the laws of the U. S. if unable to employ Counsel to defend him, the U. S. will do it, that his trial may be fair and impartial.

Article 13th

It is consented that a qualified Agent shall be appointed for the Choctaws every Four Years, unless sooner removed by the President; and he shall be removed on petition of the constituted authorities of the Nation the President being satisfied there is sufficient cause shown. The Agent shall fix his residence convenient to the great body of the people; & in the selection of an Agent immediately after the ratification of this Treaty, the wishes of the Choctaw Nation on the subject shall be entitled to great respect.

Treaty of Dancing Rabbit Creek

Article 14th

Each Choctaw head of a family being desirous to remain & become a Citizen of the States, shall be permitted to do so, by signifying his intention to the Agent within Six Months from the ratification of this Treaty & he or she shall thereupon be entitled to a reservation of one section of Six Hundred and forty Acres of Land, to be bounded by sectional lines of survey; in like manner shall be entitled to one half that quantity for each unmarried child which is living with him over Ten years of Age; & a quarter section to such child as be under 10 years of age, to adjoin the location of the Parent. If they reside upon said lands intending to become Citizens of the States for five Years after the ratification of this Treaty in that case a grant in fee simple shall issue; said reservation shall include the present improvement of the head of the family, or a portion of it. Persons who claim under this article shall not lose the privilege of a Choctaw Citizen, but if they ever remove are not to be entitled to any portion of the Choctaw Annuity;

Article 15th

To each of the Chiefs in the Choctaw Nation (to wit) Greenwood Laflore Nutackachie, and Mushulatubbe there is granted a reservation of four sections of land, two of which shall include and adjoin thier[sic] present improvement, and the other two located where they please but on unoccupied unimproved lands, such sections shall be bounded by sectional lines, & with the consent of the President they may sell the same. Also to the three principal Chiefs & to their successors in office there shall be paid Two Hundred and fifty Dollars annually while they shall continue in their respective offices, except to Mushulatubbe who as he has an annuity of One Hundred & fifty Dollars for life under a former treaty, shall receive only the additional sum of One Hundred Dollars, while he shall continue in office as Chief; & if in addition to this the Nation shall think propper[sic] to elect an additional principal Chief of the whole to superintend and govern upon republican principles he shall receive annually for his services Five Hundred Dollars, which allowance to the Chiefs and their successors in office, shall continue for Twenty Years. At any time when in Military Service, & while in service by authority of the U. S. the district Chiefs under and by selection of the President shall be entitled to the pay of Majors; the other Chief under the same circumstances shall have the pay of a Lieutenant-Colonel. The speakers of the three districts, shall receive Twenty five Dollars a year for four years each for four years each & the three secretaries one to each of the Chiefs, fifty dollars each for four years. Each Captain of the Nation, the number not to exceed ninety nine, thirty three from each District shall be furnished upon removing to the West, with each a good suit of clothes & a broad sword as an outfit, & for four years commencing with the first of thier removal, shall each receive Fifty Dollars a Year, for the trouble of

Treaty of Dancing Rabbit Creek

keeping thier people at order in settling; & whenever they shall be in military service by authority of the U. S. shall receive the pay of a captain.

Article 16th

In wagons; & with steam boats as may be found necessary the U. S. agree to remove the Indians to thier new Homes at thier expense and under the care of discreet and carefull[sic] persons, who will be kind and brotherly to them. They agree to furnish them with ample corn and beef, or pork for themselves & families for Twelve months after reaching thier new homes.

It is agreed further that the U. S. will take all thier cattle, at the valuation of some discreet person to be appointed by the President, & the same shall be paid for in money after thier arrival at thier new homes; or in other cattle such as may be desired shall be furnished them, notice being given through thier Agent of thier wishes upon this subject before thier removal that time to supply the demand may be afforded.

Article 17th

The several annuities and sums secured under former Treaties to the Choctaw Nation and People shall continue as tho. this Treaty had never been made. And it is further agreed that the U. S. in addition will pay the sum of Twenty thousand Dollars for Twenty Years, commencing after thier removal to the west, of which, in the first year after thier removal, Ten thousand Dollars shall be divided and arranged to such as may not receive reservations under this Treaty.

Article 18th

The U. S. shall cause the lands hereby ceded to be surveyed; & surveyors may enter the Choctaw Country for that purpose, conducting themselves properly & disturbing or interrupting none of the Choctaw people. But no person is to be permitted to settle within the Nation, or the lands to be sold before the Choctaws shall remove. And for the payment of the several amounts secured in this Treaty, the lands hereby ceded are to remain a fund pledged to that purpose, until the debt shall be provided for and arranged. And further it is agreed, that in the construction of this Treaty wherever well founded doubt shall arise, it shall be construed most favorably towards the Choctaws.

Treaty of Dancing Rabbit Creek

Article 19ᵗʰ

The following reservations of land are hereby admitted. To Co^l David Fulsom Four Sections of which Two shall include his present improvement, & two may be located else where, on unoccupied, unimproved land.
To I. Garland, Co^l Robert Cole, Tuppanahomer, John Pytchlynn[sic], Charles Juzan, Johokebetubbe, Eaychahobia, Ofehoma two sections, each to be include thier improvements, and to be bounded by sectional lines, & the same may be disposed of and sold with the consent of the President. And that others not provided for, may be provided for, there shall be reserved as follows:
First; One section to each head of a family not exceeding Forty in number, who during the present year, may have had in actual cultivation, with a dwelling House thereon Fifty Acres or more. Secondly three quarter sections after the manner aforesaid to each head of a family not exceeding Four Hundred and Sixty, as shall have cultivated Thirty Acres and less than Fifty, to be bounded by quarter section lines of survey, & to be contiguous and adjoining.
Third; One half section as aforesaid to those who shall have cultivated from Twenty to Thirty acres the number not to exceed Four Hundred. Fourth; a quarter section as aforesaid to such as shall have cultivated from twelve to twenty acres, the number not to exceed three hundred and fifty, and one half that quantity to such as shall have cultivated from two to twelve acres, the number also not to exceed three hundred and fifty persons. Each of said class of cases shall be subject to the limitations contained in the first class, & shall be so located as to include that part of the improvement which contains the dwelling House. If a greater number shall be found to be entitled to reservations under the several classes of this article, than is stipulated for under the limitation prescribed, then & in that case the Chiefs separeately[sic] or together shall determine the persons who shall be excluded in the respective districts.
Fifth; Any Captain the number not exceeding ninety persons, who under the provisions of this article shall receive less than a section, he shall be entitled, to an additional quantity of half a section adjoining to his other reservation. The several reservations secured under this article, may be sold with the consent of the President of the U. S; but should any prefer it, or omit to take a reservation for the quantity he may be entitled to the U. S. will on his removing pay fifty cents an acre, after reaching thier new homes, provided that before the first of January next they shall adduce to the Agent; or some other authorized person to be appointed, proof of his claim & the quantity of it. Sixth; likewise children of the Choctaw Nation residing in the Nation, who have neither Father nor Mother a list of which, with satisfactory proof of Parentage and orphanage being filed with Agent in six months to be forwarded to the War Department, shall be entitled to a quarter section of Land, to be located under the direction of the President, & with his consent the same may be sold and the proceeds applied to some beneficial purpose for the benefit of said orphans

Treaty of Dancing Rabbit Creek

Article 20th

The U. S. agree & stipulate as follows, that for the benefit and advantage of the Choctaw people, & to improve thier condition, thier[sic] shall be educated under the direction of the President & at the expense of the U. S. forty Choctaw Youths for Twenty years. This number shall be kept at school, & as they finish thier education others to supply thier places shall be received for the period stated. The U. S. agree also to erect a Council House for the Nation at some convenient central point, after thier people shall be settled; & a House for each Chief, also a church for each of the three Districts, to be used also as school Houses, until the Nation may conclude to build others; & for these purposes Ten thousand Dollars shall be appropriated; also Fifty thousand Dollars (viz) Twenty Five Hundred Dollars annually shall be given for the support of three Teachers of schools for Twenty Years. Likewise there shall be furnished to the Nation, three Blacksmiths one for each District for sixteen years, & a qualified Mill Wright for five years; Also there shall be furnished the following articles, Twenty One Hundred Blankets, To each warrior who emigrates a rifle, moulds, wipers and ammunition. One thousand axes, Ploughs, Hoes, Wheels and Cards each; and four Hundred looms. There shall also be furnished one Ton of iron & two hundred weight of steel annually to each District for sixteen years.

Article 21st

A few Choctaw Warriors yet survive who marched and fought in the Army with General Wayne the whole number stated not to exceed Twenty.
These it is agreed shall hereafter while they live receive Twenty Five dollars a year; a list of them to be early as practicable, & within six months made out, and presented to the Agent to be forwarded to the War Department.—

Article 22d

The Chiefs of the Choctaws have suggested that thier people are in a state of rapid advancement in education and refinement; and have expressed a solicitude that they might have the privilege of a Delegate on the floor of the House of Representatives extended to them. The Commissioners do not feel, that they can under a treaty stipulation accede to the request, but at thier desire, present it in the Treaty, that Congress may consider of and decide the application.

Done and signed and executed by the Commissioners of the United States and the Chiefs Captains and Head Men of the Choctaw Nation, at Dancing Rabbit Creek this 27th day of September Eighteen Hundred and Thirty.

Treaty of Dancing Rabbit Creek

			His Mark
In presence of	Jn° H. Eaton	(Seal)	
E. Breathitt Secty	Jn°. Coffee	(Seal)	
to the Commss^r =	Greenwood Leflore	(Seal)	
William Ward Agt.	Musholatubbee	(Seal)	X
for Choctaws.	Nittucachee	(Seal)	X
John Pitchlynn	Eyarhocuttubbee	(Seal)	X
US Int^r	Iyacherhopia	(Seal)	X
M Mackey	Offahoomah	(Seal)	X
US Intr.	Archalater	(Seal)	X
Geo. S. Gaines	Onnahubbee	(Seal)	X
of Alabama	Holarterhoomah	(Seal)	X
RP Currin	Hopiaunchahubbee	(Seal)	X
Luke Howard	Zishomingo	(Seal)	X
Sam. L. Worchester	Captain thalke	(Seal)	X
Jn° W Byrn	James Shield	(Seal)	X
John Bell	Pistiyubbee	(Seal)	X
Jn° Bond	Yobalarunehahubbee	(Seal)	X
	Holubbee	(Seal)	X
	Robert Cole	(Seal)	X
	Mokelareharhopin	(Seal)	X
	Lewis Perry	(Seal)	X
	Artonamarstubbe	(Seal)	X
	Hopeatubbee	(Seal)	X
	Hoshahoomah	(Seal)	X
	Chuallahoomah	(Seal)	X
	Joseph Kincaide	(Seal)	X
	Artooklubbetushpar	(Seal)	X
	Metubbee	(Seal)	X
	Arsarkatubbee	(Seal)	X
	Issaterhoomah		X
	Chohtahmatahah	(Seal)	X
	Tunnuppashubbee	(Seal)	X
	Okocharyer	(Seal)	X
	Hoshhopia	(Seal)	X
	Warsharshahopia	(Seal)	X
	Maarshunchahubbee	(Seal)	X
	Misharyubbee	(Seal)	X
	Daniel McCurtain	(Seal)	X
	Tushkerharcho	(Seal)	X
	Hoktoontubbee	(Seal)	X
	Nuknacrahookmarhee	(Seal)	X
	Mingohoomah	(Seal)	X
	Pisinhocuttubbee	(Seal)	X
	Tullarhacher	(Seal)	X
	Little leader	(Seal)	X
	Maanhutter	(Seal)	X
	Cowehoomah	(Seal)	X

Treaty of Dancing Rabbit Creek

Tillamoer	(Seal)	X
Imnullacha	(Seal)	X
Artopilachubbee	(Seal)	X
Shupherunchahubbee	(Seal)	X
Nitterhoomah	(Seal)	X
Oaklaryubbee	(Seal)	X
Pukumma	(Seal)	X
Arpalar	(Seal)	X
Holber	(Seal)	X
Hoparmingo	(Seal)	X
Isparhoomah	(Seal)	X
Tieberhoomah	(Seal)	X
Tishoholarter	(Seal)	X
Mahayarchubbee	(Seal)	X
Arlarter	(Seal)	X
Nittahubbee	(Seal)	X
Tishonouan	(Seal)	X
Warsharchaboomah	(Seal)	X
Isaac James	(Seal)	X
Hopiaintushker	(Seal)	X
Aryoshkermer		X
Shemotar		X
Hopiaisketina		X
Thomas Leflore		X
Arnokechatubbee		X
Shokoperlukna		X
Posherhoomah		X
Robert Folsom		X
Arharyotubbee		X
Kushonolarter		X
James Vaughan		X
James Karnes		X
Tishohakubbee		X
Narlanalar		X
Pennasha		X
In har yar ker		X
Motubbee		X
Narharyubbee		X
Ishmaryubbee		X
James M King		
Lewis Wilson		X
Istonarkerharcho		X
Hoshinshamartarher		X
Kinsulachubbee		X
Eyarhinstubbee		X
Saml Garlands		
Thomas Wall		
Sam. S. Worcester		

Treaty of Dancing Rabbit Creek

Jacob Folsom		
William Foster		
Ontioerharcho		X
Hugh A. Foster		
Pierre Juzan		
Jno. Pitchlynn Jr.	(Seal)	
David Folsom	(Seal)	
Sholohommastube	(Seal)	X
Tesho	(Seal)	X
Lauwechubee	(Seal)	X
Hoshehammo	(Seal)	X
Ofenowo	(Seal)	X
Ahekoche	(Seal)	X
Kaloshoube	(Seal)	X
Atoko	(Seal)	X
Ishtemeleche	(Seal)	X
Emthtohabe	(Seal)	X
Silas D. Fisher	(Seal)	
Isaac Folsom	(Seal)	X
Hekatube	(Seal)	X
Hakseche	(Seal)	X
Jerry Carney	(Seal)	X
John Washington	(Seal)	X
Phiplip	(Seal)	X
Meshameye	(Seal)	X
Ish te he ka	(Seal)	X
Heshohomme	(Seal)	X
John McKelbery	(Seal)	X
Benj^m. James	(Seal)	
Tik ba cha ham be	(Seal)	X
Aholiktube	(Seal)	X
Walking Wolf	(Seal)	X
John Waide	(Seal)	X
Big Axe	(Seal)	X
Bob	(Seal)	X
Tush ko cha u bbe	(Seal)	X
It ta be	(Seal)	X
Tish o wa ka you	(Seal)	
Folehommo	(Seal)	X
John Garland	(Seal)	X
Koshona	(Seal)	X
Ish le you ham ube	(Seal)	X
Ok la no wa	(Seal)	X
Neto	(Seal)	X
James Fletcher	(Seal)	X
Silus D Pitchlynn	(Seal)	
William Trahorn	(Seal)	
Tosh ka hem mit to	(Seal)	X

Treaty of Dancing Rabbit Creek

Te the ta yo	(Seal)	X
Emokloshahopie	(Seal)	X
Tishoimita	(Seal)	X
Thomas W Foster	(Seal)	
Zadoc Brashears		
Levi Perkins	(Seal)	X
Isaac Perry	(Seal)	X
Isblonocka Hoomah	(Seal)	X
Hiram King	(Seal)	
Ogla Enlah	(Seal)	X
Nu1tlahtubbee	(Seal)	X
Tuska Hollattuh	(Seal)	X
Panshastubbee	(Seal)	X
P. P. Pitchlynn	(Seal)	
Joel H. Nail	(Seal)	
Hopia Stonakey	(Seal)	X
Kocohomma	(Seal)	X
William Wade	(Seal)	X
Pansh stick ubbee	(Seal)	X
Ho lit tank chah ubbee	(Seal)	X
Ko th° ant chah ubbee	(Seal)	X
Eyarpulubbee	(Seal)	X
Oken tah ubbe	(Seal)	X
Living War Club	(Seal)	X
John Jones	(Seal)	X
Charles Jones	(Seal)	
Isaac Jones	(Seal)	X
Hocklucha	(Seal)	X
Muscogee	(Seal)	X
Eden Nelson	(Seal)	

And 28th Sep^t 1830
Ratified Feby 24th 1831.

In the Senate of the United States
February 21st: 1831.

Resolved, (two thirds of the Senators present concurring) That the Senate do advise and consent to the ratification of the Treaty, between the United States of America and the Mingoes, Chiefs, Captains and Warriors of the Choctaw Nation, concluded at Dancing Rabbit Creek on the 15th of September 1830, together with the Supplement thereto, concluded at the same place the 28th of September 1830: with the exception of the preamble.

Attest, Walter Lowrie

Treaty of Dancing Rabbit Creek

Andrew Jackson,
President of the United States of America,
To all and singular to whom these presents shall come,

Greeting:

Whereas a Treaty between the United States of America, and the Mingoes, Chiefs, Captains and Warriors of the Choctaw Nation was entered into at Dancing Rabbit Creek, on the twenty-seventh day of September in the Year of our Lord one thousand eight hundred and thirty, and of the Independence of the United States, the fifty-fifth, by John H. Eaton and John Coffee, Commissioners on the part of the United States, and the Chiefs, Captains and Head-Men of the Choctaw Nation on the part of said Nation; - which Treaty, together with the supplemental article thereto, is in the words following,

To wit:

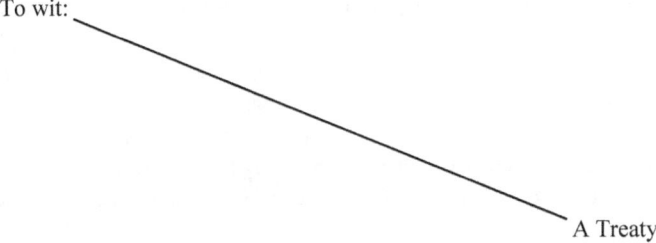

A Treaty

Various Choctaw persons have been presented by the chiefs of the Nation, with a desire that they might be provided for, Being particularly deserving, an earnestness has been manifested that provision might be made for them. It is therefore by the undersigned commissioners here assented to with the understanding that they are to have no interest in the reservations which are directed and provided for under the general Treaty to which this is a supplement.

As evidence of the liberal and kind feelings of the President and Government of the United States the Commissioners agree to the request as follows (to wit) Pierre Juzan, Peter Pitchlynn, G.W. Harkins, Jack Pitchlynn, Israel Fulsom, Louis Laflore, Benjamin James, Joel H. Nail, Hopoynjahubbee, Onorkubbee, Benjamin Laflore, Michael Laflore & Allen Yates & wife shall be entitled to a reservation of two sections of land each to include thier improvement where they at present reside, with the exception of the three first named persons & Benja. Laflore who are authorized to locate one of thier sections on any other unimproved and unoccupied land, within thier respective districts.

Article 2^d

And to each of the following persons there is allowed a reservation of a section and a half of land, (to wit) James L. McDonald, Robert Jones, Noah Wall, James Campbell, G. Nelson, ~~and~~ Vaughn Brashears, R. Harris, Little Leader, S. Foster, J.

Treaty of Dancing Rabbit Creek

Vaughn, L. Durand, Samuel Long, T. Magagha, Thos. Everge, Giles Thompson, Thomas Garland, John Bond, William Laflore, and Turner Brashears; the two first named persons, may locate one section each, and one section jointly on any unimproved and unoccupied land, these not residing in the Nation; The others are to include thier present residence and improvement.

Also one section is allowed to the following persons (to wit) Middleton Mackey, Wesley Train, Choclehomo, Moses Foster, D. W. Wall, Charles Scott, Molly Nail, Susan Colbert, who was formerly Susan James, Samuel Garland, Silas Fisher, D. McCurtain, Oaklahoma, & Polly Fillecuthey, to be located in entire sections to include thier resent residence and improvement, with the exception of Molly Nail and Susan Colbert, who are authorized to locate thiers, on any unimproved unoccupied land.

John Pitchlynn has long and faithfully served the Nation in character of U. States interpreter, he has acted as such for forty years, in consideration it is agreed, in addition to what has been done for him there shall be granted to two of his children, (to wit) Silas Pitchlynn, & Thomas Pitchlynn one section of land each to adjoin the location of thier father likewise to James Madison and Peter sons of Mushulatubbee one section of land each to include the old house and improvement ~~of~~ where thier father formerly lived on the old military road adjoining a large Prerarie[sic].

And to Henry Groves son of the Chief Natticache there is one section of land given to adjoin his father's land.

And to each of the following persons half a section of land is granted on any unoccupied and unimproved lands in the Districts where they respectively live (to wit) Willis Harkins, James D. Hamilton, William Juzan, Tobias Laflore, Jo Do~~a~~ke, Jacob Fulsom, P. Hays, Saml Worcester, Geo. Hunter, William Train ~~and~~ Robert Nail and Alexander McKee.

And there is given a quarter section of land each to Delila and her five fatherless children, she being a Choctaw woman residing out of the Nation; also the same quantity to Peggy Trihan, another Indian woman residing out of the Nation & her two fatherless children; & to the widows of Pushmilaha, & Puck she nubbee, who were formerly distinguished Chiefs of the Nation and for thier children four quarter sections of land, each in trust for themselves & thier children

All of said last mentioned reservations are to be located under and by direction of the President of the U States

Article 3

The Choctaw people now that they have ceded thier[sic] lands are solicitous to act to thier new homes early as possible & accordingly they wish that a party may be permitted to proceed this fall to ascertain where abouts will be most advantageous for thier people to be located.

Treaty of Dancing Rabbit Creek

It is therefore agreed that three or four persons (from each of the three districts) under the guidance of some discreet and well qualified person or persons ~~man~~ may proceed during this fall to the West upon an examination of the country.

For thier time and expenses the U. States agree to allow the said twelve persons Two Dollars a day each, not to exceed one hundred days, which is deemed to be ample time to make an examination.

If necessary Pilots acquainted with the country will be furnished when they arrive in the West.

Article 4th

John Donly of Alabama who has several Choctaw grand children, and who for Twenty years has carried the mail through the Choctaw Nation, a desire by the Chiefs is expressed that he may have a section of land, it is accordingly granted, to be located in one entire section, on any unimproved & unoccupied land.

Allen Glover and George S. Gaines licensed Traders in the Choctaw Nation, have accounts amounting to upwards of Nine thousand Dollars against the Indians who are unable to pay thier said debts without distressing thier families; a desire is expressed by the Chiefs that Two sections of land be set apart to be sold and the proceeds thereof to be applied toward the payment of the aforesaid debts. It is agreed that two sections of any unimproved and unoccupied land be granted to George S. Gaines who will sell the same for the best price he can obtain and apply the proceeds thereof to the credit of the Indians on thier accounts due to the before mentioned Glover and Gaines; & shall make the application to the poorest Indian first.

At the earnest and particular request of the Chief Greenwood Laflore there is granted to David Haley one half section of land to be located in a half section on any unoccupied and unimproved land as a compensation for a journey to Washington City with dispatches to the Government and returning others to the Choctaw Nation.

The foregoing is entered into, as supplemental to the treaty concluded yesterday.

Done at Dancing Rabbit creek the 28th day of September 1830.

In presence of	
E. Breathitt Secty to Com^r.	Jn° H Eaton Seal
W. Ward Agt. for Choctaws	Jn°. Coffee Seal
M Mackey US Intr.	Greenwood Leflore
John Pitchlynn	Nittucachee his x mark
US Int^r	Musholatubbee his x mark
RP Currin	Ofahoomah his x mark
Jn° W Byrn	Eyarhoeuttubbee his x mark
	Iyaeherhopia his x mark

Treaty of Dancing Rabbit Creek

Geo. S. Gaines
The following words in this supplement were interlined before being signed
1st Article "& Allen Yates & wife" also & Benj[a] Laflore
Do. Wesley Train - Choclehomo

"person or persons"

In presence of
E. Breathitt Secty to Com[r].

Holubbee   his x mark
Onarhubbee   his x mark
Robert Cole   his x mark
Hopiaunchahubbee   his x mark
David Folsom
John Garland   his x mark
Hopiahoomah   his x mark
Captain Thalko   his x mark
Pierre Juzan
Immarstarher   his x mark
Hoshimhamarter   his x mark

Now, therefore, be it known, that I, Andrew Jackson, President of the United States of America, having seen and considered said Treaty, do in pursuance of the advice and consent of the Senate, as expressed by their Resolution of the twenty-first day of February, one thousand eight hundred and thirty-one, accept, ratify and confirm the same, and every clause and article thereof, with the exception of the Preamble.

In Testimony whereof, I have caused the seal of the United States to be hereunto affixed, having signed the same with my hand.

Done at the City of Washington, this twenty fourth day of February, in the Year of our Lord one thousand eight hundred and thirty-one, and of the Independence of the United States, the fifty-fifth.

Andrew Jackson

By the President,

M. VanBuren
Secty of State

Mississippi Choctaw Census

as of

June 30, 1929

taken by R. J. Enochs, Superintendent

Census of the **Mississippi Choctaw** tribe of the _____ reservation of the **Choctaw Agency** jurisdiction, as of **June 30**, 19**29**, taken by **R. J. Enochs**, Superintendent

KEY: Surname; Census Number: Present; Last; Given Name; Sex; Date of Birth; Degree of Blood; Marital Condition; Relation to Head of Family

ALLEN

1; 1; Jim; m; 1889; Full; M; Head
2; 2; Manda; f; 1884; Full; M; Wife
3; 3; I. C.; m; 1913; Full; S; Son
4; 4; Anna Mae; f; 1914; Full; S; Daughter
5; 5; J. C.; m; 1915; Full; S; Son
6; 6; R. G.; m; 1916; Full; S; Son
7; 7; Will; m; 1923; Full; S; Son

8; 8; Joe; m; 1893; Full; S; Head

9; 9; Lacie; m; 1894; Full; S; Head

10; 10; Willis; m; 1894; Full; M; Head
11; 11; Bessie; f; 1895; Full; M; Wife
12; 12; Bob; m; 1917; Full; S; Son
13; 13; Sulum; m; 1921; Full; S; Son
14; 14; Maggie; f; 1923; Full; S; Daughter
15; 15; Nell; f; 1925; Full; S; Daughter
16; 16; Huston; m; 1924; Full; S; Son
17; 17; Willie; m; Aug-8-1927; Full; S; Son

ALEX

18; 19; Nancy; f; 1910; Full; Wd; Head
19; 20; Hubert Frank; m; Mar-25-1928; Full; S; Son

20; 21; Cooper; m; 1910; Full; S; Head

21; 22; Lee; m; 1888; Full; M; Head
22; 23; Missie; f; 1903; Full; M; Wife
23; 24; Nelson; m; 1923; Full; S; Son

ANDERSON

Census of the **Mississippi Choctaw** tribe of the _____ reservation of the **Choctaw Agency** jurisdiction, as of **June 30**, 19**29**, taken by **R. J. Enochs**, Superintendent

KEY: Surname; Census Number: Present; Last; Given Name; Sex; Date of Birth; Degree of Blood; Marital Condition; Relation to Head of Family

24; 25; Ollie; m; 1886; Full; M; Head
25; 26; Kate; f; 1881; Full; M; Wife

26; 28; Oliver; m; 1888; Full; M; Head
27; 29; Sallie; f; 1893; Full; M; Wife
28; 30; Hinton; m; 1914; Full; S; Son
29; 31; Lonie; f; 1916; Full; S; Daughter
30; 32; Phillip; m; 1919; Full; S; Son
31; 33; Houston; m; 1921; Full; S; Son
32; 34; Lucille; f; 1923; Full; S; Daughter

33; 35 Abel; m; 1906; Full; M; Head
34; 36; Nancy; f; 1886; Full; M; Wife
35; 39; Allie; f; 1916; Full; S; Step-daughter
36; 37; Ella Mae; f; 1922; Full; S; Step-daughter
37; 38; Annie Mae; f; 1924; Full; S; Step-daughter

38; 40; Bob; m; 1888; Full; M; Head
39; 41; Ella; f; 1891; Full; M; Wife
40; 43; A. G.; m; 1913; Full; S; Son
41; 44; Gladys; Full; 1919; Full; S; Daughter
42; 45; Josephine; f; 1923; Full; S; Daughter
43; 46; Selmer; f; 1926; Full; S; Daughter
44; 47; Nelson; f; Oct-29-1927; Full; S; Daughter

45; 48; John; m; 1868; Full; M; Head
46; 49; Sallie; f; 1903; Full; M; Wife
47; 50; J. C.; m; 1925; Full; S; Son

48; 51; Roy; m; 1903; Full; M; Head
49; 52; Lonie; f; 1888; Full; M; Wife

50; 53; Mattie; f; 1879; Full; Wd; Head
51; 54; Ike; m; 1906; Full; S; Son
52; 55; Irvin; m; 1908; Full; S; Son
53; 56; Bettie; f; 1910; Full; S; Daughter

Census of the **Mississippi Choctaw** tribe of the _____ reservation
of the **Choctaw Agency** jurisdiction, as of **June 30**, 19**29**,
taken by **R. J. Enochs**, Superintendent

KEY: Surname; Census Number: Present; Last; Given Name; Sex; Date of Birth; Degree of Blood; Marital Condition; Relation to Head of Family

54; 57; Lodie; f; 1912; Full; S; Daughter

55; 58; John; m; 1893; Full; M; Head
56; 59; Bettie; f; 1888; Full; M; Wife
57; 60; Bennett; m; 1908; Full; S; Son
58; 61; Siny; f; 1909; Full; S; Daughter
59; 62; L. E.; m; 1913; Full; S; Son
60; 63; Hubert; m; 1914; Full; S; Son
61; 64; Oden; m; 1921; Full; S; Son
62; 65; Wilson; m; 1924; Full; S; Son

63; 66; Phoebe; f; 1880; Full; Wd; Head

AMOS

64; 67; Sebbie; f; 1878; Full; Wd; Head

65; 68; Lampkins; m; 1880; Full; M; Head
66; 69; Ann; f; 1878; Full; M; Wife
67; 70; Bonnie; f; 1911; Full; S; Daughter
68; 71; Lonie; f; 1917; Full; S; Daughter

69; 72; Griffin; m; 1888; Full; M; Head
70; 73; Sallie; f; 1892; Full; M; Wife
71; 74; Beauty; f; 1910; Full; S; Daughter
72; 75; Julia; f; 1912; Full; S; Daughter
73; 76; John; m; 1911; Full; S; Son
74; 77; Land; m; 1916; Full; S; Son
75; 78; Julton; m; 1920; Full; S; Son
76; 79; Floyd; m; 1920; Full; S; Son
77; 80; Mose; m; 1922; Full; S; Son
79; 81; Lester; m; 1907; Full; S; Son

BAUM

80; 83; Archie; m; 1873; Full; M; Head

Census of the **Mississippi Choctaw** tribe of the _____ reservation of the **Choctaw Agency** jurisdiction, as of **June 30**, 19**29**, taken by **R. J. Enochs**, Superintendent

KEY: Surname; Census Number: Present; Last; Given Name; Sex; Date of Birth; Degree of Blood; Marital Condition; Relation to Head of Family

81; 84;   Elizabeth; f; 1873; Full; M; Wife
82; 85;   Macy; f; 1909; Full; S; Daughter

BELL

83; 86;   Nicholis; m; 1898; Full; M; Head
84;   Cleddie; f; 1912; Full; M; Wife

85; 87;   Joe; m; 1903; Full; S; Head

86; 88;   Amon; m; 1900; Full; M; Head
87; 89;   Alice; f; 1903; Full; M; Wife

88; 90;   Thompson; m; 1893; Full; M; Head
89; 91;   Ellen; f; 1898; Full; M; Wife

90; 91;   Jimus; m; 1897; Full; M; Head
91; 92;   Winnie; f; 1897; Full; M; Wife
92; 94;   Ronie; f; 1916; Full; S; Daughter
93; 95;   Woods; m; 1918; Full; S; Son
94; 96;   Mamie; f; 1920; Full; S; Daughter
95; 97;   Edmond; m; 1924; Full; S; Son
96; 98;   George; m; 1927; Full; S; Son

97; 99;   Gaston; m; 1910; Full; S; Head

98; 101; Mack; m; 1905; Full; Wd; Head
99; 102; James Cook; m; Apr-24-1928; Full; S; Son

100; 103; Nash; m; 1872; Full; M; Head
101; 104; Sallie; f; 1890; Full; M; Wife
102; 105; Emma; f; 1911; Full; S; Daughter
103; 106; Effie; f; 1919; Full; S; Daughter

104; 107; Hugh; m; 1879; Full; Wd; Head
105; 108; Viola; f; 1912; Full; S; Daughter

Census of the __Mississippi Choctaw__ tribe of the _____ reservation of the __Choctaw Agency__ jurisdiction, as of __June 30__, 19__29__, taken by __R. J. Enochs__, Superintendent

KEY: Surname; Census Number: Present; Last; Given Name; Sex; Date of Birth; Degree of Blood; Marital Condition; Relation to Head of Family

106;	109;	Oda; f; 1915; Full; S; Daughter
107;	111;	Mamie; f; 1927; Full; S; S[sic]

108; 112; John; m; 1888; Full; M; Head
109; 113; Lillian; f; 1888; Full; M; Wife
110; 114; Hattie; f; 1921; Full; S; Daughter
111; 115; Eva; f; 1925; Full; S; Daughter
112; 116; Ola; f; 1927; Full; S; Daughter

113; 117; Cornilus; m; 1859; Full; Wd; Head

114; 118; John; m; 1888; Full; S; Head

115; 119; Jim; m; 1868; Full; S; Head

116; 120; Baston; m; 1888; Full; M; Head
117; 121; Lula; f; 1903; Full; M; Wife
118; 122; Sophie; f; 1908; Full; S; Daughter
119; 123; Oda; f; 1910; Full; S; Daughter
120; 124; Effie; f; 1920; Full; S; Daughter
121; 125; Aileen; f; 1923; Full; S; Daughter
122; 126; John; m; 1922; Full; S; Son
123; 127; Emmet; m; 1925; Full; S; Son

124; 128; Lish; m; 1881; Full; M; Head
125; 129; Maggie; f; 1881; Full; M; Wife
126; 130; Minnie; f; 1908; Full; S; Daughter
127; 131; Lula; f; 1916; Full; S; Daughter
128; 132; Tom; m; 1906; Full; S; Son
129; 133; Bob; m; 1910; Full; S; Son
130; 134; Basin; m; 1925; Full; S; Son

BENN

131; 137; Tom; m; 1895; Full; M; Head
132; 138; Gladys; f; 1906; Full; M; Wife

Census of the __Mississippi Choctaw__ tribe of the _____ reservation of the __Choctaw Agency__ jurisdiction, as of __June 30__, 19__29__, taken by __R. J. Enochs__, Superintendent

---

KEY: Surname; Census Number: Present; Last; Given Name; Sex; Date of Birth; Degree of Blood; Marital Condition; Relation to Head of Family

133; 136; Fannie Lou; f; 1926; Full; S; Daughter
134;   Henry Ford; m; May-9-1929; Full; S; Son
135; 138; Hubert; m; 1927; Full; S; Son

136; 139; Lula; f; 1884; Full; Wd; Head
137; 140; Jimpson; m; 1906; Full; S; Son
138; 141; Otha; m; 1914; Full; S; Son
139; 142; Wilson; m; 1917; Full; S; Son

140; 144; Charlie; m; 1899; Full; M; Head
141; 145; Emeline; f; 1907; Full; M; Wife

142; 146; Olin; m; 1900; Full; M; Head
143; 147; Neve; f; 1905; Full; M; Wife
144; 148; Nannie Mae; Full; 1924; Full; S; Daughter
145; 149; Anna Laura; f; 1927; Full; S; Daughter
146; 150; Mattie Lou; f; Apr-5-1928; Full; S; Daughter
147; 674; **Isaac**, Lessie; f; 1913; Full; S; Sister
148; 143; **Isaac**, Coline; f; 1921; Full; S; Sister

149; 151; Wyatt; m; 1868; Full; M; Head
150; 152; Ellen; f; 1871; Full; M; Wife

151; 153; Jim; m; 1876; Full; Wd; Head
152; 154; Monroe; m; 1911; Full; S; Son
153; 156; Zelmer; f; 1916; Full; S; Daughter
154; 155; Thompson; m; 1920; Full; S; Son
155; 158; Maurice; m; 1919; Full; S; Son
156; 159; Rufus; m; 1919; Full; S; Son

<u>**BILLY**</u>

157; 161; Wade; m; 1888; Full; Wd; Head
158; 162; Marceline; f; 1907; Full; S; Daughter
159; 164; Maggie; f; 1909; Full; S; Daughter
160; 163; Joseph; m; 1927; Full; S; Son-illeg.

Census of the **Mississippi Choctaw** tribe of the _____ reservation of the **Choctaw Agency** jurisdiction, as of **June 30**, 19**29**, taken by **R. J. Enochs**, Superintendent

KEY: Surname; Census Number: Present; Last; Given Name; Sex; Date of Birth; Degree of Blood; Marital Condition; Relation to Head of Family

161; 165; Richard; m; 1911; Full; S; Son
162; 166; Augustine; f; 1912; Full; S; Daughter

163;   Jourdan; m; 1888; Full; M; Head
164; 171; Lilly; f; 1896; Full; M; Wife
165; 172; Sally Mae; f; 1917; Full; S Daughter
166; 168; Nellie; f; 1921; Full; S; Daughter
167; 169; Jim; m; 1927; Full; S; Son
168; 169; Mary Lee; f; Apr-8-1928; Full; S; Daughter

169; 173; Johnson; m; 1866; Full; M; Head
170; 174; Velaria; f; 1890; Full; M; Wife
171; 175; Gipson; m; 1911; Full; S; Son
172; 176; Ike; m; 1912; Full; S; Son
173; 177; Maude; f; 1913; Full; S; Daughter
174; 178; Wilson; m; 1918; Full; S; Son
175; 179; Greer; m; 1920; Full; S; Son
176; 180; Frank; m; 1926; Full; S; Son

177; 181; Lum; f; 1885; Full; M; Head
178; 182; Minnie; f; 1883; Full; M; Wife

179; 184; Tom; m; 1911; Full; M; Head
180; 185; Sallie; f; 1910; Full; M; Wife
181;   Johnson; m; 1927; Full; S; Son

182; 186; Willie; m; 1873; Full; S; Head

183; 187; Lewis; m; 1906; Full; M; Head
184; 188; Zelmer; f; 1904; Full; M; Wife
185; 189; Clemmie; f; 1919; Full; S; Daughter
186; 190; Mamie; f; 1921; Full; S; Daughter
187; 191; Frank; m; 1928; Full; S; Son

188; 192; Williston; m; 1894; Full; M; Head
189; 193; Jessie; f; 1905; Full; M; Wife

Census of the **Mississippi Choctaw** tribe of the _____ reservation of the **Choctaw Agency** jurisdiction, as of **June 30**, 19**29**, taken by **R. J. Enochs**, Superintendent

---

KEY: Surname; Census Number: Present; Last; Given Name; Sex; Date of Birth; Degree of Blood; Marital Condition; Relation to Head of Family

190; 194; Melton; m; 1921; Full; S; Son
191; 195; Beaman; m; 1924; Full; S; Son
192; 196; Horace; m; Aug-13-1927; Full; S; Son
193; 197; Maurice; m; 1926; Full; S; Son

194; 198; Nicy; f; 1860; Full; Wd; Head
195; 199; Leona; f; 1900; Full; S; Daughter
196; 200; Ike; m; 1907; Full; S; Son

197; 201; Will; m; 1888; Full; M; Head
198; 202; Alice; f; 1890; Full; M; Wife
199; 203; William; m; 1913; Full; S; Son
200; 204; Lee; m; 1915; Full; S; Son
201; 205; Rosie; f; 1919; Full; S; Daughter
202; 206; Irene; f; 1921; Full; S; Daughter
203; 207; Joe; m; 1923; Full; S; Son
204; 208; Will, Jr; m; Aug-15-1927; Full; S; Son
205; 209; Minche; f; 1928; Full; S; Daughter

206; 211; Jim; m; 1878; Full; S; Head

207; 212; Anderson; m; 1906; Full; S; Head

BOB

208; 213; Simon; m; 1870; Full; S; Head

BOX

209; 214; Ima; f; 1898; Full; Wd; Head
210; 215; Sam Davis; m; 1924; Full; S; Son

211; 216; Lilly; f; 1888; Full; Wd; Head
212; 217; Illman; m; 1909; Full; S; Son
213; 218; Ola; f; 1914; Full; S; Daughter
214; 219; Ollie Tat; f; 1923; Full; S; Daughter

Census of the **Mississippi Choctaw** tribe of the _____ reservation of the **Choctaw Agency** jurisdiction, as of **June 30**, 19 **29**, taken by **R. J. Enochs**, Superintendent

KEY: Surname; Census Number: Present; Last; Given Name; Sex; Date of Birth; Degree of Blood; Marital Condition; Relation to Head of Family

215; 220; Bathie; f; 1925; Full; S; Daughter
216; 221; Eula; f; 1923; Full; S; Orphan

217; 222; Betsie; f; 1920; Full; S; Orphan

218; 223; Mamie; f; 1922; Full; S; Orphan
219; 224; Hanna; m[sic]; 1924; Full; S; Orphan

BRISCO

220; 225; Tom; m; 1901; Full; M; Head
221; 226; Lucy; f; 183; Full; M; Wife
222; 227; Stephen; m; 1909; Full; S; Stepson
223; 228; Jim; m; 1912; Full; S; Stepson

BULL

224; 229; Pink, m; 1878; Full; M; Head
225; 230; Emma; f; 1880; Full; M; Wife

226; 231; Foreman; m; 1904; Full; M; Head
227; 232; Sarah; f; 1989; Full; M; Wife
228; 1215; **Tubby,** West; m; 1920; Full; S; Stepson

229; 233; George; m; 1874; Full; M; Head
230; 234; Sissie; f; 1880; Full; M; Wife

BENN

231; Aline; f; 1910; Full; S; Head

CAMPBELL

232; 236; Wiley; m; 1901; Full; M; Head
233; 237; Alice; f; 1901; Full; M; Wife
234; 235; Jennie; f; 1911; Full; S; Sister

Census of the **Mississippi Choctaw** tribe of the _____ reservation of the **Choctaw Agency** jurisdiction, as of **June 30**, 19**29**, taken by **R. J. Enochs**, Superintendent

KEY: Surname; Census Number: Present; Last; Given Name; Sex; Date of Birth; Degree of Blood; Marital Condition; Relation to Head of Family

CATES

235; 238; Alice; f; 1878; Full; Wd; Head
236; 239; Del; m; 1910; Full; S; Son
237; 240; Susieanna; f; 1914; Full; S; Daughter

238; 241; Ned; m; 1890; Full; M; Head
239; 242; Janie; f; 1893; Full; M; Wife
240; 243; Tubby; m; 1918; Full; S; Son
241; 244; Henry Marshall; m; 1922; Full; S; Son
242; 245; Willie Fulton; f; 1924; Full; S; Daughter
243; 246; Jewel Partridge; f; 1926; Full; S; Daughter
244; 247; Emma; f; 1916; Full; S; Daughter

245; 248; Bill; m; 1878; Full; M; Head
246; 249; Susan; f; 1878; Full; M; Wife
247; 250; Enis; m; 1906; Full; S; Son
248; 251; Essie; f; 1908; Full; S; Daughter
249; 252; Oscar; m; 1910; Full; S; Son
250; 253; John; m; 1912; Full; S; Son
251; 254; Lonie; f; 1913; Full; S; Daughter
252; 255; Molpus; m; 1916; Full; S; Son
253; 256; Iona; f; 1918; Full; S; Daughter

CHARLES

254; 257; Jim; m; 1898; Full; S; Head

CHARLIE

255; ; Johnson; m; 1861; Full; M; Head
256; 258; Onie Sidney; f; 1886; Full; M; Wife
257; 259; Beaman; m; 1915; Full; S; Son
258; 264; Caud; m; 1916; Full; S; Son
259; 263; Charlie; m; 1922; Full; S; Son
260; 260; Juanita; f; 1920; Full; S; Daughter

Census of the **Mississippi Choctaw** tribe of the _____ reservation of the **Choctaw Agency** jurisdiction, as of **June 30**, 19**29**, taken by **R. J. Enochs**, Superintendent

KEY: Surname; Census Number: Present; Last; Given Name; Sex; Date of Birth; Degree of Blood; Marital Condition; Relation to Head of Family

261; 261; William; m; 1851; Full; M; Head
262; 261; Fannie; f; 1865; Full; M; Wife

263; 265; John; m; 1894; Full; M; Head
264; 266; Mary; f; 1902; Full; M; Wife
265; 267; Elsie; f; 1919; Full; S; Daughter

CHICKAWAY

266; 268; Isabelle; f; 1862; Full; Wd; Head
267; 269; Ola; f; 1907; Full; S; Daughter
268; 270; Lottie; f; 1909; Full; S; Daughter

269; 271; Rufus; m; 1902; Full; M; Head
270; 272; Bessie; f; 1905; Full; M; Wife
271; 273; Ross Collins; m; Apr-11-1928; Full; S; Son

272; 274; Jim; m; 1903; Full; M; Head
273; 275; Eunice; f; 1905; Full; M; Wife
274; 277; **Grant,** Rosie Lee; f; 1923; Full; S; Step-daughter
275; 276; John Hester; m; Dec-5-1927; m; S; Son

276; 278; Sim; m; 1898; Full; M; Head
277; 279; Maggie; f; 1901; Full; M; Wife
278; 289; Clemon; m; 1919; Full; S; Son
279; 281; Nellie; f; 1921; Full; S; Daughter
280; 282; Agnes; f; 1922; Full; S; Daughter
281; 283; Albert; m; 1926; Full; S; Son
282; Maggie; f; Sept-4-1928; Full; S; Daughter

283; 284; Kelly; m; 1894; Full; M; Head
284; 285; Lillie; f; 1902; Full; M; Wife
285; 286; Mikel; m; 1923; Full; S; Son
286; 287; Anna; f; 1926; Full; S; Daughter
287; 288; Jane; Full; 1927; Full; S; Daughter

Census of the **Mississippi Choctaw** tribe of the _____ reservation of the **Choctaw Agency** jurisdiction, as of **June 30**, 19**29**, taken by **R. J. Enochs**, Superintendent

KEY: Surname; Census Number: Present; Last; Given Name; Sex; Date of Birth; Degree of Blood; Marital Condition; Relation to Head of Family

CHITTO

288; 289; Joe; m; 1901; Full; M; Head
289; 290; Callie Evans; f; 1901; Full; M; Wife
290; 291; Leo Clifton; m; Mar-8-1928; Full; S; Son

291; 292; Pat; m; 1878; Wd; Head
292;   Mary; f; 1899; Full; S; Daughter
293; 293; Henretta Annie; 1915; Full; S; Daughter
294; 294; Jefferson; m; 1917; Full; S; Son
295; 295; Ora Ann; f; 1922; Full; S; Daughter
296; 296; Isom; m; 1924; Full; S; Son

297; 297; John; m; 1890; Full; M; Head
298; 298; Sallie; f; 1891; Full; M; Wife
299; 303; Minnie; f; 1911; Full; S; Daughter
300; 299; Hattie; f; 1918; Full; S; Daughter
301; 300; Allie Nora; f; 1920; Full; S; Daughter
302; 301; Ella; f; 1922; Full; S; Daughter
303; 302; Lumbilly; m; 1926; Full; S; Son

CLARK

304; 304; Stella; f; 1895; Full; S; Head

CLEMONS

305; 305; Jeff; m; 1895; Full; M; Head
306; 306; Cora; f; 1897; Full; M; Wife
307; 307; Mattie; f; 1920; Full; S; Daughter
308; 308; Ethel; f; 1922; Full; S; Daughter
309; 309; Lethel; f; 1922; Full; S; Daughter
310; 310; John; m; 1926; Full; S; Son
311; 311; Rena Mae; f; Jan-15-1928; Full; S; Daughter

312; 312; Jim; m; 1903; Full; M; Head

Census of the **Mississippi Choctaw** tribe of the _____ reservation of the **Choctaw Agency** jurisdiction, as of **June 30**, 19**29**, taken by **R. J. Enochs**, Superintendent

KEY: Surname; Census Number: Present; Last; Given Name; Sex; Date of Birth; Degree of Blood; Marital Condition; Relation to Head of Family

313; 313; Bessie; f; 1903; Full; M; Wife
314; 314; Hester; m; Dec-12-1927; Full; S; Son

315; 315; Phillip; m; 1894; Full; S; Head

316; 316; Minch; m; 1883; Full; M; Head
317; 317; Nellie; f; 1891; Full; M; Wife
318; 318; Ruth; f; 1916; Full; S; Daughter
319; 319; Bathia; m; 1918; Full; S; Son
320; 320; Mollie; f; 1920; Full; S; Daughter
321; 321; Sleeper; m; 1927; Full; S; Son

COMBY

322; 324; Olmon; m; 1878; Full; M; Head
323; 325; Laura; f; 1881; Full; M; Wife

324; 326; William; m; 1893; Full; M; Head
325; 327; Allie; f; 1905; Full; M; Wife
326; 329; Jones; m; 1924; Full; S; Son
327; 329; Irene; f; 1926; Full; S; Daughter
328; 330; Joyce Ann; f; Jan-15-1928; Full; S; Daughter

329; 331; Seymore; m; 1901; Full; M; Head
330; 332; Edna; f; 1906; Full; M; Wife
331; 333; WC; m; 1922; Full; S; Son
332; 334; F. F.; m; 1924; Full; S; Son
333; 335; Leroy; m; 1926; Full; S; Son

334; 336; Arbin; m; 1888; Full; M; Head
335; 337; Alma; f; 1891; Full; M; Wife
336; 338; Gilbert; m; 1912; Full; S; Son
337; 339; Ella; f; 1915; Full; S; Daughter
338; 340; Rose Ella; f; 1920; Full; S; Daughter
339; 341; Maudell; f; 1923; Full; S; Daughter

Census of the **Mississippi Choctaw** tribe of the _____ reservation of the **Choctaw Agency** jurisdiction, as of **June 30**, 19**29**, taken by **R. J. Enochs**, Superintendent

KEY: Surname; Census Number: Present; Last; Given Name; Sex; Date of Birth; Degree of Blood; Marital Condition; Relation to Head of Family

COOPER

340; 342; Gaston; m; 1888; Full; M; Head
341; 343; Ada; f; 1887; Full; M; Wife
342; 344; Odell; m; 1913; Full; S; Son
343; 347; Fannie; f; 1918; Full; S; Daughter
344; 348; Hubert; m; 1920; Full; S; Son
345; 349; Christine; f; 1924; Full; S; Daughter
346; 350; Elma; f; 1926; Full; S; Daughter

347; 351; Wixon; m; 1901; Full; M; Head
348; 352; Leona; f; 1908; Full; M; Wife

COTTON

349; 354; George; m; 1900; Full; M; Head
350; 355; Ellen; f; 1900; Full; M; Wife
351; 353; John; m; 1911; Full; S; Brother

CRENSHAW

352; 356; Amos; m; 1912; S; Orphan
353; 357; Austin; m; 1916; Full; S; Orphan

DAN

354; 358; S. D.; m; 1907; Full; M; Head
355; 359; Lela; f; 1908; Full; M; Wife
356; 360; Irma; f; 1927; Full; S; Daughter

357; 361; Williston; m; 1897; Full; M; Head
358; 362; Louisana; f; 1905; Full; M; Wife
359; 363; Rose Ida; f; 1922; Full; S; Daughter

DANSBY

Census of the **Mississippi Choctaw** tribe of the _____ reservation of the **Choctaw Agency** jurisdiction, as of **June 30**, 19**29**, taken by **R. J. Enochs**, Superintendent

---

KEY: Surname; Census Number: Present; Last; Given Name; Sex; Date of Birth; Degree of Blood; Marital Condition; Relation to Head of Family

360; 364; Jacob; 1872; Full; M; Head
361; 365; Jennie; 1890; Full; M; Wife

DAVIS

362; 366; Culberson; m; 1857; Full; M; Head
363; 367; Lena; f; 1871; Full; M; Wife
364; 368; Hoby; m; 1907; Full; S; Son

365; 369; Tom; m; 1900; Full; M; Head
366; 370; Cilian; f; 1900; Full; M; Wife
367; William; m; Sept-24-1928; Full; S; Son
368; 371; Millie; f; 1921; Full; S; Daughter
369; 372; Henderson; m; 1922; Full; S; Son

370; 373; Will; m; 1868; Full; M; Head
371; 374; Lucy; f; 1900; Full; M; Wife
372; 375; Annie; f; 1920; Full; S; Daughter
373; 376; John; m; 1922; Full; S; Son
374; 377; Mary; f; 1927; Full; S; Daughter

375; 379; Malissa; f; 1866; Full; Wd; Head
376; 380; Arlis; f; 1897; Full; S; Daughter
377; 381; Bessie; f; 1909; Full; S; Daughter
378; 382; Mary; f; 1915; Full; S; Daughter
379; 383; Siny; f; 1912; Full; S; Daughter
380; 384; Ada Francis; f; 1920; Full; S; Daughter

381; 385; Sidney; m; 1888; Full; Wd; Head
382; 386; Elsmer; f; 1909; Full; S; Daughter
383; 387; Mabel; f; 1911; Full; S; Daughter
384; 388; Annie; f; 1920; Full; S; Daughter
385; 389; Johnnie; m; 1922; Full; S; Son

DENSON

Census of the __Mississippi Choctaw__ tribe of the _____ reservation of the ___Choctaw Agency___ jurisdiction, as of ___June 30___, 19_29_, taken by ___R. J. Enochs___, Superintendent

KEY: Surname; Census Number: Present; Last; Given Name; Sex; Date of Birth; Degree of Blood; Marital Condition; Relation to Head of Family

386; 390; Joe; m; 1853; Full; Wd; Head
387; 399; Winston; m; 1914; Full; S; Son
388; 400; Lula; f; 1918; Full; S; Daughter

389; 391; John; m; 1902; Full; M; Head
390; 392; Lilly; f; 1881; Full; M; Wife
391; 393; Hendrix; m; 1917; Full; S; Son
392; 394; Emma; f; 1920; Full; S; Daughter
393; 395; Charley; m; 1923; Full; S; Son
394; 396; David; m; 1925; Full; S; Son;

395; 397; Willie; m; 1908; Full; M; Head
396; 398; Beauty; f; 1911; Full; M; Wife

397; 401; Pete; m; 1890; Full; M; Head
398; 402; Rosie; f; 1899; Full; M; Wife
399; 403; Mary; f; 1917; Full; S; Daughter
400; 404; Jeffie; f; 1920; Full; S; Daughter
401; 405; Edna; f; 1924; Full; S; Daughter
402; 406; Floyd; m; 1927; Full; S; Son
403; 407; Ezell; m; 1912; Full; S; Son

DIXON

404; 408; Wilson; m; 1859; Full; M; Head
405; 409; Hope; f; 1886; Full; M; Wife
406; 410; Jim; m; 1905; Full; S; Son
407; 411; Wade; m; 1915; Full; S; Son

408; 412; Jim; m; 1904; Full; M; Head
409; 413; Sarah; f; 1905; Full; M; Wife
410; 414; Marie; f; 1924; Full; S; Daughter
411; 415; Imogene; f; 1926; Full; S; Daughter
412; 416; Ellen; f; Aug-27-1927; Full; S; Daughter

413; 417; Philip; m; 1877; Full; M; Head

Census of the **Mississippi Choctaw** tribe of the _____ reservation of the **Choctaw Agency** jurisdiction, as of **June 30**, 19 **29**, taken by **R. J. Enochs**, Superintendent

KEY: Surname; Census Number: Present; Last; Given Name; Sex; Date of Birth; Degree of Blood; Marital Condition; Relation to Head of Family

414; 418; Nannie; f; 1888; Full; M; Wife

415; 419; Kanis; m; 1883; Full; Wd; Head
416; 423; Eaby; f; 1911; Full; S; Daughter
417; 424; Lonie; f; 1914; Full; S; Daughter

418; 420; Horace; m; 1906; Full; M; Head
419; 421; Esther; f; 1907; Full; M; Wife
420; 422; Calenia; f; 1927; Full; S; Daughter

421; 425; Amon; m; 1908; Full; M; Head
422; 636; Julia; f; 1908; Full; M; Wife

423; 426; Jess; m; 1873; Full; M; Head
424; 427; Callie; f; 1878; Full; M; Wife
425; 428; Scott; m; 1909; Full; S; Son
426; 429; Young; m; 1917; Full; S; Son
427; 430; Lilly; f; 1920; Full; S; Daughter

EVANS

428; 431; John; m; 1875; Full; Wd; Head

FARMER

429; 432; Tom; m; 1866; Full; M; Head
430; 433; Lizzie; f; 1873; Full; M; Wife
431; 434; Sallie; f; 1909; Full; S; Daughter
432; 435; Hward[sic]; m; 1912; Full; S; Son

433; 436; Ishman; m; 1857; Full; M; Head
434; 437; Sweeter; f; 1873; Full; M; Wife
435; 438; Moses; m; 1900; Full; S; Son
436; 439; Emma; f; 1903; Full; S; Daughter
437; 440; Marshall; m; 1909; Full; S; Son
438; 441; Maggie; f; 1910; Full; S; Daughter

Census of the **Mississippi Choctaw** tribe of the _____ reservation of the **Choctaw Agency** jurisdiction, as of **June 30**, 19**29**, taken by **R. J. Enochs**, Superintendent

KEY: Surname; Census Number: Present; Last; Given Name; Sex; Date of Birth; Degree of Blood; Marital Condition; Relation to Head of Family

439; 442; Lena; f; 1913; Full; S; Daughter
440; 443; Bill; m; 1916; Full; S; Son
441; 444; Rainey; f; 1920; Full; S; Daughter

442; 445; Silmon; m; 1876; Full; Wd; Head
443; 446; Henry; m; 1911; Full; S; Son
444; 447; Vena; f; 1915; Full; S; Daughter
445; 448; Corrine; f; 1920; Full; S; Daughter

446; 450; Manda; f; 1883; Full; Wd; Head
447; 451; Mary Lou; f; 1917; Full; S; Daughter
448; 452; Lilly Kate; f; 1920; Full; S; Daughter
449; 453; Grace; f; 1921; Full; S; Daughter

FARVE

450; 454; Bennett; m; 1892; Full; S; Head

451; 455; Paul; m; 1888; Full; M; Head
452; 456; Renia; f; 1905; Full; M; Wife
453; 457; Phillip Jacobs; m; 1924; Full; S; Son
454; 458; Zula Mae; f; 1926; Full; S; Daughter
455; 459; Estelle; f; Sept-18-1927; Full; S; Daughter

456; 460; Joseph Simons; m; 1912; Full; m; Head
457; 461; Rachel; f; 1879; Full; M; Wife

458; 462; Western; m; 1890; Full; M; Head
459; 463; Chester; m; 1905; Full; S; Son
460; 464; Josie; f; 1907; Full; S; Daughter
461; 465; John; m; 1908; Full; S; Son
462; 466; Lillian; f; 1911; Full; S; Daughter
463; 467; Ima; f; 1916; Full; S; Daughter
464; 468; Hilda; f; 1924; Full; S; Daughter

465; 471; Antwine; m; 1877; Full; M; Head

Census of the **Mississippi Choctaw** tribe of the _____ reservation of the **Choctaw Agency** jurisdiction, as of **June 30**, 19**29**, taken by **R. J. Enochs**, Superintendent

KEY: Surname; Census Number: Present; Last; Given Name; Sex; Date of Birth; Degree of Blood; Marital Condition; Relation to Head of Family

466; 469; Liseeda; f; 1874; Full; M; Wife
467; 470; Edna; f; 1910; Full; S; Daughter
468; 472; Cecilia; f; 1912; Full; S; Daughter
469; 473; Isileen; f; 1913; Full; S; Daughter
470; 474; Earl; m; 1918; Full; S; Son
471; 475; Mamie; f; 1920; Full; S; Daughter
472; 476; Corbrin; f; 1923; Full; S; Daughter

473; 477; Dave; m; 1878; Full; Wd; Head
474; 478; William; m; 1901; Full; S; Son
475; 479; Lena; f; 1900; Full; S; Daughter
476; 480; Sarah Alma; f; 1911; Full; S; Daughter
477; 481; Georgia; f; 1919; Full; S; Daughter
478; 482; John; m; 1922; Full; S; Son

479; 483; Rosine Hudson; m; 1883; Full; m; Head
480; 484; Winoa; f; 1878; Full; M; Wife

481; 485; Charles; m; 1888; Full; M; Head
482; 486; Edwina; f; 1891; Full; M; Wife
483; 487; Retha; f; 1918; Full; S; Daughter
484; 488; Alvin; m; 1920; Full; S; Son
485; 489; Irvin; m; 1922; Full; S; Son
486; 490; Aubrey; f; 1925; Full; S Daughter
487; 491; Vivian; f; 1926; Full; S; Daughter

488; 497; Thomas; m; 1882; Full; M; Head
489; 492; Mary; f; 1898; Full; M; Wife
490; 493; Hazel; f; 1918; Full; S; Daughter
491; 494; Robert; m; 1919; Full; S; Son
492; 496; Gertrude; f; 1921; Full; S; Daughter
493; 495; Ruth; f; 1924; Full; S; Daughter

493; 498; Sylvesta; m; 1888; Full; S; Head

495; 499; Joe Tole; m; 1865; Full; M; Head

Census of the **Mississippi Choctaw** tribe of the _____reservation of the **Choctaw Agency** jurisdiction, as of **June 30**, 19 **29**, taken by **R. J. Enochs**, Superintendent

KEY: Surname; Census Number: Present; Last; Given Name; Sex; Date of Birth; Degree of Blood; Marital Condition; Relation to Head of Family

496; 500; Lela; f; 1868; Full; M; Wife
497; 501; Dora; f; 1893; Full; S; Daughter
498; 502; Victoria; f; 1900; Full; S; Daughter

499; 503; Gilmore; m; 1902; Full; M; Head
500; 504; Gertrude; f; 1904; Full; M; Wife

501; 505; Joe; m; 1906; Full; M; Head
502; 506; Lillian; f; 1908; Full; M; Wife

503; 507; Basie; m; 1911; Full; S; Head

504; 508; Jessie; Full; 1912; Full; S; Head

505; 509; Corrine; m; 1895; Full; M; Head
506; 510; Viola; f; 1897; Full; M; Wife
507; 511; William; m; 1916; Full; S; Son
508; 512; Francis; m; 1922; Full; S; Son
509; 513; JC; m; 1924; Full; S; Son
510; 514; Wilma; f; 1926; Full; S; Daughter

511; 515; John Tole; m; 1883; Full; S; Head

512; 516; Charles T.; m; 1884; Full; M; Head
513; 517; Alfonsine; f; 1898; Full; M; Wife

514; 518; Emeline; f; 1890; Full; S; Head

515; 519; Mary; f; 1896; Full; S; Head

516; 520; Julia; f; 1885; Full; S; Head

517; 521; RC; m; 1901; Full; S; Head

518; 522; Dennie; m; 1888; Full; S; Head

Census of the **Mississippi Choctaw** tribe of the _____ reservation of the **Choctaw Agency** jurisdiction, as of **June 30**, 19**29**, taken by **R. J. Enochs**, Superintendent

KEY: Surname; Census Number: Present; Last; Given Name; Sex; Date of Birth; Degree of Blood; Marital Condition; Relation to Head of Family

519; 523; Western; m; 1880; Full; S; Head

520; 524; Noah; m; 1892; Full; S; Head

521; 525; Bennett; m; 1894; Full; S; Head

522; 526; William; m; 1898; Full; S; Head

523; 527; Seman; m; 1866; Full; Wd; Head

524; 528; Elinor; f; 1894; Full; S; Head

525; 529; Joe; m; 1879; Full; S; Head

526; 530; Albert; m; 1881; Full; M; Head
527; 531; Iktial; f; 1883; Full; M; Wife

528; 532; Lucile; f; 1902; Full; S; Head

529; 533; Ethel; f; 1904; Full; S; Head

530; 534; Ida; f; 1880; Full; S; Head

531; 535; Roselle; f; 1876; Full; S; Head

532; 536; Amelia; f; 1894; Full; S; Head

533; 537; Renrites; f; 1898; Full; S; Head

534; 538; Bay Turner; m; 1905; Full; S; Head

535; 539; Ceciline; m; 1906; Full; S; Head

536; 540; Charles; m; 1880; Full; S; Head

Census of the __Mississippi Choctaw__ tribe of the _____ reservation of the ___Choctaw Agency___ jurisdiction, as of ___June 30___, 19_29_, taken by ___R. J. Enochs___, Superintendent

KEY: Surname; Census Number: Present; Last; Given Name; Sex; Date of Birth; Degree of Blood; Marital Condition; Relation to Head of Family

FORBES

537; 541; Wesley; m; 1863; Full; M; Head
538; 542; Sallie; f; 1868; Full; M; Wife
539; 543; Ella; f; 1898; Full; S; Daughter
540; 544; Clent; m; 1902; Full; S; Son
541; 545; Josie; f; 1900; Full; S; Daughter
542; 546; Ida Mae; f; 1917; Full; S; Daughter
543; 547; Gaston; m; 1922; Full; S; Son

FRAZIER

544; 549; Eckel; m; 1876; Full; M; Head
545; 548; Eliza; f; 1873; Full; M; Wife

546; 550; Mollie; f; 1878; Full; Wd; Head
547; 551; Fobes; m; 1908; Full; S; Son
548; 552; John; m; 1910; Full; S; Son

549; 553; Will; m; 1898; Full; M; Head
550; 554; Lavina; f; 1903; Full; M; Wife

551; 555; Henson; m; 1873; Full; M; Head
552; 556; Liza; f; 1870; Full; M; Wife

553; 558; West; m; 1903; Full; M; Head
554; 559; Nannie; f; 1908; Full; M; Wife
555; 557; Corrine; f; 1920; Full; S; Daughter

556; 560; Ellis; m; 1897; Full; M; Head
557; 561; Emma; f; 1902; Full; M; Wife
558; 562; Susan; f; 1918; Full; S; Daughter
559; 563; Simpson; m; 1920; Full; S; Son
560; 564; Herman; m; 1924; Full; S; Son
561; 565; Frazier; m; 1926; Full; S; Son
562; 566; Velma; f; Jan-24-1928; Full; S; Daughter

Census of the **Mississippi Choctaw** tribe of the _____ reservation of the **Choctaw Agency** jurisdiction, as of **June 30**, 19**29**, taken by **R. J. Enochs**, Superintendent

KEY: Surname; Census Number: Present; Last; Given Name; Sex; Date of Birth; Degree of Blood; Marital Condition; Relation to Head of Family

563; 567; Ligman; m; 1894; Full; Wd; Head
564; 568; Edmond; m; 1922; Full; S; Son
565; 569; Sallie; f; 1924; Full; S; Daughter
566; 570; Willie; m; 1926; Full; S; Son

567; 571; Jim; m; 1903; Full; M; Head
568; 572; Anna; f; 1905; Full; M; Wife
569; 573; Foreman; m; 1926; Full; S; Son
570; 574; A. B.; m; Nov-3-1927; Full; S; Son

571; 575; Seals; m; 1873; Full; Wd; Head

GARDNER

572; 576; Jim; m; 1899; Full; M; Head
573; 577; Celie; f; 1905; Full; M; Wife
574; 578; Arleta; f; 921; Full; S; Daughter
575; 579; Alton; m; 1927; Full; S; Son

GIPSON

576; 580; Steve; m; 1860; Full; M; Head
577; 581; Jennie; f; 1868; Full; M; Wife
578; 582; Minnie; f; 1913; Full; S; Daughter
579; 583; Willie; m; 1918; Full; S; Son

580; 584; Annie; f; 1909; Full; S; Daughter-Head
581; 585; Hugh; m; 1926; Full; S; Son (Illegit.)
582; 586; Aron; m; Oct-16-1927; Full; S; Son (Illegit.)

583; 587; Ikey; m; 1903; Full; M; Head
584; 588; Fannie; f; 1908; Full; M; Wife

585; 589; Bart; m; 1876; Full; M; Head
586; 590; Lucy; f; 1878; Full; M; Wife
587; 591; Maggie; f; 1906; Full; S; Daughter

Census of the **Mississippi Choctaw** tribe of the _____ reservation of the ____**Choctaw Agency**____ jurisdiction, as of ___**June 30**___, 19__29__, taken by ____**R. J. Enochs**____, Superintendent

KEY: Surname; Census Number: Present; Last; Given Name; Sex; Date of Birth; Degree of Blood; Marital Condition; Relation to Head of Family

588; 592; Beauty; f; 1908; Full; S; Daughter
589; 593; Hansley; m; 1910; Full; S; Son
590; 594; Homer; m; 1914; Full; S; Son
591; 595; Amber; m; 1905; Full; S; Brother
592; 596; Gus; m; 1908; Full; S; Brother

593; 597; Nolie; m; 1902; Full; M; Head
594; 598; Frances; f; 1900; Full; M; Wife
595; 599; Paul; m; 1926; Full; S; Son

HALL

596; 600; Eliza; f; 1843; Full; Wd; Head

597; 601; George; m 1907; Full; M; Head
598; 602; Pauline; f; 1909; Full; M; Wife
1512; Herbert Hoover; m; Mar-4-1929; Full; S; Son

599; 603; Langford; m; 1901; Full; M; Head
600; 604; Lou; f; 1905; Full; M; Wife
601; 605; Travius; m; 1923; Full; S; Son
602; 606; Arlone; f; 1925; Full; S; Daughter
603; 607; Frank; m; 1927; Full; S; Son

604; 608; Henry; m; 1909; Full; M; Head
605; 1168; Bessie; f; 1912; Full; M; Wife

HARPER

606; 609; Lena; f; 1912; Full; S; Orphan

HARRIS

607; 610; Elismore; f; 1908; Full; S; Head

Census of the **Mississippi Choctaw** tribe of the _____ reservation of the **Choctaw Agency** jurisdiction, as of **June 30**, 19**29**, taken by **R. J. Enochs**, Superintendent

KEY: Surname; Census Number: Present; Last; Given Name; Sex; Date of Birth; Degree of Blood; Marital Condition; Relation to Head of Family

HAWKINS

608; 612; John; m; 1868; Full; M; Head
609; 611; Alice; f; 1893; Full; M; Wife
610; **Shoemaker**, Mary; f; 1911; Full; S; Step-daughter
611; **Shoemaker**, Lesta; f; 1914; Full; S; Step-daughter

HENRY

612; 613; Robert; m; 1874; Full; M; Head
613; 614; Nellie; f; 1878; Full; M; Wife
614; 615; Bob; m; 1908; Full; S; Son
615; 616; Mattie; f; 1912; Full; S; Daughter
616; 617; Jasper; m; 1917; Full; S; Son
617; 618; Dolphus; m; 1920; Full; S; Son

618; 620; Albert; m; 1878; Full; M; Head
619; 621; Martha; f; 1886; Full; M; Wife
620; 623; Beulah; f; 1900; Full; S; Daughter
621; 624; Lige; m; 1910; Full; S; Son
622; 625; Melvin; m; 1913; Full; S; Son
623; 626; Nettie; f; 1915; Full; S; Daughter
624; 627; Sis; f; 1918; Full; S; Daughter
625; 622; Guiser; f; 1904; Full; S; Daughter
626; Ellen Maurine; f; Aug-17-1928; Full; S; Daughter (illegit.)

627; 628; Jim; m; 1904; Full; M; Head
628; 629; Sallie; f; 1903; Full; M; Wife
629; 630; Frank; m; 1927; Full; S; Son
630; John; m; Feb-15-1929; Full; S
631; 632; Susie; f; 1919; Full; S; Daughter No. 618
632; 633; I. D.; m; 1924; Full; S; Daughter No. 618

HICKMAN

633; 634; Billie; m; 1886; Full; M; Head

Census of the **Mississippi Choctaw** tribe of the _____ reservation of the **Choctaw Agency** jurisdiction, as of **June 30**, 19**29**, taken by **R. J. Enochs**, Superintendent

---

KEY: Surname; Census Number: Present; Last; Given Name; Sex; Date of Birth; Degree of Blood; Marital Condition; Relation to Head of Family

634; 635; Radie; f; 1882; Full; M; Wife
635; 637; Willie; m; 1911; Full; S; Son
636; 638; Sim; m; 1913; Full; S; Son
637; 639; Susan; f; 1919; Full; S; Daughter
638; 640; Lela; f; 1921; Full; S; Daughter

639; 641; Mary; f; 1856; Full; Wd; Head
640;   **Charley**, Beckey; f; 1919; Full; S; Granddaughter

641; 642; Stennie; m; 1903; Full; M; Head
642; 643; Winnie; f; 1906; Full; M; Wife
643; 644; Eula; f; 1926; Full; S; Daughter
644; 645; Mary Ellen; f; May-1-1928; Full; S; Daughter

645; 646; Dock; m; 1904; Full; S; Head

646; 647; Wallace; m; 1906; Full; M; Head
647; 648; Lonie; f; 1909; Full; M; Wife
648; 649; Robinson; m; 1927; Full; S; Son

649; 650; Enoch; m; 1874; Full; M; Head
650; 651; Malinda; f; 1886; Full; M; Wife
651; 653; Sallie; f; 1910; Full; S; Daughter
652; 654; Sadie; f; 1911; Full; S; Daughter
653; 652; Tubby; m; 1913; Full; S; Son
654; 655; Eliza Jane; f; 1914; Full; S; Daughter
655; 656; Mary Long; f; 1916; Full; S; Daughter
656; 661; Sam; m; 1919; Full; S; Son
657; 657; Annie; f; 1921; Full; S; Daughter
658; 658; Varderman; m; 1922; Full; S; Son
659; 659; William Penn; m; 1923; Full; S; Son
660; 660; John; m; 1925; Full; S; Son

HUDSON

661; 662; Celia; f; 1907; Full; S; Head

Census of the **Mississippi Choctaw** tribe of the _____ reservation of the **Choctaw Agency** jurisdiction, as of **June 30**, 19**29**, taken by **R. J. Enochs**, Superintendent

KEY: Surname; Census Number: Present; Last; Given Name; Sex; Date of Birth; Degree of Blood; Marital Condition; Relation to Head of Family

ISAAC

662; 663; Byrd; m; 1895; Full; Wd; Head
663; 664; Oda Mae; f; 1916; Full; S; Daughter
664; 665; Bernice; f; 1918; Full; S; Daughter
665; 666; Catherine; f; 1920; Full; S; Daughter
666; 667; Edwin; m; 1927; Full; S; Son

667; 668; Simon; m; 1884; Full; M; Head
668; 669; Nannie; f; 1881; Full; M; Wife
669; 670; Hugh; m; 1910; Full; S; Son
670; 671; Beaman; m; 1913; Full; S; Son
671; 672; Florine; f; 1912; Full; S; Daughter
672; 673; Effus; f; 1923; Full; S; Daughter

673; 682; Jim; m; 1994[sic]; Full; M; Head
674; 683; Bessie; f; 1902; Full; M; Wife

675; 684; Davied; m; 1907; Full; M; Head
676; 685; Lesper; f; 1908; Full; M; Wife
677; 686; Joe Day; m; July-20-1927; Full; S; Son
678; Franklin; m; May-11-1929; Full; S; Son

679; 687; Wilson; m; 1854; Full; M; Head
680; 688; Martha; f; 1867; Full; M; Wife
681; Jackson; m; 1905; Full; S; Son
682; 689; John Day; m; 1914; Full; S; Son

683; 690; William; m; 1898; Full; M; Head
684; 691; Louisa; f; 1903; Full; M; Wife
685; 692; Annie; f; 1918; Full; S; Daughter
686; 693; Cornelia; f; July-19-1927; Full; S; Daughter

687; 695; Isaac; m; 1901; Full; M; Head
688; 27; Maggie; f; 1909; Full; M; Wife
689; 696; Claudine; f; 1922; Full; S; Daughter

Census of the __Mississippi Choctaw__ tribe of the _____ reservation of the ___Choctaw Agency___ jurisdiction, as of __June 30__, 19__29__, taken by ___R. J. Enochs___, Superintendent

KEY: Surname; Census Number: Present; Last; Given Name; Sex; Date of Birth; Degree of Blood; Marital Condition; Relation to Head of Family

690; 697; Wilbur; m; 1924; Full; S; Son
691; 694; Claud Preston; m; June-20-1928; Full; S; Son
692; Enoch; m; May-15-1929; Full; S; Son

1510; Hickman; m; 1910; Full; S; Orphan

ISOM

693; 698; Isom; m; 1900; Full; S; Head
694; 699; Willis; m; 1914; Full; S; Brother

JACKSON

695; 700; Mack; m; 1900; Full; S; Head

696; 701; Tom; m; 1888; Full; Wd; Head
697; 702; Woodrow; m; 1917; Full; S; Son
698; 703; Eva; f; 1920; Full; S; Daughter

699; 704; Sam; m; 1884; Full; M; Head
700; 705; Martha; f; 1883; Full; M; Wife

701; 706; Alex; m; 1863; Full; M; Head
702; 707; Betty; f; 1876; Full; M; Wife
703; 708; Rosie; f; 1912; Full; S; Daughter
704; 709; Nancy; f; 1914; Full; S; Daughter
705; 710; Carlson; m; 1920; Full; S; Son

706; 711; Lena; f; 1888; Full; Wd; Head
707; 100; **Bell**, Ella; f; 1914; Full; S; Daughter
708; 712; Gipson; m; 1911; Full; S; Son
709; 713; Gulton; m; 1913; Full; S; Son
710; 714; Emmett; m; 1922; Full; S; Son
711; 715; Lucille; f; 1923; Full; S; Daughter
712; 716; Prentiss; m; 1909; Full; S; Son

Census of the **Mississippi Choctaw** tribe of the _____ reservation of the **Choctaw Agency** jurisdiction, as of **June 30**, 19**29**, taken by **R. J. Enochs**, Superintendent

KEY: Surname; Census Number: Present; Last; Given Name; Sex; Date of Birth; Degree of Blood; Marital Condition; Relation to Head of Family

JEFFERSON

713; 717; Addie; f; 1910; Full; S; Orphan

714; 718; Esther; f; 1912; Full; S; Orphan
715; 719; Nute; m; 1914; Full; S; Orphan

716; 720; Otis; m; 1900; Full; M; Head
717; 721; Ona; f; 1903; Full; M; Wife
718; 722; Otho; m; 1925; Full; S; Son
719; 723; Andy; m; 1926; Full; S; Son

720; 724; Oscar; m; 1902; Full; M; Head
721; 725; Salina; f; 1905; Full; M; Wife
722; 726; Malcum; m; 1927; Full; S; Son

723; 727; Braxton; m; 1904; Full; S; Widowed

724; 729; Amos; m; 1906; Full; M; Head
725; 730; Ida; f; 1910; Full; M; Wife

726; 731; Willis; m; 1877; Full; M; Head
727; 732; Elsie; f; 1886; Full; M; Wife

JIM

728; 733; Harvey; m; 1915; Full; S; Orphan

729; 734; Mattie; f; 1898; Full; S; Head

730; 736; Logan; m; 1848; Full; S; Widowed

731; 737; George; m; 1868; Full; M; Head
732; 738; Eliza; f; 1878; Full; M; Wife

733; 739; Lee; f; 1906; Full; S; Head

Census of the __Mississippi Choctaw__ tribe of the _____ reservation of the ___Choctaw Agency___ jurisdiction, as of ___June 30___, 19__29__, taken by ___R. J. Enochs___, Superintendent

KEY: Surname; Census Number: Present; Last; Given Name; Sex; Date of Birth; Degree of Blood; Marital Condition; Relation to Head of Family

734; 740; Sidney; m; 1916; Full; S; Son
735; 741; John; m; 1907; Full; S; Son

736; 742; Cooley; m; 1870; Full; M; Head
737; 743; Lorena; f; 1908; Full; M; Wife
738; 744; William; m; 1922; Full; S; Son
739; 745; Tom; m; 1925; Full; S; Son

740; 746; Henry; m; 1885; Full; M; Head
741; 747; Mollie; f; 1876; Full; M; Wife

742; 748; Ben; m; 1868; Full; M; Head
743; 749; Dora; f; 1890; Full; M; Wife
744; Bobbie Sue; f; Jan-25-1929; F; S; Daughter
745; Frank; m; June-25-1927; Full; S; Son
746; 751; Annie May; f; 1915; Full; S; Daughter
747; 752; Rainey; m; 1923; Full; S; Son

748; 753; Amon; m; 1884; Full; M; Head
749; 754; Lucy; f; 1890; Full; M; Wife
750; 755; Opal; f; 1919; Full; S; Daughter
751; Carter; m; Sept-27-1928; Full; S; Son

752; 756; Whitman; m; 1910; Full; S; Head

753; 757; Victor; m; 1900; Full; M; Head
754; 758; Lena; f; 1908; Full; M; Wife
755; 759; Foy; m; 1927; Full; S; Son

756; 760; Goodman; m; 1858; Full; M; Head
757; 761; Leona; f; 1902; Full; M; Wife
758; 762; Clifton; m; 1923; Full; S; Son
759; 763; Frank McKinley; m; 1925; Full; S; Son
760; Goodman; m; Aug-18-1928; Full; S; Son

761; 764; Henry; m; 1901; Full; M; Head

Census of the **Mississippi Choctaw** tribe of the _____ reservation of the **Choctaw Agency** jurisdiction, as of **June 30**, 19**29**, taken by **R. J. Enochs**, Superintendent

KEY: Surname; Census Number: Present; Last; Given Name; Sex; Date of Birth; Degree of Blood; Marital Condition; Relation to Head of Family

762; 765; Maggie; f; 1896; Full; M; Wife

763; 766; Albert; m; 1906; Full; M; Head
764; 767; Dora; f; 1906; Full; M; Wife

JIMMIE

765; 768; Melton; m; 1904; Full; M; Head
766; 769; Mary; f; 1907; Full; M; Wife
767; 770; Ona O.; f; 1928; Full; S; Daughter
768; 771; Frank; m; 1911; Full; S; Brother

769; 772; Will; m; 1878; Full; M; Head
770; 773; Hester; f; 1883; Full; M; Wife
771; 774; Mack; m; 1905; Full; S; Son
772; 775; Homer; m; 1909; Full; S; Son

JOE

773; 776; Nicholas; m; 1890; Full; M; Head
774; 777; Esley; f; 1890; Full; M; Wife
775; 778; Aston; m; 1914; Full; S; Son
776; 779; Henry; m; 1916; Full; S; Son
777; 780; Emily; f; 1912; Full; S; Daughter
778; 781; Widge; f; 1921; Full; S; Daughter
779; 782; Bessie; f; 1923; Full; S; Daughter
780; 783; Billie Joe; m; 1925; Full; S; Son
781; 784; Noah; m; 1927; Full S; Son

782; 785; Langley; m; 1848; Full; S; Widower

783; 786; John; m; 1898; Full; M; Head
784; 787; Emma; f; 1900; Full; M; Wife
785; Lillie; f; 1925; Full; S; Daughter
786; Claud; m; 1928; Full; S; Son

Census of the **Mississippi Choctaw** tribe of the _____ reservation of the **Choctaw Agency** jurisdiction, as of **June 30**, 19**29**, taken by **R. J. Enochs**, Superintendent

KEY: Surname; Census Number: Present; Last; Given Name; Sex; Date of Birth; Degree of Blood; Marital Condition; Relation to Head of Family

787; 788; Jasper; m; 1888; Full; M; Head
788; 789; Sallie; f; 1893; Full; M; Wife
789; 780; Lula; f; 1913; Full; S; Daughter
790; 791; Houston; m; 1918; Full; S; Son
791; 792; Watkins; m; 1922; Full; S; Son

792; 793; Emily; f; 1856; Full; S; Widow

JOHN

793; 794; Josh; m; 1878; Full; S; Widower

794; 795; Empsey; m; 1886; Full; M; Head
795; 796; Betsie; f; 1898; Full; M; Wife
796; 797; Bilbo; m; 1917; Full; S; Son
797; 798; Mabel; f; 1920; Full; S; Daughter
798; 799; Renia; f; 1922; Full; S; Daughter
799; 800; Vardeman; m; 1925; Full; S; Son
800; Lisette Helen; f; June-29-1929; Full; S; Daughter
801; 801; Smith; m; 1927; Full; S; Son

802; 802; Jack; m; 1874; Full; M; Head
803; 803; Amanda; f; 1899; Full; M; Wife
804; 804; Callie; f; 1913; Full; S; Daughter
805; 805; Jefferson; m; 1823; Full; S; Son
806; 806; Mary; f; 1924; Full; S; Daughter

807; 807; Mack; m; 1873; Full; M; Head
808; 809; Lizzie; f; 1858; Full; M; Wife

809; 810; Clint; m; 1888; Full; S; Head

810; 811; Bob; m; 1875; Full; M; Head
811; 812; Ona; f; 1885; Full; M; Wife
812; 813; Ira; m; 1906; Full; S; Son
813; 814; Oliver; m; 1914; Full; S; Son

Census of the **Mississippi Choctaw** tribe of the _____ reservation of the **Choctaw Agency** jurisdiction, as of **June 30**, 19**29**, taken by **R. J. Enochs**, Superintendent

KEY: Surname; Census Number: Present; Last; Given Name; Sex; Date of Birth; Degree of Blood; Marital Condition; Relation to Head of Family

814; 815; Otis; m; 1917; Full; S; Son
815; 816; Roby; m; 1921; Full; S; Son
816; 817; Rosie; f; 1922; Full; S; Daughter

JOHNSON

817; 818; Willie; m; 1872; Full; M; Head
818; 819; Dixie; f; 1902; Full; M; Wife
819; 322; **Comby**, Vena; f; 1918; Full; S; Step-daughter
820; 323; **Comby**, Guss; m; 1925; Full; S; Step-Son

821; 820; Frank; m; 1892; Full; M; Head
822; 821; Lorina; f; 1900; Full; M; Wife
823; 822; Otha; m; 1916; Full; S; Son
824; 823; Athens; m; 1918; Full; S; Son
825; 824; Sudia; f; 1920; Full; S; Daughter
826; 825; Bertha; f; 1922; Full; S; Daughter
827; 826; Nevon; m; 1924; Full; S; Son
828; 827; Sudan; f; 1926; Full; S; Daughter
829; 828; Bana; f; 1928; Full; S; Daughter

830; Afton; m; 1902; Full; M; Head
831; 829; Savana; f; 1908; Full; M; Wife
832; 830; Callie; f; 1928; Full; S; Daughter

833; 831; Edgar; m; 1899; Full; m Head
834; 832; Beatrice; f; 1903; Full; M; Wife
835; 833; Callie; f; 1924; Full; S; Daughter
836; 834; Francis; f; 1926; Full; S; Daughter
837; 835; Egbert; m; 1927; Full; S; Son
838; 836; Sallie; f; 1850; Full; S; Widow

JOSHUA

839; 837; Sam; m; 1856; Full; M; Head
840; 838; Jennie; f; 1863; Full; M; Wife

Census of the **Mississippi Choctaw** tribe of the _____ reservation of the **Choctaw Agency** jurisdiction, as of **June 30**, 19**29**, taken by **R. J. Enochs**, Superintendent

KEY: Surname; Census Number: Present; Last; Given Name; Sex; Date of Birth; Degree of Blood; Marital Condition; Relation to Head of Family

KING

841; 840; Betsy; f; 1886; Full; Wd; Head
842; 841; Christine; f; 1914; Full; S; Daughter
843; 842; Joseph; m; 1922; Full; S; Son
844; 843; Joe; m; 1924; Full; S; Son
845; 844; Barkum; m; 1926; Full; S; Son

846; 845; John Wesley; m; 1855; Full; m; Head
847; 847; Mollie; f; 1903; Full; S; Daughter
848; 848; Clay Irvin; m; 1905; Full; S; Son
849; 849; Burman; m; 1911; Full; S; Son
850; 850; Enos; m; 1911; Full; S; Son
851; 851; Luvenia; f; 1920; Full; S; Daughter

852; 852; Banks; m; 1904; Full; M; Head
853; 853; Betsie; f; 1900; f; m; Wife

LEBAN

854; 854; Ben; m; 1872; Full; M; Head
855; 855; Lena; f; 1873; Full; M; Wife
856; 856; Mary; f; 1900; Full; S; Daughter

LeFLORE

857; 857; John; m; 1871; Full; M; Head
858; 858; Emma; f; 1880; f; m; Wife
859; 859; Richard Earl; m; 1893; Full; S; Son
860; 860; Willie; f; 1904; Full; S; Daughter
861; 861; Bertha Lee; f; 1908; Full; S; Daughter
862; 862; John; m; 1911; Full; S; Son
863; 863; Lewis; m; 1912; Full; S; Son
864; 864; S. D.; m; 1906; Full; S; Son

Census of the **Mississippi Choctaw** tribe of the _____ reservation of the **Choctaw Agency** jurisdiction, as of **June 30**, 19**29**, taken by **R. J. Enochs**, Superintendent

KEY: Surname; Census Number: Present; Last; Given Name; Sex; Date of Birth; Degree of Blood; Marital Condition; Relation to Head of Family

LEWIS

865; 865; Duffie; m; 1899; Full; M; Head
866; 866; Lilly; f; 1883; Full; M; Wife
867; 867; **Billy**, Egbert; m; 1920; Full; S; Step-son

868; 868; Mamie; f; 1898; Full; S; Head

869; 869; Calvin; m; 1880; Full; M; Head
870; 870; Lola; f; 1896; Full; M; Wife
871; 871; Lum; m; 1926; Full; S; Son

872; 872; Albert; m; 1895; Full; M; Head
873; 873; Mollie; f; 1898; Full; M; Wife
874; 874; Indiana; f; 1914; Full; S; Daughter
875; 875; Bernice; f; 1917; Full; S; Daughter
876; 876; Eastland; m; 1919; Full; S; Son
877; 877; Ivena; f; 1921; Full; S; Daughter

878; 878; Jim; m; 1903; Full; M; Head
879; 879; Jennie; f; 1908; Full; M; Wife
880; Jennie Lin; f; Sept-1-1928; Full; S; Daughter

881; 880; Marshall; m; 1875; Full; M; Head
882; 881; Martha; f; 1886; Full; M; Wife
883; 882; Lizzie; f; 1916; Full; S; Daughter
884; 883; Belfa; f; 1917; Full; S; Daughter
885; 884; Houston; m; 1920; Full; S; Son
886; 885; Lee; m; 1922; Full; S; Son
887; 886; Bettie; f; 1924; Full; S; Daughter
888; 887; Hodges; m; 1925; Full; S; Son
889; 888; Leon; m; 1927; Full; S; Son

890; 889; Adam; m; 1907; Full; M; Head
891; 890; Sallie; f; 1908; Full; M; Wife
892; 891; Nannie; f; Feb-1-1928; Full; S; Daughter

Census of the **Mississippi Choctaw** tribe of the _____ reservation of the **Choctaw Agency** jurisdiction, as of **June 30**, 19**29**, taken by **R. J. Enochs**, Superintendent

KEY: Surname; Census Number: Present; Last; Given Name; Sex; Date of Birth; Degree of Blood; Marital Condition; Relation to Head of Family

893; 892; Jim; m; 1868; Full; M; Head
894; 893; Fannie; f; 1890; Full; M; Wife
895; 894; Alma; f; 1916; Full; S; Daughter

896; 896; Johnnie; m; 1898; Full; Wd; Head
897; 897; Marzine; f; 1924; Full; S; Daughter

898; 898; Elon; m; 1881; Full; M; Head
899; 899; Lula; f; 1878; Full; M; Wife

900; 900; Ruben; m; 1848; Full; Wd; Head
901; 901; Lennis; m; 1906; Full; S; Son
902; 902; Ola; f; 1912; Full; S; Daughter
903; 903; Hollis; m; 1916; Full; S; Son

904; 904; Ed m; 1878; Full; M; Head
905; 905; Edna; f; 1875; Full; M; Wife
906; 906; Winton; m; 1910; Full; S; Son

MARTIN

907; 907; Willie; m; 1890; Full; M; Head
908; 908; Mary; f; 1896; Full; M; Wife
909; 909; Raymond; m; 1920; Full; S; Son
910; 910; Edmond Joseph; m; 1924; Full; S; Son
911; 911; Philip; m; 1926; Full; S; Son
912; Ann Mae; f; July-26-1928; Full; S; Daughter
913; 912; Anis; m; 1906; Full; S; Cousin

McMILLEN

914; 915; Oscar; m; 1893; Full; M; Head
915; 916; Bennie; f; 1899; Full; M; Wife
916; 917; Arnold; m; 1914; Full; S; Son
917; 918; Leslie; f; 1922; Full; S; Daughter
918; 919; Bert; m; 1924; Full; S; Son

Census of the **Mississippi Choctaw** tribe of the _____ reservation of the **Choctaw Agency** jurisdiction, as of **June 30**, 19**29**, taken by **R. J. Enochs**, Superintendent

KEY: Surname; Census Number: Present; Last; Given Name; Sex; Date of Birth; Degree of Blood; Marital Condition; Relation to Head of Family

919; 920; Frances; f; 1927; Full; S; Daughter
920; John; m; Sept-25-1928; Full; S; Son

921; 921; Egbert; m; 1901; Full; M; Head
922; 922; Nola; f; 1909; Full; M; Wife
923; 923; A. J.; m; 1922; Full; S; Son
924; 924; Odie Mae; f; 1924; Full; S; Daughter
925; 925; John; m; 1927; Full; S; Son

926; 926; Cephus; m; 1882; Full; M; Head
927; 927; Mina; f; 1894; Full; M; Wife
928; 928; Anthony; m; 1908; Full; S; Son
929; 929; Mary; f; 1913; Full; S; Daughter
930; 930; Willie; m; 1916; Full; S; Son
931; 931; Enochs; m; Oct-8-1927; Full; S; Son
932; 167; **Billy**, Clemon; m; 1914; Full; S; Stepson
933; 913; Jimmie; m; 1912; Full; S; Nephew
934; 914; Jimpson; m; 1915; Full; S; Nephew

935; 932; Sorsby; m; 1875; Full; M; Head
936; 933; Annie; f; 1897; Full; M; Wife
937; 934; Luna; f; 1913; Full; S; Daughter
938; 935; Mary; f; 1914; Full; S; Daughter
939; 936; Emma; f; 1915; Full; S; Daughter
940; 937; Clarence; m; 1916; Full; S; Son
941; 938; Bessie; f; 1919; Full; S; Daughter
942; 939; Gipson; m; 1923; Full; S; Son
943; 940; Pauline; f; Jan-26-1928; Full; S; Daughter

944; 941; Lina Solomon; f; 1888; Full; Wd; Head
945; 942; Eva; f; 1914; Full; S; Daughter
946; 943; Mary; f; 1920; Full; S; Daughter

MINGO

947; 944; Horace; m; 1881; Full; M; Head

Census of the **Mississippi Choctaw** tribe of the _____ reservation of the **Choctaw Agency** jurisdiction, as of **June 30**, 19**29**, taken by **R. J. Enochs**, Superintendent

KEY: Surname; Census Number: Present; Last; Given Name; Sex; Date of Birth; Degree of Blood; Marital Condition; Relation to Head of Family

948; 945; Lilly; f; 1878; Full; M; Wife
949; 946; Lin; f; 1915; Full; S; Daughter
950; 947; Jim; m; 1917; Full; S; Son
951; 948; Olin; m; 1919; Full; S; Son
952; 949; Nettie; f; 1921; Full; S; Daughter

953; 950; Oscar; m; 1909; Full; M; Head
954; 951; Lindy; f; 1899; Full; M; Wife

955; 952; Rich; m; 1905; Full; M; Head
956; 953; Annie; f; 1904; Full; M; Wife
957; 954; Davidson; m; 1923; Full; S; Son
958; 955; Effie; f; 1924; Full; S; Daughter

959; 956; John; m; 1883; Full; M; Head
960; 957; Hattie; f; 1905; Full; M; Wife
961; 958; Arch; m; 1922; Full; S; Son
962; 959; Otis; m; 1924; Full; S; Son
963; 960; Sis; f; 1927; Full; S; Daughter

MITCH

964; 962; Sarah; f; 1884; Full; Wd; Head
965; 963; Elea; m; 1902; Full; S; Son
966; 964; Divan; m; 1904; Full; S; Son
967; 965; Wilson; m; 1906; Full; S; Son
968; 966; Gilmer; m; 1915; Full; S; Son
969; 967; Annie; f; 1919; Full; S; Daughter

MORRIS

970; 968; Mosley; m; 1869; Full; M; Head
971; 969; Ida; f; 1870; Full; M; Wife
972; 970; Wilson; m; 1903; Full; S; Son
973; 971; Joe; m; 1908; Full; S; Son

Census of the **Mississippi Choctaw** tribe of the _____ reservation of the **Choctaw Agency** jurisdiction, as of **June 30**, 19**29**, taken by **R. J. Enochs**, Superintendent

KEY: Surname; Census Number: Present; Last; Given Name; Sex; Date of Birth; Degree of Blood; Marital Condition; Relation to Head of Family

974; 972; Dimpsey; m; 1900; Full; M; Head
975; 973; Janie; f; 1902; Full; M; Wife
976; 974; Ora; f; 1921; Full; S; Daughter
977; 975; Vesney; m; 1924; Full; S; Son
978; 976; Davis; m; 1927; Full; S; Son

979; 977; Sallie; f; 1868; Full; Wd; Head
980; 978; Seward; m; 1900; Full; S; Son

981; 979; Howard; m; 1907; Full; M; Head
982; 980; Bertie; f; 1910; Full; M; Wife
983; 981; Jimmie; m; 1926; Full; S; Son

984; 982; Houston; m; 1906; Full; M; Head
985; 983; Bertha; f; 1908; Full; M; Wife

986; 984; Boston; m; 1903; Full; M; Head
987; 985; Nola; f; 1905; Full; M; Wife

988; 986; Rich; m; 1906; Full; M; Head
989; 987; Callie; f; 1907; Full; M; Wife

990; 988; Felma; m; 1909; Full; S; Head

MOSES

991; 989; Allen; m; 1907; Full; S; Head
1511; 990; Alma; f; 1911; Full; S; Sister

NICKEY

992; 991; Sam; m; 1885; Full; M; Head
993; 992; Malissie; f; 1887; Full; M; Wife
994; 993; Dora; f; 1915; Full; S; Daughter
995; 994; Sherman; m; 1922; Full; S; Son
996; 995; Copeland; m; Apr-1-1928; Full; S; Son

Census of the **Mississippi Choctaw** tribe of the _____ reservation of the **Choctaw Agency** jurisdiction, as of **June 30**, 19**29**, taken by **R. J. Enochs**, Superintendent

---

KEY: Surname; Census Number: Present; Last; Given Name; Sex; Date of Birth; Degree of Blood; Marital Condition; Relation to Head of Family

997; 996; Billy; m; 1890; Full; M; Head
998; 997; Frauney; f; 1881; Full; M; Wife
999; 998; Ode; f; 1909; Full; S; Daughter
1000; 999; Zema; f; 1912; Full; S; Daughter
1001; 1000; Zone; f; 1918; Full; S; Daughter
1002; 1001; Hughie; m; 1915; Full; S; Son
1003; 1002; Cozette; m; 1920; Full; S; Son
1004; 1003; Thomas; m; 1923; Full; S; Son

NOAH

1005; 1005; Elizabeth; f; 1872; Full; Wd; Head

1006; 1006; Lula; f; 1872; Full; Wd; Head

NUBBY

1007; 1007; Billy; m; 1860; Full; M; Head

1008; 1008; Lilly; Full; 1880; Full; M; Head

PHILLIPS

1009; 1009; Raliegh[sic]; m; 1907; Full; M; Head
1010; Human; m; 1926; Full; S; Son
1011; M. C.; m; July-3-1928; Full; S; Son

POLK

1012; 1012; George; m; 1862; Full; Wd; Head
1013; 1014; Francis; m; 1909; Full; S; Son

1014; 1015; Henry; m; 1908; Full; M; Head
1015; 1016; Lucy; f; 1900; Full; M; Wife
1016; 1017; Zula; f; June-7-1928; Full; S; Daughter

Census of the **Mississippi Choctaw** tribe of the _____ reservation of the **Choctaw Agency** jurisdiction, as of **June 30**, 19 **29**, taken by **R. J. Enochs**, Superintendent

KEY: Surname; Census Number: Present; Last; Given Name; Sex; Date of Birth; Degree of Blood; Marital Condition; Relation to Head of Family

1017; 1018; Josie; m; 1890; Full; M; Head
1018; 1019; Lenie; f; 1888; Full; M; Wife
1019; 1020; Edna; f; 1916; Full; S; Daughter

1020; 1021; Tom; m; 1880; Full; Wd; Head
1021; 1022; Comelia; m; 1909; Full; S; Son
1022; 1023; Alma; f; 1912; Full; S; Daughter
1023; 1024; Osburn; m; 1914; Full; S; Son

POOLSON

1024; 1025; Alic; m; 1872; Full; S; Head

1025; 1026; Frank; m; 1900; Full; M; Head
1026; 1027; Mary; f; 1902; Full; M; Wife

1027; 1029; Eddie; m; 1906; Full; M; Head
1028; 1028; Cornelia; f; 1904; Full; M; Wife

1029; 1030; Julius; m; 1907; Full; S; Head

1030; 1031; Johnnie; m; 1909; Full; S; Head

1031; 1032; Charley; m; 1911; Full; S; Head

ROBINSON

1032; 1033; Mary; f; 1848; Full; Wd; Head

1033; 1034; Thomas; m; 1893; Full; M; Head
1034; 1035; Sybol; f; 1894; Full; M; Wife
1035; 1036; Jimmie; m; 1912; Full; S; Son
1036; 1037; Georgia; f; 1914; Full; S; Daughter
1037; 1038; Sallie; f; 1916; Full; S; Daughter
1038; 1039; Carl; m; 1919; Full; S; Son

Census of the **Mississippi Choctaw** tribe of the _____ reservation of the **Choctaw Agency** jurisdiction, as of **June 30**, 19_29_, taken by **R. J. Enochs**, Superintendent

KEY: Surname; Census Number: Present; Last; Given Name; Sex; Date of Birth; Degree of Blood; Marital Condition; Relation to Head of Family

1039; 1040; Willis; m; 1903; Full; M; Head
1040; 1041; Sibley; f; 1905; Full; M; Wife
1041; 1042; Campbell; f; 1927; Full; S; Daughter

RUTHFORD

1042; 1043; Henritta[sic]; f; 1898; Full; S; Head

SAM

1043; 1044; Willie; m; 1899; Full; M; Head
1044; 1045; Eva; f; 1901; Full; M; Wife
1045; 1046; Nettie; f; 1921; Full; S; Daughter
1046; 1047; Able; m; 1922; Full; S; Son
1047; 1048; Lonie; m; 1924; Full; S; Son

1048; 1051; Oscar; m; 1858; Full; M; Head
1049; 1050; Mattie; f; 1873; Full; M; Wife
1050; 1053; Raymond; m; 1888; Full; S; Son
1051; 1054; Seer; f; 1914; Full; S; Daughter
1052; 1057; Truman; m; 1909; Full; S; Son

1053; 1055; Jimpsy; m; 1900; Full; S; Head

1054 1058; Levada; f; 1914; Full; S; Orphan

1055; 1059; Walter; m; 1890; Full; Wd; Head
1056; 1060; Grace; f; 1917; Full; S; Daughter
1057; 1061; Tom; m; 1919; Full; S; Son
1058; 2062; Manza; f; 1923; Full; S; Daughter
  78;-   Edna; f; 1921; Full; S; Daughter

1059; 1063; Charlie; m; 1914; Full; S; Orphan

1060; 1064; Beeman; m; 1920; Full; S; Orphan

Census of the **Mississippi Choctaw** tribe of the _____ reservation of the **Choctaw Agency** jurisdiction, as of **June 30**, 19**29**, taken by **R. J. Enochs**, Superintendent

KEY: Surname; Census Number: Present; Last; Given Name; Sex; Date of Birth; Degree of Blood; Marital Condition; Relation to Head of Family

SHOEMAKE

1061; 1065;   Buck; m; 1887; Full; M; Head
1062; 1066;   Annie; f; 1901; Full; M; Wife
1063; 1067;   Leona; f; 1920; Full; S; Daughter
1064; 1068;   Eliza; f; 1922; Full; S; Daughter
1065; 1069;   Martha; f; 1923; Full; S; Daughter
1066; 1070;   Daisy; f; 1926; Full; S; Daughter
1067; 1071;   Carrie Mae; f; 1927; Full; S; Daughter

1068; 1072;   Alonzo; m; 1900; Full; M; Head
1069; 1073;   Susan; f; 1900; Full; M; Wife
1070; 1074;   Dempsie; m; 1921; Full; S; Son
1071; 1075;   Lemon; m; 1923; Full; S; Son
1072; 1076;   Ruben; m; 1926; Full; S; Son

1073; 1077;   Lester; f[sic]; 1914; Full; S; Orphan

SIMPSON

1074; 1078;   John; m; 1878; Full; M; Head
1075; 1079;   Sallie; f; 1874; Full; S; Wife
1076; 1080;   Pauline; f; 1917; Full; S; Daughter
1077; 1081;   Celia; f; 1919; Full; S; Daughter

SMITH

1078; 1082;   Sebe; m; 1889; Full; M; Head
1079; 1083;   Sina; f; 1891; Full; M; Wife
1080; 1084;   Sophia; f; 1915; Full; S; Daughter
1081; 1085;   Clemon; m; 1918; Full; S; Son

1082; 1086;   Wesley; m; 1878; Full; M; Head
1083; 1087;   Mary; f; 1873; Full; M; Wife

1084; 1088;   George; m; 1876; Full; Wd; Head

Census of the __Mississippi Choctaw__ tribe of the _____ reservation of the ___Choctaw Agency___ jurisdiction, as of ___June 30___, 19_29_, taken by ___R. J. Enochs___, Superintendent

KEY: Surname; Census Number: Present; Last; Given Name; Sex; Date of Birth; Degree of Blood; Marital Condition; Relation to Head of Family

1085; 1089;   Flay; m; 1906; Full; M; Head
1086; 1090;   Nettie; f; 1904; Full; M; Wife

1087; 1091;   Robert; m; 1893; Full; M; Head
1088; 1092;   Minnie; f; 1900; Full; M; Wife

SOCKEY

1089; 1093;   Mike; m; 1902; Full; M; Head
1090; 1094;   Nephus; f; 1903; Full; M; Wife
1091; 1095;   Odell; m; 1924; Full; S; Son
1092; 1096;   Ellis; f; 1922; Full; S; Daughter
1093; 1097;   Enochs; m; 1927; Full; S; Son

1094; 1098;   John; m; 1886; Full; M; Head
1095; 1099;   Lula; f; 1895; Full; M; Wife
1096; 1100;   Benny; m; 1908; Full; S; Son
1097; 1101;   Homer; m; 1923; Full; S; Son
1098; 1102;   Ile; m; 1927; Full; S; Son

SOLOMON

1099; 1103;   Raymond; m; 1892; Full; M; Head
1100; 1104;   Bessie; f; 1894; Full; M; Wife

1101; 1105;   Marshall; m; 1903; Full; S; Head

1102; 1106;   Ernest; m; 1917; Full; S; Orphan

1103; 1107;   W. M.; m; 1884; Full; Wd; Head

SONA

1104; 1109;   Emily; f; 1896; Full; Wd; Head

1105; 1110;   Fontaine; m; 1889; Full; Wd; Head

Census of the __Mississippi Choctaw__ tribe of the _____ reservation
of the ___Choctaw Agency___ jurisdiction, as of ___June 30___, 19_29_,
taken by ___R. J. Enochs___, Superintendent

KEY: Surname; Census Number: Present; Last; Given Name; Sex; Date of Birth; Degree of Blood; Marital Condition; Relation to Head of Family

1106; 1111; Leona; f; 1922; Full; S; Daughter
1107; 1112; Jennie; f; 1926; Full; S; Daughter
1108; 1113; Ella Ruth; f; Sept-10-1927; Full; S; Daughter

STAR

1109; 1114; Bill; m; 1889; Full; Wd; Head

1110; 1115; Necie; f; 1888; Full; Wd; Head
1111; 1116; Summers; m; 1916; Full; S; Son
1112; 1117; Edna; f; 1918; Full; S; Daughter
1113; 1118; Nannie; f; 1921; Full; S; Daughter
1114; 1119; Mary; f; 1923; Full; S; Daughter

1115; 1120; Dave; m; 1891; Full; M; Head
1116; 1121; Lucy; f; 1888; Full; M; Wife

STEPHENS

1117; 1122; Felix; m; 1907; Full; M; Head
1118; 1123; Martha; f; 1909; Full; M; Wife

1119; 1124; Tom; m; 1863; Full; Wd; Head
1120; 1125; Cornelia; f; 1904; Full; S; Daughter
1121; 1127; Willie; m; 1910; Full; S; Son

1122; 1128; Silmon; m; 1896; Full; Wd; Head

1123; 1129; Nathan; m; 1900; Full; M; Head
1124; 1130; Annie; f; 1900; Full; M; Wife
1125; 1131; Maxton; m; 1925; Full; S; Son
1126; 1132; Cutie Mae; f; 1926; Full; S; Daughter
1127; 1133; Dorothy Mae; f; Feb-3-1928; Full; S; Daughter

STEVE

Census of the **Mississippi Choctaw** tribe of the _____ reservation of the **Choctaw Agency** jurisdiction, as of **June 30**, 19**29**, taken by **R. J. Enochs**, Superintendent

---

KEY: Surname; Census Number: Present; Last; Given Name; Sex; Date of Birth; Degree of Blood; Marital Condition; Relation to Head of Family

1128; 1134;   Murphy; m; 1878; Full; M; Head
1129; 1135;   Patsy; f; 1908; Full; M; Wife
1130; 1136;   Helen; f; Oct-8-1927; Full; S; Daughter

1131; 1137;   Josie; m; 1902; Full; M; Head
1132; 1138;   Maggie; f; 1909; Full; M; Wife
1133; 1139;   Ruby; f; 1925; Full; S; Daughter
1134; 1140;   Jane; f; 1927; Full; S; Daughter

1135; 1141;   Houston; m; 1888; Full; M; Head
1136; 1142;   Lena; f; 1888; Full; M; Wife
1137; 1143;   Enis; m; 1911; Full; S; Son
1138; 1144;   McKinley; m; 1921; Full; S; Son
1139; 1145;   Yates; m; 1923; Full; S; Son
1140; 1146;   Marabelle; f; 1927; Full; S; Daughter

1141; 1147;   Bobo; m; 1905; Full; M; Head
1142; 1148;   Lucile; f; 1910; Full; M; Wife
1143; 1149;   Morris; m; 1926; Full; S; Son
1144; 1150;   Aubrey; f; 1927; Full; S; Daughter
1145;   Vivian; f; May-11-1929; Full; S; Daughter

1146; 1151;   Smith; f; 1896; Full; M; Head
1147; 1152;   Winnie; f; 1897; Full; M; Wife
1148; 1153;   Zona; f; 1920; Full; S; Daughter
1149; 1154;   Pauline; f; 1921; Full; S; Daughter
1150; 1155;   Mollie; f; 1924; Full; S; Daughter
1151;   Earline; f; Nov-23-1928; Full; S; Daughter

STOLIBY

1152; 1156;   John; m; 1875; Full; Wd; Head
1153; 1157;   Nancy; f; 1911; Full; S; Daughter
1154; 1158;   Will Banks; m; 1919; Full; S; Son
1155; 1159;   Otis; m; 1922; Full; S; Son
1156; 1160;   Sona Wilber; f; 1925; Full; S; Daughter

Census of the **Mississippi Choctaw** tribe of the _____ reservation of the **Choctaw Agency** jurisdiction, as of **June 30**, 19**29**, taken by **R. J. Enochs**, Superintendent

KEY: Surname; Census Number: Present; Last; Given Name; Sex; Date of Birth; Degree of Blood; Marital Condition; Relation to Head of Family

1157; 1161; Tom; m; 1902; Full; S; Head
1158; 1162; Elum Ferum; m; 1926; Full; S; Orphan

STRIBLING

1159; 1163; Malissa; f; 1884; Full; Wd; Head
1160; 1164; Varderman; m; 1902; Full; S; Son
1161; 1166; Marvin; m; 1906; Full; S; Son

SOLOMON

1162; Will; m; 1863; Full; M; Head
1163; Minnie Lee; f; 1907; Full; M; Wife
1164; Eva; f; 1920; Full; S; Daughter
1165; Mary; f; 1914; Full; S; Daughter
1166; Mollie Lee; f; Feb-19-1929; Full; S; Daughter

THOMAS

1167; 1167; Louis; m; 1884; Full; M; Head
1168; 1168; Mamie; f; 1887; Full; M; Wife
1169; 1169; Lula; f; 1917; Full; S; Daughter
1170; 1170; Newman; m; 1919; Full; S; Son
1171; 1171; Isaac; m; 1924; Full; S; Son
1172; 1172; Mina; f; 1925; Full; S; Daughter

1173; 1173; Riley; m; 1905; Full; S; Head

1174; 1174; Cleve; m; 1903; Full; M; Head
1175; 1175; Pheobe[sic]; f; 1908; Full; M; Wife

1176; 1176; William; m; 1893; Full; M; Head
1177; 1177; Sallie; f; 1907; Full; M; Wife
1178; 1178; Woodrow; m; 1919; Full; S; Son
1179; 1179; Mollie; f; 1921; Full; S; Daughter
1180; 1180; Golden; m 1923; Full; S; Son

Census of the **Mississippi Choctaw** tribe of the _____ reservation of the **Choctaw Agency** jurisdiction, as of **June 30**, 19 **29**, taken by **R. J. Enochs**, Superintendent

KEY: Surname; Census Number: Present; Last; Given Name; Sex; Date of Birth; Degree of Blood; Marital Condition; Relation to Head of Family

1181; 1181; Amos; m; 1898; Full; M; Head
1182; 1183; Rosie; f; 1893; Full; M; Wife

1183; 1184; Lena; f; 1895; Full; S; Head

1184; 1185; Arline; f; 1897; Full; S; Head

1185; George; m; 1849; Full; Wd; Head

THOMPSON

1186; 1186; Mose; m; 1902; Full; M; Head
1187; 1187; Janie; f; 1902; Full; M; Wife
1188; 1188; Jim; m; 1921; Full; S; Son
1189; 1189; Annie; f; 1922; Full; S; Daughter
1190; 1190; Thurman; m; 1924; Full; S; Son

1191; 1191; John; m; 1896; Full; M; Head
1192; 1192; Lilly; f; 1898; Full; M; Wife
1193; 1193; Moline; f; 1921; Full; S; Daughter
1194; 1194; Onie; f; 1922; Full; S; Daughter
1195; 1195; Tom; m; 1927; Full; S; Son

1196; 1196; Amilda; f; 1870; Full; Wd; Head
1197; 1197; Beneva; f; 1911; Full; S; Daughter

1198; 1198; Will; m; 1904; Full; M; Head
1199; 631; Zena; f; 1907; Full; M; Wife
1200; 619; Claudie; m; 1927; Full; S; Son
1201; Henry; m; Dec-22-1928; Full; S; Son
1202; 1199; Otis; m; 1924; Full; S; Son

1203; 1200; Cephus; m; 1890; Full; M; Head
1204; 1201; Emma; f; 1906; Full; M; Wife
1205; 1202; Dixon; m; 1915; Full; S; Son
1206; 1203; Farmer; m; 1923; Full; S; Son

Census of the **Mississippi Choctaw** tribe of the _____ reservation of the **Choctaw Agency** jurisdiction, as of **June 30**, 19**29**, taken by **R. J. Enochs**, Superintendent

KEY: Surname; Census Number: Present; Last; Given Name; Sex; Date of Birth; Degree of Blood; Marital Condition; Relation to Head of Family

1207; 1204; Steve; m; Nov-26-1927; Full; S; Son

TUBBY

1208; 1205; Edgar; m; 1900; Full; M; Head
1209; 1206; Annie; f; 1902; Full; M; Wife
1210; 1207; Steve; m; 1921; Full; S; Son
1211; 1208; Willie; m; 1922; Full; S; Son
1212; 1209; Odis; m; 1924; Full; S; Son
1213; 1210; Parlimo; f; 1927; Full; S; Daughter

1214; 1211; Dick; m; 1871; Full; M; Head
1215; 1212; Eline; f; 1880; Full; M; Wife

1216; 1213; Coline; f; 1825; Full; Wd; Head

1217; 1214; Jeff; m; 1906; Full; S; Head

1218; 1216; Simpson; m; 1861; Full; M; Head
1219; 1217; Minnie; f; 1893; Full; M; Wife
1220; 1218; Sue; f; 1911; Full; S; Daughter
1221; 1219; Ica; m; 1912; Full; S; Son
1222; 1220; Henry; m; 1913; Full; S; Son
1223; 1221; Eva; f; 1914; Full; S; Daughter
1224; 1222; Lewis; m; 1917; Full; S; Son
1225; 1223; McKinley; m; 1920; Full; S; Son
1226; 1224; Hudson; m; 1923; Full; S; Son
1227; 1225; Sullivan; m; 1924; Full; S; Son
1228; 1226; Collie; f; 1926; Full; S; Daughter
1229; 1227; Nelie; f; 1927; Full; S; Daughter

1230; 1228; Dewitt; m; 1906; Full; M; Head
1231; 1229; Kate; f; 1906; Full; M; Wife
1232; Kate; f; Feb-6-1929; Full; S; Daughter

1233; 1230; Moley; m; 1903; Full; M; Head

Census of the **Mississippi Choctaw** tribe of the _____ reservation of the **Choctaw Agency** jurisdiction, as of **June 30**, 19 **29**, taken by **R. J. Enochs**, Superintendent

KEY: Surname; Census Number: Present; Last; Given Name; Sex; Date of Birth; Degree of Blood; Marital Condition; Relation to Head of Family

1234; 183;   Sallie; f; 1907; Full; M; Wife

1235; 1231;   Henderson; m; 1905; Full; Wd; Head
1236; 1233;   Lessmore; m; 1926; Full; S; Son
1237; 1234;   Lenie; f; 1927; Full; S; Daughter

1238; 1235;   Helen; m; 1878; Full; Wd; Head

1239; 1236;   Clement; m; 1886; Full; M; Head
1240; 1237;   Alice; f; 1882; Full; M; Wife

1241; 1238;   Sidney; m; 1897; Full; M; Head
1242; 1239;   Katie; f; 1905; Full; M; Wife
1243; 1239[sic] Rufus; m; 1919; Full; S; Son
1244; 1240;   Felie; f; 1922; Full; S; Daughter
1245; 1241;   Katie Mae; f; 1925; Full; S; Daughter

1246; 1242;   Lefus; m; 1893; Full; M; Head
1247; 1243;   Frances; f; 1903; Full; M; Wife
1248; 1244;   Ina; f; 1922; Full; S; Daughter
1249; 1245;   Irene; f; 1924; Full; S; Daughter
1250; 1246;   Leona; f; Sept-28-1927; Full; S; Daughter

1251; 1247;   Pat; m; 1893; Full; M; Head
1252; 1248;   Francis; f; 1894; Full; M; Wife
1253; 1249;   Vernon; m; 1913; Full; S; Son
1254; 1250;   Honest; m; 1919; Full; S; Son
1255; 1251;   Lorene; f; 1922; Full; S; Daughter
1256; 1252;   Addice; f; 1924; Full; S; Daughter
1257; 1253;   Elsie Mae; f; 1927; Full; S; Daughter

1258; 1254;   Annis; m; 1897; Full; M; Head
1259; 1255;   Annie; f; 1899; Full; M; Wife

1260; 1256;   Liza; f; 1850; Full; Wd; Head

Census of the **Mississippi Choctaw** tribe of the _____ reservation of the **Choctaw Agency** jurisdiction, as of **June 30**, 19**29**, taken by **R. J. Enochs**, Superintendent

KEY: Surname; Census Number: Present; Last; Given Name; Sex; Date of Birth; Degree of Blood; Marital Condition; Relation to Head of Family

1261; 1257; George; m; 1908; Full; M; Head
1262; 1258; Mary; f; 1911; Full; M; Wife
1263; 1281; Jennie; f; 1918; Full; S; Orphan

1264; 1259; Anderson; m; 1901; Full; M; Head
1265; 1260; Tom; f; 1905; Full; M; Wife
1266; 1261; Burton; m; 1923; Full; S; Son
1267; 1262; Omar; f; 1924; Full; S; Daughter
1268; 1263; Buracy; m; 1926; Full; S; Son

1269; 1264; Rainey; f; 1863; Full; Wd; Head
1270; 1265; Adam; m; 1898; Full; S; Son
1271; 1266; Lena; f; 1900; Full; S; Daughter
1272; 1267; Mollie; f; 1903; Full; S; Daughter
1273; 1268; Hubert; m; 1905; Full; S; Son

1274; 1269; Jimpson; m; 1863; Full; Wd; Head

1275; 1270; Nichols; m; 1898; Full; M; Head
1276; 1271; Esther; f; 1903; Full; M; Wife
1277; 1272; Alice; f; 1923; Full; S; Daughter
1278; 1273; Sullivan; m; 1922; Full; S; Son
1279; 1274; Catherine; f; 1927; Full; S; Daughter
1280; 1275; Minnie; f; 1925; Full; S; Daughter

1281; 1276; Evans; m; 1893; Full; M; Head
1282; 1277; Jennie; f; 1888; Full; M; Wife
1283; 1278; Annie; f; 1923; Full; S; Daughter

1284; 1279; Jackson; m; 1908; Full; M; Head
1285; 1280; Malissa; f; 1907; Full; M; Wife

1286; 1282; Jackson; m; 1909; Full; M; Head
1287; 1283; Missey; f; 1911; Full; M; Wife

1288; 1288; William Tom; m; 1909; Full; S; Head

Census of the **Mississippi Choctaw** tribe of the _____ reservation of the **Choctaw Agency** jurisdiction, as of **June 30**, 19**29**, taken by **R. J. Enochs**, Superintendent

---

KEY: Surname; Census Number: Present; Last; Given Name; Sex; Date of Birth; Degree of Blood; Marital Condition; Relation to Head of Family

1289; 1289; Henderson; m; 1896; Full; M; Head
1290; 1290; Maggie; f; 1905; Full; M; Wife
1291; 1294; Sam; m; 1916; Full; S; Son
1292; 1291; Otis; m; 1924; Full; S; Son
1293; 1292; W. C.; m; 1925; Full; S; Son
1294; 1293; Gladys Mae; f; 1927 Full; S; Daughter

1295; 1295; Charlie; m; 1899; Full; M; Head
1296; Bessie; f; 1901; Full; M; Wife
1297; 1284; Katie Sam; f; 1921; Full; S; Daughter
1298; 1285; Alice; f; 1924; Full; S; Daughter
1299; 1286; Jack; m; 1925; Full; S; Son
1300; 1287; J. C.; m; 1927; Full; S; Son

1301; 1296; Elis; m; 1924; Full; S; Orphan

1302; 1297; Anderson; m; 1894; Full; S; Head

1303; 1298; Lysander; m; 1888; Full; M; Head
1304; Annie Mae; f; 1909; Full; M; Wife

1305; 1299; Hazel; f; 1917; Full; S; Orphan

1306; 1300; Smith; m; 1918; Full; S; Orphan

1307; 1301; Icy; f; 1920; Full; S; Orphan

1308; 1302; John; m; 1920; Full; S; Orphan

1309; 1304; I. B.; m; 1907; Full; S; Head

1310; 1305; Allen; m; 1848; Full; Wd; Head
1311; 1306; Mary; f; 1903; Full; S; Daughter
1312; 1307; Lilly; f; 1905; Full; S; Daughter

Census of the **Mississippi Choctaw** tribe of the _____ reservation of the **Choctaw Agency** jurisdiction, as of **June 30**, 19 **29**, taken by **R. J. Enochs**, Superintendent

KEY: Surname; Census Number: Present; Last; Given Name; Sex; Date of Birth; Degree of Blood; Marital Condition; Relation to Head of Family

TUCKALOO

1313; 1308; Frances; f; 1863; Full; Wd; Head
1314; 1310; Enia; m[sic]; 1924; Full; S; Granddaughter
1315; 1309; Mason; m; 1915; Full; S; Grandson
1316; 1311; Sarah; f; 1926; Full; S; Granddaughter
1317; 1312; Alice; f; 1924; Full; S; Granddaughter

VAUGHN

1318; 1313; John; m; 1862; Full; S; Widow

1319; 1314; John; m; 1906; Full; M; Head
1320; 1315; Malissa; f; 1893; Full; M; Wife
1321; 1316; Mollie; f; 1913; Full; S; Daughter
1322; 1317; Annie; f; 1915; Full; S; Daughter
1323; 1318; Lester; m; 1907; Full; S; Head

1324; 1319; Howard; m; 1905; Full; M; Head
1325; 1320; Betty; f; 1903; Full; M; Wife
1326; 1321; Clifton; m; 1926; Full; S; Son

1327; 1322; Greer; m; 1878; Full; M; Head
1328; 1323; Jane; f; 1888; Full; M; Wife
1329; 1324; Agnes Cheatham; f; 1926; Full; S; Daughter

1330; 1325; Cooksey; m; 1869; Full; M; Head
1331; 1326; Susan; 1873; Full; M; Wife
1332; 1327; Lena; f; 1894; Full; S; Daughter
1333; 1328; Luddie; f; 1904; Full; S; Daughter
1334; 1329; Silmon; m; 1910; Full; S; Son

WAITER

1335; 1330; Gipson; m; 1862; Full; M; Head
1336; 1331; Minnie; f; 1876; Full; M; Wife

Census of the **Mississippi Choctaw** tribe of the _____ reservation of the **Choctaw Agency** jurisdiction, as of **June 30**, 19**29**, taken by **R. J. Enochs**, Superintendent

KEY: Surname; Census Number: Present; Last; Given Name; Sex; Date of Birth; Degree of Blood; Marital Condition; Relation to Head of Family

1337; 1332; Lonia; m; 1905; Full; S; Son
1338; 1333; Ruby; f; 1910; Full; S; Daughter
1339; 1334; Lilly Mae; f; 1911; Full; S; Daughter

WALLACE

1340; 1335; Comby; m; 1883; Full; M; Head
1341; 1336; Betty; f; 1888; Full; M; Wife
1342; 1337; Sula; f; 1910; Full; S; Daughter
1343; 1338; Lucy; f; 1912; Full; S; Daughter
1344; 1339; Emma; f; 1914; Full; S; Daughter
1345; 1340; Maggie; f; 1916; Full; S; Daughter
1346; 1341; Tom; m; 1918; Full; S; Son
1347; 1342; Alton; m; 1920; Full; S; Son

1348; 1343; Rachel; f; 1878; Full; S; Widow
1349; 1344; Columbus; m; 1910; Full; S; Son
1350; 1345; Leona; f; 1912; Full; S; Daughter
1351; 1346; Stenot; m; 1906; Full; S; Son

1352; 1348; Eunice; f; 1890; Full; S; Widow
1353; 1349; Henry; m; 1916; Full; S; Son
1354; 1350; Sally; f; 1919; Full; S; Daughter
1355; 1351; Houston; m; 1927; Full; S; Son

WARNER

1356; 1352; Ellen; f; 1840; Full; S; Widow
1357; 1353; Johnnie Lee; m; 1912; Full; S; Son

WESLEY

1358; 1354; Sue; f; 1898; Full; S; Daughter

1359; 1355; Rufus; m; 1888; Full; M; Head

Census of the **Mississippi Choctaw** tribe of the _____ reservation of the **Choctaw Agency** jurisdiction, as of **June 30**, 19 **29**, taken by **R. J. Enochs**, Superintendent

KEY: Surname; Census Number: Present; Last; Given Name; Sex; Date of Birth; Degree of Blood; Marital Condition; Relation to Head of Family

WILEY

1360; 1356; Liza; f; 1870; Full; S; Head

WILSON

1361; 1357; John; m; 1895; Full; M; Head
1362; 1358; Eva; f; 1902; Full; M; Wife
1514; 1359; Selmon; m; 1919; Full; S; Son
1363; 1360; Mollie; f; 1921; Full; S; Daughter
1364; 1361; Sidney; m; 1922; Full; S; Son
1365; 1362; Leo; m; 1925; Full; S; Son

1366; 1363; Martha; f; 1848; Full; S; Widow

1367; 1364; Will; m; 1888; Full; M; Head
1368; 1365; Martha; f; 1900; Full; M; Wife
1369; 1366; Fannie; f; 1921; Full; S; Daughter
1370; 1367; Lennie; f; 1922; Full; S; Daughter
1371; 1369; Louisanna; f; 1924; Full; S; Daughter
1372; 1370; Joseph; m; 1927; Full; S; Son

WILLIAMS

1373; 1371; Louis; m; 1876; Full; M; Head
1374; 1372; Mamie; f; 1899; Full; M; Wife
1375; 1374; Maurine; f; 1925; Full; S; Daughter

1376; 1375; Fate; m; 1893; Full; S; Head
1377; 1376; Jennie; f; 1844; Full; S; Widow

1378; 1377; Jones; m; 1878; Full; M; Head
1379; 1378; Maggie; f; 1883; Full; M; Wife
1380; 1379; Zonia; m; 1909; Full; S; Son

1381; 1380; Rufus; m; 1907; Full; M; Head

Census of the **Mississippi Choctaw** tribe of the _____ reservation of the **Choctaw Agency** jurisdiction, as of **June 30**, 19**29**, taken by **R. J. Enochs**, Superintendent

KEY: Surname; Census Number: Present; Last; Given Name; Sex; Date of Birth; Degree of Blood; Marital Condition; Relation to Head of Family

1382; 1381; Nellie; f; 1902; Full; M; Wife
1383; 1382; Evan; m; 1921; Full; S; Son
1384; 1383; Phillip; m; 1923; Full; S; Son
1385; 1384; Thelma; m; 1927; Full; S; Son

WILLIAMSON

1386; 1385; Bike; m; 1891; Full; M; Head
1387; 1386; Effie; f; 1904; Full; M; Wife
1388; 1387; Mary; f; 1920; Full; S; Daughter
1389; 1388; Lola; f; 1922; Full; S; Daughter

1390; 1389; Mack; m; 1863; Full; M; Head
1391; 1390; Ida; f; 1878; Full; M; Wife
1392; 1391; Arnold; m; 1919; Full; S; Son

WILLIS

1393; 1392; Hugh; m; 1883; Full; M; Head
1394; 1393; Mollie; f; 1896; Full; M; Wife
1395; 1394; Thompson; m; 1915; Full; S; Son
1396; 1395; Clemon; m; 1917; Full; S; Son
1397; 1396; JC; m; 1918; Full; S; Son
1398; 1397; Collins; m; 1920; Full; S; Son
1399; 1398; Lillie; f; 1922; Full; S; Daughter
1400; 1399; Walter; m; 1924; Full; S; Son
1401; 1400; Lola; f; 1926; Full; S; Daughter

1402; 1401; Henry; m; 1832; Full; M; Head
1403; 1402; Mary; f; 1853; Full; M; Wife
1404; 1403; Wickson; m; 1904; Full; S; Son
1405; 1404; Lola; f; 1903; Full; S; Daughter
1406; 1405; Kelly; m; 1925; Full; S; Son

1407; 1406; Wesley; m; 1866; Full; S; Widower

Census of the __Mississippi Choctaw__ tribe of the _____ reservation
of the __Choctaw Agency__ jurisdiction, as of __June 30__, 19_29_,
taken by __R. J. Enochs__, Superintendent

KEY: Surname; Census Number: Present; Last; Given Name; Sex; Date of Birth; Degree of Blood; Marital Condition; Relation to Head of Family

1408; 1407; Ella; m; 1900; Full; M; Head
1409; 1408; Otis; f; 1903; Full; M; Wife
1410; 1409; Vanola; f; 1920; Full; S; Daughter
1411; 1410; Flora; f; 1922; Full; S; Daughter
1412; 1411; Kittie; f; 1924; Full; S; Daughter
1413; 1412; Bonnie; f; 1926; Full; S; Daughter

1414; 1413; Ike; m; 1905; Full; M; Head
1415; 1414; Ellen; f; 1903; Full; M; Wife

1416; 1415; Salum; m; 1905; Full; S; Head

1417; 1416; Edmond; m; 1908; Full; M; Head
1418; 1417; Sallie; f; 1913; Full; M; Wife
1419; John; m; 1929; Full; S; Son

1420; 1418; Gamlin; m; 1900; Full; M; Head
1421; 1419; Helen; f; 1902; Full; M; Wife
1422; 1420; Mattie; f; 1919; Full; S; Daughter
1423; 1421; G. C.; m; 1920; Full; S; Son
1424; 1422; Eula; f; 1922; Full; S; Daughter
1425; 1423; Maruice; f; 1924; Full; S; Daughter
1426; Marabelle; f; Jan-23-1929; Full; S; Daughter

1427; 1425; Robert; m; 1888; Full; M; Head
1428; 1426; Sallie; f; 1899; Full; M; Wife
1429; 1427; Mollie; f; 1912; Full; S; Daughter

1513; 157; **Benn,** Wilson; m; 1910; Full; S; Orphan

1430; 1428; Jim; m; 1878; Full; M; Head
1431; 1429; Louisa; f; 1880; Full; M; Wife
1432; 1430; Tom; m; 1902; Full; S; Son
1433; 1431; Dennis; m; 1904; Full; S; Son
1434; 1432; Waggoner; m; 1909; Full; S; Son
1435; 1433; Deiley[sic]; f; 1911; Full; S; Daughter

Census of the **Mississippi Choctaw** tribe of the _____ reservation of the **Choctaw Agency** jurisdiction, as of **June 30**, 19**29**, taken by **R. J. Enochs**, Superintendent

KEY: Surname; Census Number: Present; Last; Given Name; Sex; Date of Birth; Degree of Blood; Marital Condition; Relation to Head of Family

1436; 1434; Dora; f; 1912; Full; S; Daughter
1437; 1435; Rosie; f; 1913; Full; S; Daughter
1438; 1436; Smith; m; 1915; Full; S; Son
1439; 1437; Woodrow Wilson; m; 1920; Full; S; Son

1440; 1438; Joe; m; 1862; Full; M; Head
1441; 1439; Adeline; f; 1870; Full; M; Wife

1442; 1440; Nath; m; 1904; Full; M; Head
1443; 1441; Esther; f; 1904; Full; M; Wife
1444; 1442; Silva; f; 1927; Full S; Daughter

1445; 1443; Elias; m; 1902; Full; S; Head

1446; 1444; Edd[sic]; m; 1871; Full; M; Head
1447; 1445; Passie; f; 1878; Full; M; Wife

1448; 1446; Bill; m; 1896; Full; M; Head
1449; 1447; Savenia; f; 1902; Full; M; Wife
1450; 1448; Claud Yates; m; 1919; Full; S; Son
1451; 1449; Elsie; f; 1920; Full; S; Daughter
1452; 1450; William Burkley; m; 1922; Full; S; Son
1453; Lucy; f; Sept-19-1928; Full; S; Daughter

1454; 1451; Gus; m; 1873; Full; M; Head
1455; 1452; Rainey; f; 1901; Full; M; Wife
1456; 677; **Isaac**, Wilson; m; 1913; Full; S; Step-son
1457; 675; **Isaac**, Isom; m; 1922; Full; S; Step-son
1458; 676; **Isaac**, Malton; m; 1920; Full; S; Step-son
1459; 678; **Isaac**, Nannie; f; 1919; Full; S; Step-daughter
1460; 679; **Isaac**, Eunice; Full; 1920; Full; S; Step-daughter
1461; 680; **Isaac**, Rosie; f; 1925; Full; S; Step-daughter
1462; 681; **Isaac**, Tom; m; 1912; Full; S; Step-son
1463; Hester; f; 1926; Full; S; Daughter

1464; 1453; Finis; m; 1898; Full; M; Head

Census of the **Mississippi Choctaw** tribe of the _____ reservation of the **Choctaw Agency** jurisdiction, as of **June 30**, 19**29**, taken by **R. J. Enochs**, Superintendent

KEY: Surname; Census Number: Present; Last; Given Name; Sex; Date of Birth; Degree of Blood; Marital Condition; Relation to Head of Family

1465; 1454; Sallie; f; 1900; Full; M; Wife
1466; 1455; Nola; f; 1925; Full; S; Daughter
1467; 1456; Hester; m; 1927; Full; S; Son

1468; 1458; Dina; f; 1912; Full; S; Orphan

1469; 1459; Spinks; m; 1894; Full; M; Head
1470; 1460; Susie; f; 1900; Full; M; Wife
1471; 1461; Wilson; m; 1919; Full; S; Son
1472; 1462; Flonie; f; 1921; Full; S; Daughter
1473; 1463; Meley; f; 1924; Full; S; Daughter
1474; 1464; John Banks; m; Sept-2-1927; Full; S; Son

1475; 1465; Cohan; m; 1898; Full; M; Head
1476; 1466; Sissie; f; 1902; Full; M; Wife
1477; 1467; Annie; f; 1918; Full; S; Daughter
1478; 1468; Una; f; 1920; Full; S; Daughter
1479; 1469; Sallie; f; 1923; Full S; Daughter
1480; 1470; Harrison; m; 1925; Full; S; Son
1481; 1471; AJ; m; 1927; Full; S; Son

1482; 1472; Johnson; m; 1861; Full; Wd; Head

WISHORK

1483; 1473; Massey; m; 1896; Full; M; Head
1484; 1474; Alpha; f; 1902; Full; M; Wife
1485; 1475; Zelia; f; 1921; Full; S; Daughter
1486; 1476; Avelina; f; 1922; Full; S; Daughter
1487; 1477; Nugar; f; 1925; Full; S; Daughter

1488; 1478; Sampson; m; 1864; Full; Wd; Head

WICKSON

1489; Jimmie; m; 1905; Full; M; Head

Census of the **Mississippi Choctaw** tribe of the _____ reservation of the __Choctaw Agency__ jurisdiction, as of __June 30__, 19_29_, taken by__ R. J. Enochs__, Superintendent

KEY: Surname; Census Number: Present; Last; Given Name; Sex; Date of Birth; Degree of Blood; Marital Condition; Relation to Head of Family

1490;   Lola; f; 1904; Full; M; Wife
1491;   Kelly; m; 1924; Full; S; Son
1492;   Yates; m; July-24-1928; Full; S; Son

YORK

1493; 1479;   Ben; m; 1893; Full; M; Head
1494; 1480;   Louella; f; 1888; Full; M; Wife
1495; 1481;   Elsie; f; 1918; Full; S; Daughter
1496; 1485;   Lena Pearl; f; 1915; Full; S; Daughter

1497; 1482;   Scott; m; 1853; Full; M; Head
1498; 1483;   Celie; f; 1849; Full; M; Wife
1499; 1484;   Burkley; m; 1911; Full; S; Grandson

1500; 1486;   Bennett; m; 1891; Full; M; Head
1501; 1487;   Lacey; f; 1907; Full; M; Wife
1502; 1488;   D. B.; m; 1925; Full; S; Son
1503; 1489;   Colie; f; July-1-1927; Full; S; Daughter

1504; 1490;   Emmett; m; 1904; Full; S; Head
1505; 1491;   Baxter; m; 1907; Full; S; Brother
1506; 1492;   Addie; f; 1909; Full; S; Sister
1507; 1493;   Gasler; m; 1912; Full; S; Brother
1508; 1494;   Eunice; f; 1914; Full; S; Sister
1509; 1495;   Beaman; m; 1917; Full; S; Brother

NOTE: The numbers listed [below] are given to the names listed [below] in their alphabetical order, their names being omitted when making the original census roll. Our total census for June 30, 1929, is 1515.

  78;   **Sam**, Edna; f; 1921; Full; S; Daughter
1510;   **Isaac**, Hickman; m; 1910; Full; S; Orphan
1511;   990;   **Moses**, Alma; f; 1911; Full; S; Sister
1512;   **Hall**, Herbert Hoover; m; Mar-4-1929; Full; S; Son

Census of the **Mississippi Choctaw** tribe of the _____ reservation of the **Choctaw Agency** jurisdiction, as of **June 30**, 19**29**, taken by **R. J. Enochs**, Superintendent

KEY: Surname; Census Number: Present; Last; Given Name; Sex; Date of Birth; Degree of Blood; Marital Condition; Relation to Head of Family

1513; 157; **Benn**, Wilson; m; 1910; Full; S; Orphan
1514; 1359; **Wilson**, Selma; m; 1919; Full; S; Son
1515; **Tubby**, Sallie Mae; f; Feb-26-1928; Full; S;
                                                                                      Daughter of 1303 & 1304

Mississippi Choctaw Census

as of

April 30, 1930

taken by R. J. Enochs, Superintendent

Census of the ~~Miss. Choctaw~~ reservation of the **Choctaw Agency** jurisdiction, as of **April 30**, 19**30**, taken by **R. J. Enochs**, Superintendent. Purchased Lands   MISSISSIPPI

KEY: Surname; Census Number; Given Name; Sex; Age at Last Birthday; Tribe; Degree of Blood; Marital Status; Relationship to Head of Family; At Jurisdiction Where Enrolled (Yes or No); (If No Where); Ward (Yes unless given otherwise.)

ALEX

Miss Choctaws are Wards because of being eligible for al[sic] of purchased lands. MW Stewart

1; Cooper; m; 20; Miss. Choctaw; F; S; Head; Yes

2; Lee; m; 50; Miss. Choctaw; F; M; Head; Yes
3; Missie; f; 50; Miss. Choctaw; F; M; Wife; Yes
4; Nelson; m; 7; Miss. Choctaw; F; S; Son; Yes
5; **Dixon**, Lonie; f; 16; Miss. Choctaw; F; S; Step-daughter; Yes

ALLEN

6; Willis; m; 36; Miss. Choctaw; F; M; Head; Yes
7; Bessie; f; 35; Miss. Choctaw; F; M; Wife; Yes
8; Bob; m; 13; Miss. Choctaw; F; S; Son; Yes
9; Sulum; m; 9; Miss. Choctaw; F; S; Son; Yes
10; Maggie; f; 7; Miss. Choctaw; F; S; Daughter; Yes
11; Nell; f; 5; Miss. Choctaw; F; S; Daughter; Yes
12; Huston; m; 6; Miss. Choctaw; F; S; Son; Yes
13; Willie; m; 2; Miss. Choctaw; F; S; Son; Yes
14; B. C.; m; 7/12; Miss. Choctaw; F; S; Son; Yes

15; Jim; m; 44; Miss. Choctaw; F; M; Head; Yes
16; Manda; f; 46; Miss. Choctaw; F; M; Wife; Yes
17; I. C.; f; 16; Miss. Choctaw; F; S; Daughter; Yes
18; Annie Mae; f; 16; Miss. Choctaw; F; S; Daughter; Yes
19; J. C.; m; 15; Miss. Choctaw; F; S; Son; Yes
20; R. G.; m; 14; Miss. Choctaw; F; S; Son; Yes
21; Will; m; 7; Miss. Choctaw; F; S; Son; Yes

22; Joseph; m; 37; Miss. Choctaw; F; S; Head; Yes

23; Lacey; m; 36; Miss. Choctaw; F; S; Head; Yes

Census of the ~~Miss. Choctaw~~ reservation of the **Choctaw Agency** jurisdiction, as of **April 30**, 19**30**, taken by **R. J. Enochs**, Superintendent. Purchased Lands   MISSISSIPPI

KEY: Surname; Census Number; Given Name; Sex; Age at Last Birthday; Tribe; Degree of Blood; Marital Status; Relationship to Head of Family; At Jurisdiction Where Enrolled (Yes or No); (If No Where); Ward (Yes unless given otherwise.)

AMOS

24;   Sebbie; f; 52; Miss. Choctaw; F; Wd; Head; Yes

25;   Albert; m; 26; Miss. Choctaw; F; S; Head; Yes

26;   Griffin; m; 42; Miss. Choctaw; F; M; Head; Yes
27;   Sallie; f; 38; Miss. Choctaw; F; M; Wife; Yes
28;   Beauty; f; 20; Miss. Choctaw; F; S; Daughter; Yes
29;   Julia; f; 18; Miss. Choctaw; F; S; Daughter; Yes
30;   John; m; 16; Miss. Choctaw; F; S; Son; Yes
31;   Land; m; 14; Miss. Choctaw; F; S; Son; Yes
32;   Fulton; m; 10; Miss. Choctaw; F; S; Son; Yes
33;   Floyed; m; 10; Miss. Choctaw; F; S; Son; Yes
34;   Mose; m; 8; Miss. Choctaw; F; S; Son; Yes

35;   Lampkin; m; 52; Miss. Choctaw; F; M; Head; Yes
36;   Ann; f; 52; Miss. Choctaw; F; M; Wife; Yes
37;   Bonnie; f; 19; Miss. Choctaw; F; S; Daughter; Yes
38;   Lonie; f; 13; Miss. Choctaw; F; S; Daughter; Yes
39;   **Isom**, Mary; f; 3; Miss. Choctaw; F; S; Grand-daughter; Yes

ANDERSON

40;   Bob; m; 45; Miss. Choctaw; F; M; Head; Yes
41;   Ella; f; 42; Miss. Choctaw; F; M; Wife; Yes
42;   A. J; m; 18; Miss. Choctaw; F; S; Son; Yes
43;   Chuty; f; 12; Miss. Choctaw; F; S; Daughter; Yes
44;   Josephine; f; 8; Miss. Choctaw; F; S; Daughter; Yes
45;   Sallie Mae; f; 5; Miss. Choctaw; F; S; Daughter; Yes
46;   Burnice; f; 2; Miss. Choctaw; F; S; Daughter; Yes

47;   John; m; 62; Miss. Choctaw; F; M; Head; Yes
48;   Sallie; f; 27; Miss. Choctaw; F; M; Wife; Yes

Census of the ~~Miss. Choctaw~~ reservation of the Choctaw Agency jurisdiction, as of   April 30   , 19 30 , taken by   R. J. Enochs   , Superintendent. Purchased Lands   MISSISSIPPI

KEY: Surname; Census Number; Given Name; Sex; Age at Last Birthday; Tribe; Degree of Blood; Marital Status; Relationship to Head of Family; At Jurisdiction Where Enrolled (Yes or No); (If No Where); Ward (Yes unless given otherwise.)

49;   J. C; m; 5; Miss. Choctaw; F; S; Son; Yes
50;   Flonie; f; 2; Miss. Choctaw; F; S; Daughter; Yes

51;   Mattie; f; 60; Miss. Choctaw; F; Wd; Head; Yes
52;   Ike; m; 28; Miss. Choctaw; F; S; Son; Yes
53;   Evan; m; 26; Miss. Choctaw; F; S; Son; Yes
54;   Vada; m; 24; Miss. Choctaw; F; S; Son; Yes
55;   Lodie Mae; f; 22; Miss. Choctaw; F; S; Daughter; Yes

56;   Roy; m; 34; Miss. Choctaw; F; M; Head; Yes
57;   Lonie; f; 30; Miss. Choctaw; F; M; Wife; Yes
58;   Francis B; f; 1; Miss. Choctaw; F; S; Daughter; Yes

59;   Ollie; m; 44; Miss. Choctaw; ~~7/8~~ 1/4+; M; Head; Yes
60;   Kate; f; 49; Miss. Choctaw; F; M; Wife; Yes
61;   Grace; f; 7; 15/16; Miss. Choctaw; S; Daughter; Yes
62;   **Campbell**, Ginnie; f; 18; Miss. Choctaw; F; S; Step-daughter; Yes

63;   Oliver; m; 44; Miss. Choctaw; F; M; Head; Yes
64;   Sallie; f; 37; Miss. Choctaw; F; M; Wife; Yes
65;   Hinton; m; 16; Miss. Choctaw; F; S; Son; Yes
66;   Lonie; f; 15; Miss. Choctaw; F; S; Daughter; Yes
67;   Phillip; m; 11; Miss. Choctaw; F; S; Son; Yes
68;   Houston; m; 9; Miss. Choctaw; F; S; Son; Yes
69;   Lucille; f; 7; Miss. Choctaw; F; S; Daughter; Yes

70;   Abel; m; 24; Miss. Choctaw; F; M; Head; Yes
71;   Nancy; f; 44; Miss. Choctaw; F; M; Wife; Yes
72;   **Farmer**, Allie; f; 14; Miss. Choctaw; F; S; Step-daughter; Yes
73;   **Farmer**, Ella Mae; f; 8; Miss. Choctaw; F; S; Step-daughter; Yes
74;   **Farmer**, Annie Mae; f; 6; Miss. Choctaw; F; S; Step-daughter; Yes

Census of the ~~Miss. Choctaw~~ reservation of the **Choctaw Agency** jurisdiction, as of **April 30**, 19 **30**, taken by **R. J. Enochs**, Superintendent. Purchased Lands   MISSISSIPPI

KEY: Surname; Census Number; Given Name; Sex; Age at Last Birthday; Tribe; Degree of Blood; Marital Status; Relationship to Head of Family; At Jurisdiction Where Enrolled (Yes or No); (If No Where); Ward (Yes unless given otherwise.)

BELL

75; Hugh; m; 51; Miss. Choctaw; F; Wd; Head; Yes
76; Viola; f; 18; Miss. Choctaw; F; S; Daughter; Yes
77; Mamie; f; 4; Miss. Choctaw; F; S; Daughter; Yes

78; John; m; 40; Miss. Choctaw; F; M; Head; Yes
79; Lillian; f; 40; Miss. Choctaw; F; M; Wife; Yes
80; Hattie; f; 9; Miss. Choctaw; F; S; Daughter; Yes
81; Eva; f; 5; Miss. Choctaw; F; S; Daughter; Yes
82; Ola; f; 3; Miss. Choctaw; F; S; Daughter; Yes

83; Sallie; f; 40; Miss. Choctaw; F; Wd; Head; Yes
84; Emma; f; 19; Miss. Choctaw; F; S; Daughter; Yes
85; Effie; f; 11; Miss. Choctaw; F; S; Daughter; Yes

86; Junus; m; 33; Miss. Choctaw; F; M; Head; Yes
87; Winnie; f; 29; Miss. Choctaw; F; M; Wife; Yes
88; Ronie; f; 13; Miss. Choctaw; F; S; Daughter; Yes
89; Woods; m; 10; Miss. Choctaw; F; S; Son; Yes
90; Minnie; f; 8; Miss. Choctaw; F; S; Daughter; Yes
91; Edmond; f; 5; Miss. Choctaw; F; S; Son; Yes
92; George; m; 3; Miss. Choctaw; F; S; Son; Yes

93; Evan; m; 28; Miss. Choctaw; F; M; Head; Yes
94; Willie; f; 18; Miss. Choctaw; F; M; Wife; Yes
95; Homer; m; 3; Miss. Choctaw; F; S; Son; Yes
96; Nancy L; f; 1; Miss. Choctaw; F; S; Daughter; Yes

97; Mack; m; 25; Miss. Choctaw; F; M; Head; Yes
98; Lin; f; 16; Miss. Choctaw; F; M; Wife; Yes
99; James; m; 2; Miss. Choctaw; F; S; Son; Yes

100; Thompson; m; 32; Miss. Choctaw; F; M; Head; Yes

Census of the ~~Miss. Choctaw~~ reservation of the **Choctaw Agency** jurisdiction, as of **April 30**, 19 **30**, taken by **R. J. Enochs**, Superintendent. Purchased Lands   MISSISSIPPI

KEY: Surname; Census Number; Given Name; Sex; Age at Last Birthday; Tribe; Degree of Blood; Marital Status; Relationship to Head of Family; At Jurisdiction Where Enrolled (Yes or No); (If No Where); Ward (Yes unless given otherwise.)

101; Ellen; f; 32; Miss. Choctaw; F; M; Wife; Yes
102; Frank King; m; 16; Miss. Choctaw; F; S; Son; Yes

103; Nicholas; m; 30; Miss. Choctaw; F; M; Head; Yes
104; Cleddie; f; 18; Miss. Choctaw; F; M; Wife; Yes
105; Rubie; f; 4/12; Miss. Choctaw; F; S; Daughter; Yes

106; Amon; m; 28; Miss. Choctaw; F; M; Head; Yes
107; Alice; f; 27; Miss. Choctaw; F; M; Wife; Yes

108; Jim; m; 60; Miss. Choctaw; F; S; Head; Yes

109; Joe; m; 38; Miss. Choctaw; F; M; Head; Yes
110; Susie; f; 30; Miss. Choctaw; F; M; Wife; Yes
111; Tom; m; 10; Miss. Choctaw; F; S; Son; Yes
112; Bill; m; 6; Miss. Choctaw; F; S; Son; Yes
113; Henry; m; 4; Miss. Choctaw; F; S; Son; Yes
114; Polly Ann; f; 2; Miss. Choctaw; F; S; Daughter; Yes
115; **Jackson**, Sallie; f; 53; Miss. Choctaw; F; Wd; Mother-in-law; Yes

116; Boston; m; 45; Miss. Choctaw; F; M; Head; Yes
117; Lela; f; 30; Miss. Choctaw; F; M; Wife; Yes
118; Sopha; f; 22; Miss. Choctaw; F; S; Daughter; Yes
119; Ola; f; 20; Miss. Choctaw; F; S; Daughter; Yes
120; Effie; f; 18; Miss. Choctaw; F; S; Daughter; Yes
121; John; m; 8; Miss. Choctaw; F; S; Son; Yes
122; Emma; f; 6; Miss. Choctaw; F; S; Daughter; Yes
123; Emmet; m; 5; Miss. Choctaw; F; S; Son; Yes
124; Marshall; m; 5/12; Miss. Choctaw; F; S; Grand-son; Yes

125; Cornelius; m; 71; Miss. Choctaw; F; Wd; Head; Yes
126; John; m; 23; Miss. Choctaw; F; S; Son; Yes

127; Jim; 68; Miss. Choctaw; F; S; Head; Yes

Census of the ~~Miss. Choctaw~~ reservation of the **Choctaw Agency** jurisdiction, as of ____April 30____, 19_30_, taken by __R. J. Enochs__, Superintendent. Purchased Lands   MISSISSIPPI

KEY: Surname; Census Number; Given Name; Sex; Age at Last Birthday; Tribe; Degree of Blood; Marital Status; Relationship to Head of Family; At Jurisdiction Where Enrolled (Yes or No); (If No Where); Ward (Yes unless given otherwise.)

128; Lish; m; 40; Miss. Choctaw; F; M; Head; Yes
129; Martha; f; 36; Miss. Choctaw; F; M; Wife; Yes
130; Willie; m; 15; Miss. Choctaw; F; S; Son; Yes
131; Huston; m; 10; Miss. Choctaw; F; S; Son; Yes
132; Minnie; f; 9; Miss. Choctaw; F; S; Daughter; Yes
133; Less C; m; 7; Miss. Choctaw; F; S; Son; Yes
134; Gene D; m; 5; Miss. Choctaw; F; S; Son; Yes
135; Jay; m; 3; Miss. Choctaw; F; S; Son; Yes
136; Gaston; m; 22; Miss. Choctaw; F; S; Brother; Yes

137; Bob; m; 20; Miss. Choctaw; F; M; Head; Yes
138; Beneva; f; 19; Miss. Choctaw; F; M; Wife; Yes
139; Sudie; f; 6/12; Miss. Choctaw; F; S; Daughter; Yes

140; Lish; m; 49; Miss. Choctaw; F; M; Head; Yes
141; Maggie; f; 49; Miss. Choctaw; F; M; Wife; Yes
142; Minnie; f; 22; Miss. Choctaw; F; S; Daughter; Yes
143; Lula; f; 14; Miss. Choctaw; F; S; Daughter; Yes
144; Tom; m; 24; Miss. Choctaw; F; S; Son; Yes
145; Bob; m; 20; Miss. Choctaw; F; S; Son; Yes
146; Basin; m; 5; Miss. Choctaw; F; S; Son; Yes

BEN

147; Olan; m; 30; Miss. Choctaw; F; M; Head; Yes
148; Neva; f; 23; Miss. Choctaw; F; M; Wife; Yes
149; Nannie Mae; f; 6; Miss. Choctaw; F; S; Daughter; Yes
150; Annie Laura; f; 4; Miss. Choctaw; F; S; Daughter; Yes
151; Mattie Lou; f; 2; Miss. Choctaw; F; S; Daughter; Yes
152; **Isaac**, Lessie; f; 17; Miss. Choctaw; F; S; Sister-in-law; Yes
153; **Isaac**, Coline; f; 11; Miss. Choctaw; F; S; Sister-in-law; Yes

154; Wyatt; m; 62; Miss. Choctaw; F; M; Head; Yes
155; Ellen; f; 58; Miss. Choctaw; F; M; Wife; Yes

Census of the **Miss. Choctaw** reservation of the **Choctaw Agency** jurisdiction, as of **April 30**, 19**30**, taken by **R. J. Enochs**, Superintendent. Purchased Lands   MISSISSIPPI

KEY: Surname; Census Number; Given Name; Sex; Age at Last Birthday; Tribe; Degree of Blood; Marital Status; Relationship to Head of Family; At Jurisdiction Where Enrolled (Yes or No); (If No Where); Ward (Yes unless given otherwise.)

156; Jimpson; m; 24; Miss. Choctaw; F; S; Head; Yes
157; Lula; f; 46; Miss. Choctaw; F; Wd; Mother; Yes
158; Otha; m; 16; Miss. Choctaw; F; S; Son; Yes
159; Wilson; m; 13; Miss. Choctaw; F; S; Son; Yes

160; Tom; m; 35; Miss. Choctaw; F; M; Head; Yes
161; Gladys; f; 24; Miss. Choctaw; F; M; Wife; Yes
162; Fannie Lou; f; 5; Miss. Choctaw; F; S; Daughter; Yes
163; Hubert; m; 3; Miss. Choctaw; F; S; Son; Yes
164; Henry Ford; m; 11/12; Miss. Choctaw; F; S; Son; Yes

165; Charlie; m; 31; Miss. Choctaw; F; M; Head; Yes
166; Emeline; f; 23; Miss. Choctaw; F; M; Wife; Yes
167; Jim; m; 54; Miss. Choctaw; F; Wd; Father; Yes
168; Monroe; m; 19; Miss. Choctaw; F; S; Son; Yes
169; Thompson; m; 11; Miss. Choctaw; F; S; Son; Yes
170; Zelmer; f; 14; Miss. Choctaw; F; S; Niece; Yes

BILLY

171; Lum; m; 45; Miss. Choctaw; F; M; Head; Yes
172; Minnie; f; 47; Miss. Choctaw; F; M; Wife; Yes
173; **Charles**, Jim; m; 32; Miss. Choctaw; F; S; Brother-in-law; Yes

174; Tom; m; 19; Miss. Choctaw; F; M; Head; Yes
175; Sallie; f; 20; Miss. Choctaw; F; M; Wife; Yes
176; Robert; m; 2; Miss. Choctaw; F; S; Son; Yes

177; Will; m; 53; Miss. Choctaw; F; S; Head; Yes

178; Williston; m; 36; Miss. Choctaw; F; M; Head; Yes
179; Jessie; f; 26; Miss. Choctaw; F; M; Wife; Yes
180; Melton; m; 9; Miss. Choctaw; F; S; Son; Yes
181; Beamon; m; 6; Miss. Choctaw; F; S; Son; Yes

Census of the ~~Miss. Choctaw~~ reservation of the **Choctaw Agency** jurisdiction, as of **April 30**, 19 **30**, taken by **R. J. Enochs**, Superintendent. Purchased Lands   MISSISSIPPI

KEY: Surname; Census Number; Given Name; Sex; Age at Last Birthday; Tribe; Degree of Blood; Marital Status; Relationship to Head of Family; At Jurisdiction Where Enrolled (Yes or No); (If No Where); Ward (Yes unless given otherwise.)

182; Maurice; m; 4; Miss. Choctaw; F; S; Son; Yes
183; Horace; m; 3; Miss. Choctaw; F; S; Son; Yes
184; Nicy; f; 70; Miss. Choctaw; F; Wd; Mother; Yes
185; Leona; f; 30; Miss. Choctaw; F; S; Daughter; Yes
186; Earl; m; 4; Miss. Choctaw; F; S; Grand-daughter[sic]; Yes
187; Ike; m; 20; Miss. Choctaw; F; S; Son; Yes

188; Augustan; m; 20; Miss. Choctaw; F; M; Head; Yes
189; Louena; f; 20; Miss. Choctaw; F; M; Wife; Yes

190; Johnson; m; 64; Miss. Choctaw; F; M; Head; Yes
191; Belaria; f; 40; Miss. Choctaw; F; M; Wife; Yes
192; Gipson; m; 19; Miss. Choctaw; F; S; Son; Yes
193; Ike; m; 18; Miss. Choctaw; F; S; Son; Yes
194; Maud; f; 17; Miss. Choctaw; F; S; Daughter; Yes
195; Wilson; m; 13; Miss. Choctaw; F; S; Son; Yes
196; Greer; m; 11; Miss. Choctaw; F; S; Son; Yes
197; Frank; m; 6; Miss. Choctaw; F; S; Son; Yes
198; Phillip; m; 6/12; Miss. Choctaw; F; S; Grand-son; Yes

199; Lewis; m; 25; Miss. Choctaw; F; M; Head; Yes
200; Zelma; f; 25; Miss. Choctaw; F; M; Wife; Yes
201; **Willis**, Clennie; f; 10; Miss. Choctaw; F; S; Step-daughter; Yes
202; **Willis**, Mamie; f; 8; Miss. Choctaw; F; S; Step-daughter; Yes
203; Frank; m; 4; Miss. Choctaw; F; S; Son; Yes
204; Annie; f; 1; Miss. Choctaw; F; S; Daughter; Yes

205; Will; m; 42; Miss. Choctaw; F; M; Head; Yes
206; Alice; f; 40; Miss. Choctaw; F; M; Wife; Yes
207; William; m; 17; Miss. Choctaw; F; S; Son; Yes
208; Leo; m; 15; Miss. Choctaw; F; S; Son; Yes
209; Rosie; f; 11; Miss. Choctaw; F; S; Daughter; Yes
210; Irene; f; 9; Miss. Choctaw; F; S; Daughter; Yes
211; Joe; m; 7; Miss. Choctaw; F; S; Son; Yes

Census of the ~~Miss. Choctaw~~ reservation of the **Choctaw Agency** jurisdiction, as of **April 30**, 19 **30**, taken by **R. J. Enochs**, Superintendent. Purchased Lands   MISSISSIPPI

KEY: Surname; Census Number; Given Name; Sex; Age at Last Birthday; Tribe; Degree of Blood; Marital Status; Relationship to Head of Family; At Jurisdiction Where Enrolled (Yes or No); (If No Where); Ward (Yes unless given otherwise.)

212; Will, Jr; m; 3; Miss. Choctaw; F; S; Son; Yes
213; Marchie; f; 2; Miss. Choctaw; F; S; Daughter; Yes
214; Charlie; m; 2/12; Miss. Choctaw; F; S; Son; Yes

215; Jordan; m; 45; Miss. Choctaw; F; M; Head; Yes
216; Lilly; f; 27; Miss. Choctaw; F; M; Wife; Yes
217; Sallie Mae; f; 12; Miss. Choctaw; F; S; Daughter; Yes
218; Nellie; f; 9; Miss. Choctaw; F; S; Daughter; Yes
219; Jim; m; 4; Miss. Choctaw; F; S; Son; Yes
220; Mary Lou; f; 2; Miss. Choctaw; F; S; Daughter; Yes

221; Richard; m; 20; Miss. Choctaw; F; m; Head; Yes
222; Eva; f; 15; Miss. Choctaw; F; M; Wife; Yes

223; Wade; m; 51; Miss. Choctaw; F; M; Head; Yes
224; Lina; f; 33; Miss. Choctaw; F; M; Wife; Yes
225; **McMillian**, Mary; f; 10; Miss. Choctaw; F; S; Step-daughter; Yes

BOB

226; Simon; m; 60; Miss. Choctaw; F; S; Head; Yes

BOX

227; Illiman; m; 24; Miss. Choctaw; F; M; Head; Yes
228; Rosie; f; 18; Miss. Choctaw; F; M; Wife; Yes

229; Lillie; f; 42; Miss. Choctaw; F; Wd; Head; Yes
230; Ollie T; m; 15; Miss. Choctaw; F; S; Son; Yes
231; Bathie; f; 7; Miss. Choctaw; F; S; Daughter; Yes
232; Bethy; f; 5; Miss. Choctaw; F; S; Daughter; Yes
233; **Joe**, Emly; f; 70; Miss. Choctaw; F; Wd; Mother; Yes

Census of the ~~Miss. Choctaw~~ reservation of the **Choctaw Agency** jurisdiction, as of **April 30**, 19**30**, taken by **R. J. Enochs**, Superintendent. Purchased Lands   MISSISSIPPI

KEY: Surname; Census Number; Given Name; Sex; Age at Last Birthday; Tribe; Degree of Blood; Marital Status; Relationship to Head of Family; At Jurisdiction Where Enrolled (Yes or No); (If No Where); Ward (Yes unless given otherwise.)

BOYD

234; Archie; m; 66; Miss. Choctaw; F; M; Head; Yes
235; Elizabeth; f; 70; Miss. Choctaw; F; M; Wife; Yes

BRISCOE

236; Tom; m; 39; Miss. Choctaw; F; M; Head; Yes
237; Lucy; f; 47; Miss. Choctaw; F; M; Wife; Yes
238; **Polk**, Frances; m; 20; Miss. Choctaw; F; S; Uncle; Yes

BULL

239; Pink; m; 52; Miss. Choctaw; F; M; Head; Yes
240; Emma; f; 55; Miss. Choctaw; F; M; Wife; Yes

241; George; m; 56; Miss. Choctaw; F; M; Head; Yes
242; Sissy; f; 48; Miss. Choctaw; F; M; Wife; Yes

243; Foreman; m; 27; Miss. Choctaw; F; M; Head; Yes
244; Sarah; f; 26; Miss. Choctaw; F; M; Wife; Yes

CAMPBELL

245; Wiley; m; 29; Miss. Choctaw; F; M; Head; Yes
246; Alice; f; 29; Miss. Choctaw; F; M; Wife; Yes

CATES

247; Susan; f; 52; Miss. Choctaw; F; Wd; Head; Yes
248; Enis; m; 25; Miss. Choctaw; F; S; Son; Yes
249; Essie; f; 22; Miss. Choctaw; F; S; Daughter; Yes
250; **Vaughn**, John; m; 2; Miss. Choctaw; F; S; Grand-son; Yes
251; John; m; 18; Miss. Choctaw; F; S; Son; Yes

Census of the ~~Miss. Choctaw~~ reservation of the **Choctaw Agency** jurisdiction, as of **April 30**, 19 **30**, taken by **R. J. Enochs**, Superintendent. Purchased Lands   MISSISSIPPI

KEY: Surname; Census Number; Given Name; Sex; Age at Last Birthday; Tribe; Degree of Blood; Marital Status; Relationship to Head of Family; At Jurisdiction Where Enrolled (Yes or No); (If No Where); Ward (Yes unless given otherwise.)

252; Lonie; f; 17; Miss. Choctaw; F; S; Daughter; Yes
253; Molpus; m; 16; Miss. Choctaw; F; S; Son; Yes
254; Iona; f; 12; Miss. Choctaw; F; S; Daughter; Yes

255; Oscar; m; 20; Miss. Choctaw; F; S; Head; Yes

256; Alice; f; 25; Miss. Choctaw; F; Wd; Head; Yes
257; Dock; m; 28; Miss. Choctaw; F; S; Son; Yes
258; Dee; m; 22; Miss. Choctaw; F; S; Son; Yes

259; Ned; m; 32; Miss. Choctaw; F; M; Head; Yes
260; Janie; f; 28; Miss. Choctaw; F; M; Wife; Yes
261; Susan Mabel; f; 17; Miss. Choctaw; F; S; Daughter; Yes
262; Emma; f; 14; Miss. Choctaw; F; S; Daughter; Yes
263; Tubby; m; 12; Miss. Choctaw; F; S; Son; Yes
264; Henry M; m; 10; Miss. Choctaw; F; S; Son; Yes
265; Willie F; M; 7; Miss. Choctaw; F; S; Son; Yes
266; Nannie; f; 5; Miss. Choctaw; F; S; Daughter; Yes
267; Julia; f; 4; Miss. Choctaw; F; S; Daughter; Yes

CHAPMAN

268; Will; m; 43; Miss. Choctaw; F; M; Head; Yes
269; Bettie; f; 46; Miss. Choctaw; F; M; Wife; Yes
270; Asa; m; 12; Miss. Choctaw; F; S; Son; Yes
271; Ralston; m; 11; Miss. Choctaw; F; S; Son; Yes
272; Hattie; f; 7; Miss. Choctaw; F; S; Daughter; Yes
273; Ronie; f; 6; Miss. Choctaw; F; S; Daughter; Yes
274; Lilly; f; 5; Miss. Choctaw; F; S; Daughter; Yes
275; Raymond; m; f; Miss. Choctaw; F; S; Son; Yes
276; Cris; m; 3; Miss. Choctaw; F; S; Son; Yes
277; Minnie; f; 2; Miss. Choctaw; F; S; Daughter; Yes

Census of the ~~Miss. Choctaw~~ reservation of the **Choctaw Agency** jurisdiction, as of **April 30**, 19**30**, taken by **R. J. Enochs**, Superintendent. Purchased Lands   MISSISSIPPI

KEY: Surname; Census Number; Given Name; Sex; Age at Last Birthday; Tribe; Degree of Blood; Marital Status; Relationship to Head of Family; At Jurisdiction Where Enrolled (Yes or No); (If No Where); Ward (Yes unless given otherwise.)

CHARLIE

278; Onie; f; 44; Miss. Choctaw; F; Wd; Head; Yes
279; Beamon; m; 15; Miss. Choctaw; F; S; Son; Yes
280; Juanita; f; 10; Miss. Choctaw; F; S; Daughter; Yes
281; Charlie C; m; 8; Miss. Choctaw; F; S; Son; Yes

282; William; m; 79; Miss. Choctaw; F; M; Head; Yes
283; Fannie; f; 65; Miss. Choctaw; F; M; Wife; Yes

284; John; m; 36; Miss. Choctaw; F; M; Head; Yes
285; Mary; f; 28; Miss. Choctaw; F; M; Wife; Yes
286; Elsie; f; 11; Miss. Choctaw; F; S; Daughter; Yes

CHICKAWAY

287; Sim; m; 32; Miss. Choctaw; F; M; Head; Yes
288; Maggie; f; 29; Miss. Choctaw; F; M; Wife; Yes
289; Clemon; m; 11; Miss. Choctaw; F; S; Son; Yes
290; Nellie; f; 9; Miss. Choctaw; F; S; Daughter; Yes
291; Agnes; f; 8; Miss. Choctaw; F; S; Daughter; Yes
292; Albert; m; 4; Miss. Choctaw; F; S; Son; Yes
293; Maggie Kate; f; 2; Miss. Choctaw; F; S; Daughter; Yes
294; Isabell; f; 68; Miss. Choctaw; F; Wd; Mother; Yes
295; Ola; f; 23; Miss. Choctaw; F; S; Sister; Yes

296; Jim; m; 27; Miss. Choctaw; F; M; Head; Yes
297; Eunice; f; 24; Miss. Choctaw; F; M; Wife; Yes
298; **Grant**, Rosie Lee; f; 8; Miss. Choctaw; F; S; Step-daughter; Yes
299; John Hester; m; 2; Miss. Choctaw; F; S; Son; Yes

300; Kelly; m; 37; Miss. Choctaw; F; M; Head; Yes
301; Lilla; f; 28; Miss. Choctaw; F; M; Wife; Yes
302; Mikel; m; 7; Miss. Choctaw; F; S; Son; Yes

Census of the **Miss. Choctaw** reservation of the **Choctaw Agency** jurisdiction, as of **April 30**, 19**30**, taken by **R. J. Enochs**, Superintendent. Purchased Lands   MISSISSIPPI

KEY: Surname; Census Number; Given Name; Sex; Age at Last Birthday; Tribe; Degree of Blood; Marital Status; Relationship to Head of Family; At Jurisdiction Where Enrolled (Yes or No); (If No Where); Ward (Yes unless given otherwise.)

303;   Annah; f; 5; Miss. Choctaw; F; S; Daughter; Yes
304;   Jane; f; 3; Miss. Choctaw; F; S; Daughter; Yes
305;   Rufus; m; 28; Miss. Choctaw; F; S; Son; Yes
306;   Bessie; f; 25; Miss. Choctaw; F; S; Daughter; Yes
307;   Ross C; m; 2; Miss. Choctaw; F; S; Son; Yes
308;   Elizabeth; 3/12; Miss. Choctaw; F; S; Daughter; Yes

CHITTO

309;   Joe; m; 30; Miss. Choctaw; F; M; Head; Yes
310;   Callie; f; 30; Miss. Choctaw; F; M; Wife; Yes
311;   Leo Clifton; m; 2; Miss. Choctaw; F; S; Son; Yes
312;   Lucy D; f; 9/12; Miss. Choctaw; F; S; Daughter; Yes
313;   Linnie Mc; f; 9/12; Miss. Choctaw; F; S; Daughter; Yes

314;   Pat; m; 53; Miss. Choctaw; F; Wd; Head; Yes
315;   Henrietta; f; 15; Miss. Choctaw; F; S; Daughter; Yes
316;   Jefferson; m; 13; Miss. Choctaw; F; S; Son; Yes
317;   Erean; f; 8; Miss. Choctaw; F; S; Daughter; Yes
318;   Isom; m; 6; Miss. Choctaw; F; S; Son; Yes

319;   John; m; 40; Miss. Choctaw; F; M; Head; Yes
320;   Sallie; f; 39; Miss. Choctaw; F; M; Wife; Yes
321;   Minnie; f; 19; Miss. Choctaw; F; S; Daughter; Yes
322;   Hattie; f; 12; Miss. Choctaw; F; S; Daughter; Yes
323;   Allie Nora; f; 10; Miss. Choctaw; F; S; Daughter; Yes
324;   Ella; f; 8; Miss. Choctaw; F; S; Daughter; Yes
325;   Lum Billy; m; 4; Miss. Choctaw; F; S; Son; Yes

326;   Tom; m; 70; Miss. Choctaw; F; M; Head; Yes
327;   Laura; f; 62; Miss. Choctaw; F; M; Wife; Yes
328;   Aliene; f; 20; Miss. Choctaw; F; S; Step-daughter; Yes

Census of the ~~Miss. Choctaw~~ reservation of the **Choctaw Agency** jurisdiction, as of **April 30**, 19**30**, taken by **R. J. Enochs**, Superintendent. Purchased Lands   MISSISSIPPI

KEY: Surname; Census Number; Given Name; Sex; Age at Last Birthday; Tribe; Degree of Blood; Marital Status; Relationship to Head of Family; At Jurisdiction Where Enrolled (Yes or No); (If No Where); Ward (Yes unless given otherwise.)

CLEMONS

329;   Phillip; m; 35; Miss. Choctaw; F; S; Head; Yes

CLEMONS or COWED

330;   Jim; m; 25; Miss. Choctaw; F; M; Head; Yes
331;   Bessie; f; 23; Miss. Choctaw; F; M; Wife; Yes
332;   Margie; f; 2; Miss. Choctaw; F; S; Daughter; Yes
333;   Lewisman; m; 6/12; Miss. Choctaw; F; S; Son; Yes

CLARK

334;   Stella; f; 35; Miss. Choctaw; F; S; Head; Yes

CLEMONS

335;   Jeff; m; 33; Miss. Choctaw; F; M; Head; Yes
336;   Cora; f; 29; Miss. Choctaw; F; M; Wife; Yes
337;   Mattie; f; 8; Miss. Choctaw; F; S; Daughter; Yes
338;   Ethel; f; 7; Miss. Choctaw; F; S; Daughter; Yes
339;   Letha; f; 5; Miss. Choctaw; F; S; Daughter; Yes
340;   John; m; 4; Miss. Choctaw; F; S; Son; Yes
341;   Rena Mae; f; 2; Miss. Choctaw; F; S; Daughter; Yes

342;   Munch; m; 47; Miss. Choctaw; F; M; Head; Yes
343;   Nellie; f; 39; Miss. Choctaw; F; M; Wife; Yes
344;   Ruth; f; 12; Miss. Choctaw; F; S; Daughter; Yes
345;   Bathia; f; 11; Miss. Choctaw; F; S; Daughter; Yes
346;   Mollie; f; 9; Miss. Choctaw; F; S; Daughter; Yes
347;   Sleeper; m; 5; Miss. Choctaw; F; S; Son; Yes

COMBY

Census of the ~~Miss. Choctaw~~ reservation of the **Choctaw Agency** jurisdiction, as of **April 30**, 19**30**, taken by **R. J. Enochs**, Superintendent. Purchased Lands   MISSISSIPPI

KEY: Surname; Census Number; Given Name; Sex; Age at Last Birthday; Tribe; Degree of Blood; Marital Status; Relationship to Head of Family; At Jurisdiction Where Enrolled (Yes or No); (If No Where); Ward (Yes unless given otherwise.)

348; Alma; f; 38; Miss. Choctaw; F; Wd; Head; Yes
349; **McMillian**, Jimmie; m; 19; Miss. Choctaw; F; S; Son; Yes
350; **McMillian**, Jimpson; m; 17; Miss. Choctaw; F; S; Son; Yes
351; **McMillian**, Ella; f; 15; Miss. Choctaw; F; S; Daughter; Yes
352; **McMillian**, Jordan; m; 2/12; Miss. Choctaw; F; S; Son; Yes

353; Arbin; m; 42; Miss. Choctaw; F; M; Head; Yes
354; Gilbert; m; 18; Miss. Choctaw; F; S; Son; Yes
355; Rozella; f; 10; Miss. Choctaw; F; S; Daughter; Yes
356; Maudell; f; 7; Miss. Choctaw; F; S; Daughter; Yes

357; Seymour; m; 29; Miss. Choctaw; F; M; Head; Yes
358; Edna; f; 24; Miss. Choctaw; F; M; Wife; Yes
359; W. C; m; 8; Miss. Choctaw; F; S; Son; Yes
360; B. C; m; 6; Miss. Choctaw; F; S; Son; Yes
361; Leroy; m; 4; Miss. Choctaw; F; S; Son; Yes

362; William; m; 34; Miss. Choctaw; F; M; Head; Yes
363; Allie; f; 25; Miss. Choctaw; F; M; Wife; Yes
364; Jones; m; 6; Miss. Choctaw; F; S; Son; Yes
365; Irene; f; 4; Miss. Choctaw; F; S; Daughter; Yes
366; Joyce Ann; f; 2; Miss. Choctaw; F; S; Daughter; Yes
367; R. L; m; 4/12; Miss. Choctaw; F; S; Son; Yes
368; **Chitto**, Mary; f; 31; Miss. Choctaw; F; S; Sister-in-law; Yes

369; Wallace; m; 58; Miss. Choctaw; F; M; Head; Yes
370; Bettie; f; 54; Miss. Choctaw; F; M; Wife; Yes
371; Lucy; f; 17; Miss. Choctaw; F; S; Daughter; Yes
372; Emma; f; 15; Miss. Choctaw; F; S; Daughter; Yes
373; Maggie; f; 13; Miss. Choctaw; F; S; Daughter; Yes
374; Tom; m; 9; Miss. Choctaw; F; S; Son; Yes
375; Fulton; m; 6; Miss. Choctaw; F; S; Son; Yes

376; Ben; m; 68; Miss. Choctaw; F; Wd; Head; Yes

Census of the ~~Miss. Choctaw~~ reservation of the **Choctaw Agency** jurisdiction, as of **April 30**, 19**30**, taken by **R. J. Enochs**, Superintendent. Purchased Lands   MISSISSIPPI

KEY: Surname; Census Number; Given Name; Sex; Age at Last Birthday; Tribe; Degree of Blood; Marital Status; Relationship to Head of Family; At Jurisdiction Where Enrolled (Yes or No); (If No Where); Ward (Yes unless given otherwise.)

377; Olmon; m; 52; Miss. Choctaw; F; M; Head; Yes
378; Laura; f; 49; Miss. Choctaw; F; M; Wife; Yes

COOPER

379; Wixon; m; 29; Miss. Choctaw; F; M; Head; Yes
380; Leana; f; 22; Miss. Choctaw; F; M; Wife; Yes

381; Gaston; m; 44; Miss. Choctaw; F; M; Head; Yes
382; Ada; f; 46; Miss. Choctaw; F; M; Wife; Yes
383; Odell; f; 17; Miss. Choctaw; F; S; Daughter; Yes
384; Fannie; f; 12; Miss. Choctaw; F; S; Daughter; Yes
385; Hubert; m; 9; Miss. Choctaw; F; S; Son; Yes
386; Christine; f; 6; Miss. Choctaw; F; S; Daughter; Yes
387; Elma; f; 3; Miss. Choctaw; F; S; Daughter; Yes

COTTON

388; John; m; 20; Miss. Choctaw; F; S; Head; Yes

389; George; m; 30; Miss. Choctaw; F; M; Head; Yes
390; Ellen; f; 29; Miss. Choctaw; F; M; Wife; Yes
391; Minnie; f; 4; Miss. Choctaw; F; S; Daughter; Yes

CRENSHAW

392; Amos; m; 18; Miss. Choctaw; F; S; Orphan; Yes
393; Austin; m; 14; Miss. Choctaw; F; S; Orphan; Yes

DAN

394; S. D; m; 24; Miss. Choctaw; F; M; Head; Yes
395; Lela; f; 22; Miss. Choctaw; F; M; Wife; Yes
396; Irene; f; 4; Miss. Choctaw; F; S; Daughter; Yes

Census of the ~~Miss. Choctaw~~ reservation of the Choctaw Agency jurisdiction, as of April 30, 19 30, taken by R. J. Enochs, Superintendent. Purchased Lands   MISSISSIPPI

KEY: Surname; Census Number; Given Name; Sex; Age at Last Birthday; Tribe; Degree of Blood; Marital Status; Relationship to Head of Family; At Jurisdiction Where Enrolled (Yes or No); (If No Where); Ward (Yes unless given otherwise.)

397; Albert B; m; 4/12; Miss. Choctaw; F; S; Son; Yes

398; Williston; m; 33; Miss. Choctaw; F; Wd; Head; Yes
399; Rose Ida; f; 8; Miss. Choctaw; F; S; Daughter; Yes

DANSBY

400; Jacob; m; 58; Miss. Choctaw; F; M; Head; Yes
401; Jennie; f; 45; Miss. Choctaw; F; M; Wife; Yes
402; **Tubby**, R. B; m; 23; Miss. Choctaw; F; S; Brother-in-law; Yes
403; **Tubby**, Jim; m; 57; Miss. Choctaw; F; S; Brother-in-law; Yes

DAVIS

404; Culberson; m; 68; Miss. Choctaw; F; M; Head; Yes
405; Leona; f; 54; Miss. Choctaw; F; M; Wife; Yes
406; Hobbie; m; 24; Miss. Choctaw; F; S; Son; Yes

407; Will; m; 56; Miss. Choctaw; F; M; Head; Yes
408; Mattie; f; 28; Miss. Choctaw; F; M; Wife; Yes
409; Annie; f; 11; Miss. Choctaw; F; S; Daughter; Yes
410; John; m; 9; Miss. Choctaw; F; S; Son; Yes
411; Mary; f; 2; Miss. Choctaw; F; S; Daughter; Yes
412; Mack; m; 1; Miss. Choctaw; F; S; Son; Yes

413; Sidney; m; 42; Miss. Choctaw; F; Wd; Head; Yes
414; Elsmer; f; 21; Miss. Choctaw; F; S; Daughter; Yes
415; Mabel; f; 19; Miss. Choctaw; F; S; Daughter; Yes
416; Anna; f; 10; Miss. Choctaw; F; S; Daughter; Yes
417; Johnie; m; 8; Miss. Choctaw; F; S; Son; Yes

418; Malissie; f; 60; Miss. Choctaw; F; Wd; Head; Yes
419; Alice; f; 33; Miss. Choctaw; F; S; Daughter; Yes
420; Bessie; f; 20; Miss. Choctaw; F; S; Daughter; Yes

Census of the ~~Miss. Choctaw~~ reservation of the Choctaw Agency jurisdiction, as of April 30, 19 30, taken by R. J. Enochs, Superintendent. Purchased Lands   MISSISSIPPI

KEY: Surname; Census Number; Given Name; Sex; Age at Last Birthday; Tribe; Degree of Blood; Marital Status; Relationship to Head of Family; At Jurisdiction Where Enrolled (Yes or No); (If No Where); Ward (Yes unless given otherwise.)

421;   Sina; f; 18; Miss. Choctaw; F; S; Grand-daughter; Yes
422;   Ada Francis; f; 10; Miss. Choctaw; F; S; Grand-daughter; Yes
423;   Mary; f; 15; Miss. Choctaw; F; S; Grand-daughter; Yes

424;   Tom; m; 30; Miss. Choctaw; F; M; Head; Yes
425;   Cilian; f; 30; Miss. Choctaw; F; M; Wife; Yes
426;   Millie; f; 10; Miss. Choctaw; F; S; Daughter; Yes
427;   Henderson; m; 8; Miss. Choctaw; F; S; Son; Yes

DENSON

428;   Lilly; f; 42; Miss. Choctaw; F; Wd; Head; Yes
429;   Hendrix; m; 13; Miss. Choctaw; F; S; Son; Yes
430;   Emma; f; 10; Miss. Choctaw; F; S; Daughter; Yes
431;   Charley; m; 7; Miss. Choctaw; F; S; Son; Yes
432;   David; m; 5; Miss. Choctaw; F; S; Son; Yes

433;   Pete; m; 42; Miss. Choctaw; F; M; Head; Yes
434;   Rosie; f; 29; Miss. Choctaw; F; M; Wife; Yes
435;   Mary; f; 14; Miss. Choctaw; F; S; Daughter; Yes
436;   Jeffie; f; 12; Miss. Choctaw; F; S; Daughter; Yes
437;   Edna; f; 7; Miss. Choctaw; F; S; Daughter; Yes
438;   Floyd; m; 3; Miss. Choctaw; F; S; Son; Yes
439;   Nancy; f; 1; Miss. Choctaw; F; S; Daughter; Yes

440;   Willie; m; 22; Miss. Choctaw; F; M; Head; Yes
441;   Beauty; f; 18; Miss. Choctaw; F; M; Wife; Yes
442;   Joe; m; 76; Miss. Choctaw; F; Wd; Father; Yes
443;   Winston; m; 16; Miss. Choctaw; F; S; Brother; Yes

DIXON

444;   Phillip; m; 53; Miss. Choctaw; F; M; Head; Yes
445;   Nannie; f; 50; Miss. Choctaw; F; M; Wife; Yes

Census of the ~~Miss. Choctaw~~ reservation of the Choctaw Agency jurisdiction, as of April 30, 19 30, taken by R. J. Enochs, Superintendent. Purchased Lands   MISSISSIPPI

KEY: Surname; Census Number; Given Name; Sex; Age at Last Birthday; Tribe; Degree of Blood; Marital Status; Relationship to Head of Family; At Jurisdiction Where Enrolled (Yes or No); (If No Where); Ward (Yes unless given otherwise.)

446; **Sam**, Charlie; m; 16; Miss. Choctaw; F; S; Nephew; Yes

447; Jim; m; 29; Miss. Choctaw; F; M; Head; Yes
448; Sarah; f; 27; Miss. Choctaw; F; M; Wife; Yes
449; Marie; f; 7; Miss. Choctaw; F; S; Daughter; Yes
450; Imogene; f; 4; Miss. Choctaw; F; S; Daughter; Yes
451; Ellen; f; 2; Miss. Choctaw; F; S; Daughter; Yes

452; Jess; m; 52; Miss. Choctaw; F; M; Head; Yes
453; Callie; f; 60; Miss. Choctaw; F; M; Wife; Yes
454; Scott; m; 19; Miss. Choctaw; F; S; Son; Yes
455; **Thompson**, Mary Jane; f; 80; Miss. Choctaw; F; Wd; Mother-in-law; Yes
456; Young; m; 13; Miss. Choctaw; F; S; Son; Yes
457; Lilly; f; 10; Miss. Choctaw; F; S; Daughter; Yes

458; Horace; m; 24; Miss. Choctaw; F; M; Head; Yes
459; Esther; f; 23; Miss. Choctaw; F; M; Wife; Yes
460; Calenia; f; 3; Miss. Choctaw; F; S; Daughter; Yes

461; Emmond; m; 22; Miss. Choctaw; F; M; Head; Yes
462; Julia; f; 21; Miss. Choctaw; F; M; Wife; Yes
463; Addie Mae; f; 6/12; Miss. Choctaw; F; S; Daughter; Yes

464; Wilson; m; 71; Miss. Choctaw; F; M; Head; Yes
465; Hope; f; 44; Miss. Choctaw; F; M; Wife; Yes

466; Kanis; m; 38; Miss. Choctaw; F; Wd; Head; Yes
467; Eaby; f; 19; Miss. Choctaw; F; S; Daughter; Yes
468; Lonie; f; 16; Miss. Choctaw; F; S; Daughter; Yes
469; Jim; m; 25; Miss. Choctaw; F; S; Son; Yes
470; Wade; m; 15; Miss. Choctaw; F; S; Son; Yes

Census of the ~~Miss. Choctaw~~ reservation of the **Choctaw Agency** jurisdiction, as of **April 30**, 19 **30**, taken by **R. J. Enochs**, Superintendent. Purchased Lands   MISSISSIPPI

KEY: Surname; Census Number; Given Name; Sex; Age at Last Birthday; Tribe; Degree of Blood; Marital Status; Relationship to Head of Family; At Jurisdiction Where Enrolled (Yes or No); (If No Where); Ward (Yes unless given otherwise.)

EVANS

471; John; m; 55; Miss. Choctaw; F; Wd; Head; Yes
472; **Wickson**, Kelly; m; 5; Miss. Choctaw; F; S; Grand-Son; Yes

FARMER

473; Silmon; m; 56; Miss. Choctaw; F; Wd; Head; Yes
474; Henry; f; 18; Miss. Choctaw; F; S; Son; Yes
475; Bennie; f; 12; Miss. Choctaw; F; S; Daughter; Yes
476; Corine; f; 9; Miss. Choctaw; F; S; Daughter; Yes

477; Ishman; m; 85; Miss. Choctaw; F; M; Head; Yes
478; Sweeter; f; 57; Miss. Choctaw; F; M; Wife; Yes
479; Emma; f; 27; Miss. Choctaw; F; S; Daughter; Yes
480; Marshall; m; 25; Miss. Choctaw; F; S; Son; Yes
481; Maggie; f; 20; Miss. Choctaw; F; S; Daughter; Yes
482; Lena; f; 17; Miss. Choctaw; F; S; Daughter; Yes
483; Bill; m; 14; Miss. Choctaw; F; S; Son; Yes
484; Rainey; f; 10; Miss. Choctaw; F; S; Daughter; Yes

485; Moses; m; 30; Miss. Choctaw; F; M; Head; Yes
486; Lottie; f; 22; Miss. Choctaw; F; M; Wife; Yes

487; Thomas; m; 64; Miss. Choctaw; F; M; Head; Yes
488; Mallissa; f; 57; Miss. Choctaw; F; M; Wife; Yes

489; Howard; m; 18; Miss. Choctaw; F; M; Head; Yes
490; Lena; f; 16; Miss. Choctaw; F; M; Wife; Yes

FARVE

491; Bennett; m; 37; Miss. Choctaw; F; S; Head; Yes

Census of the ~~Miss. Choctaw~~ reservation of the **Choctaw Agency** jurisdiction, as of **April 30**, 19**30**, taken by **R. J. Enochs**, Superintendent. Purchased Lands   MISSISSIPPI

KEY: Surname; Census Number; Given Name; Sex; Age at Last Birthday; Tribe; Degree of Blood; Marital Status; Relationship to Head of Family; At Jurisdiction Where Enrolled (Yes or No); (If No Where); Ward (Yes unless given otherwise.)

491; Paul; m; 42; Miss. Choctaw; F; M; Head; Yes
493; Renia; f; 25; Miss. Choctaw; F; M; Wife; Yes
494; Phillip J; m; 6; Miss. Choctaw; F; S; Son; Yes
495; Zula Mae; f; 4; Miss. Choctaw; F; S; Daughter; Yes
496; Estelle; f; 2; Miss. Choctaw; F; S; Daughter; Yes
497; Viola; f; 6/12; Miss. Choctaw; F; S; Daughter; Yes

498; Joseph S; m; 18; Miss. Choctaw; F; M; Head; Yes
499; Rachel; f; 51; Miss. Choctaw; F; M; Wife; Yes

500; Western; m; 40; Miss. Choctaw; F; Wd; Head; Yes
501; Chester; m; 25; Miss. Choctaw; F; S; Son; Yes
502; Josie; f; 22; Miss. Choctaw; F; S; Daughter; Yes
503; John; m; 22; Miss. Choctaw; F; S; Son; Yes
504; Lillian; f; 19; Miss. Choctaw; F; S; Daughter; Yes
505; Ima; f; 14; Miss. Choctaw; F; S; Daughter; Yes
506; Hilda; f; 6; Miss. Choctaw; F; S; Daughter; Yes

507; Antwine; m; 53; Miss. Choctaw; F; M; Head; Yes
508; Liseeda; f; 56; Miss. Choctaw; F; M; Wife; Yes
509; Edna; f; 20; Miss. Choctaw; F; S; Daughter; Yes
510; Cecilia; f; 18; Miss. Choctaw; F; S; Daughter; Yes
511; Isileen; f; 17; Miss. Choctaw; F; S; Daughter; Yes
512; Earl; m; 12; Miss. Choctaw; F; S; Son; Yes
513; Mamie; f; 10; Miss. Choctaw; F; S; Daughter; Yes
514; Corbrin; m; 7; Miss. Choctaw; F; S; Son; Yes

515; Dave; m; 52; Miss. Choctaw; F; Wd; Head; Yes
516; William; m; 29; Miss. Choctaw; F; S; Son; Yes
517; Lena; f; 30; Miss. Choctaw; F; S; Daughter; Yes
518; Sarah Alma; f; 19; Miss. Choctaw; F; S; Daughter; Yes
519; Georgia; f; 11; Miss. Choctaw; F; S; Daughter; Yes
520; John; m; 8; Miss. Choctaw; F; S; Son; Yes

Census of the ~~Miss. Choctaw~~ reservation of the **Choctaw Agency** jurisdiction, as of **April 30**, 19**30**, taken by **R. J. Enochs**, Superintendent. Purchased Lands   MISSISSIPPI

KEY: Surname; Census Number; Given Name; Sex; Age at Last Birthday; Tribe; Degree of Blood; Marital Status; Relationship to Head of Family; At Jurisdiction Where Enrolled (Yes or No); (If No Where); Ward (Yes unless given otherwise.)

521; Rosine H; m; 47; Miss. Choctaw; F; M; Head; Yes
522; Winoa; f; 52; Miss. Choctaw; F; M; Wife; Yes

523; Charles; m; 42; Miss. Choctaw; F; M; Head; Yes
524; Edwina; f; 39; Miss. Choctaw; F; M; Wife; Yes
525; Retha; f; 12; Miss. Choctaw; F; S; Daughter; Yes
526; Alvin; m; 10; Miss. Choctaw; F; S; Son; Yes
527; Irvin; m; 8; Miss. Choctaw; F; S; Son; Yes
528; Aubrey; f; 5; Miss. Choctaw; F; S; Daughter; Yes
529; Vivian; f; 4; Miss. Choctaw; F; S; Daughter; Yes

530; Thomas; m; 48; Miss. Choctaw; F; M; Head; Yes
531; Mary; f; 32; Miss. Choctaw; F; M; Wife; Yes
532; Hazel; f; 12; Miss. Choctaw; F; S; Daughter; Yes
533; Robert; m; 11; Miss. Choctaw; F; S; Son; Yes
534; Gertrude; f; 9; Miss. Choctaw; F; S; Daughter; Yes
535; Ruth; f; 6; Miss. Choctaw; F; S; Daughter; Yes

536; Sylvesta; m; 42; Miss. Choctaw; F; S; Head; Yes

537; Joe Tole; m; 65; Miss. Choctaw; F; M; Head; Yes
538; Lela; f; 62; Miss. Choctaw; F; M; Wife; Yes
539; Dora; f; 37; Miss. Choctaw; F; S; Daughter; Yes
540; Victoria; f; 30; Miss. Choctaw; F; S; Daughter; Yes

541; Gilmore; m; 28; Miss. Choctaw; F; M; Head; Yes
542; Gertrude; f; 26; Miss. Choctaw; F; M; Wife; Yes

543; Joe; m; 24; Miss. Choctaw; F; M; Head; Yes
544; Lillian; f; 22; Miss. Choctaw; F; M; Wife; Yes

545; Basie; m; 19; Miss. Choctaw; F; S; Head; Yes

546; Jessie; f; 18; Miss. Choctaw; F; S; Head; Yes

Census of the ~~Miss. Choctaw~~ reservation of the **Choctaw Agency** jurisdiction, as of **April 30**, 19 **30**, taken by **R. J. Enochs**, Superintendent. Purchased Lands   MISSISSIPPI

KEY: Surname; Census Number; Given Name; Sex; Age at Last Birthday; Tribe; Degree of Blood; Marital Status; Relationship to Head of Family; At Jurisdiction Where Enrolled (Yes or No); (If No Where); Ward (Yes unless given otherwise.)

547; Corrine; m; 35; Miss. Choctaw; F; M; Head; Yes
548; Viola; f; 33; Miss. Choctaw; F; M; Wife; Yes
549; William; m; 14; Miss. Choctaw; F; S; Son; Yes
550; Francis; m; 8; Miss. Choctaw; F; S; Son; Yes
551; J. C; m; 6; Miss. Choctaw; F; S; Son; Yes
552; Wilma; f; 4; Miss. Choctaw; F; S; Daughter; Yes

553; John Tole; m; 47; Miss. Choctaw; F; S; Head; Yes

554; Charles T; m; 46; Miss. Choctaw; F; M; Head; Yes
555; Alfonsine; f; 32; Miss. Choctaw; F; M; Wife; Yes

556; Emeline; f; 40; Miss. Choctaw; F; S; Head; Yes

557; Mary; f; 34; Miss. Choctaw; F; S; Head; Yes

558; Julia; f; 45; Miss. Choctaw; F; S; Head; Yes

559; R. C; m; 29; Miss. Choctaw; F; S; Head; Yes

560; Dennie; m; 42; Miss. Choctaw; F; S; Head; Yes

561; Western; m; 50; Miss. Choctaw; F; S; Head; Yes

562; Noah; m; 38; Miss. Choctaw; F; S; Head; Yes

563; Bennett; m; 36; Miss. Choctaw; F; S; Head; Yes

564; William; m; 32; Miss. Choctaw; F; S; Head; Yes

565; Seman; m; 64; Miss. Choctaw; F; Wd; Head; Yes

566; Elinor; f; 36; Miss. Choctaw; F; S; Head; Yes

Census of the ~~Miss. Choctaw~~ reservation of the **Choctaw Agency** jurisdiction, as of **April 30**, 19 **30**, taken by **R. J. Enochs**, Superintendent. Purchased Lands   MISSISSIPPI

KEY: Surname; Census Number; Given Name; Sex; Age at Last Birthday; Tribe; Degree of Blood; Marital Status; Relationship to Head of Family; At Jurisdiction Where Enrolled (Yes or No); (If No Where); Ward (Yes unless given otherwise.)

567; Joe; m; 57; Miss. Choctaw; F; S; Head; Yes

568; Albert; m; 49; Miss. Choctaw; F; M; Head; Yes
569; Iktial; f; 47; Miss. Choctaw; F; M; Wife; Yes

570; Lucille; f; 28; Miss. Choctaw; F; S; Head; Yes

571; Ethel; f; 26; Miss. Choctaw; F; S; Head; Yes

572; Ida; f; 50; Miss. Choctaw; F; S; Head; Yes

573; Roselle; f; 54; Miss. Choctaw; F; S; Head; Yes

574; Amelia; f; 36; Miss. Choctaw; F; S; Head; Yes

575; Renrites; f; 32; Miss. Choctaw; F; S; Head; Yes

576; Bay Turner; m; 25; Miss. Choctaw; F; S; Head; Yes

577; Ceciline; m; 24; Miss. Choctaw; F; S; Head; Yes

578; Charles; m; 50; Miss. Choctaw; F; S; Head; Yes

FORBES

579; Wesley; m; 66; Miss. Choctaw; F; M; Head; Yes
580; Sallie; f; 65; Miss. Choctaw; F; M; Wife; Yes
581; Ella; f; 20; Miss. Choctaw; F; S; Daughter; Yes

582; Clint; m; 28; Miss. Choctaw; F; M; Head; Yes
583; Josey; f; 30; Miss. Choctaw; F; M; Wife; Yes
584; Ida Mae; f; 13; Miss. Choctaw; F; S; Daughter; Yes
585; Gaston; m; 8; Miss. Choctaw; F; S; Son; Yes
586; Henry; m; 4/12; Miss. Choctaw; F; S; Son; Yes

Census of the ~~Miss. Choctaw~~ reservation of the **Choctaw Agency** jurisdiction, as of **April 30**, 19**30**, taken by **R. J. Enochs**, Superintendent. Purchased Lands   MISSISSIPPI

KEY: Surname; Census Number; Given Name; Sex; Age at Last Birthday; Tribe; Degree of Blood; Marital Status; Relationship to Head of Family; At Jurisdiction Where Enrolled (Yes or No); (If No Where); Ward (Yes unless given otherwise.)

FRAZIER

587; Mollie; f; 55; Miss. Choctaw; F; Wd; Head; Yes
588; Essie; f; 23; Miss. Choctaw; F; S; Daughter; Yes
589; John; m; 19; Miss. Choctaw; F; S; Son; Yes

590; West; m; 22; Miss. Choctaw; F; M; Head; Yes
591; Nannie; f; 21; Miss. Choctaw; F; M; Wife; Yes
592; Marshall; m; 1; Miss. Choctaw; F; S; Son; Yes

593; Forbes; m; 25; Miss. Choctaw; F; M; Head; Yes
594; Ima; f; 25; Miss. Choctaw; F; M; Wife; Yes
595; **Fox**, Sam Davis; m; 6; Miss. Choctaw; F; S; Step-son; Yes
596; Homer; m; 6; Miss. Choctaw; F; S; Son; Yes

597; Will; m; 30; Miss. Choctaw; F; M; Head; Yes
598; Lavena; f; 27; Miss. Choctaw; F; M; Wife; Yes

599; Seale; m; 60; Miss. Choctaw; F; M; Head; Yes
600; Eliza; f; 75; Miss. Choctaw; F; M; Wife; Yes
601; Willie; f; 6; Miss. Choctaw; F; S; Grand-daughter; Yes

602; Jim; m; 24; Miss. Choctaw; F; M; Head; Yes
603; Nannie; f; 27; Miss. Choctaw; F; M; Wife; Yes
604; A. B; m; 3; Miss. Choctaw; F; S; Son; Yes
605; Henry; m; 4; Miss. Choctaw; F; S; Son; Yes
606; Nancy; f; 1; Miss. Choctaw; F; S; Daughter; Yes

607; Ligman; m; 36; Miss. Choctaw; F; M; Head; Yes
608; Sina; f; 21; Miss. Choctaw; F; M; Wife; Yes
609; Edmon; m; 8; Miss. Choctaw; F; S; Son; Yes
610; Sallie; f; 6; Miss. Choctaw; F; S; Daughter; Yes

611; Emma; f; 32; Miss. Choctaw; F; Wd; Head; Yes

Census of the ~~Miss. Choctaw~~ reservation of the **Choctaw Agency** jurisdiction, as of **April 30**, 19 **30**, taken by **R. J. Enochs**, Superintendent. Purchased Lands   MISSISSIPPI

KEY: Surname; Census Number; Given Name; Sex; Age at Last Birthday; Tribe; Degree of Blood; Marital Status; Relationship to Head of Family; At Jurisdiction Where Enrolled (Yes or No); (If No Where); Ward (Yes unless given otherwise.)

612;   Susie; f; 14; Miss. Choctaw; F; S; Daughter; Yes
613;   Simpson; m; 10; Miss. Choctaw; F; S; Son; Yes
614;   Herman; m; 9; Miss. Choctaw; F; S; Son; Yes
615;   Frazier; m; 7; Miss. Choctaw; F; S; Son; Yes
616;   Velma; f; 5; Miss. Choctaw; F; S; Daughter; Yes

617;   Henson; m; 62; Miss. Choctaw; F; M; Head; Yes
618;   Fenie; f; 60; Miss. Choctaw; F; M; Wife; Yes
619;   Lucy; f; 12; Miss. Choctaw; F; S; Daughter; Yes
620;   Wade; m; 12; Miss. Choctaw; F; S; Nephew; Yes
621;   Jake; m; 8; Miss. Choctaw; F; S; Nephew; Yes

GARDNER

622;   Jim; m; 31; Miss. Choctaw; F; M; Head; Yes
623;   Celia; f; 26; Miss. Choctaw; F; M; Wife; Yes
624;   Arleta; f; 9; Miss. Choctaw; F; S; Daughter; Yes
625;   Alton; m; 3; Miss. Choctaw; F; S; Son; Yes

GIPSON

626;   Bart; m; 54; Miss. Choctaw; F; M; Head; Yes
627;   Lucy; f; 50; Miss. Choctaw; F; M; Wife; Yes
628;   Maggie; f; 22; Miss. Choctaw; F; S; Daughter; Yes
629;   Homer; m; 17; Miss. Choctaw; F; S; Son; Yes

630;   Hensley; m; 19; Miss. Choctaw; F; M; Head; Yes
631;   Elizabeth; f; 19; Miss. Choctaw; F; M; Wife; Yes

632;   Andrew; m; 25; Miss. Choctaw; F; S; Head; Yes

633;   Gus; m; 21; Miss. Choctaw; F; S; Head; Yes

634;   Nolie; m; 28; Miss. Choctaw; F; M; Head; Yes

Census of the ~~Miss. Choctaw~~ reservation of the **Choctaw Agency** jurisdiction, as of **April 30**, 19**30**, taken by **R. J. Enochs**, Superintendent. Purchased Lands   MISSISSIPPI

KEY: Surname; Census Number; Given Name; Sex; Age at Last Birthday; Tribe; Degree of Blood; Marital Status; Relationship to Head of Family; At Jurisdiction Where Enrolled (Yes or No); (If No Where); Ward (Yes unless given otherwise.)

635;   Frances; f; 30; Miss. Choctaw; F; M; Wife; Yes
636;   Huston; m; 5; Miss. Choctaw; F; S; Son; Yes
637;   Paul; m; 4; Miss. Choctaw; F; S; Son; Yes
638;   Annie; f; 1; Miss. Choctaw; F; S; Daughter; Yes

639;   Steve; m; 66; Miss. Choctaw; F; M; Head; Yes
640;   Jennie; f; 62; Miss. Choctaw; F; M; Wife; Yes
641;   Minnie; f; 17; Miss. Choctaw; F; S; Daughter; Yes
642;   Willie; m; 12; Miss. Choctaw; F; S; Son; Yes
643;   Ikey; f; 27; Miss. Choctaw; F; S; Daughter; Yes
644;   Fannie; f; 22; Miss. Choctaw; F; S; Daughter; Yes
645;   Annie; f; 21; Miss. Choctaw; F; S; Daughter; Yes
646;   Hugh; m; 4; Miss. Choctaw; F; S; Grand-son; Yes
647;   **Unknown**, Aron; m; 3; Miss. Choctaw; F; S; Grand-son; Yes

HALL

648;   Bessie; f; 18; Miss. Choctaw; F; Wd; Head; Yes
649;   Henrietta; f; 2; Miss. Choctaw; F; S; Daughter; Yes
650;   **Thomas**, Lula; f; 16; Miss. Choctaw; F; S; Sister

651;   Langford; m; 35; Miss. Choctaw; F; M; Head; Yes
652;   Lou; f; 25; Miss. Choctaw; F; M; Wife; Yes
653;   Travis; m; 7; Miss. Choctaw; F; S; Son; Yes
654;   Arlone; f; 6; Miss. Choctaw; F; S; Daughter; Yes
655;   Frank; m; 4; Miss. Choctaw; F; S; Son; Yes

HARPER

656;   Lena; f; 18; Miss. Choctaw; F; S; Head; Yes

HARRIS

657;   Elsmore; f; 22; Miss. Choctaw; F; S; Head; Yes

Census of the ~~Miss. Choctaw~~ reservation of the **Choctaw Agency** jurisdiction, as of **April 30**, 19**30**, taken by **R. J. Enochs**, Superintendent. Purchased Lands   MISSISSIPPI

KEY: Surname; Census Number; Given Name; Sex; Age at Last Birthday; Tribe; Degree of Blood; Marital Status; Relationship to Head of Family; At Jurisdiction Where Enrolled (Yes or No); (If No Where); Ward (Yes unless given otherwise.)

HAWKINS

658; John; m; 70; Miss. Choctaw; F; M; Head; Yes
659; Alice; f; 48; Miss. Choctaw; F; M; Wife; Yes
660; Mary; f; 19; Miss. Choctaw; F; S; Step-daughter; Yes
661; **Shoemaker**, Lester; f[sic]; 17; Miss. Choctaw; F; S; Step-daughter; Yes
662; **Lewis**, Mamie; f; 38; Miss. Choctaw; F; S; Sister-in-law; Yes

HENRY

663; Albert; m; 52; Miss. Choctaw; F; M; Head; Yes
664; Martha; f; 42; Miss. Choctaw; F; M; Wife; Yes
665; Guiser; f; 26; Miss. Choctaw; F; S; Daughter; Yes
666; Ellen M; f; 1; Miss. Choctaw; F; S; Grand-daughter; Yes
667; Beulah; f; 22; Miss. Choctaw; F; S; Daughter; Yes
668; Lige; m; 20; Miss. Choctaw; F; S; Son; Yes
669; Melvin; m; 17; Miss. Choctaw; F; S; Son; Yes
670; Nettie; f; 15; Miss. Choctaw; F; S; Daughter; Yes
671; Sis; f; 12; Miss. Choctaw; F; S; Daughter; Yes
672; Susie; f; 10; Miss. Choctaw; F; S; Daughter; Yes
673; R. D; m; 8; Miss. Choctaw; F; S; Son; Yes

674; Jim; m; 27; Miss. Choctaw; F; M; Head; Yes
675; Sallie; f; 25; Miss. Choctaw; F; M; Wife; Yes
676; Frank; m; 3; Miss. Choctaw; F; S; Son; Yes
677; Wicks; m; 1; Miss. Choctaw; F; S; Son; Yes

678; Robert; m; 56; Miss. Choctaw; F; S; Son[sic]; Yes
679; Nellie; f; 46; Miss. Choctaw; F; M; Wife; Yes
680; Bob; m; 22; Miss. Choctaw; F; S; Son; Yes
681; Mattie; f; 18; Miss. Choctaw; F; S; Daughter; Yes
682; Jasper; m; 13; Miss. Choctaw; F; S; Son; Yes
683; Dolphus; m; 10; Miss. Choctaw; F; S; Son; Yes

Census of the ~~Miss. Choctaw~~ reservation of the **Choctaw Agency** jurisdiction, as of **April 30**, 19 **30**, taken by **R. J. Enochs**, Superintendent. Purchased Lands   MISSISSIPPI

KEY: Surname; Census Number; Given Name; Sex; Age at Last Birthday; Tribe; Degree of Blood; Marital Status; Relationship to Head of Family; At Jurisdiction Where Enrolled (Yes or No); (If No Where); Ward (Yes unless given otherwise.)

HICKMAN

684;   Billy; m; 44; Miss. Choctaw; F; M; Head; Yes
685;   Rhodie; f; 46; Miss. Choctaw; F; M; Wife; Yes
686;   Willie; m; 20; Miss. Choctaw; F; S; Son; Yes
687;   Sim; m; 18; Miss. Choctaw; F; S; Son; Yes
688;   Susan; f; 12; Miss. Choctaw; F; S; Daughter; Yes
689;   Lula; f; 10; Miss. Choctaw; F; S; Daughter; Yes

690;   Ellis; m; 60; Miss. Choctaw; F; M; Head; Yes
691;   Susan; f; 55; Miss. Choctaw; F; M; Wife; Yes
692;   **Bell**, Burton; m; 10; Miss. Choctaw; F; S; Grand-son; Yes
693;   **Bell**, Henry; m; 8; Miss. Choctaw; F; S; Grand-son; Yes

694;   Johnkin; m; 30; Miss. Choctaw; F; M; Head; Yes
695;   Minnie; f; 25; Miss. Choctaw; F; M; Wife; Yes

696;   Enoch; m; 56; Miss. Choctaw; F; M; Head; Yes
697;   Malinda; f; 54; Miss. Choctaw; F; M; Wife; Yes
698;   Sallie; f; 20; Miss. Choctaw; F; S; Daughter; Yes
699;   Sadie; f; 19; Miss. Choctaw; F; S; Daughter; Yes
700;   Tubby; m; 17; Miss. Choctaw; F; S; Son; Yes
701;   Eliza Jane; f; 16; Miss. Choctaw; F; S; Daughter; Yes
702;   Mary Long; f; 14; Miss. Choctaw; F; S; Daughter; Yes
703;   Annie; f; 9; Miss. Choctaw; F; S; Daughter; Yes
704;   Wm. Penn; m; 9; Miss. Choctaw; F; S; Son; Yes
705;   Vardaman; m; 6; Miss. Choctaw; F; S; Son; Yes
706;   John; m; 5; Miss. Choctaw; F; S; Son; Yes

707;   Wallace; m; 24; Miss. Choctaw; F; M; Head; Yes
708;   Dona; f; 21; Miss. Choctaw; F; M; Wife; Yes
709;   Robinson; m; 4; Miss. Choctaw; F; S; Son; Yes

710;   Stennis; m; 26; Miss. Choctaw; F; M; Head; Yes

Census of the ~~Miss. Choctaw~~ reservation of the **Choctaw Agency** jurisdiction, as of **April 30**, 19**30**, taken by **R. J. Enochs**, Superintendent. Purchased Lands   MISSISSIPPI

KEY: Surname; Census Number; Given Name; Sex; Age at Last Birthday; Tribe; Degree of Blood; Marital Status; Relationship to Head of Family; At Jurisdiction Where Enrolled (Yes or No); (If No Where); Ward (Yes unless given otherwise.)

711; Winnie; f; 25; Miss. Choctaw; F; M; Wife; Yes
712; Eula; f; 3; Miss. Choctaw; F; S; Daughter; Yes
713; Snooks; m; 2; Miss. Choctaw; F; S; Son; Yes

714; Mary; f; 74; Miss. Choctaw; F; Wd; Head; Yes
715; **Charlie**, Beckie; f; 13; Miss. Choctaw; F; S; Grand-daughter; Yes

HUDSON

716; Celia; f; 23; Miss. Choctaw; F; S; Head; Yes

ISAAC

717; Jim; m; 35; Miss. Choctaw; F; M; Head; Yes
718; Bessie; f; 29; Miss. Choctaw; F; M; Wife; Yes

719; Steve; m; 75; Miss. Choctaw; F; Wd; Head; Yes

720; Byrd; m; 34; Miss. Choctaw; F; Wd; Head; Yes
721; Odie Mae; f; 14; Miss. Choctaw; F; S; Daughter; Yes
722; Bernice; f; 12; Miss. Choctaw; F; S; Daughter; Yes
723; Catherine; f; 10; Miss. Choctaw; F; S; Daughter; Yes
724; Edwin; m; 3; Miss. Choctaw; F; S; Son; Yes

725; Hickman; m; 23; Miss. Choctaw; F; S; Head; Yes

726; Simon; m; 46; Miss. Choctaw; F; M; Head; Yes
727; Nannie; f; 49; Miss. Choctaw; F; M; Wife; Yes
728; Beeman; m; 17; Miss. Choctaw; F; S; Son; Yes
729; Effie; f; 7; Miss. Choctaw; F; S; Daughter; Yes
730; Lillie Mae; f; 5; Miss. Choctaw; F; S; Grand-daughter; Yes

733; Isaac; m; 29; Miss. Choctaw; F; M; Head; Yes
734; Maggie; f; 21; Miss. Choctaw; F; M; Wife; Yes

Census of the ~~Miss. Choctaw~~ reservation of the **Choctaw Agency** jurisdiction, as of **April 30**, 19**30**, taken by **R. J. Enochs**, Superintendent. Purchased Lands   MISSISSIPPI

KEY: Surname; Census Number; Given Name; Sex; Age at Last Birthday; Tribe; Degree of Blood; Marital Status; Relationship to Head of Family; At Jurisdiction Where Enrolled (Yes or No); (If No Where); Ward (Yes unless given otherwise.)

735; Claudine; f; 8; Miss. Choctaw; F; S; Daughter; Yes
736; Wilbur; m; 6; Miss. Choctaw; F; S; Son; Yes
737; Claud P; m; 2; Miss. Choctaw; F; S; Son; Yes
738; Enochs; m; 11/12; Miss. Choctaw; F; S; Son; Yes

739; Will; m; 32; Miss. Choctaw; F; M; Head; Yes
740; Louisa; f; 31; Miss. Choctaw; F; M; Wife; Yes
741; Annie; f; 12; Miss. Choctaw; F; S; Daughter; Yes
742; Cornelia; f; 3; Miss. Choctaw; F; S; Daughter; Yes

743; Wilson; m; 76; Miss. Choctaw; F; M; Head; Yes
744; Martha; f; 63; Miss. Choctaw; F; M; Wife; Yes
745; John Day; m; 16; Miss. Choctaw; F; S Son; Yes
746; Jackson; m; 25; Miss. Choctaw; F; S; Son; Yes
747; **Sam**, Edna; f; 8; Miss. Choctaw; F; S; Unknown; Yes

748; David; m; 23; Miss. Choctaw; F; M; Head; Yes
749; Lesper; f; 22; Miss. Choctaw; F; M; Wife; Yes
750; Joe Day; m; 3; Miss. Choctaw; F; S; Son; Yes
751; Franklin; m; 1; Miss. Choctaw; F; S; Son; Yes

752; Dixon; m; 78; Miss. Choctaw; F; M; Head; Yes
753; Love; f; 25; Miss. Choctaw; F; M; Wife; Yes
754; Asley; f; 13; Miss. Choctaw; F; S; Daughter; Yes
755; Rainey; f; 9; Miss. Choctaw; F; S; Daughter; Yes
756; Manda; f; 7; Miss. Choctaw; F; S; Daughter; Yes
757; Lester; f; 6; Miss. Choctaw; F; S; Daughter; Yes
758; **Billy**, Emma; f; 24; Miss. Choctaw; F; S; Sister-in-law; Yes

ISOM

759; Willie; m; 16; Miss. Choctaw; F; S; Head; Yes

760; Isom; m; 30; Miss. Choctaw; F; S; Head; Yes

Census of the ~~Miss. Choctaw~~ reservation of the Choctaw Agency jurisdiction, as of April 30, 19 30, taken by R. J. Enochs, Superintendent. Purchased Lands   MISSISSIPPI

KEY: Surname; Census Number; Given Name; Sex; Age at Last Birthday; Tribe; Degree of Blood; Marital Status; Relationship to Head of Family; At Jurisdiction Where Enrolled (Yes or No); (If No Where); Ward (Yes unless given otherwise.)

JACKSON

761; Betty; f; 54; Miss. Choctaw; F; Wd; Head; Yes
762; Rosie; f; 18; Miss. Choctaw; F; S; Daughter; Yes
763; Nancie; f; 16; Miss. Choctaw; F; S; Daughter; Yes
764; Carlson; m; 10; Miss. Choctaw; F; S; Son; Yes

765; Lena; f; 42; Miss. Choctaw; F; Wd; Head; Yes
766; Ella; f; 16; Miss. Choctaw; F; S; Daughter; Yes
767; Gipson; m; 17; Miss. Choctaw; F; S; Son; Yes
768; Floyd F; M; 15; Miss. Choctaw; F; S; Son; Yes
769; Jackson; m; 12; Miss. Choctaw; F; S; Son; Yes
770; Emmett; m; 10; Miss. Choctaw; F; S; Son; Yes
771; Lucille; f; 9; Miss. Choctaw; F; S; Daughter; Yes

772; Tom; m; 42; Miss. Choctaw; F; Wd; Head; Yes
773; Woodrow; m; 12; Miss. Choctaw; F; S; Son; Yes
774; Eva; f; 11; Miss. Choctaw; F; S; Daughter; Yes

775; Sam; m; 46; Miss. Choctaw; F; M; Head; Yes
776; Martha; f; 48; Miss. Choctaw; F; M; Wife; Yes

777; Tubby; m; 20; Miss. Choctaw; F; M; Head; Yes
778; Missie; f; 20; Miss. Choctaw; F; M; Wife; Yes

779; Prentiss; m; 27; Miss. Choctaw; F; M; Head; Yes
780; Mary; f; 27; Miss. Choctaw; F; M; Wife; Yes

781; Mike; m; 29; Miss. Choctaw; F; S; Head; Yes

JEFFERSON

782; Braxton; m; 24; Miss. Choctaw; F; Wd; Head; Yes
783; Addie; f; 20; Miss. Choctaw; F; S; Sister; Yes

Census of the ~~Miss. Choctaw~~ reservation of the **Choctaw Agency** jurisdiction, as of **April 30**, 19**30**, taken by **R. J. Enochs**, Superintendent. Purchased Lands   MISSISSIPPI

KEY: Surname; Census Number; Given Name; Sex; Age at Last Birthday; Tribe; Degree of Blood; Marital Status; Relationship to Head of Family; At Jurisdiction Where Enrolled (Yes or No); (If No Where); Ward (Yes unless given otherwise.)

784; Amos; m; 23; Miss. Choctaw; F; M; Head; Yes
785; Ida; f; 18; Miss. Choctaw; F; M; Wife; Yes

786; Willis; m; 55; Miss. Choctaw; F; S; Head; Yes
787; Elsie; f; 43; Miss. Choctaw; F; S; Sister; Yes

788; Oscar; m; 25; Miss. Choctaw; F; M; Head; Yes
789; Saline; f; 23; Miss. Choctaw; F; M; Wife; Yes
790; Malcolm; m; 4; Miss. Choctaw; F; S; Son; Yes

791; Otis; m; 27; Miss. Choctaw; F; M; Head; Yes
792; Onie; f; 25; Miss. Choctaw; F; M; Wife; Yes
793; Otto; m; 5; Miss. Choctaw; F; S; Son; Yes
794; Andy; m; 4; Miss. Choctaw; F; S; Son; Yes

JIM

795; George; m; 62; Miss. Choctaw; F; M; Head; Yes
796; Eliza; f; 52; Miss. Choctaw; F; M; Wife; Yes
797; Lee; m; 24; Miss. Choctaw; F; S; Son; Yes
798; Sidney; m; 14; Miss. Choctaw; F; S; Son; Yes
799; **Hall**, Pauline; f; 18; Miss. Choctaw; F; Wd; Niece; Yes
800; **Hall**, Herbert H; m; 1; Miss. Choctaw; F; S; Grand-son; Yes

801; Cooley; m; 60; Miss. Choctaw; F; M; Head; Yes
802; Lorena; f; 32; Miss. Choctaw; F; M; Wife; Yes
803; William; m; 9; Miss. Choctaw; F; S; Son; Yes
804; Tom; m; 7; Miss. Choctaw; F; S; Son; Yes

805; John; m; 24; Miss. Choctaw; F; M; Head; Yes
806; Bessie; f; 21; Miss. Choctaw; F; M; Wife; Yes

807; Henry; f; 45; Miss. Choctaw; F; M; Head; Yes
808; Mollie; f; 58; Miss. Choctaw; F; M; Wife; Yes

Census of the ~~Miss. Choctaw~~ reservation of the **Choctaw Agency** jurisdiction, as of ____April 30____, 19 30, taken by ____R. J. Enochs____, Superintendent. Purchased Lands   MISSISSIPPI

KEY: Surname; Census Number; Given Name; Sex; Age at Last Birthday; Tribe; Degree of Blood; Marital Status; Relationship to Head of Family; At Jurisdiction Where Enrolled (Yes or No); (If No Where); Ward (Yes unless given otherwise.)

809; Harvey; m; 15; Miss. Choctaw; F; M; Head; Yes
810; Mattie; f; 32; Miss. Choctaw; F; M; Wife; Yes

811; Ben; m; 52; Miss. Choctaw; F; M; Head; Yes
812; Dora; f; 40; Miss. Choctaw; F; M; Wife; Yes
813; Annie Mae; f; 16; Miss. Choctaw; F; S; Daughter; Yes
814; Rena; f; 8; Miss. Choctaw; F; S; Daughter; Yes
815; Frank; m; 2; Miss. Choctaw; F; S; Grand-son; Yes
816; Bobbie Sue; f; 1; Miss. Choctaw; F; S; Grand-daughter; Yes

817; Logan; m; 82; Miss. Choctaw; F; Wd; Head; Yes

818; Amon; m; 54; Miss. Choctaw; F; M; Head; Yes
819; Lucy; f; 45; Miss. Choctaw; F; M; Wife; Yes
820; Opal; f; 11; Miss. Choctaw; F; S; Daughter; Yes
821; Carter; m; 1; Miss. Choctaw; F; S; Son; Yes
822; **Dan**, Louisana; f; 25; Miss. Choctaw; F; Wd; Daughter; Yes

823; Goodman; m; 65; Miss. Choctaw; F; M; Head; Yes
824; Leona; f; 28; Miss. Choctaw; F; M; Wife; Yes
825; Clifton; m; 9; Miss. Choctaw; F; S; Son; Yes
826; Frank McKinley; m; 4; Miss. Choctaw; F; S; Son; Yes
827; Claud Yates; m; 2; Miss. Choctaw; F; S; Son; Yes
828; **Farmer**, Sallie; f; 75; Miss. Choctaw; F; Wd; Sister; Yes

829; Albert; m; 24; Miss. Choctaw; F; M; Head; Yes
830; Dora; f; 24; Miss. Choctaw; F; M; Wife; Yes
831; Grace; f; 5/12; Miss. Choctaw; F; S; Daughter; Yes

832; Henry; m; 30; Miss. Choctaw; F; M; Head; Yes
833; Maggie; f; 36; Miss. Choctaw; F; M; Wife; Yes

834; Victor; m; 29; Miss. Choctaw; F; M; Head; Yes
835; Lena; f; 20; Miss. Choctaw; F; M; Wife; Yes

Census of the ~~Miss. Choctaw~~ reservation of the **Choctaw Agency** jurisdiction, as of **April 30**, 19 **30**, taken by **R. J. Enochs**, Superintendent. Purchased Lands   MISSISSIPPI

KEY: Surname; Census Number; Given Name; Sex; Age at Last Birthday; Tribe; Degree of Blood; Marital Status; Relationship to Head of Family; At Jurisdiction Where Enrolled (Yes or No); (If No Where); Ward (Yes unless given otherwise.)

836;   Loy; m; 4; Miss. Choctaw; F; S; Son; Yes
837;   Egbert; m; 10/12; Miss. Choctaw; F; S; Son; Yes

838;   Winston; m; 20; Miss. Choctaw; F; S; Head; Yes

JIMMIE

839;   Melton; m; 26; Miss. Choctaw; F; M; Head; Yes
840;   Mary; f; 23; Miss. Choctaw; F; M; Wife; Yes
841;   Ona O; f; 2; Miss. Choctaw; F; S; Daughter; Yes
842;   Delores; f; 6/12; Miss. Choctaw; F; S; Daughter; Yes
843;   Frank M; m; 19; Miss. Choctaw; F; S; Brother; Yes

844;   Ike; m; 60; Miss. Choctaw; F; S; Head; Yes

845;   Mack; m; 24; Miss. Choctaw; F; S; Head; Yes

846;   Will; m; 50; Miss. Choctaw; F; M; Head; Yes
847;   Hester; m; 48; Miss. Choctaw; F; M; Wife; Yes
848;   Homer; m; 21; Miss. Choctaw; F; S; Son; Yes

JOE

849;   Nicholas; m; 40; Miss. Choctaw; F; M; Head; Yes
850;   Ella; f; 35; Miss. Choctaw; F; M; Wife; Yes
851;   Austin; m; 16; Miss. Choctaw; F; S; Son; Yes
852;   Henry; m; 12; Miss. Choctaw; F; S; Son; Yes
853;   Widge; f; 9; Miss. Choctaw; F; S; Daughter; Yes
854;   Bessie; f; 7; Miss. Choctaw; F; S; Daughter; Yes
855;   Billie Joe; m; 6; Miss. Choctaw; F; S; Son; Yes
856;   Mary; f; 5/12; Miss. Choctaw; F; S; Daughter; Yes
857;   **Lewis**, Susie; f; 7; Miss. Choctaw; F; S; Step-daughter; Yes
858;   **Lewis**, Elsie; f; 5; Miss. Choctaw; F; S; Step-daughter; Yes

Census of the ~~Miss. Choctaw~~ reservation of the **Choctaw Agency** jurisdiction, as of **April 30**, 19**30**, taken by **R. J. Enochs**, Superintendent. Purchased Lands   MISSISSIPPI

KEY: Surname; Census Number; Given Name; Sex; Age at Last Birthday; Tribe; Degree of Blood; Marital Status; Relationship to Head of Family; At Jurisdiction Where Enrolled (Yes or No); (If No Where); Ward (Yes unless given otherwise.)

859; Jasper; m; 42; Miss. Choctaw; F; M; Head; Yes
860; Sallie; f; 37; Miss. Choctaw; F; M; Wife; Yes
861; Lula; f; 17; Miss. Choctaw; F; S; Daughter; Yes
862; Huston; m; 12; Miss. Choctaw; F; S; Son; Yes
863; Watkins; m; 8; Miss. Choctaw; F; S; Son; Yes

864; Emily; f; 74; Miss. Choctaw; F; Wd; Head; Yes

865; John; m; 32; Miss. Choctaw; F; M; Head; Yes
866; Emma; f; 30; Miss. Choctaw; F; M; Wife; Yes
867; Bessie; f; 9; Miss. Choctaw; F; S; Daughter; Yes
868; Lillie; f; 5; Miss. Choctaw; F; S; Daughter; Yes
869; Claud; m; 2; Miss. Choctaw; F; S; Son; Yes

870; Langley; m; 82; Miss. Choctaw; F; Wd; Head; Yes

JOHN

871; Mike; m; 57; Miss. Choctaw; F; M; Head; Yes
872; Lizzie; f; 72; Miss. Choctaw; F; M; Wife; Yes
873; **Willis**, Dina; f; 16; Miss. Choctaw; F; S; Grand-daughter; Yes

874; Josh; m; 54; Miss. Choctaw; F; Wd; Head; Yes

875; Anderson; m; 53; Miss. Choctaw; F; M; Head; Yes
876; Bettie; f; 42; Miss. Choctaw; F; M; Wife; Yes
877; Bennett; m; 21; Miss. Choctaw; F; S; Son; Yes
878; Sina; f; 18; Miss. Choctaw; F; S; Daughter; Yes
879; L. E; m; 15; Miss. Choctaw; F; S; Son; Yes
880; Hubert; m; 14; Miss. Choctaw; F; S; Son; Yes
881; Oden; m; 9; Miss. Choctaw; F; S; Son; Yes
882; Wilson; m; 2; Miss. Choctaw; F; S; Son; Yes

883; Clint; m; 39; Miss. Choctaw; F; S; Head; Yes

Census of the ~~Miss. Choctaw~~ reservation of the **Choctaw Agency** jurisdiction, as of **April 30**, 19**30**, taken by **R. J. Enochs**, Superintendent. Purchased Lands   MISSISSIPPI

KEY: Surname; Census Number; Given Name; Sex; Age at Last Birthday; Tribe; Degree of Blood; Marital Status; Relationship to Head of Family; At Jurisdiction Where Enrolled (Yes or No); (If No Where); Ward (Yes unless given otherwise.)

884;   Ira; m; 25; Miss. Choctaw; F; M; Head; Yes
885;   Leda; f; 17; Miss. Choctaw; F; M; Wife; Yes

886;   Bob; m; 56; Miss. Choctaw; F; M; Head; Yes
887;   Onie; f; 45; Miss. Choctaw; F; M; Wife; Yes
888;   Oliver; m; 15; Miss. Choctaw; F; S; Son; Yes
889;   Otis; m; 13; Miss. Choctaw; F; S; Son; Yes
890;   Roby; m; 9; Miss. Choctaw; F; S; Son; Yes
891;   Rose; f; 7; Miss. Choctaw; F; S; Daughter; Yes

892;   Jack; m; 56; Miss. Choctaw; F; M; Head; Yes
893;   Amanda; f; 35; Miss. Choctaw; F; M; Wife; Yes
894;   Jefferson; m; 8; Miss. Choctaw; F; S; Son; Yes
895;   Mary; f; 6; Miss. Choctaw; F; S; Daughter; Yes

896;   Betsie; f; 32; Miss. Choctaw; F; Wd; Mother; Yes
897;   Belba; m; 13; Miss. Choctaw; F; S; Son; Yes
898;   Mable; f; 10; Miss. Choctaw; F; S; Daughter; Yes
899;   Renie; f; 8; Miss. Choctaw; F; S; Daughter; Yes
900;   Varderman; m; 5; Miss. Choctaw; F; S; Son; Yes
901;   Smith; m; 3; Miss. Choctaw; F; S; Son; Yes
902;   Lisette H; f; 9/12; Miss. Choctaw; F; S; Daughter; Yes

JOHNSON

903;   Quitman; m; 19; Miss. Choctaw; F; S; Head; Yes

904;   Will; m; 58; Miss. Choctaw; F; M; Head; Yes
905;   Dixie; f; 36; Miss. Choctaw; F; M; Wife; Yes
906;   **Comby**, Venie; f; 14; Miss. Choctaw; F; S; Step-daughter; Yes
907;   **Comby**, Gus; m; 5; Miss. Choctaw; F; S; Step-son; Yes
908;   Sallie; f; 75; Miss. Choctaw; F; Wd; Mother; Yes

909;   Afton; m; 26; Miss. Choctaw; F; M; Head; Yes

Census of the ~~Miss. Choctaw~~ reservation of the Choctaw Agency jurisdiction, as of April 30, 19 30, taken by R. J. Enochs, Superintendent. Purchased Lands   MISSISSIPPI

KEY: Surname; Census Number; Given Name; Sex; Age at Last Birthday; Tribe; Degree of Blood; Marital Status; Relationship to Head of Family; At Jurisdiction Where Enrolled (Yes or No); (If No Where); Ward (Yes unless given otherwise.)

910; Sevenia; f; 24; Miss. Choctaw; F; M; Wife; Yes
911; Callie; f; 1; Miss. Choctaw; F; S; Daughter; Yes

912; Edgar; m; 31; Miss. Choctaw; F; M; Head; Yes
913; Beatrice; f; 27; Miss. Choctaw; F; M; Wife; Yes
914; Callie; f; 7; Miss. Choctaw; F; S; Daughter; Yes
915; Frances; f; 5; Miss. Choctaw; F; S; Daughter; Yes
916; Egbert; m; 3; Miss. Choctaw; F; S; Son; Yes

917; Frank; m; 38; Miss. Choctaw; F; M; Head; Yes
918; Lorine; f; 30; Miss. Choctaw; F; M; Wife; Yes
919; Otha; m; 14; Miss. Choctaw; F; S; Son; Yes
920; Athens; m; 12; Miss. Choctaw; F; S; Son; Yes
921; Sudie; f; 10; Miss. Choctaw; F; S; Daughter; Yes
922; Bertha; f; 8; Miss. Choctaw; F; S; Daughter; Yes
923; Naven; m; 6; Miss. Choctaw; F; S; Son; Yes
924; Sudan; f; 4; Miss. Choctaw; F; S; Daughter; Yes
925; Bena; f; 2; Miss. Choctaw; F; S; Daughter; Yes

JOSHUA

926; Sam; m; 80; Miss. Choctaw; F; M; Head; Yes
927; Jennie; f; 60; Miss. Choctaw; F; M; Wife; Yes
928; **John**, Callie; f; 19; Miss. Choctaw; F; S; Grand-daughter; Yes
929; **John**, Edison; m; 2; Miss. Choctaw; F; S; Great-grand-son; Yes

KING

930; John W; m; 70; Miss. Choctaw; F; Wd; Head; Yes
931; **Kings**[sic], Mollie; f; 27; Miss. Choctaw; F; S; Daughter; Yes
932; Enos; m; 18; Miss. Choctaw; F; S; Son; Yes
933; Varnam; m; 18; Miss. Choctaw; F; S; Son; Yes
934; John Lee; m; 16; Miss. Choctaw; F; S; Great-nephew; Yes
935; Lavenia; f; 11; Miss. Choctaw; F; S; Great-niece; Yes

Census of the ~~Miss. Choctaw~~ reservation of the **Choctaw Agency** jurisdiction, as of **April 30**, 19**30**, taken by **R. J. Enochs**, Superintendent. Purchased Lands   MISSISSIPPI

KEY: Surname; Census Number; Given Name; Sex; Age at Last Birthday; Tribe; Degree of Blood; Marital Status; Relationship to Head of Family; At Jurisdiction Where Enrolled (Yes or No); (If No Where); Ward (Yes unless given otherwise.)

936; Clay I; m; 24; Miss. Choctaw; F; M; Head; Yes
937; Alice; f; 28; Miss. Choctaw; F; M; Wife; Yes

938; Betsie; f; 48; Miss. Choctaw; F; Wd; Mother
939; Christine; f; 20; Miss. Choctaw; F; S; Daughter; Yes
940; Joseph; m; 13; Miss. Choctaw; F; S; Son; Yes
941; Joe; m; 11; Miss. Choctaw; F; S; Son; Yes
942; Barkum; m; 9; Miss. Choctaw; F; S; Son; Yes

943; Banks; m; 25; Miss. Choctaw; F; M; Head; Yes
944; Betsie; f; 35; Miss. Choctaw; F; M; Wife; Yes

LEBAN

945; Ben; m; 58; Miss. Choctaw; F; M; Head; Yes
946; Lena; f; 57; Miss. Choctaw; F; M; Wife; Yes
947; Mary; f; 30; Miss. Choctaw; F; S; Daughter; Yes

LEFLORE

948; John; m; 59; Miss. Choctaw; F; M; Head; Yes
949; Emma; f; 50; Miss. Choctaw; F; M; Wife; Yes
950; Richard Earl; m; 37; Miss. Choctaw; F; S; Son; Yes
951; S. D; m; 24; Miss. Choctaw; F; S; Son; Yes
952; Willie; f; 26; Miss. Choctaw; F; S; Daughter; Yes
953; Bertha Lee; f; 22; Miss. Choctaw; F; S; Daughter; Yes
954; John; m; 19; Miss. Choctaw; F; S; Son; Yes
955; Lewis; m; 18; Miss. Choctaw; F; S; Son; Yes

LEWIS

956; Jim; m; 62; Miss. Choctaw; F; M; Head; Yes
957; Fannie; f; 40; Miss. Choctaw; F; M; Wife; Yes

Census of the ~~Miss. Choctaw~~ reservation of the **Choctaw Agency** jurisdiction, as of **April 30**, 19**30**, taken by **R. J. Enochs**, Superintendent. Purchased Lands   MISSISSIPPI

KEY: Surname; Census Number; Given Name; Sex; Age at Last Birthday; Tribe; Degree of Blood; Marital Status; Relationship to Head of Family; At Jurisdiction Where Enrolled (Yes or No); (If No Where); Ward (Yes unless given otherwise.)

958; Ezell; m; 18; Miss. Choctaw; F; M; Head; Yes
959; Beauty; f; 18; Miss. Choctaw; F; M; Wife; Yes

960; Adam; m; 25; Miss. Choctaw; F; M; Head; Yes
961; Sillie; f; 23; Miss. Choctaw; F; M; Wife; Yes
962; Nannie; f; 2; Miss. Choctaw; F; S; Daughter; Yes
963; Nammie; f; 2/12; Miss. Choctaw; F; S; Daughter; Yes
964; Tom; m; 4; Miss. Choctaw; F; S; Step-son; Yes

965; Elon; m; 49; Miss. Choctaw; F; M; Head; Yes
966; Lula; f; 52; Miss. Choctaw; F; M; Wife; Yes
967; **Jefferson**, Esther; f; 17; Miss. Choctaw; F; S; Step-daughter; Yes
968; **Jefferson**, Nute; m; 14; Miss. Choctaw; F; S; Step-son; Yes

969; Johnnie; m; 32; Miss. Choctaw; F; Wd; Head; Yes
970; Marzine; f; 6; Miss. Choctaw; F; S; Daughter; Yes

971; Marshall; m; 55; Miss. Choctaw; F; M; Head; Yes
972; Martha; f; 44; Miss. Choctaw; F; M; Wife; Yes
973; Eliza; f; 15; Miss. Choctaw; F; S; Daughter; Yes
974; Belfa; f; 14; Miss. Choctaw; F; S; Daughter; Yes
975; Houston; m; 11; Miss. Choctaw; F; S; Son; Yes
976; Lee; m; 9; Miss. Choctaw; F; S; Son; Yes
977; Bettie; f; 6; Miss. Choctaw; F; S; Daughter; Yes
978; Hodges; m; Miss. Choctaw; F; S; Son; Yes
979; Leon; m; 2; Miss. Choctaw; F; S; Son; Yes
980; Lucille R; f; 7/12; Miss. Choctaw; F; S; Daughter; Yes

981; Joe; m; 56; Miss. Choctaw; F; Wd; Head; Yes

982; Reuben; m; 70; Miss. Choctaw; F; Wd; Head; Yes
983; Amos; m; 18; Miss. Choctaw; F; S; Grand-son; Yes

984; Lennis; m; 23; Miss. Choctaw; F; M; Head; Yes

Census of the ~~Miss. Choctaw~~ reservation of the **Choctaw Agency** jurisdiction, as of ____April 30____, 19_30_, taken by **R. J. Enochs**, Superintendent. Purchased Lands   MISSISSIPPI

KEY: Surname; Census Number; Given Name; Sex; Age at Last Birthday; Tribe; Degree of Blood; Marital Status; Relationship to Head of Family; At Jurisdiction Where Enrolled (Yes or No); (If No Where); Ward (Yes unless given otherwise.)

985;   Ola; f; 19; Miss. Choctaw; F; M; Wife; Yes
986;   Nervie; f; 1; Miss. Choctaw; F; S; Daughter; Yes

987;   Ed; m; 56; Miss. Choctaw; F; M; Head; Yes
988;   Edna; f; 48; Miss. Choctaw; F; M; Wife; Yes
989;   Hollis; m; 14; Miss. Choctaw; F; S; Son; Yes

990;   Albert; m; 36; Miss. Choctaw; F; M; Head; Yes
991;   Mollie; f; 33; Miss. Choctaw; F; M; Wife; Yes
992;   Indiana; f; 15; Miss. Choctaw; F; S; Daughter; Yes
993;   Bernice; f; 13; Miss. Choctaw; F; S; Daughter; Yes
994;   Eastland; m; 11; Miss. Choctaw; F; S; Son; Yes
995;   Ivena; f; 9; Miss. Choctaw; F; S; Daughter; Yes

996;   Calvin; m; 50; Miss. Choctaw; F; Wd; Head; Yes

997;   Jim; m; 27; Miss. Choctaw; F; M; Head; Yes
998;   Jennie; f; 22; Miss. Choctaw; F; M; Wife; Yes
999;   Jennie Lin; f; 1; Miss. Choctaw; F; S; Daughter; Yes

1000; Duffie; m; 34; Miss. Choctaw; F; M; Head; Yes
1001; Lilly; f; 50; Miss. Choctaw; F; M; Wife; Yes
1002; **Briscoe**, Stephens; m; 21; Miss. Choctaw; F; S; Step-son; Yes
1003; **Briscoe**, Jim; m; 15; Miss. Choctaw; F; S; Step-son; Yes
1004; **Briscoe**, Egbert; m; 7; Miss. Choctaw; F; S; Step-son; Yes
1005; **Farmer**, Henry; m; 19; Miss. Choctaw; F; S; Nephew; Yes
1006; **Wickson**, Ollie or Yates; m; 1; Miss. Choctaw; F; S; Nephew; Yes

MARTIN

1007; Willie; m; 40; Miss. Choctaw; F; M; Head; Yes
1008; Mary; f; 34; Miss. Choctaw; F; M; Wife; Yes
1009; Raymond; m; 10; Miss. Choctaw; F; S; Son; Yes

Census of the ~~Miss. Choctaw~~ reservation of the **Choctaw Agency** jurisdiction, as of **April 30**, 19**30**, taken by **R. J. Enochs**, Superintendent. Purchased Lands   MISSISSIPPI

KEY: Surname; Census Number; Given Name; Sex; Age at Last Birthday; Tribe; Degree of Blood; Marital Status; Relationship to Head of Family; At Jurisdiction Where Enrolled (Yes or No); (If No Where); Ward (Yes unless given otherwise.)

1010; Edmond J; m; 7; Miss. Choctaw; F; S; Son; Yes
1011; Phillip; m; 4; Miss. Choctaw; F; S; Son; Yes
1012; Annie Mae; f; 2; Miss. Choctaw; F; S; Daughter; Yes

1013; Ennis; m; 21; Miss. Choctaw; F; M; Head; Yes
1014; Nancy; f; 20; Miss. Choctaw; F; M; Wife; Yes
1015; **Alex**, Herbert F; m; 3; Miss. Choctaw; F; S; Step-son; Yes

McMILLEN

1016; Sorsby; m; 54; Miss. Choctaw; F; Wd; Head; Yes
1017; Mary; f; 16; Miss. Choctaw; F; S; Daughter; Yes
1018; Emma; f; 15; Miss. Choctaw; F; S; Daughter; Yes
1019; Clarence; m; 14; Miss. Choctaw; F; S; Son; Yes
1020; Bessie; f; 11; Miss. Choctaw; F; S; Daughter; Yes
1021; Gipson; m; 6; Miss. Choctaw; F; S; Son; Yes
1022; Pauline; f; 2; Miss. Choctaw; F; S Daughter; Yes

1023; Lemmie; m; 20; Miss. Choctaw; F; M; Head; Yes
1024; Maggie; f; 21; Miss. Choctaw; F; M; Wife; Yes

1025; Cephus; m; 48; Miss. Choctaw; F; M; Head; Yes
1026; Mina; f; 36; Miss. Choctaw; F; M; Wife; Yes
1027; Anthony; m; 22; Miss. Choctaw; F; S; Son; Yes
1028; Mary; f; 17; Miss. Choctaw; F; S; Daughter; Yes
1029; Jimpson; m; 15; Miss. Choctaw; F; S; Nephew; Yes
1030; **Billy**, Clemon; m; 16; Miss. Choctaw; F; S; Step-son; Yes
1031; Willie; m; 14; Miss. Choctaw; F; S; Son; Yes
1032; Enochs; m; 2; Miss. Choctaw; F; S; Son; Yes

1033; Egbert; m; 29; Miss. Choctaw; F; M; Head; Yes
1034; Nola; f; 25; Miss. Choctaw; F; M; Wife; Yes
1035; A. J; m; 8; Miss. Choctaw; F; S; Son; Yes
1036; Odie Mae; f; 6; Miss. Choctaw; F; S; Daughter; Yes

Census of the ~~Miss. Choctaw~~ reservation of the **Choctaw Agency** jurisdiction, as of **April 30**, 19 **30**, taken by **R. J. Enochs**, Superintendent. Purchased Lands   MISSISSIPPI

KEY: Surname; Census Number; Given Name; Sex; Age at Last Birthday; Tribe; Degree of Blood; Marital Status; Relationship to Head of Family; At Jurisdiction Where Enrolled (Yes or No); (If No Where); Ward (Yes unless given otherwise.)

1037;   John; m; 3; Miss. Choctaw; F; S; Son; Yes

1038;   Oscar; m; 36; Miss. Choctaw; F; M; Head; Yes
1039;   Bennie; f; 31; Miss. Choctaw; F; M; Wife; Yes
1040;   Arnold; m; 16; Miss. Choctaw; F; S; Son; Yes
1041;   Leslie; f; 8; Miss. Choctaw; F; S; Daughter; Yes
1042;   Bert; m; 6; Miss. Choctaw; F; S; Son; Yes
1043;   Frances; f; 4; Miss. Choctaw; F; S; Daughter; Yes
1044;   John; m; 1; Miss. Choctaw; F; S; Son; Yes

MINGO

1045;   Rich; m; 25; Miss. Choctaw; F; M; Head; Yes
1046;   Annie; f; 26; Miss. Choctaw; F; M; Wife; Yes
1047;   Davidson; m; 7; Miss. Choctaw; F; S; Son; Yes
1048;   Effie; f; 6; Miss. Choctaw; F; S; Daughter; Yes

1049;   John; m; 54; Miss. Choctaw; F; M; Head; Yes
1050;   Hattie; f; 28; Miss. Choctaw; F; M; Wife; Yes
1051;   Arch; m; 8; Miss. Choctaw; F; S; Son; Yes
1052;   Odis; m; 5; Miss. Choctaw; F; S; Son; Yes
1053;   Sister; f; 3; Miss. Choctaw; F; S; Daughter; Yes
1054;   Mary; f; 9/12; Miss. Choctaw; F; S; Daughter; Yes

1055;   Horace; m; 48; Miss. Choctaw; F; M; Head; Yes
1056;   Lilly; f; 52; Miss. Choctaw; F; M; Wife; Yes
1057;   Jim; m; 15; Miss. Choctaw; F; S; Son; Yes
1058;   Olin; m; 12; Miss. Choctaw; F; S; Son; Yes
1059;   Nettie; f; 9; Miss. Choctaw; F; S; Daughter; Yes

1060;   Oscar; m; 20; Miss. Choctaw; F; M; Head; Yes
1061;   Linday; f; 25; Miss. Choctaw; F; M; Wife; Yes

Census of the ~~Miss. Choctaw~~ reservation of the **Choctaw Agency** jurisdiction, as of **April 30**, 19 **30**, taken by **R. J. Enochs**, Superintendent. Purchased Lands   MISSISSIPPI

KEY: Surname; Census Number; Given Name; Sex; Age at Last Birthday; Tribe; Degree of Blood; Marital Status; Relationship to Head of Family; At Jurisdiction Where Enrolled (Yes or No); (If No Where); Ward (Yes unless given otherwise.)

MITCH

1062; Sarah; f; 46; Miss. Choctaw; F; Wd; Head; Yes
1063; Elea; m; 28; Miss. Choctaw; F; S; Son; Yes
1064; Divan; m; 26; Miss. Choctaw; F; S; Son; Yes
1065; Wilson; m; 24; Miss. Choctaw; F; S; Son; Yes
1066; Gilmore; m; 15; Miss. Choctaw; F; S; Son; Yes
1067; Annie; f; 11; Miss. Choctaw; F; S; Daughter; Yes

MORRIS

1068; Rich; m; 23; Miss. Choctaw; F; M; Head; Yes
1069; Callie; f; 18; Miss. Choctaw; F; M; Wife; Yes
1070; Arwin; f; 3; Miss. Choctaw; F; S; Daughter; Yes

1071; Julius; m; 28; Miss. Choctaw; F; M; Head; Yes
1072; Beauty; f; 25; Miss. Choctaw; F; M; Wife; Yes
1073; Eddie; f; 6; Miss. Choctaw; F; S; Daughter; Yes
1074; Lena; f; 3; Miss. Choctaw; F; S; Daughter; Yes
1075; Water Olin; m; 6/12; Miss. Choctaw; F; S; Son; Yes

1076; Mosley; m; 64; Miss. Choctaw; F; M; Head; Yes
1077; Ida; f; 49; Miss. Choctaw; F; M; Wife; Yes
1078; Lilly; f; 30; Miss. Choctaw; F; S; Daughter; Yes
1079; Sue; f; 28; Miss. Choctaw; F; Wd; Daughter; Yes
1080; Wilson; m; 26; Miss. Choctaw; F; S; Son; Yes
1081; Joe; m; 9; Miss. Choctaw; F; S; Son; Yes
1082; **Wesley**, Rufus; m; 5; Miss. Choctaw; F; S; Grand-son; Yes

1083; Dempsey; m; 29; Miss. Choctaw; F; M; Head; Yes
1084; Janie; f; 28; Miss. Choctaw; F; M; Wife; Yes
1085; Ora; f; 0; Miss. Choctaw; F; S; Daughter; Yes
1086; Vesney; m; 6; Miss. Choctaw; F; S; Son; Yes
1087; Davis; m; 4; Miss. Choctaw; F; S; Son; Yes

Census of the ~~Miss. Choctaw~~ reservation of the **Choctaw Agency** jurisdiction, as of **April 30**, 19**30**, taken by **R. J. Enochs**, Superintendent.   Purchased Lands   MISSISSIPPI

KEY: Surname; Census Number; Given Name; Sex; Age at Last Birthday; Tribe; Degree of Blood; Marital Status; Relationship to Head of Family; At Jurisdiction Where Enrolled (Yes or No); (If No Where); Ward (Yes unless given otherwise.)

1088;   Champs; m; 1; Miss. Choctaw; F; S; Son; Yes

1089;   Sallie; f; 61; Miss. Choctaw; F; Wd; Head; Yes
1090;   Seward; m; 20; Miss. Choctaw; F; S; Son; Yes

1091;   Howard; m; 23; Miss. Choctaw; F; M; Head; Yes
1092;   Bettie; f; 20; Miss. Choctaw; F; M; Wife; Yes
1093;   Jimmie; m; 4; Miss. Choctaw; F; S; Son; Yes

1094;   Huston; m; 24; Miss. Choctaw; F; M; Head; Yes
1095;   Bertha; f; 22; Miss. Choctaw; F; M; Wife; Yes

1096;   Boston; m; 27; Miss. Choctaw; F; M; Head; Yes
1097;   Nola; f; 25; Miss. Choctaw; F; M; Wife; Yes

1098;   Velma; f; 21; Miss. Choctaw; F; S; Head; Yes

MOSES

1099;   Alma; f; 19; Miss. Choctaw; F; S; Head; Yes

1100;   Allen; m; 24; Miss. Choctaw; F; M; Head; Yes
1101;   Florene; f; 24; Miss. Choctaw; F; M; Wife; Yes

NICKEY

1102;   Sam; m; 45; Miss. Choctaw; F; M; Head; Yes
1103;   Malissie; f; 43; Miss. Choctaw; F; M; Wife; Yes
1104;   Dora; f; 15; Miss. Choctaw; F; S; Daughter; Yes
1105;   Sherman; m; 8; Miss. Choctaw; F; S; Son; Yes
1106;   Copeland; m; 2; Miss. Choctaw; F; S; Son; Yes

1107;   Billy; m; 45; Miss. Choctaw; F; M; Head; Yes
1108;   Fronie; f; 49; Miss. Choctaw; F; M; Wife; Yes

Census of the ~~Miss. Choctaw~~ reservation of the **Choctaw Agency** jurisdiction, as of **April 30**, 19 **30**, taken by **R. J. Enochs**, Superintendent. Purchased Lands   MISSISSIPPI

KEY: Surname; Census Number; Given Name; Sex; Age at Last Birthday; Tribe; Degree of Blood; Marital Status; Relationship to Head of Family; At Jurisdiction Where Enrolled (Yes or No); (If No Where); Ward (Yes unless given otherwise.)

1109; Ode; f; 21; Miss. Choctaw; F; S; Daughter; Yes
1110; Zema; f; 18; Miss. Choctaw; F; S; Daughter; Yes
1111; Hughie; m; 15; Miss. Choctaw; F; S; Son; Yes
1112; Jona; f; 13; Miss. Choctaw; F; S; Daughter; Yes
1113; Cossette; m; 11; Miss. Choctaw; F; S; Son; Yes
1114; Thomas; m; 7; Miss. Choctaw; F; S; Son; Yes

NOAH

1115; Elizabeth; f; 58; Miss. Choctaw; F; Wd; Head; Yes
1116; Celia; f; 30; Miss. Choctaw; F; S; Daughter; Yes

1117; Lizzie; f; 40; Miss. Choctaw; F; Wd; Head; Yes
1118; Nancie; f; 14; Miss. Choctaw; F; S; Daughter; Yes
1119; Annie; f; 11; Miss. Choctaw; F; S; Daughter; Yes

NUBBY

1120; Billy; m; 70; Miss. Choctaw; F; M; Head; Yes
1121; Lilly; f; 50; Miss. Choctaw; F; M; Wife; Yes

PHILLIPS

1122; Riley; m; 23; Miss. Choctaw; F; Wd; Head; Yes
1123; Edmon; m; 3; Miss. Choctaw; F; S; Son; Yes
1124; Empsey; m; 1; Miss. Choctaw; F; S; Son; Yes

POLK

1125; Henry; m; 22; Miss. Choctaw; F; M; Head; Yes
1126; Susie; f; 28; Miss. Choctaw; F; M; Wife; Yes
1127; Zula; f; 1; Miss. Choctaw; F; S; Daughter; Yes

1128; George; m; 68; Miss. Choctaw; F; Wd; Head; Yes

Census of the ~~Miss. Choctaw~~ reservation of the **Choctaw Agency** jurisdiction, as of **April 30**, 19__30__, taken by **R. J. Enochs**, Superintendent. Purchased Lands   MISSISSIPPI

KEY: Surname; Census Number; Given Name; Sex; Age at Last Birthday; Tribe; Degree of Blood; Marital Status; Relationship to Head of Family; At Jurisdiction Where Enrolled (Yes or No); (If No Where); Ward (Yes unless given otherwise.)

1129; Josie; m; 49; Miss. Choctaw; F; M; Head; Yes
1130; Lennie; f; 50; Miss. Choctaw; F; M; Wife; Yes
1131; Ada; f; 12; Miss. Choctaw; F; S; Daughter; Yes
1132; Frances; f; 12; Miss. Choctaw; F; S; Daughter; Yes

1133; Tom; m; 52; Miss. Choctaw; F; Wd; Head; Yes
1134; Comelia; m; 20; Miss. Choctaw; F; S; Son; Yes
1135; Alma; f; 16; Miss. Choctaw; F; S; Daughter; Yes
1136; Osborn; m; 14; Miss. Choctaw; F; S; Son; Yes

POULSON

1137; Allie; f; 57; Miss. Choctaw; F; S; Head; Yes

1138; Frank; m; 30; Miss. Choctaw; F; M; Head; Yes
1139; Mary; f; 28; Miss. Choctaw; F; M; Wife; Yes

1140; Eddie M; m; 24; Miss. Choctaw; F; M; Head; Yes
1141; Cornelia; f; 26; Miss. Choctaw; F; M; Wife; Yes

1142; Julius; m; 23; Miss. Choctaw; F; S; Head; Yes

1143; Johnnie; m; 21; Miss. Choctaw; F; S; Head; Yes

1144; Charlie; m; 19; Miss. Choctaw; F; S; Head; Yes

ROBINSON

1145; Thomas; m; 40; Miss. Choctaw; F; M; Head; Yes
1146; Syble; f; 35; Miss. Choctaw; F; M; Wife; Yes
1147; Jimmie; m; 16; Miss. Choctaw; F; S; Son; Yes
1148; Georgie; f; 14; Miss. Choctaw; F; S; Daughter; Yes
1149; Sallie; f; 13; Miss. Choctaw; F; S; Daughter; Yes
1150; Carl; m; 11; Miss. Choctaw; F; S; Son; Yes

Census of the ~~Miss. Choctaw~~ reservation of the **Choctaw Agency** jurisdiction, as of **April 30**, 19 **30**, taken by **R. J. Enochs**, Superintendent. Purchased Lands   MISSISSIPPI

KEY: Surname; Census Number; Given Name; Sex; Age at Last Birthday; Tribe; Degree of Blood; Marital Status; Relationship to Head of Family; At Jurisdiction Where Enrolled (Yes or No); (If No Where); Ward (Yes unless given otherwise.)

1151; Mamie; f; 10; Miss. Choctaw; F; S; Daughter; Yes
1152; Betsey; f; 8; Miss. Choctaw; F; S; Daughter; Yes
1153; Homer; m; 6; Miss. Choctaw; F; S; Son; Yes
1154; Teach; m; 1; Miss. Choctaw; F; S; Son; Yes

1155; Belia; f; 23; Miss. Choctaw; F; Wd; Head; Yes
1156; Campbell; m; 3; Miss. Choctaw; F; S; Son; Yes

1157; Mary; f; 82; Miss. Choctaw; F; Wd; Head; Yes

RUTHERFORD

1158; Henrietta; f; 32; Miss. Choctaw; F; S; Head; Yes

SAM

1159; Truman; m; 21; Miss. Choctaw; F; S; Head; Yes

1160; Raymond; m; 49; Miss. Choctaw; F; S; Head; Yes

1161; Oscar; m; 76; Miss. Choctaw; F; M; Head; Yes
1162; Mattie; f; 50; Miss. Choctaw; F; M; Wife; Yes
1163; Seer; f; 16; Miss. Choctaw; F; S; Grand-daughter; Yes
1164; Lavada; f; 18; Miss. Choctaw; F; S; Grand-daughter; Yes

1165; Jimpsey; m; 27; Miss. Choctaw; F; S; Head; Yes

1166; Walter; m; 40; Miss. Choctaw; F; Wd; Head; Yes
1167; Grace; f; 13; Miss. Choctaw; F; S; Daughter; Yes
1168; Tom; m; 11; Miss. Choctaw; F; S; Son; Yes
1169; Manzie; f; 7; Miss. Choctaw; F; S; Daughter; Yes

1170; Fontain; m; 44; Miss. Choctaw; F; M; Head; Yes
1171; Emily; f; 40; Miss. Choctaw; F; M; Wife; Yes

Census of the ~~Miss. Choctaw~~ reservation of the Choctaw Agency jurisdiction, as of April 30, 19 30, taken by R. J. Enochs, Superintendent. Purchased Lands   MISSISSIPPI

KEY: Surname; Census Number; Given Name; Sex; Age at Last Birthday; Tribe; Degree of Blood; Marital Status; Relationship to Head of Family; At Jurisdiction Where Enrolled (Yes or No); (If No Where); Ward (Yes unless given otherwise.)

1172;   Leona; f; 8; Miss. Choctaw; F; S; Daughter; Yes
1173;   Ellis; m; 5; Miss. Choctaw; F; S; Son; Yes
1174;   Fannie; f; 4; Miss. Choctaw; F; S; Daughter; Yes
1175;   Ella Ruth; f; 2; Miss. Choctaw; F; S; Daughter; Yes
1176;   Armond; m; 3/12; Miss. Choctaw; F; S; Son; Yes
1177;   Beemon; m; 10; Miss. Choctaw; F; S; Nephew; Yes

1178;   Willie; m; 31; Miss. Choctaw; F; M; Head; Yes
1179;   Eva; f; 29; Miss. Choctaw; F; M; Wife; Yes
1180;   Nettie; f; 9; Miss. Choctaw; F; S; Daughter; Yes
1181;   Abel; m; 8; Miss. Choctaw; F; S; Son; Yes
1182;   Lonie; f; 6; Miss. Choctaw; F; S; Daughter; Yes
1183;   Grisaline; f; 4/12; Miss. Choctaw; F; S; Daughter; Yes

SCOTT

1184;   Marshall; m; 60; Miss. Choctaw; F; M; Head; Yes
1185;   Lona; f; 25; Miss. Choctaw; F; M; Wife; Yes
1186;   Rachel; f; 4; Miss. Choctaw; F; S; Daughter; Yes

SHOEMAKER

1187;   Alonzo; m; 42; Miss. Choctaw; F; M; Head; Yes
1188;   Susan; f; 30; Miss. Choctaw; F; M; Wife; Yes
1189;   Dempsey; m; 9; Miss. Choctaw; F; S; Son; Yes
1190;   Layman; m; 7; Miss. Choctaw; F; S; Son; Yes
1191;   Ruben; m; 4; Miss. Choctaw; F; S; Son; Yes
1192;   Noleen; f; 1; Miss. Choctaw; F; S; Daughter; Yes

1193;   Buck; m; 45; Miss. Choctaw; F; M; Head; Yes
1194;   Annie; f; 30; Miss. Choctaw; F; M; Wife; Yes
1195;   Leona; f; 10; Miss. Choctaw; F; S; Daughter; Yes
1196;   Eliza; f; 8; Miss. Choctaw; F; S; Daughter; Yes
1197;   Martha; f; 6; Miss. Choctaw; F; S; Daughter; Yes

Census of the ~~Miss. Choctaw~~ reservation of the **Choctaw Agency** jurisdiction, as of **April 30**, 19 **30**, taken by **R. J. Enochs**, Superintendent. Purchased Lands   MISSISSIPPI

KEY: Surname; Census Number; Given Name; Sex; Age at Last Birthday; Tribe; Degree of Blood; Marital Status; Relationship to Head of Family; At Jurisdiction Where Enrolled (Yes or No); (If No Where); Ward (Yes unless given otherwise.)

1198; Daisy; f; 4; Miss. Choctaw; F; S; Daughter; Yes
1199; Carry Mae; f; 3; Miss. Choctaw; F; S; Daughter; Yes

SIMPSON

1200; John; m; 52; Miss. Choctaw; F; M; Head; Yes
1201; Sallie; f; 50; Miss. Choctaw; F; M; Wife; Yes
1202; Pauline; f; 14; Miss. Choctaw; F; S; Daughter; Yes
1203; Celie; f; 12; Miss. Choctaw; F; S; Daughter; Yes

SMITH

1204; George; m; 58; Miss. Choctaw; F; M; Head; Yes
1205; Mandy; f; 44; Miss. Choctaw; F; M; Wife; Yes
1206; **Farmer**, Mary Lou; f; 12; Miss. Choctaw; F; S; Step-daughter; Yes
1207; **Farmer**, Lilly Kate; f; 10; Miss. Choctaw; F; S; Step-daughter; Yes
1208; **Farmer**, Grace; f; 7; Miss. Choctaw; F; S; Step-daughter; Yes

1209; Sebe; m; 40; Miss. Choctaw; F; M; Head; Yes
1210; Sinie; f; 39; Miss. Choctaw; F; M; Wife; Yes
1211; Sophie; f; 17; Miss. Choctaw; F; S; Daughter; Yes
1212; Clemon; m; 11; Miss. Choctaw; F; S; Son; Yes

1213; John Wesley; m; 55; Miss. Choctaw; F; M; Head; Yes
1214; Mary; f; 70; Miss. Choctaw; F; M; Wife; Yes

1215; Minnie; f; 35; Miss. Choctaw; F; Wd; Head; Yes
1216; Melton; m; 4; Miss. Choctaw; F; S; Son; Yes
1217; Elton; m; 2; Miss. Choctaw; F; S; Son; Yes
1218; **Stephens**, Phoeba; f; 10; Miss. Choctaw; F; S; Grand-daughter; Yes

Census of the ~~Miss. Choctaw~~ reservation of the __Choctaw Agency__ jurisdiction, as of ___April 30___, 19__30__, taken by __R. J. Enochs__, Superintendent. Purchased Lands   MISSISSIPPI

KEY: Surname; Census Number; Given Name; Sex; Age at Last Birthday; Tribe; Degree of Blood; Marital Status; Relationship to Head of Family; At Jurisdiction Where Enrolled (Yes or No); (If No Where); Ward (Yes unless given otherwise.)

1219;   Clay; m; 25; Miss. Choctaw; F; M; Head; Yes
1220;   Mattie; f; 28; Miss. Choctaw; F; M; Wife; Yes

SOCKEY

1221;   Irvin; m; 48; Miss. Choctaw; F; M; Head; Yes
1222;   Lula; f; 35; Miss. Choctaw; F; M; Wife; Yes
1223;   Benny; m; 22; Miss. Choctaw; F; S; Son; Yes
1224;   Homer; m; 7; Miss. Choctaw; F; S; Son; Yes
1225;   Ill; m; 2; Miss. Choctaw; F; S; Son; Yes

1226;   Mike; m; 28; Miss. Choctaw; F; M; Head; Yes
1227;   Nephus; f; 27; Miss. Choctaw; F; M; Wife; Yes
1228;   Verelia; f; 8; Miss. Choctaw; F; S; Daughter; Yes
1229;   Odell; m; 6; Miss. Choctaw; F; S; Son; Yes
1230;   Enochs; m; 3; Miss. Choctaw; F; S; Son; Yes
1231;   Arnold; m; 5/12; Miss. Choctaw; F; S; Son; Yes

SOLOMON

1232;   Willie; m; 46; Miss. Choctaw; F; Wd; Head; Yes

1233;   Marshall; m; 26; Miss. Choctaw; F; M; Head; Yes
*783;   ~~(Jefferson), Addie; f; 21; Miss. Choctaw; F; M; Wife; Yes~~
       *Do not count Addie Solomon. She was listed as #783, under the Jeffersons.

1234;   Willie; m; 67; Miss. Choctaw; F; M; Head; Yes
1235;   Winnie L; f; 25; Miss. Choctaw; F; M; Wife; Yes
1236;   Mollie Lee; f; 1; Miss. Choctaw; F; S; Daughter; Yes

1237;   Raymond; m; 36; Miss. Choctaw; F; M; Head; Yes
1238;   Bessie; f; 36; Miss. Choctaw; F; M; Wife; Yes
1239;   Earnest; m; 14; Miss. Choctaw; F; S; Son; Yes

Census of the ~~Miss. Choctaw~~ reservation of the **Choctaw Agency** jurisdiction, as of **April 30**, 19 **30**, taken by **R. J. Enochs**, Superintendent. Purchased Lands   MISSISSIPPI

KEY: Surname; Census Number; Given Name; Sex; Age at Last Birthday; Tribe; Degree of Blood; Marital Status; Relationship to Head of Family; At Jurisdiction Where Enrolled (Yes or No); (If No Where); Ward (Yes unless given otherwise.)

1240; Murphy; m; 11; Miss. Choctaw; F; S; Son; Yes
1241; Mollie; f; 8; Miss. Choctaw; F; S; Daughter; Yes

STAR

1242; Lucy; f; 42; Miss. Choctaw; F; Wd; Head; Yes

1243; Bill; m; 41; Miss. Choctaw; F; Wd; Head; Yes
1244; Summers; m; 14; Miss. Choctaw; F; S; Son; Yes
1245; Edna; f; 12; Miss. Choctaw; F; S; Daughter; Yes
1246; Nannie; f; 9; Miss. Choctaw; F; S; Daughter; Yes
1247; Mary; f; 7; Miss. Choctaw; F; S; Daughter; Yes

STEPHENS

1248; Nathan; m; 27; Miss. Choctaw; F; M; Head; Yes
1249; Annie; f; 32; Miss. Choctaw; F; M; Wife; Yes
1250; Maxton; m; 5; Miss. Choctaw; F; S; Son; Yes
1251; Cutie Mae; f; 3; Miss. Choctaw; F; S; Daughter; Yes
1252; Dorthy D; f; 2; Miss. Choctaw; F; S; Daughter; Yes
1253; Bonnie B; f; 6/12; Miss. Choctaw; F; S; Daughter; Yes

1254; Tom; m; 67; Miss. Choctaw; F; Wd; Head; Yes

1255; Silmon; m; 35; Miss. Choctaw; F; S; Head; Yes

1256; Felix; m; 24; Miss. Choctaw; F; M; Head; Yes
1257; Martha; f; 22; Miss. Choctaw; F; M; Wife; Yes
1258; Martha Lee; f; 9/12; Miss. Choctaw; F; S; Daughter; Yes

1259; Willie; m; 20; Miss. Choctaw; F; S; Head; Yes

1260; Cornelia; f; 24; Miss. Choctaw; F; S; Head; Yes

Census of the ~~Miss. Choctaw~~ reservation of the **Choctaw Agency** jurisdiction, as of **April 30**, 19 **30**, taken by **R. J. Enochs**, Superintendent. Purchased Lands   MISSISSIPPI

KEY: Surname; Census Number; Given Name; Sex; Age at Last Birthday; Tribe; Degree of Blood; Marital Status; Relationship to Head of Family; At Jurisdiction Where Enrolled (Yes or No); (If No Where); Ward (Yes unless given otherwise.)

STEVE

1261; Murphy; m; 56; Miss. Choctaw; F; M; Head; Yes
1262; Patsy; f; 23; Miss. Choctaw; F; M; Wife; Yes
1263; Helen; f; 2; Miss. Choctaw; F; S; Daughter; Yes
1264; George; m; 1/36; Miss. Choctaw; F; S; Son; Yes
1265; Winston; m; 1/36; Miss. Choctaw; F; S; Son; Yes

1266; Josie; m; 28; Miss. Choctaw; F; M; Head; Yes
1267; Maggie; f; 21; Miss. Choctaw; F; M; Wife; Yes
1268; Ruby; f; 4; Miss. Choctaw; F; S; Daughter; Yes
1269; Jane; f; 3; Miss. Choctaw; F; S; Daughter; Yes

1270; Huston; m; 42; Miss. Choctaw; F; M; Head; Yes
1271; Lena; f; 38; Miss. Choctaw; F; M; Wife; Yes
1272; Ennis; m; 21; Miss. Choctaw; F; S; Son; Yes
1273; McKinley; m; 11; Miss. Choctaw; F; S; Son; Yes
1274; Yates; m; 7; Miss. Choctaw; F; S; Son; Yes
1275; Marabelle; f; 3; Miss. Choctaw; F; S; Daughter; Yes

1276; Bobo; m; 23; Miss. Choctaw; F; M; Head; Yes
1277; Lucille; f; 18; Miss. Choctaw; F; M; Wife; Yes
1278; Maurice; f; 4; Miss. Choctaw; F; S; Daughter; Yes
1279; Aubrey; f; 2; Miss. Choctaw; F; S; Daughter; Yes
1280; Vivian; f; 11/12; Miss. Choctaw; F; S; Daughter; Yes

1281; Smith; m; 36; Miss. Choctaw; F; M; Head; Yes
1282; Winnie; f; 33; Miss. Choctaw; F; M; Wife; Yes
1283; Tonie; f; 10; Miss. Choctaw; F; S; Daughter; Yes
1284; Pauline; f; 9; Miss. Choctaw; F; S; Daughter; Yes
1285; Mollie; f; 5; Miss. Choctaw; F; S; Daughter; Yes
1286; Aileen; f; 1; Miss. Choctaw; F; S; Daughter; Yes

Census of the ~~Miss. Choctaw~~ reservation of the Choctaw Agency jurisdiction, as of April 30, 19 30, taken by R. J. Enochs, Superintendent. Purchased Lands   MISSISSIPPI

KEY: Surname; Census Number; Given Name; Sex; Age at Last Birthday; Tribe; Degree of Blood; Marital Status; Relationship to Head of Family; At Jurisdiction Where Enrolled (Yes or No); (If No Where); Ward (Yes unless given otherwise.)

STOLIBY

1287;   Missouri; f; 62; Miss. Choctaw; F; Wd; Head; Yes
1288;   Tom; m; 27; Miss. Choctaw; F; S; Son; Yes
1289;   Elum Ferum; m; 4; Miss. Choctaw; F; S; Grand-son; Yes

1290;   John; m; 40; Miss. Choctaw; F; Wd; Head; Yes
1291;   Nancy; f; 19; Miss. Choctaw; F; S; Daughter; Yes
1292;   Will Banks; m; 11; Miss. Choctaw; F; S; Son; Yes
1293;   Otis; m; 9; Miss. Choctaw; F; S; Son; Yes
1294;   Zona Milker; f[sic]; 5; Miss. Choctaw; F; S; Son; Yes

STRIBLING

1295;   Malissie; f; 58; Miss. Choctaw; F; Wd; Head; Yes
1296;   Varderman; m; 28; Miss. Choctaw; F; Wd; Son; Yes
1297;   Marvin; m; 24; Miss. Choctaw; F; S; Son; Yes

THOMAS

1298;   Lewis; m; 46; Miss. Choctaw; F; M; Head; Yes
1299;   Mamie; f; 43; Miss. Choctaw; F; M; Wife; Yes
1300;   Newman; m; 11; Miss. Choctaw; F; S; Son; Yes
1301;   Isaac; m; 7; Miss. Choctaw; F; S; Son; Yes
1302;   Mina; f; 5; Miss. Choctaw; F; S; Daughter; Yes

1303;   George; m; 81; Miss. Choctaw; F; Wd; Head; Yes

1304;   Riley; m; 25; Miss. Choctaw; F; S; Head; Yes

1305;   Cleve; m; 27; Miss. Choctaw; F; M; Head; Yes
1306;   Phoebe; f; 22; Miss. Choctaw; F; M; Wife; Yes

1307;   Willman; m; 30; Miss. Choctaw; F; M; Head; Yes

Census of the ~~Miss. Choctaw~~ reservation of the Choctaw Agency jurisdiction, as of April 30, 19 30, taken by R. J. Enochs, Superintendent. Purchased Lands   MISSISSIPPI

KEY: Surname; Census Number; Given Name; Sex; Age at Last Birthday; Tribe; Degree of Blood; Marital Status; Relationship to Head of Family; At Jurisdiction Where Enrolled (Yes or No); (If No Where); Ward (Yes unless given otherwise.)

1308; Sallie; f; 29; Miss. Choctaw; F; M; Wife; Yes
1309; Woodrow; m; 11; Miss. Choctaw; F; S; Son; Yes
1310; Mollie; f; 9; Miss. Choctaw; F; S; Daughter; Yes
1311; Golden; m; 7; Miss. Choctaw; F; S; Son; Yes
1312; Amos; m; 5; Miss. Choctaw; F; S; Son; Yes
1313; Single; m; 1; Miss. Choctaw; F; S; Son; Yes

1314; Lester; m; 21; Miss. Choctaw; F; M; Head; Yes
1315; Rosie; f; 19; Miss. Choctaw; F; M; Wife; Yes

1316; Rosie; f; 35; Miss. Choctaw; F; S; Head; Yes

1317; Leona; f; 30; Miss. Choctaw; F; M; Wife; Yes

1318; Evaline; f; 34; Miss. Choctaw; F; M; Wife; Yes

NOTE: Leona and Evaline Thomas listed above are married to white men. No children. Husbands not listed.

THOMPSON

1319; Will; m; 26; Miss. Choctaw; F; M; Head; Yes
1320; Sina; f; 23; Miss. Choctaw; F; M; Wife; Yes
1321; Otis; m; 6; Miss. Choctaw; F; S; Son; Yes
1322; Claudine; f; 3; Miss. Choctaw; F; S; Daughter; Yes
1323; Henry; m; 1; Miss. Choctaw; F; S; Son; Yes

1324; Cephus; m; 40; Miss. Choctaw; F; M; Head; Yes
1325; Amie; f; 25; Miss. Choctaw; F; M; Wife; Yes
1326; Dixon; m; 16; Miss. Choctaw; F; S; Son; Yes
1327; Farmer; m; 6; Miss. Choctaw; F; S; Son; Yes
1328; Alice; f; 5; Miss. Choctaw; F; S; Daughter; Yes
1329; Annie; f; 2; Miss. Choctaw; F; S; Daughter; Yes

Census of the ~~Miss. Choctaw~~ reservation of the **Choctaw Agency** jurisdiction, as of **April 30**, 19**30**, taken by **R. J. Enochs**, Superintendent. Purchased Lands   MISSISSIPPI

KEY: Surname; Census Number; Given Name; Sex; Age at Last Birthday; Tribe; Degree of Blood; Marital Status; Relationship to Head of Family; At Jurisdiction Where Enrolled (Yes or No); (If No Where); Ward (Yes unless given otherwise.)

1330; Malinda; f; 65; Miss. Choctaw; F; Wd; Head; Yes
1331; Beneva; f; 19; Miss. Choctaw; F; S; Daughter; Yes

1332; Mose; m; 33; Miss. Choctaw; F; M; Head; Yes
1333; Jean; f; 34; Miss. Choctaw; F; M; Wife; Yes
1334; Jim; m; 10; Miss. Choctaw; F; S; Son; Yes
1335; Annie; f; 7; Miss. Choctaw; F; S; Daughter; Yes
1336; Therman; m; 5; Miss. Choctaw; F; S; Son; Yes
1337; Steve; m; 3; Miss. Choctaw; F; S; Son; Yes

1338; John; m; 38; Miss. Choctaw; F; M; Head; Yes
1339; Lula; f; 36; Miss. Choctaw; F; M; Wife; Yes
1340; Moline; f; 9; Miss. Choctaw; F; S; Daughter; Yes
1341; Onie; f; 8; Miss. Choctaw; F; S; Daughter; Yes
1342; Tom; m; 3; Miss. Choctaw; F; S; Son; Yes

1343; Tommie; m; 31; Miss. Choctaw; F; M; Head; Yes
1344; Bonnie; f; 28; Miss. Choctaw; F; M; Wife; Yes

TUBBY

1345; Dan; m; 28; Miss. Choctaw; F; M; Head; Yes
1346; Lola; f; 34; Miss. Choctaw; F; M; Wife; Yes
1347; **Lewis**, Lum; m; 4; Miss. Choctaw; F; S; Step-son; Yes
1349; Mary; Miss. Choctaw; F; 19; Miss. Choctaw; F; M; Wife; Yes
1350; Thomas; m; 1; Miss. Choctaw; F; S; Son; Yes
1351; Jennie; f; 12; Miss. Choctaw; F; S; Sister; Yes

1352; Lefus; m; 37; Miss. Choctaw; F; M; Head; Yes
1353; Frances; f; 30; Miss. Choctaw; F; M; Wife; Yes
1354; Ina; f; 8; Miss. Choctaw; F; S; Daughter; Yes
1355; Irene; f; 6; Miss. Choctaw; F; S; Daughter; Yes
1356; Leona; f; 3; Miss. Choctaw; F; S; Daughter; Yes
1357; **Ben**, Rufus; m; 12; Miss. Choctaw; F; S; Step-son; Yes

Census of the ~~Miss. Choctaw~~ reservation of the Choctaw Agency jurisdiction, as of April 30, 19 30, taken by R. J. Enochs, Superintendent. Purchased Lands   MISSISSIPPI

KEY: Surname; Census Number; Given Name; Sex; Age at Last Birthday; Tribe; Degree of Blood; Marital Status; Relationship to Head of Family; At Jurisdiction Where Enrolled (Yes or No); (If No Where); Ward (Yes unless given otherwise.)

1358; Sidney; m; 30; Miss. Choctaw; F; M; Head; Yes
1359; Kate; f; 29; Miss. Choctaw; F; M; Wife; Yes
1360; Rufus; m; 11; Miss. Choctaw; F; S; Son; Yes
1361; Phelia; f; 8; Miss. Choctaw; F; S; Daughter; Yes
1362; Eva Kate; f; 5; Miss. Choctaw; F; S; Daughter; Yes
1363; Edmon; m; 2; Miss. Choctaw; F; S; Son; Yes

1364; Annis; m; 51; Miss. Choctaw; F; M; Head; Yes
1365; Annie; f; 30; Miss. Choctaw; F; M; Wife; Yes

1366; Edgar; m; 30; Miss. Choctaw; F; M; Head; Yes
1367; Annie; f; 28; Miss. Choctaw; F; M; Wife; Yes
1368; Steve; m; 9; Miss. Choctaw; F; S; Son; Yes
1369; Willie; m; 8; Miss. Choctaw; F; S; Son; Yes
1370; Odie; m; 6; Miss. Choctaw; F; S; Son; Yes
1371; Parline; f; 3; Miss. Choctaw; F; S; Daughter; Yes

1372; Dick; m; 59; Miss. Choctaw; F; M; Head; Yes
1373; Eline; f; 50; Miss. Choctaw; F; M; Wife; Yes
1374; Jeff; m; 24; Miss. Choctaw; F; S; Nephew; Yes

1375; Allen; m; 74; Miss. Choctaw; F; Wd; Head; Yes
1376; Mary; f; 27; Miss. Choctaw; F; S; Daughter; Yes
1377; Lilly; f; 25; Miss. Choctaw; F; S; Daughter; Yes

1378; Pat; m; 36; Miss. Choctaw; F; M; Head; Yes
1379; Frances; f; 36; Miss. Choctaw; F; M; Wife; Yes
1380; Vernal; m; 18; Miss. Choctaw; F; S; Son; Yes
1381; Earnest; m; 10; Miss. Choctaw; F; S; Son; Yes
1382; Lorraine; f; 8; Miss. Choctaw; F; S; Daughter; Yes
1383; Alice; f; 6; Miss. Choctaw; F; S; Daughter; Yes
1384; Aileen; f; 3; Miss. Choctaw; F; S; Daughter; Yes

1385; Lysander; m; 42; Miss. Choctaw; F; M; Head; Yes

Census of the ~~Miss. Choctaw~~ reservation of the **Choctaw Agency** jurisdiction, as of **April 30**, 19**30**, taken by **R. J. Enochs**, Superintendent. Purchased Lands   MISSISSIPPI

KEY: Surname; Census Number; Given Name; Sex; Age at Last Birthday; Tribe; Degree of Blood; Marital Status; Relationship to Head of Family; At Jurisdiction Where Enrolled (Yes or No); (If No Where); Ward (Yes unless given otherwise.)

1386;   Annie Mae; f; 21; Miss. Choctaw; F; M; Wife; Yes

1387;   Moley; m; 27; Miss. Choctaw; F; M; Head; Yes
1388;   Sallie; f; 23; Miss. Choctaw; F; M; Wife; Yes

1389;   Adam; m; 28; Miss. Choctaw; F; S; Head; Yes

1390;   Dewitt; m; 23; Miss. Choctaw; F; M; Head; Yes
1391;   Katie; f; 24; Miss. Choctaw; F; M; Wife; Yes

1392;   Rainey; f; 60; Miss. Choctaw; F; Wd; Mother; Yes
1393;   Lena; f; 30; Miss. Choctaw; F; S; Daughter; Yes
1394;   Mollie; f; 25; Miss. Choctaw; F; S; Daughter; Yes
1395;   Herbert; m; 22; Miss. Choctaw; F; S; Son; Yes

1396;   Jimpson; m; 66; Miss. Choctaw; F; Wd; Head; Yes

1397;   Anderson; m; 30; Miss. Choctaw; F; M; Head; Yes
1398;   Nancy; f; 20; Miss. Choctaw; F; M; Wife; Yes
1399;   Jim; m; 6; Miss. Choctaw; F; S; Son; Yes
1400;   Omarr; f; 4; Miss. Choctaw; F; S; Daughter; Yes
1401;   Buracy; f; 2; Miss. Choctaw; F; S; Daughter; Yes
1402;   Etoyle; f; 1/12; Miss. Choctaw; F; S; Daughter; Yes

1403;   Evan; m; 37; Miss. Choctaw; F; M; Head; Yes
1404;   Jennie; f; 42; Miss. Choctaw; F; M; Wife; Yes
1405;   Annie; f; 7; Miss. Choctaw; F; S; Daughter; Yes

1406;   Charlie; m; 34; Miss. Choctaw; F; M; Head; Yes
1407;   Betsy; f; 29; Miss. Choctaw; F; M; Wife; Yes
1408;   Alice; f; 7; Miss. Choctaw; F; S; Daughter; Yes
1409;   Kate; f; 9; Miss. Choctaw; F; S; Step-daughter; Yes
1410;   Jack; m; 5; Miss. Choctaw; F; S; Son; Yes
1411;   J. C; m; 3; Miss. Choctaw; F; S; Son; Yes

Census of the ~~Miss. Choctaw~~ reservation of the **Choctaw Agency** jurisdiction, as of   April 30   , 19 30 , taken by   **R. J. Enochs** , Superintendent. Purchased Lands   MISSISSIPPI

KEY: Surname; Census Number; Given Name; Sex; Age at Last Birthday; Tribe; Degree of Blood; Marital Status; Relationship to Head of Family; At Jurisdiction Where Enrolled (Yes or No); (If No Where); Ward (Yes unless given otherwise.)

1412;   Colie; f; 1; Miss. Choctaw; F; S; Daughter; Yes

1413;   Ellis; m; 6; Miss. Choctaw; F; S; Orphan; Yes

1414;   Henderson; m; 37; Miss. Choctaw; F; M; Head; Yes
1415;   Maggie; f; 25; Miss. Choctaw; F; M; Wife; Yes
1416;   Sam; m; 14; Miss. Choctaw; F; S; Orphan; Yes
1417;   Otis; f; 7; Miss. Choctaw; F; S; Daughter; Yes
1418;   W. C; m; 5; Miss. Choctaw; F; S; Son; Yes
1419;   Gladys; f; 3; Miss. Choctaw; F; S; Daughter; Yes
1420;   Finis; m; 1; Miss. Choctaw; F; S; Son; Yes

1421;   Clemon; m; 55; Miss. Choctaw; F; M; Head; Yes
1422;   Alice; f; 55; Miss. Choctaw; F; M; Wife; Yes
1423;   Joe; m; 21; Miss. Choctaw; F; S; Step-son; Yes
1424;   Lash; m; 4; Miss. Choctaw; F; S; Great-nephew; Yes
1425;   Sarah; f; 3; Miss. Choctaw; F; S; Great-niece; Yes

1426;   Jackson; m; 22; Miss. Choctaw; F; M; Head; Yes
1427;   Mallissa; f; 23; Miss. Choctaw; F; M; Wife; Yes

1428;   Nichols; m; 32; Miss. Choctaw; F; M; Head; Yes
1429;   Esther; f; 27; Miss. Choctaw; F; M; Wife; Yes
1430;   Sullivan; m; 8; Miss. Choctaw; F; S Son; Yes
1431;   Alice; f; 7; Miss. Choctaw; F; S; Daughter; Yes
1432;   Minnie; f; 5; Miss. Choctaw; F; S; Daughter; Yes
1433;   Catherine; f; 3; Miss. Choctaw; F; S; Daughter; Yes

1434;   Alice; f; 40; Miss. Choctaw; F; Wd; Mother; Yes
1435;   **Johnson**, Lee; m; 18; Miss. Choctaw; F; S; Son; Yes

1436;   Tom; m; 21; Miss. Choctaw; F; M; Head; Yes
1437;   Marceline; f; 23; Miss. Choctaw; F; M; Wife; Yes
1438;   Inis; m; 6/12; Miss. Choctaw; F; S; Son; Yes

Census of the ~~Miss. Choctaw~~ reservation of the Choctaw Agency jurisdiction, as of April 30, 19 30, taken by R. J. Enochs, Superintendent. Purchased Lands   MISSISSIPPI

KEY: Surname; Census Number; Given Name; Sex; Age at Last Birthday; Tribe; Degree of Blood; Marital Status; Relationship to Head of Family; At Jurisdiction Where Enrolled (Yes or No); (If No Where); Ward (Yes unless given otherwise.)

1439; Joseph; m; 3; Miss. Choctaw; F; S; Step-son; Yes

1440; Anderson; m; 38; Miss. Choctaw; F; M; Head; Yes
1441; Louisiana; f; 40; Miss. Choctaw; F; M; Wife; Yes
1442; Hazel; f; 16; Miss. Choctaw; F; S; Daughter; Yes
1443; Smith; f; 14; Miss. Choctaw; F; S; Daughter; Yes
1444; Icy; f; 12; Miss. Choctaw; F; S; Daughter; Yes
1445; John; m; 10; Miss. Choctaw; F; S; Son; Yes

1446; Simpson; m; 70; Miss. Choctaw; F; M; Head; Yes
1447; Minnie; f; 37; Miss. Choctaw; F; M; Wife; Yes
1448; Iko; m; 18; Miss. Choctaw; F; S; Son; Yes
1449; Henry; m; 17; Miss. Choctaw; F; S; Son; Yes
1450; Eva; f; 16; Miss. Choctaw; F; S; Daughter; Yes
1451; Lewis; m; 13; Miss. Choctaw; F; S; Son; Yes
1452; McKinley; m; 10; Miss. Choctaw; F; S; Son; Yes
1453; Hudson; m; 7; Miss. Choctaw; F; S; Son; Yes
1454; Sullivan; m; 6; Miss. Choctaw; F; S; Son; Yes
1455; Callie; f; 4; Miss. Choctaw; F; S; Daughter; Yes
1456; Nellie; f; 3; Miss. Choctaw; F; S; Daughter; Yes

TUCKALLOO

1457; Frances; f; 67; Miss. Choctaw; F; Wd; Head; Yes
1458; **Tubby**, Wesley; m; 11; Miss. Choctaw; F; S; Grand-son; Yes
1459; Mason; m; 16; Miss. Choctaw; F; S; Grand-son; Yes
1460; Enia; m; 6; Miss. Choctaw; F; S; Grand-son; Yes
1461; Alice; f; 5; Miss. Choctaw; F; S; Grand-daughter; Yes
1462; Sarah; f; 4; Miss. Choctaw; F; S; Grand-daughter; Yes

VAUGHN

1463; John; m; 65; Miss. Choctaw; F; Wd; Head; Yes

Census of the ~~Miss. Choctaw~~ reservation of the **Choctaw Agency** jurisdiction, as of **April 30**, 19**30**, taken by **R. J. Enochs**, Superintendent.   Purchased Lands   MISSISSIPPI

KEY: Surname; Census Number; Given Name; Sex; Age at Last Birthday; Tribe; Degree of Blood; Marital Status; Relationship to Head of Family; At Jurisdiction Where Enrolled (Yes or No); (If No Where); Ward (Yes unless given otherwise.)

1464; Greer; m; 55; Miss. Choctaw; F; M; Head; Yes
1465; Jane; f; 50; Miss. Choctaw; F; M; Wife; Yes
1466; Agnes; f; 4; Miss. Choctaw; F; S; Daughter; Yes

1467; Cooksie; m; 65; Miss. Choctaw; F; M; Head; Yes
1468' Susan; f; 58; Miss. Choctaw; F; M; Wife; Yes
1469; Lena; f; 35; Miss. Choctaw; F; S; Daughter; Yes
1470; Ludie; f; 23; Miss. Choctaw; F; S; Daughter; Yes

1471; Silmon; m; 18; Miss. Choctaw; F; M; Head; Yes
1472; Seta; f; 14; Miss. Choctaw; F; M; Wife; Yes

1473; Howard; m; 28; Miss. Choctaw; F; M; Head; Yes
1474; Bessie; f; 28; Miss. Choctaw; F; M; Wife; Yes
1475; Clifton; m; 4; Miss. Choctaw; F; S; Son; Yes
1476; Mary Rose; f; 2; Miss. Choctaw; F; S; Daughter; Yes

1477; John; m; 24; Miss. Choctaw; F; M; Head; Yes
1478; Mallisa; f; 37; Miss. Choctaw; F; M; Wife; Yes
1479; Mollie; f; 17; Miss. Choctaw; F; S; Step-daughter; Yes
1480; Annie; f; 12; Miss. Choctaw; F; S; Step-daughter; Yes

WAITER

1481; Gipson; m; 67; Miss. Choctaw; F; Wd; Head; Yes

1482; Minnie; f; 54; Miss. Choctaw; F; Wd; Head; Yes
1483; Ruby; f; 20; Miss. Choctaw; F; S; Daughter; Yes
1484; Lillie Mae; f; 19; Miss. Choctaw; F; S; Daughter; Yes

1485; Lonnie; m; 25; Miss. Choctaw; F; M; Head; Yes
1486; Sue; f; 20; Miss. Choctaw; F; M; Wife; Yes

Census of the ~~Miss. Choctaw~~ reservation of the **Choctaw Agency** jurisdiction, as of **April 30**, 19 **30**, taken by **R. J. Enochs**, Superintendent. Purchased Lands   MISSISSIPPI

KEY: Surname; Census Number; Given Name; Sex; Age at Last Birthday; Tribe; Degree of Blood; Marital Status; Relationship to Head of Family; At Jurisdiction Where Enrolled (Yes or No); (If No Where); Ward (Yes unless given otherwise.)

WALLACE

1487; Eunice; f; 40; Miss. Choctaw; F; Wd; Head; Yes
1488; Susie; f; 17; Miss. Choctaw; F; S; Daughter; Yes
1489; Henry; m; 15; Miss. Choctaw; F; S; Son; Yes
1490; Celia; f; 14; Miss. Choctaw; F; S; Daughter; Yes
1491; Austin; m; 3; Miss. Choctaw; F; S; Son; Yes

1492; Rachel; f; 45; Miss. Choctaw; F; Wd; Head; Yes
1493; Leona; f; 15; Miss. Choctaw; F; S; Daughter; Yes

1494; Columbus; m; 20; Miss. Choctaw; F; M; Head; Yes
1495; Essie; f; 18; Miss. Choctaw; F; M; Wife; Yes

1496; Stenot; m; 22; Miss. Choctaw; F; M; Head; Yes
1497; Annie; f; 17; Miss. Choctaw; F; M; Wife; Yes

1498; Alton; m; 10; Miss. Choctaw; F; S; Orphan; Yes

WARNER

1499; Ellen; f; 90; Miss. Choctaw; F; Wd; Head; Yes
1500; Johnnie Lee; m; 18; Miss. Choctaw; F; S; Son; Yes

WESLEY

1501; Sidney; m; 65; Miss. Choctaw; F; Wd; Head; Yes

1502; Cameron; m; 40; Miss. Choctaw; F; M; Head; Yes
1503; Julie; f; 26; Miss. Choctaw; F; M; Wife; Yes
1504; Bennie; m; 13; Miss. Choctaw; F; S; Son; Yes
1505; John; m; 5; Miss. Choctaw; F; S; Son; Yes
1506; Willie B; m; 3; Miss. Choctaw; F; S; Son; Yes

Census of the ~~Miss. Choctaw~~ reservation of the Choctaw Agency jurisdiction, as of April 30, 19 30, taken by R. J. Enochs, Superintendent. Purchased Lands   MISSISSIPPI

KEY: Surname; Census Number; Given Name; Sex; Age at Last Birthday; Tribe; Degree of Blood; Marital Status; Relationship to Head of Family; At Jurisdiction Where Enrolled (Yes or No); (If No Where); Ward (Yes unless given otherwise.)

WICKSON

1507;   Jim; m; 22; Miss. Choctaw; F; M; Head; Yes
1508;   Alma; f; 25; Miss. Choctaw; F; M; Wife; Yes

WILEY

1509;   Lizza; f; 60; Miss. Choctaw; F; S; Head; Yes

WILLIAMS

1510;   Jonas; m; 55; Miss. Choctaw; F; M; Head; Yes
1511;   Maggie; f; 45; Miss. Choctaw; F; M; Wife; Yes
1512;   Tony; m; 21; Miss. Choctaw; F; S; Son; Yes

1513;   Rufus; m; 24; Miss. Choctaw; F; M; Head; Yes
1514;   Nellie; f; 29; Miss. Choctaw; F; M; Wife; Yes
1515;   Evan; m; 8; Miss. Choctaw; F; S; Son; Yes
1516;   Phillip; m; 7; Miss. Choctaw; F; S; Son; Yes
1517;   Fillman; m; 3; Miss. Choctaw; F; S; Son; Yes
1518;   Coy; m; 1; Miss. Choctaw; F; S; Son; Yes

1519;   Jennie; f; 86; Miss. Choctaw; F; Wd; Head; Yes
1520;   Fate; m; 41; Miss. Choctaw; F; S; Son; Yes

1521;   Lewis; m; 53; Miss. Choctaw; F; M; Head; Yes
1522;   Mamie; f; 31; Miss. Choctaw; F; M; Wife; Yes
1523;   Mary Ann; f; 5; Miss. Choctaw; F; S; Daughter; Yes
1523;   Sarah; f; 1; Miss. Choctaw; F; S; Daughter; Yes

WILLIAMSON

1525;   Mack; m; 55; Miss. Choctaw; F; M; Head; Yes
1526;   Ida; f; 55; Miss. Choctaw; F; M; Wife; Yes

Census of the ~~Miss. Choctaw~~ reservation of the **Choctaw Agency** jurisdiction, as of **April 30**, 19**30**, taken by **R. J. Enochs**, Superintendent. Purchased Lands   MISSISSIPPI

KEY: Surname; Census Number; Given Name; Sex; Age at Last Birthday; Tribe; Degree of Blood; Marital Status; Relationship to Head of Family; At Jurisdiction Where Enrolled (Yes or No); (If No Where); Ward (Yes unless given otherwise.)

1527;   Arnold; m; 11; Miss. Choctaw; F; S; Son; Yes
1528;   **Lewis**, Marceline; f; 6; Miss. Choctaw; F; S; Grand-daughter; Yes

1529;   Bike; m; 38; Miss. Choctaw; F; M; Head; Yes
1530;   Effie; f; 26; Miss. Choctaw; F; M; Wife; Yes
1531;   Mary; f; 10; Miss. Choctaw; F; S; Daughter; Yes
1532;   Lallie; f; 8; Miss. Choctaw; F; S; Daughter; Yes

WILLIS

1533;   Bill; m; 34; Miss. Choctaw; F; M; Head; Yes
1534;   Savenia; f; 28; Miss. Choctaw; F; M; Wife; Yes
1535;   Claud Yates; m; 11; Miss. Choctaw; F; S; Son; Yes
1536;   Elsie; f; 10; Miss. Choctaw; F; S; Daughter; Yes
1537;   William B; m; 7; Miss. Choctaw; F; S; Son; Yes
1538;   Lucy; f; 2; Miss. Choctaw; F; S; Daughter; Yes

1539;   Nath; m; 23; Miss. Choctaw; F; M; Head; Yes
1540;   Ester; f; 27; Miss. Choctaw; F; M; Wife; Yes
1541;   Silma; f; 2; Miss. Choctaw; F; S; Daughter; Yes
1542;   Joe; m; 10/12; Miss. Choctaw; F; S; Son; Yes

1543;   Ike; m; 23; Miss. Choctaw; F; M; Head; Yes
1544;   Ellen; f; 21; Miss. Choctaw; F; M; Wife; Yes
1545;   Adam; m; 4; Miss. Choctaw; F; S; Son; Yes
1546;   Jasper; m; 1; Miss. Choctaw; F; S; Son; Yes

1547;   Robert; m; 42; Miss. Choctaw; F; M; Head; Yes
1548;   Celie; f; 29; Miss. Choctaw; F; M; Wife; Yes
1549;   Mallie; f; 18; Miss. Choctaw; F; S; Daughter; Yes
1550;   **Ben**, Wilson; m; 10; Miss. Choctaw; F; S; Orphan; Yes

1551;   Finis; m; 28; Miss. Choctaw; F; M; Head; Yes

Census of the ~~Miss. Choctaw~~ reservation of the **Choctaw Agency** jurisdiction, as of **April 30**, 19 **30**, taken by **R. J. Enochs**, Superintendent. Purchased Lands   MISSISSIPPI

KEY: Surname; Census Number; Given Name; Sex; Age at Last Birthday; Tribe; Degree of Blood; Marital Status; Relationship to Head of Family; At Jurisdiction Where Enrolled (Yes or No); (If No Where); Ward (Yes unless given otherwise.)

1552;   Nora; f; 23; Miss. Choctaw; F; M; Wife; Yes
1553;   Onie; f; 5; Miss. Choctaw; F; S; Daughter; Yes
1554;   Leona; f; 1; Miss. Choctaw; F; S; Daughter; Yes

1555;   John; m; 24; Miss. Choctaw; F; M; Head; Yes
1556;   Susiana; f; 16; Miss. Choctaw; F; M; Wife; Yes

1557;   Johnson; m; 65; Miss. Choctaw; F; Wd; Head; Yes

1558;   Gus; m; 57; Miss. Choctaw; F; M; Head; Yes
1559;   Rainey; f; 33; Miss. Choctaw; F; M; Wife; Yes
1560;   Hester; m; 3; Miss. Choctaw; F; S; Son; Yes
1561;   **Isaac**, Nannie; f; 12; Miss. Choctaw; F; S; Step-daughter; Yes
1562;   **Isaac**, Eunice; f; 10; Miss. Choctaw; F; S; Step-daughter; Yes
1563;   **Isaac**, Rosie; f; 6; Miss. Choctaw; F; S; Step-daughter; Yes
1564;   **Isaac**, Wilson; m; 17; Miss. Choctaw; F; S; Step-son; Yes

1565;   Gamblin; m; 30; Miss. Choctaw; F; M; Head; Yes
1566;   Ellen; f; 32; Miss. Choctaw; F; M; Wife; Yes
1567;   Dina; f; 18; Miss. Choctaw; F; S; Orphan; Yes
1568;   Mattie; f; 12; Miss. Choctaw; F; S; Daughter; Yes
1569;   G. C; m; 9; Miss. Choctaw; F; S; Son; Yes
1570;   Eula; f; 7; Miss. Choctaw; F; S; Daughter; Yes
1571;   Maurice; f; 6; Miss. Choctaw; F; S; Daughter; Yes
1572;   Marabelle; f; 1; Miss. Choctaw; F; S; Daughter; Yes
1573;   **York**, Lena Pearl; f; 15; Miss. Choctaw; F; S; Step-daughter; Yes

1574;   Ed; m; 59; Miss. Choctaw; F; M; Head; Yes
1575;   Panzie; f; 58; Miss. Choctaw; F; M; Wife; Yes

1576;   Joe; m; 61; Miss. Choctaw; F; M; Head; Yes
1577;   Adaline; f; 58; Miss. Choctaw; F; M; Wife; Yes
1578;   Nannie; f; 20; Miss. Choctaw; F; S; Grand-daughter; Yes

Census of the ~~Miss. Choctaw~~ reservation of the **Choctaw Agency** jurisdiction, as of **April 30**, 19**30**, taken by **R. J. Enochs**, Superintendent. Purchased Lands   MISSISSIPPI

KEY: Surname; Census Number; Given Name; Sex; Age at Last Birthday; Tribe; Degree of Blood; Marital Status; Relationship to Head of Family; At Jurisdiction Where Enrolled (Yes or No); (If No Where); Ward (Yes unless given otherwise.)

1579; Elias; m; 27; Miss. Choctaw; F; S; Head; Yes

1580; Jim; m; 52; Miss. Choctaw; F; M; Head; Yes
1581; Louisa; f; 50; Miss. Choctaw; F; M; Wife; Yes
1582; Tom; m; 28; Miss. Choctaw; F; S; Son; Yes
1583; Dennis; m; 26; Miss. Choctaw; F; S; Son; Yes
1584; Waggoner; m; 21; Miss. Choctaw; F; S; Son; Yes
1585; Deiley; f; 19; Miss. Choctaw; F; S; Daughter; Yes
1586; Dora; f; 18; Miss. Choctaw; F; S; Daughter; Yes
1587; Rosie; f; 17; Miss. Choctaw; F; S; Daughter; Yes
1588; Smith; m; 15; Miss. Choctaw; F; S; Son; Yes
1589; Woodrow Wilson; m; 10; Miss. Choctaw; F; S; Grand-son; Yes

1590; Edmon; m; 22; Miss. Choctaw; F; M; Head; Yes
1591; Sallie; f; 17; Miss. Choctaw; F; M; Wife; Yes
1592; John; m; 1; Miss. Choctaw; F; S; Son; Yes

1593; Elea; m; 29; Miss. Choctaw; F; M; Head; Yes
1594; Otis; f; 23; Miss. Choctaw; F; M; Wife; Yes
1595; Vanola; f; 10; Miss. Choctaw; F; S; Daughter; Yes
1596; Flora; f; 8; Miss. Choctaw; F; S; Daughter; Yes
1597; Kittie; f; 7; Miss. Choctaw; F; S; Daughter; Yes
1598; Bonnie; m; 5; Miss. Choctaw; F; S; Son; Yes

1599; Cohan; m; 32; Miss. Choctaw; F; M; Head; Yes
1600; Sis; f; 28; Miss. Choctaw; F; M; Wife; Yes
1601; Ancie; f; 12; Miss. Choctaw; F; S; Daughter; Yes
1602; Una; f; 10; Miss. Choctaw; F; S; Daughter; Yes
1603; Sallie; f; 7; Miss. Choctaw; F; S; Daughter; Yes
1604; Harrison; m; 5; Miss. Choctaw; F; S; Son; Yes
1605; A. J; m; 2; Miss. Choctaw; F; S; Son; Yes

1606; Hugh; m; 47; Miss. Choctaw; F; M; Head; Yes
1607; Mollie; f; 34; Miss. Choctaw; F; M; Wife; Yes

Census of the ~~Miss. Choctaw~~ reservation of the **Choctaw Agency** jurisdiction, as of **April 30**, 19**30**, taken by **R. J. Enochs**, Superintendent.   Purchased Lands   MISSISSIPPI

KEY: Surname; Census Number; Given Name; Sex; Age at Last Birthday; Tribe; Degree of Blood; Marital Status; Relationship to Head of Family; At Jurisdiction Where Enrolled (Yes or No); (If No Where); Ward (Yes unless given otherwise.)

1608; Thompson; m; 15; Miss. Choctaw; F; S; Son; Yes
1609; Clemon; m; 13; Miss. Choctaw; F; S; Son; Yes
1610; J. C; m; 9; Miss. Choctaw; F; S; Son; Yes
1611; Collins; m; 7; Miss. Choctaw; F; S; Son; Yes
1612; Lillie; f; 6; Miss. Choctaw; F; S; Daughter; Yes
1613; Walter; m; 5; Miss. Choctaw; F; S; Son; Yes
1614; Lola; f; 4; Miss. Choctaw; F; S Daughter; Yes

1615; Spinks, m; 40; Miss. Choctaw; F; M; Head; Yes
1616; Susie; f; 31; Miss. Choctaw; F; M; Wife; Yes
1617; Wilson; m; 11; Miss. Choctaw; F; S; Son; Yes
1618; Flennie; f; 8; Miss. Choctaw; F; S; Daughter; Yes

1619; Wesley M; m; 64; Miss. Choctaw; F; Wd; Head; Yes
1620; Meley; f; 6; Miss. Choctaw; F; S; Daughter; Yes
1621; John Banks; m; 3; Miss. Choctaw; F; S; Son; Yes
1622; Leighton; m; 6/12; Miss. Choctaw; F; S; Son; Yes

1623; Salum; m; 25; Miss. Choctaw; F; S; Head; Yes

WILSON

1624; John; m; 35; Miss. Choctaw; F; M; Head; Yes
1625; Eva; f; 28; Miss. Choctaw; F; M; Wife; Yes
1626; Silman; m; 11; Miss. Choctaw; F; S; Son; Yes
1627; Mollie; f; 9; Miss. Choctaw; F; S; Daughter; Yes
1628; Sidney; m; 8; Miss. Choctaw; F; S; Son; Yes
1629; Leo; m; 5; Miss. Choctaw; F; S; Son; Yes
1630; Edna; f; 1; Miss. Choctaw; F; S; Daughter; Yes
1631; Marth[sic]; f; 82; Miss. Choctaw; F; Wd; Mother; Yes

1632; Will; m; 42; Miss. Choctaw; F; M; Head; Yes
1633; Martha; f; 36; Miss. Choctaw; F; M; Wife; Yes
1634; Sammie; m; 9; Miss. Choctaw; F; S; Son; Yes

Census of the ~~Miss. Choctaw~~ reservation of the **Choctaw Agency** jurisdiction, as of **April 30**, 19 **30**, taken by **R. J. Enochs**, Superintendent. Purchased Lands   MISSISSIPPI

KEY: Surname; Census Number; Given Name; Sex; Age at Last Birthday; Tribe; Degree of Blood; Marital Status; Relationship to Head of Family; At Jurisdiction Where Enrolled (Yes or No); (If No Where); Ward (Yes unless given otherwise.)

1635; Linnie; f; 8; Miss. Choctaw; F; S; Daughter; Yes
1636; Louisiana; f; 7; Miss. Choctaw; F; S; Daughter; Yes
1637; R. L; m; 1; Miss. Choctaw; F; S; Son; Yes
1638; Jim; m; 1/12; Miss. Choctaw; F; S; Son; Yes

WISHORK

1639; Massey; m; 34; Miss. Choctaw; F; M; Head; Yes
1640; Alpha; f; 28; Miss. Choctaw; F; M; Wife; Yes
1641; Zelia; f; 9; Miss. Choctaw; F; S; Daughter; Yes
1642; Evelyn; f; 8; Miss. Choctaw; F; S; Daughter; Yes
1643; Nugar; m; 5; Miss. Choctaw; F; S; Son; Yes
1644; Lyn Presley; m; 1; Miss. Choctaw; F; S; Son; Yes

1645; Sampson; m; 66; Miss. Choctaw; F; Wd; Head; Yes

YORK

1646; Ben; m; 39; Miss. Choctaw; F; M; Head; Yes
1647; Louella; f; 45; Miss. Choctaw; F; M; Wife; Yes
1648; Elsie; f; 13; Miss. Choctaw; F; S; Daughter; Yes
1649; Hester; m; 8; Miss. Choctaw; F; S; Son; Yes

1650; Scott; m; 75; Miss. Choctaw; F; M; Head; Yes
1651; Celie; f; 80; Miss. Choctaw; F; M; Wife; Yes
1652; Burkley; m; 18; Miss. Choctaw; F; S; Grand-son; Yes

1653; Bennett; m; 40; Miss. Choctaw; F; M; Head; Yes
1654; Lacie; f; 22; Miss. Choctaw; F; M; Wife; Yes
1655; G. B; m; 4; Miss. Choctaw; F; S; Son; Yes
1656; Colie; f; 3; Miss. Choctaw; F; S; Daughter; Yes

1657; Necie; f; 42; Miss. Choctaw; F; Wd; Head; Yes
1658; Emmet; m; 26; Miss. Choctaw; F; S; Son; Yes

Census of the ~~Miss. Choctaw~~ reservation of the **Choctaw Agency** jurisdiction, as of **April 30**, 19 **30**, taken by **R. J. Enochs**, Superintendent. Purchased Lands   MISSISSIPPI

KEY: Surname; Census Number; Given Name; Sex; Age at Last Birthday; Tribe; Degree of Blood; Marital Status; Relationship to Head of Family; At Jurisdiction Where Enrolled (Yes or No); (If No Where); Ward (Yes unless given otherwise.)

1659; Boxter; m; 23; Miss. Choctaw; F; S; Son; Yes
1660; Addie; f; 21; Miss. Choctaw; F; S; Daughter; Yes
1661; Gasler; m; 18; Miss. Choctaw; F; S; Son; Yes
1662; Eunice; f; 16; Miss. Choctaw; F; S; Daughter; Yes
1663; Beaman; m; 13; Miss. Choctaw; F; S; Son; Yes

1664; **Box**, Ola; f; 16; Miss. Choctaw; F; S; Orphan; Yes
1665; **Box**, Eula; f; 7; Miss. Choctaw; F; S; Orphan; Yes
1666; **Box**, Mamie; f; 8; Miss. Choctaw; F; S; Orphan; Yes

Mississippi Choctaw Census

as of

April 1, 1931

taken by R. J. Enochs, Superintendent

Census of the **Mississippi Choctaw** reservation of the **Choctaw Agency** jurisdiction, as of **April 1**, 19**31**, taken by **R. J. Enochs**, Superintendent.

KEY; Surname; Census Number; Given Name; Sex; Age at Last Birthday; Tribe; Degree of Blood; Marital Status; Relationship to Head of Family; Last Census Roll Number; At Jurisdiction Where Enrolled (Yes, unless given otherwise)

ALEX

1; Cooper; m; 21; Miss. Choctaw; S; Head; 1

2; Lee; m; 51; Miss. Choctaw; M; Head; 2
3; Missie; f; 51; Miss. Choctaw; M; Wife; 3
4; Nelson; m; 8; Miss. Choctaw; S; Son; 4
5; **Dixon**, Lonie; f; 17; Miss. Choctaw; S; Step-dau; 5

ALLEN

6; Willis; m; 37; Miss. Choctaw; M; Head; 6
7; Bessie; f; 36; Miss. Choctaw; M; Wife; 7
8; Bob; m; 14; Miss. Choctaw; S; Son; 8
9; Sulum; m; 10; Miss. Choctaw; S; Son; 9
10; Maggie; f; 8; Miss. Choctaw; S; Dau; 10
11; Huston; m; 7; Miss. Choctaw; S; Son; 12
12; Nell; f; 6; Miss. Choctaw; S; Dau; 11
13; Willie; m; 3; Miss. Choctaw; F; S; Son; 13

14; Jim; m; 45; Miss. Choctaw; M; Head; 15
15; Manda; f; 47; Miss. Choctaw; M; Wife; 16
16; I. C.; f; 17; Miss. Choctaw; S; Dau; 17
17; Annie Mai; f; 17; Miss. Choctaw; S; Dau; 18
18; J. C.; m; 16; Miss. Choctaw; S; Son; 19
19; R. G.; m; 15; Miss. Choctaw; S; Son; 20
20; Will; m; 8; Miss. Choctaw; S; Son; 21

21; Joseph; m; 38; Miss. Choctaw; S; Head; 22

22; Lacey; m; 37; Miss. Choctaw; S; Head; 23

AMOS

Census of the **Mississippi Choctaw** reservation of the **Choctaw Agency** jurisdiction, as of **April 1**, 19**31**, taken by **R. J. Enochs**, Superintendent.

KEY; Surname; Census Number; Given Name; Sex; Age at Last Birthday; Tribe; Degree of Blood; Marital Status; Relationship to Head of Family; Last Census Roll Number; At Jurisdiction Where Enrolled (Yes, unless given otherwise)

23; Sebbie; f; 53; Miss. Choctaw; Wd; Head; 24

24; Albert; m; 27; Miss. Choctaw; S; Head; 25

25; Griffin; m; 43; Miss. Choctaw; M; Head; 26
26; Sallie; f; 39; Miss. Choctaw; M; Wife; 27
27; Beauty; f; 21; Miss. Choctaw; S; Dau; 28
28; Julia; f; 19; Miss. Choctaw; S; Dau; 29
29; John; m; 17; Miss. Choctaw; S; Son; 30
30; Land; m; 15; Miss. Choctaw; S; Son; 31
31; Fulton; m; 10; Miss. Choctaw; S; Son; 32
32; Floyed; m; 10; Miss. Choctaw; S; Son; 33
33; Mose; m; 9; Miss. Choctaw; S; Son; 34

34; Lampkin; m; 53; Miss. Choctaw; M; Head; 35
35; Ann; f; 53; Miss. Choctaw; M; Wife; 36
36; Bonnie; f; 20; Miss. Choctaw; S; Dau; 37
37; Lonie; f; 14; Miss. Choctaw; S; Dau; 38
38; **Isom**, Mary; f; 4; Miss. Choctaw; S; Grand-dau; 39

ANDERSON

39; Bob; m; 46; Miss. Choctaw; M; Head; 40
40; Ella; f; 43; Miss. Choctaw; M; Wife; 41
41; A. J.; m; 19; Miss. Choctaw; S; Son; 42
42; Chuty; f; 13; Miss. Choctaw; S; Dau; 43
43; Josephine; f; 9; Miss. Choctaw; S; Dau; 44
44; Sallie Mae; f; 6; Miss. Choctaw; S; Dau; 45
45; Burncie[sic]; f; 3; Miss. Choctaw; S; Dau; 46

46; John; m; 63; Miss. Choctaw; M; Head; 47
47; Sallie; f; 29; Miss. Choctaw; M; Wife; 48
48; J. C.; m; 6; Miss. Choctaw; S; Son; 49

Census of the **Mississippi Choctaw** reservation of the **Choctaw Agency** jurisdiction, as of **April 1**, 19**31**, taken by **R. J. Enochs**, Superintendent.

KEY; Surname; Census Number; Given Name; Sex; Age at Last Birthday; Tribe; Degree of Blood; Marital Status; Relationship to Head of Family; Last Census Roll Number; At Jurisdiction Where Enrolled (Yes, unless given otherwise)

49; Mattie; f; 61; Miss. Choctaw; Wd; Head; 51
50; Ike; m; 29; Miss. Choctaw; S; Son; 52
51; Vada; f; f; 25; Miss. Choctaw; S; Dau; 54

52; Evan; m; 27; Miss. Choctaw; M; Head; 53
53; Thelma; f; 15; Miss. Choctaw; M; Wife; 170

54; Roy; m; 35; Miss. Choctaw; M; Head; 56
55; Lonie; f; 31; Miss. Choctaw; M; Wife; 57
56; Frances B; f; 2; Miss. Choctaw; S; Dau; 58

57; Ollie; m; 45; 7/8; M; Head; 59
58; Kate; f; 50; Miss. Choctaw; M; Wife; 60
59; Grace; f; 8; 15/16; S; Dau; 61
60; Gimmie; f; 19; Miss. Choctaw; S; Step-dau; 62

61; Oliver; m; 45; Miss. Choctaw; M; Head; 63
62; Sallie; f; 38; Miss. Choctaw; M; Wife; 64
63; Hinton; m; 27; Miss. Choctaw; S; Son; 65
64; Lonie; f; 16; Miss. Choctaw; S; Dau; 66
65; Philipp[sic]; m; 12; Miss. Choctaw; S; Son; 67
66; Houston; m; 10; Miss. Choctaw; S; Son; 68
67; Lucille; f; 8; Miss. Choctaw; S; Dau; 69

68; Abel; m; 25; Miss. Choctaw; M; Head; 70
69; Nancy; f; 45; Miss. Choctaw; M; Wife; 71
70; **Farmer**, Allie; f; 15; Miss. Choctaw; S; Step-dau; 72
71; **Farmer**, Ella Mae; f; 9; Miss. Choctaw; S; Step-dau; 73
72; **Farmer**, Annie Mae; f; 7; Miss. Choctaw; S; Dau[sic]; 74

BELL

73; Hugh; m; 52; Miss. Choctaw; Wd; Father; 75
74; Viola; f; 19; Miss. Choctaw; S; Dau; 76

Census of the Mississippi Choctaw reservation of the Choctaw Agency jurisdiction, as of April 1, 19 31, taken by R. J. Enochs, Superintendent.

KEY; Surname; Census Number; Given Name; Sex; Age at Last Birthday; Tribe; Degree of Blood; Marital Status; Relationship to Head of Family; Last Census Roll Number; At Jurisdiction Where Enrolled (Yes, unless given otherwise)

   75;   Mamie; f; 5; Miss. Choctaw; S; Dau; 77

   76;   John; m; 41; Miss. Choctaw; M; Head; 78
   77;   Lillian; f; 41; Miss. Choctaw; M; Wife; 79
   78;   Hattie; f; 10; Miss. Choctaw; S; Dau; 80
   79;   Eva; f; 6; Miss. Choctaw; S; Dau; 81
   80;   Ola; f; 4; Miss. Choctaw; S; Dau; 82

   81;   Sallie; f; 41; Miss. Choctaw; Wd; Head; 83
   82;   Emma; f; 20; Miss. Choctaw; S; Dau; 84
   83;   Effie; f; 12; Miss. Choctaw; S; Dau; 85

   84;   Junus; m; 34; Miss. Choctaw; M; Head; 86
   85;   Winnie; f; 30; Miss. Choctaw; F[sic]; Wife; 87
   86;   Ronie; f; 14; Miss. Choctaw; S; Dau; 88
   87;   Woods; m; 11; Miss. Choctaw; S; Son; 89
   88;   Minnie; f; 9; Miss. Choctaw; S; Dau; 90
   89;   Edmond; m; 6; Miss. Choctaw; S; Son; 91
   90;   George; m; 4; Miss. Choctaw; S; Son; 92

   91;   Evan; m; 29; Miss. Choctaw; M; Head; 93
   92;   Willie; f; 19; Miss. Choctaw; M; Wife; 94
   93;   Homer; m; 4; Miss. Choctaw; S; Son; 95
   94;   Nancy L; f; 2; Miss. Choctaw; S; Dau; 96

   95;   Mack; m; 26; Miss. Choctaw; M; Head; 97
   96;   Lin; f; 17; Miss. Choctaw; M; Wife; 98
   97;   James; m; 3; Miss. Choctaw; S; Son; 99

   98;   Thompson; m; 33; Miss. Choctaw; M; Head; 100
   99;   Ellen; f; 33; Miss. Choctaw; M; Wife; 101
  100;   Frank King; m; 17; Miss. Choctaw; S; Son; 102

  101;   Nicholas; m; 31; Miss. Choctaw; M; Head; 103

Census of the **Mississippi Choctaw** reservation of the **Choctaw Agency** jurisdiction, as of **April 1**, 19**31**, taken by **R. J. Enochs**, Superintendent.

KEY; Surname; Census Number; Given Name; Sex; Age at Last Birthday; Tribe; Degree of Blood; Marital Status; Relationship to Head of Family; Last Census Roll Number; At Jurisdiction Where Enrolled (Yes, unless given otherwise)

102; Cleddie; f; 19; Miss. Choctaw; M; Wife; 104
103; Rubie; f; 1; Miss. Choctaw; S; Dau; 105

104; Amon; m; 29; Miss. Choctaw; M; Head; 106
105; Alice; f; 28; Miss. Choctaw; M; Wife; 107

106; Jim; m; 61; Miss. Choctaw; S; Alone; 108

107; Joe; m; 39; Miss. Choctaw; M; Head; 109
108; Susie; f; 31; Miss. Choctaw; M; Wife; 110
109; Tom; m; 11; Miss. Choctaw; S; Son; 111
110; Bill; m; 7; Miss. Choctaw; S; Son; 112
111; Henry; m; 5; Miss. Choctaw; S; Son; 113
112; Polly Ann; f; 3; Miss. Choctaw; S; Dau; 114
113; Sallie; f; 54; Miss. Choctaw; W; Mother-in-Law; 115

114; Boston; m; 46; Miss. Choctaw; M; Head; 116
115; Lela; f; 31; Miss. Choctaw; M; Wife; 117
116; Sopha; f; 23; Miss. Choctaw; S; Dau; 118
117; Ola; f; 21; Miss. Choctaw; S; Dau; 119
118; Effie; f; 19; Miss. Choctaw; S; Dau; 120
119; John; m; 9; Miss. Choctaw; S; Son; 121
120; Emma; f; 7; Miss. Choctaw; S; Dau; 122
121; Emmet; m; 6; Miss. Choctaw; S; Son; 123
122; Marshall; m; 1; Miss. Choctaw; S; Grandson; 124

123; Cornelius; m; 73; Miss. Choctaw; Wd; Head; 125
124; John; m; 24; Miss. Choctaw; S; Son; 126

125; Jim; m; 69; Miss. Choctaw; S; Alone; 127

126; Lish; m; 41; Miss. Choctaw; M; Head; 128
127; Martha; f; 36; Miss. Choctaw; M; Wife; 129
128; Willie; m; 16; Miss. Choctaw; S; Son; 130

Census of the **Mississippi Choctaw** reservation of the **Choctaw Agency** jurisdiction, as of **April 1**, 19**31**, taken by **R. J. Enochs**, Superintendent.

KEY; Surname; Census Number; Given Name; Sex; Age at Last Birthday; Tribe; Degree of Blood; Marital Status; Relationship to Head of Family; Last Census Roll Number; At Jurisdiction Where Enrolled (Yes, unless given otherwise)

129; Huston; m; 11; Miss. Choctaw; S; Son; 131
130; Minnie; f; 10; Miss. Choctaw; S; Dau; 132
131; Less C; m; 8; Miss. Choctaw; S; Son; 133
132; Gene D; m; 6; Miss. Choctaw; S; Son; 134
133; Jay; m; 4; Miss. Choctaw; S; Son; 135
134; Gaston; m; 22; Miss. Choctaw; S; Bro; 136

135; Bob; m; 21; Miss. Choctaw; M; Head; 137
136; Beneva; f; 20; Miss. Choctaw; M; Wife; 138
137; Sadie; f; 1; Miss. Choctaw; S; Dau; 139

138; Lish; m; 50; Miss. Choctaw; M; Head; 140
139; Maggie; f; 50; Miss. Choctaw; M; Wife; 141
140; Minnie; f; 23; Miss. Choctaw; S; Dau; 142
141; Lula; f; 15; Miss. Choctaw; S; Dau; 143
142; Tom; m; 25; Miss. Choctaw; S; Son; 144
143; Bob; m; 21; Miss. Choctaw; S; Son; 145
144; Basin; m; 6; Miss. Choctaw; S; Son; 146

BEN

145; Olan; m; 31; Miss. Choctaw; M; Head; 147
146; Neva; f; 24; Miss. Choctaw; M; Wife; 148
147; Nannie Mae; f; 7; Miss. Choctaw; S; Dau; 149
148; Annie Laura; f; 5; Miss. Choctaw; S; Dau; 150
149; Mattie Lou; f; 3; Miss. Choctaw; S; Dau; 151
150; **Isaac**, Lessie; f; 18; Miss. Choctaw; S; Sister in Law; 152
151; **Isaac**, Coline; f; 12; Miss. Choctaw; S; Sister in Law; 153

152; Wyatt; m; 63; Miss. Choctaw; M; Head; 154
153; Ellen; f; 59; Miss. Choctaw; M; Wife; 155

154; Lula; f; 47; Miss. Choctaw; Wd; Head; 157
155; Jimpson; m; 25; Miss. Choctaw; S; Son; 156

Census of the **Mississippi Choctaw** reservation of the **Choctaw Agency** jurisdiction, as of **April 1**, 19 **31**, taken by **R. J. Enochs**, Superintendent.

KEY; Surname; Census Number; Given Name; Sex; Age at Last Birthday; Tribe; Degree of Blood; Marital Status; Relationship to Head of Family; Last Census Roll Number; At Jurisdiction Where Enrolled (Yes, unless given otherwise)

156; Otha; m; 17; Miss. Choctaw; S; Son; 158
157; Wilson; m; 14; Miss. Choctaw; S; Son; 159

158; Tom; m; 36; Miss. Choctaw; M; Head; 160
159; Gladys; f; 25; Miss. Choctaw; M; Wife; 161
160; Fannie Lou; f; 6; Miss. Choctaw; S; Dau; 162
161; Hubert; m; 4; Miss. Choctaw; S; Son; 163
162; Henry Ford; m; 2; Miss. Choctaw; S; Son; 164

163; Charlie; m; 32; Miss. Choctaw; M; Head; 165
164; Emeline; f; 24; Miss. Choctaw; M; Wife; 166

165; Jim; m; 55; Miss. Choctaw; Wd; Alone; 167
166; Monroe; m; 20; Miss. Choctaw; S[sic]; Head; 168
167; Lillie May; f; 20; Miss. Choctaw; M; Wife; 1484

BILLY

168; Lum; m; 46; Miss. Choctaw; M; Head; 171
169; Minnie; f; 48; Miss. Choctaw; M; Wife; 172
170; **Charles**, Jim; m; 33; Miss. Choctaw; S; Bro in Law; 173

171; Tom; m; 20; Miss. Choctaw; M; Head; 174
172; Sallie; f; 21; Miss. Choctaw; M; Wife; 175
173; Robert; m; 3; Miss. Choctaw; S; Son; 176
174; Jim; m; 3/12; Miss. Choctaw; S; Son

175; Will; m; 54; Miss. Choctaw; S; Alone; 177

176; Williston; m; 37; Miss. Choctaw; M; Head; 178
177; Jessie; f; 27; Miss. Choctaw; M; Wife; 179
178; Melton; m; 10; Miss. Choctaw; S; Son; 180
179; Beaman; m; 7; Miss. Choctaw; S; Son; 181
180; Maurice; m; 5; Miss. Choctaw; S; Son; 182

Census of the **Mississippi Choctaw** reservation of the **Choctaw Agency** jurisdiction, as of **April 1**, 19**31**, taken by **R. J. Enochs**, Superintendent.

KEY; Surname; Census Number; Given Name; Sex; Age at Last Birthday; Tribe; Degree of Blood; Marital Status; Relationship to Head of Family; Last Census Roll Number; At Jurisdiction Where Enrolled (Yes, unless given otherwise)

181; Horace; m; 4; Miss. Choctaw; S; Son; 183
182; Betty Jean; f; 3/12; Miss. Choctaw; S; Dau

183; Nicy; f; 71; Miss. Choctaw; Wd; Head; 184
184; Leona; f; 31; Miss. Choctaw; S; Dau; 185
185; Earl; f; 5; Miss. Choctaw; S; Grand dau; 186
186; Ike; m; 21; Miss. Choctaw; S; Son; 187

187; Augustan; m; 21; Miss. Choctaw; M; Head; 188
188; Louena; f; 21; Miss. Choctaw; M; Wife; 189

189; Johnson; m; 65; Miss. Choctaw; M; Head; 190
190; Belaria; f; 50; Miss. Choctaw; M; Wife; 191
191; Gipson; m; 20; Miss. Choctaw; S; Son; 192
192; Ike; m; 19; Miss. Choctaw; S; Son; 193
193; Maud; f; 18; Miss. Choctaw; S; Dau; 194
194; Wilson; m; 14; Miss. Choctaw; S; Son; 195
195; Greer; m; 12; Miss. Choctaw; S; Son; 196
196; Frank; m; 7; Miss. Choctaw; S; Son; 197
197; Phillip; m; 1; Miss. Choctaw; S; Grand-son; 198

198; Lewis; m; 26; Miss. Choctaw; M; Head; 199
199; Zelma; f; 26; Miss. Choctaw; M; Wife; 200
200; **Willis**, Clennie; f; 11; Miss. Choctaw; S; Step-dau; 201
201; **Willis**, Mamie; f; 9; Miss. Choctaw; S; Step-dau; 202
202; Frank; m; 5; Miss. Choctaw; S; Son; 203
203; Annie; f; 2; Miss. Choctaw; S; Dau; 204

204; Will; m; 43; Miss. Choctaw; M; Head; 205
205; Alice; f; 41; Miss. Choctaw; M; Wife; 206
206; William; m; 18; Miss. Choctaw; S; Son; 207
207; Lee; m; 15; Miss. Choctaw; S; Son; 208
208; Rosie; f; 12; Miss. Choctaw; S; Dau; 209
209; Irene; f; 9; Miss. Choctaw; S; Dau; 210

Census of the **Mississippi Choctaw** reservation of the **Choctaw Agency** jurisdiction, as of **April 1**, 19**31**, taken by **R. J. Enochs**, Superintendent.

KEY; Surname; Census Number; Given Name; Sex; Age at Last Birthday; Tribe; Degree of Blood; Marital Status; Relationship to Head of Family; Last Census Roll Number; At Jurisdiction Where Enrolled (Yes, unless given otherwise)

210; Joe; m; 8; Miss. Choctaw; S; Son; 211
211; Will, Jr; m; 4; Miss. Choctaw; S; Son; 212
212; Marchie; f; 3; Miss. Choctaw; S; Dau; 213
213; Charlie; m; 1; Miss. Choctaw; S; Son; 214

214; Jordon; m; 46; Miss. Choctaw; M; Head; 215
215; Lilly; f; 28; Miss. Choctaw; M; Wikfe[sic]; 216
216; Sallie Mae; f; 13; Miss. Choctaw; S; Dau; 217
217; Nellie; f; 10; Miss. Choctaw; S; Dau; 218
218; Jim; m; 5; Miss. Choctaw; S; Son; 219
219; Mary Lou; f; 3; Miss. Choctaw; S; Dau; 220
220; Paul; m; 9/12; Miss. Choctaw; S; Son

221; Richard; m; 20; Miss. Choctaw; M; Head; 221
222; Eva; f; 16; Miss. Choctaw; M; Wife; 222

223; Wade; m; 52; Miss. Choctaw; M; Head; 223
224; Lina; f; 34; Miss. Choctaw; M; Wife; 224
225; **McMillian**, Mary; f; 11; Miss. Choctaw; S; Step-dau; 225

BOB

226; Simon; m; 61; Miss. Choctaw; S; Alone; 226

BOX

227; Illiman; m; 25; Miss. Choctaw; M; Head; 227
228; Rosie; f; 19; Miss. Choctaw; M; Wife; 228

229; Lillie; f; 43; Miss. Choctaw; Wd; Head; 229
230; Ollie T.; m; 16; Miss. Choctaw; S; Son; 230
231; Bathie; f; 8; Miss. Choctaw; S; Dau; 231
232; Bethy; f; 6; Miss. Choctaw; S; Dau; 232
233; **Joe**, Emly; f; 71; Miss. Choctaw; Wd; Mother; 233

Census of the **Mississippi Choctaw** reservation of the **Choctaw Agency** jurisdiction, as of **April 1**, 19 **31**, taken by **R. J. Enochs**, Superintendent.

KEY; Surname; Census Number; Given Name; Sex; Age at Last Birthday; Tribe; Degree of Blood; Marital Status; Relationship to Head of Family; Last Census Roll Number; At Jurisdiction Where Enrolled (Yes, unless given otherwise)

234; Ola; f; 17; Miss. Choctaw; S; Orphan; 1664

BOYD

235; Archie; m; 67; Miss. Choctaw; M; Head; 234
236; Elizabeth; f; 71; Miss. Choctaw; M; Wife; 235

BRISCOE

237; Tom; m; 30; Miss. Choctaw; M; Head; 236
238; Lucy; f; 48; Miss. Choctaw; M; Wife; 237
239; **Polk**, Francis; m; 21; Miss. Choctaw; S; Nephew; 238

240; Stephens; m; 22; Miss. Choctaw; M; Head; 1002
241; Maggie; f; 23; Miss. Choctaw; M; Wife; 628

BULL

242; Pink; m; 53; Miss. Choctaw; M; Head; 239
243; Emma; f; 55; Miss. Choctaw; M; Wife; 240

244; George; m; 57; Miss. Choctaw; M; Head; 241
245; Sissy; f; 49; Miss. Choctaw; M; Wife; 242

246; Foreman; m; 28; Miss. Choctaw; M; Head; 243
247; Sarah; f; 27; Miss. Choctaw; M; Wife; 244

CAMPBELL

248; Wiley; m; 30; Miss. Choctaw; Wd; Alone; 245

CATES

249; Susan; f; 53; Miss. Choctaw; Wd; Head; 247

Census of the **Mississippi Choctaw** reservation of the **Choctaw** **Agency** jurisdiction, as of **April 1**, 19**31**, taken by **R. J. Enochs**, Superintendent.

KEY; Surname; Census Number; Given Name; Sex; Age at Last Birthday; Tribe; Degree of Blood; Marital Status; Relationship to Head of Family; Last Census Roll Number; At Jurisdiction Where Enrolled (Yes, unless given otherwise)

250; Enis; m; 26; Miss. Choctaw; S; Son; 248
251; Essie; f; 23; Miss. Choctaw; S; Dau; 249
252; John; m; 19; Miss. Choctaw; S; Son; 251
253; Lonie; f; 18; Miss. Choctaw; S; Dau; 252
254; Molpus; m; 17; Miss. Choctaw; S; Son; 253
255; Iona; f; 13; Miss. Choctaw; S; Dau; 254
256; John; m; 3; Miss. Choctaw; S; Grand-son; 250

257; Oscar; m; 21; Miss. Choctaw; S; Alone; 255

258; Alice; f; [?]; Miss. Choctaw; Wd; Head; 256
259; Dock; m; 29; Miss. Choctaw; S; Son; 257
260; Dee; m; 23; Miss. Choctaw; S; Son; 258

261; Ned; m; 33; Miss. Choctaw; M; Head; 259
262; Janie; f; 29; Miss. Choctaw; M; Wife; 260
263; Susan Mabel; f; 14; Miss. Choctaw; S; Dau; 261
264; Emma; f; 14; Miss. Choctaw; S; Dau; 262
265; Tubby; m; 13; Miss. Choctaw; S; Son; 263
266; Henry M; m; 11; Miss. Choctaw; S; Son; 264
267; Willie F; m; 8; Miss. Choctaw; S; Son; 265
268; Nannie; f; 6; Miss. Choctaw; S; Dau; 266
269; Julia; f; 5; Miss. Choctaw; S; Dau; 267

CHAPMAN

270; Will; m; 44; Miss. Choctaw; M; Head; 268
271; Bettie; f; 47; Miss. Choctaw; M; Wife; 269
272; Asa; m; 13; Miss. Choctaw; S; Son; 270
273; Ralston; m; 12; Miss. Choctaw; S; Son; 271
274; Hattie; f; 8; Miss. Choctaw; S; Dau; 272
275; Ronie; f; 7; Miss. Choctaw; S; Dau; 273
276; Lilly; f; 6; Miss. Choctaw; S; Dau; 274
277; Raymond; m; 5; Miss. Choctaw; S; Son; 275

Census of the **Mississippi Choctaw** reservation of the **Choctaw Agency** jurisdiction, as of **April 1**, 19**31**, taken by **R. J. Enochs**, Superintendent.

KEY; Surname; Census Number; Given Name; Sex; Age at Last Birthday; Tribe; Degree of Blood; Marital Status; Relationship to Head of Family; Last Census Roll Number; At Jurisdiction Where Enrolled (Yes, unless given otherwise)

278; Cris; m; 4; Miss. Choctaw; S; Son; 276
279; Minnie; f; 3; Miss. Choctaw; S; Dau; 277

CHARLIE

280; Onie; f; 45; Miss. Choctaw; Wd; Head; 278
281; Beamon; m; 16; Miss. Choctaw; S; Son; 279
282; Juanita; f; 11; Miss. Choctaw; S; Dau; 280
283; Charlie C; m; 9; Miss. Choctaw; S; Son; 281

284; William; m; 80; Miss. Choctaw; M; Head; 282
285; Fannie; f; 66; Miss. Choctaw; M; Wife; 283

286; John; m; 37; Miss. Choctaw; M; Head; 284
287; Mary; f; 29; Miss. Choctaw; M; Wife; 285
288; Elsie; f; 12; Miss. Choctaw; S; Dau; 286

CHICKAWAY

289; Sim; m; 33; Miss. Choctaw; M; Head; 287
290; Maggie; f; 30; Miss. Choctaw; M; Wife; 288
291; Clemon; m; 12; Miss. Choctaw; S; Son; 289
292; Nellie; f; 10; Miss. Choctaw; S; Dau; 290
293; Agnes; f; 8; Miss. Choctaw; S; Dau; 291
294; Albert; m; 5; Miss. Choctaw; D; Son; 292
295; Maggie Kate; f; 3; Miss. Choctaw; S; Dau; 293
296; Isabell; m[sic]; 69; Miss. Choctaw; Wd; Mother; 294
297; Ola; f; 24; Miss. Choctaw; S; Sister; 295

298; Jim; m; 28; Miss. Choctaw; M; Head; 296
299; Eunice; f; 25; Miss. Choctaw; M; Wife; 297
300; John Hester; m; 3; Miss. Choctaw; S; Son; 299
301; Henry; m; 3/12; Miss. Choctaw; S; Son
302; **Grant**, Rosie Lee; f; 9; Miss. Choctaw; S; Step-dau; 298

Census of the **Mississippi Choctaw** reservation of the **Choctaw** **Agency** jurisdiction, as of **April 1**, 19**31**, taken by **R. J. Enochs**, Superintendent.

KEY; Surname; Census Number; Given Name; Sex; Age at Last Birthday; Tribe; Degree of Blood; Marital Status; Relationship to Head of Family; Last Census Roll Number; At Jurisdiction Where Enrolled (Yes, unless given otherwise)

303; Kelly; m; 38; Miss. Choctaw; M; Head; 300
304; Lilla; f; 29; Miss. Choctaw; M; Wife; 301
305; Mikel; m; 8; Miss. Choctaw; S; Son; 302
306; Annah; f; 6; Miss. Choctaw; S; Dau; 303
307; Jane; f; 4; Miss. Choctaw; S; Dau; 304

308; Rufus; m; 29; Miss. Choctaw; M; Head; 305
309; Bessie; f; 26; Miss. Choctaw; M; Wife; 306
310; Ross C; m; 3; Miss. Choctaw; S Son; 307
311; Elizabeth; f; 1; Miss. Choctaw; S; Dau; 308

CHITTO

312; Joe; m; 31; Miss. Choctaw; M; Head; 309
313; Callie; f; 31; Miss. Choctaw; M; Wife; 310
314; Leo Clifton; m; 3; Miss. Choctaw; S; Son; 311

315; Pat; m; 54; Miss. Choctaw; Wd; Head; 314
316; Henrietta; f; 16; Miss. Choctaw; S; Dau; 315
317; Jefferson; m; 14; Miss. Choctaw; S; Son; 316
318; Erma; f; 9; Miss. Choctaw; S; Dau; 317
319; Isom; m; 7; Miss. Choctaw; S; Son; 318

320; John; m; 41; Miss. Choctaw; M; Head; 319
321; Sallie; f; 40; Miss. Choctaw; M; Wife; 320
322; Minnie; f; 20; Miss. Choctaw; S; Dau; 321
323; Hattie; f; 13; Miss. Choctaw; S; Dau; 322
324; Allie Nora; f; 11; Miss. Choctaw; S; Dau; 323
325; Ella; f; 9; Miss. Choctaw; S; Dau; 324
326; Lum Billy; m; 5; Miss. Choctaw; S; Son; 325

327; Laura; f; 63; Miss. Choctaw; Wd; Head; 327
328; Alyne; f; 21; Miss. Choctaw; S; Dau; 328

Census of the **Mississippi Choctaw** reservation of the **Choctaw Agency** jurisdiction, as of **April 1**, 19**31**, taken by **R. J. Enochs**, Superintendent.

KEY; Surname; Census Number; Given Name; Sex; Age at Last Birthday; Tribe; Degree of Blood; Marital Status; Relationship to Head of Family; Last Census Roll Number; At Jurisdiction Where Enrolled (Yes, unless given otherwise)

CLEMONS

329;   Phillip; m; 36; Miss. Choctaw; S; Alone; 329

330;   **Tubby**, Sam; m; 15; Miss. Choctaw; S; Orphan; 1416

CLEMONS or COWED

331;   Jim; m; 26; Miss. Choctaw; M; Head; 330
332;   Bessie; f; 24; Miss. Choctaw; M; Wife; 331
333;   Margie; f; 3; Miss. Choctaw; S; Dau; 332
334;   Lewisman; m; 1; Miss. Choctaw; S; Son; 333

CLARK

335;   Stella; f; 36; Miss. Choctaw; S; Alone; 334

CLEMONS

336;   Jeff; m; 34; Miss. Choctaw; M; Head; 335
337;   Cora; f; 30; Miss. Choctaw; M; Wife; 336
338;   Mattie; f; 9; Miss. Choctaw; S; Dau; 337
339;   Ethel; f; 8; Miss. Choctaw; S; Dau; 338
340;   Letha; f; 6; Miss. Choctaw; S; Dau; 339
341;   John; m; 5; Miss. Choctaw; S; Dau; 340
342;   Rena Mae; f; 3; Miss. Choctaw; S; Dau; 341

343;   Munch; m; 48; Miss. Choctaw; M; Head; 342
344;   Nellie; f; 40; Miss. Choctaw; M; Wife; 343
345;   Ruth; f; 13; Miss. Choctaw; S; Dau; 344
346;   Bathia; f; 12; Miss. Choctaw; S; Dau; 345
347;   Mollie; f; 10; Miss. Choctaw; S; Dau; 346

Census of the **Mississippi Choctaw** reservation of the **Choctaw Agency** jurisdiction, as of **April 1**, 19**31**, taken by **R. J. Enochs**, Superintendent.

KEY; Surname; Census Number; Given Name; Sex; Age at Last Birthday; Tribe; Degree of Blood; Marital Status; Relationship to Head of Family; Last Census Roll Number; At Jurisdiction Where Enrolled (Yes, unless given otherwise)

COMBY

348; Alma; f; 39; Miss. Choctaw; Wd; Head; 348
349; **McMillian**, Jimmie; m; 20; Miss. Choctaw; S; Son; 349
350; **McMillian**, Ella; f; 16; Miss. Choctaw; S; Dau; 351
351; **McMillian**, Jordan; m; 1; Miss. Choctaw; S; Grand-son; 352

353; Arbin; m; 43; Miss. Choctaw; Wd; Head; 353
354; Gilbert; m; 19; Miss. Choctaw; S; Son; 354
355; Rosella; f; 11; Miss. Choctaw; S; Dau; 355
356; Maudell; f; 8; Miss. Choctaw; S; Dau; 356

357; Seymour; m; 30; Miss. Choctaw; M; Head; 357
358; Edna; f; 25; Miss. Choctaw; M; Wife; 358
359; W. C; m; 9; Miss. Choctaw; S; Son; 359
360; B. C; m; 7; Miss. Choctaw; S; Son; 360
361; Leroy; m; 5; Miss. Choctaw; S; Son; 361

362; Allie; f; 26; Miss. Choctaw; Wd; Head; 363
363; Jones; m; 7; Miss. Choctaw; S; Son; 364
364; Irene; f; 5; Miss. Choctaw; S; Dau; 365
365; Joyce Ann; f; 3; Miss. Choctaw; S; Dau; 366
366; R. L.; m; 1; Miss. Choctaw; S; Son; 357
367; **Chitto**, Mary; f; 32; Miss. Choctaw; S; Sister; 368

368; Wallace; m; 59; Miss. Choctaw; M; Head; 369
369; Betty; f; 55; 55; Miss. Choctaw; M; Wife; 370
370; Lucy; f; 18; Miss. Choctaw; S; Dau; 371
371; Emma; f; 16; Miss. Choctaw; S; Dau; 372
372; Maggie; f; 14; Miss. Choctaw; S; Dau; 373
373; Tom; m; 10; Miss. Choctaw; S; Son; 374
374; Fulton; m; 7; Miss. Choctaw; S; Son; 375

375; Ben; m; 69; Miss. Choctaw; Wd; Alone; 376

Census of the **Mississippi Choctaw** reservation of the **Choctaw Agency** jurisdiction, as of **April 1**, 19**31**, taken by **R. J. Enochs**, Superintendent.

KEY; Surname; Census Number; Given Name; Sex; Age at Last Birthday; Tribe; Degree of Blood; Marital Status; Relationship to Head of Family; Last Census Roll Number; At Jurisdiction Where Enrolled (Yes, unless given otherwise)

376;   Olmon; m; 53; Miss. Choctaw; M; Head; 377
377;   Laura; f; 50; Miss. Choctaw; M; Wife; 378

COOPER

378;   Wixon; m; 30; Miss. Choctaw; M; Head; 379
379;   Leana; f; 23; Miss. Choctaw; M; Wife; 380

380;   Gaston; m; 45; Miss. Choctaw; M; Head; 381
381;   Ada; f; 47; Miss. Choctaw; M; Wife; 382
382;   Odell; f; 18; Miss. Choctaw; S; Dau; 383
383;   Fannie; f; 13; Miss. Choctaw; S; Day[sic]; 384
384;   Hubert; m; 10; Miss. Choctaw; S; Son; 385
385;   Christine; f; 7; Miss. Choctaw; S; Dau; 386
386;   Alma; f; 4; Miss. Choctaw; S; Dau; 387

COTTON

387;   John; m; 21; Miss. Choctaw; S; Alone; 388

388;   George; m; 31; Miss. Choctaw; M; Head; 389
389;   Ellen; f; 30; Miss. Choctaw; M; Wife; 390
390;   Minnie; f; 5; Miss. Choctaw; S; Dau; 391
391;   **Crenshaw**, Amos; m; 19; Miss. Choctaw; S; Orphan; 392
392;   **Crenshaw**, Austin; m; 15; Miss. Choctaw; S; Orphan; 393

DAN

393;   S. D; m; 25; Miss. Choctaw; M; Head; 394
394;   Lela; f; 23; Miss. Choctaw; M; Wife; 395
395;   Irene; f; 5; Miss. Choctaw; S; Dau; 396
396;   Albert B; m; 1; Miss. Choctaw; S; Son; 397

397;   Williston; m; 34; Miss. Choctaw; M; Head; 398

Census of the **Mississippi Choctaw** reservation of the **Choctaw Agency** jurisdiction, as of **April 1**, 19 **31**, taken by **R. J. Enochs**, Superintendent.

KEY; Surname; Census Number; Given Name; Sex; Age at Last Birthday; Tribe; Degree of Blood; Marital Status; Relationship to Head of Family; Last Census Roll Number; At Jurisdiction Where Enrolled (Yes, unless given otherwise)

398; Dinah; f; 19; Miss. Choctaw; M; Wife; 1567
399; Rose Ida; f; 9; Miss. Choctaw; S; Dau; 399

DANSBY

400; Jacob; m; 59; Miss. Choctaw; M; Head; 400
401; Jennie; f; 46; Miss. Choctaw; M; Wife; 401
402; **Tubby**, R. B; m; 24; Miss. Choctaw; S; Brother in-law; 402
403; **Tubby**, Jim; m; 58; Miss. Choctaw; S; Brother in-law; 403

DAVIS

404; Culberson; m; 69; Miss. Choctaw; M; Head; 404
405; Leona; f; 55; Miss. Choctaw; M; Wife; 405
406; Hobbie; m; 25; Miss. Choctaw; S; Son; 406

407; Will; m; 57; Miss. Choctaw; M; Head; 407
408; Mattie; f; 29; Miss. Choctaw; M; Wife; 408
409; Annie; f; 12; Miss. Choctaw; S; Dau; 409
410; John; m; 10; Miss. Choctaw; S; Son; 410
411; Mary; f; 3; Miss. Choctaw; S; Dau; 411
412; Mack; m; 2; Miss. Choctaw; S; Son; 412
413; Lewis; m; 6/12; Miss. Choctaw; S; Son

414; Sidney; m; 43; Miss. Choctaw; Wd; Head; 413
415; Elsmer; f; 22; Miss. Choctaw; S; Dau; 414
416; Mabel; f; 20; Miss. Choctaw; S; Dau; 415
417; Anna; f; 11; Miss. Choctaw; S; Dau; 416
418; Johnnie; m; 9; Miss. Choctaw; S; Son; 417

419; Malissie; f; 61; Miss. Choctaw; Wd; Head; 418
420; Alice; f; 34; Miss. Choctaw; S; Dau; 419
421; Bessie; f; 21; Miss. Choctaw; S; Dau; 420
422; Sina; f; 19; Miss. Choctaw; S; Grand-dau; 421

Census of the **Mississippi Choctaw** reservation of the **Choctaw Agency** jurisdiction, as of **April 1**, 19 **31**, taken by **R. J. Enochs**, Superintendent.

KEY; Surname; Census Number; Given Name; Sex; Age at Last Birthday; Tribe; Degree of Blood; Marital Status; Relationship to Head of Family; Last Census Roll Number; At Jurisdiction Where Enrolled (Yes, unless given otherwise)

423; Ada Francis; f; 11; Miss. Choctaw; S; Grand-dau; 422
424; Mary; f; 16; Miss. Choctaw; S; Grand-dau; 423

425; Tom; m; 31; Miss. Choctaw; M; Head; 424
426; Cilian; f; 30; Miss. Choctaw; M; Wife; 425
427; Millie; f; 11; Miss. Choctaw; S; Dau; 426
428; Henderson; m; 9; Miss. Choctaw; S; Son; 427

DENSON

429; Lilly; f; 43; Miss. Choctaw; Wd; Head; 428
430; Hendrix; m; 14; Miss. Choctaw; S; Son; 429
431; Emma; f; 11; Miss. Choctaw; S; Dau; 430
432; Charley; m; 8; Miss. Choctaw; S; Son; 431
433; David; m; 6; Miss. Choctaw; S; Son; 432

434; Pete; m; 43; Miss. Choctaw; M; Head; 433
435; Rosie; f; 30; Miss. Choctaw; M; Wife; 434
436; Mary; f; 15; Miss. Choctaw; S; Dau; 435
437; Jeffie; f; 13; Miss. Choctaw; S; Dau; 436
438; Edna; f; 8; Miss. Choctaw; S; Dau; 437
439; Nancy; f; 2; Miss. Choctaw; S; Dau; 439

440; Willis; m; 23; Miss. Choctaw; M; Head; 440
441; Beauty; f; 19; Miss. Choctaw; M; Wife; 441

442; Joe; m; 77; Miss. Choctaw; Wd; Head; 442
443; Winston; m; 17; Miss. Choctaw; S; Son; 443

444; Ezell; m; 19; Miss. Choctaw; M; Head; 958
445; Beauty; f; 19; Miss. Choctaw; M; Wife; 959
446; Ruth; f; 4/12; Miss. Choctaw; S; Dau

Census of the **Mississippi Choctaw** reservation of the **Choctaw Agency** jurisdiction, as of **April 1**, 19**31**, taken by **R. J. Enochs**, Superintendent.

KEY; Surname; Census Number; Given Name; Sex; Age at Last Birthday; Tribe; Degree of Blood; Marital Status; Relationship to Head of Family; Last Census Roll Number; At Jurisdiction Where Enrolled (Yes, unless given otherwise)

DIXON

447; Nannie; f; 51; Miss. Choctaw; Wd; Head; 445
448; **Sam**, Charlie; m; 16; Miss. Choctaw; S; Nephew; 446

449; Jim; m; 30; Miss. Choctaw; M; Head; 447
450; Sarah; f; 28; Miss. Choctaw; M; Wife; 448
451; Marie; f; 8; Miss. Choctaw; S; Dau; 449
452; Imogene; f; 5; Miss. Choctaw; S; Dau; 450
453; Ellen; f; 3; Miss. Choctaw; S; Dau; 451
454; Mable C; f; 7/12; Miss. Choctaw; S; Dau

455; Jess; m; 53; Miss. Choctaw; M; Head; 452
456; Callie; f; 61; Miss. Choctaw; M; Wife; 453
457; Scott; m; 20; Miss. Choctaw; S; Son; 454
458; Young; m; 14; Miss. Choctaw; S; Son; 456
459; Lilly; f; 11; Miss. Choctaw; S; Dau; 457
460; **Thompson**, Mary Jane; f; 81; Miss. Choctaw; Wd; Mother in-Law; 455

461; Horace; m; 25; Miss. Choctaw; M; Head; 458
462; Esther; f; 24; Miss. Choctaw; M; Wife; 459
463; Calonia; f; 4; Miss. Choctaw; S; Dau; 460

464; Edmond; m; 23; Miss. Choctaw; M; Head; 461
465; Julia; f; 22; Miss. Choctaw; M; Wife; 462
466; Addie May; f; 1; Miss. Choctaw; S; Dau; 463

467; Wilson; m; 72; Miss. Choctaw; M; Head; 464
468; Hope; f; 45; Miss. Choctaw; M; Wife; 465

469; Kanis; m; 39; Miss. Choctaw; Wd; Head; 466
470; Esby; f; 20; Miss. Choctaw; S; Dau; 467
471; Lonie; f; 17; Miss. Choctaw; S; Dau; 468

Census of the **Mississippi Choctaw** reservation of the **Choctaw Agency** jurisdiction, as of **April 1**, 19**31**, taken by **R. J. Enochs**, Superintendent.

KEY; Surname; Census Number; Given Name; Sex; Age at Last Birthday; Tribe; Degree of Blood; Marital Status; Relationship to Head of Family; Last Census Roll Number; At Jurisdiction Where Enrolled (Yes, unless given otherwise)

472; Jim; m; 26; Miss. Choctaw; S; Son; 469
473; Wade; m; 16; Miss. Choctaw; S; Son; 470

EVANS

474; John; m; 56; Miss. Choctaw; Wd; Head; 471
475; **Wickson**, Kelly; m; 6; Miss. Choctaw; S; Grand-son; 472

FARMER

476; Silmon; m; 57; Miss. Choctaw; Wd; Head; 473
477; Henry; m; 19; Miss. Choctaw; S; Son; 474
478; Bennie; f; 13; Miss. Choctaw; S; Dau; 475
479; Corine; f; 10; Miss. Choctaw; S; Dau; 476

480; Ishman; m; 86; Miss. Choctaw; M; Head; 477
481; Sweeter; f; 58; Miss. Choctaw; M; Wife; 478
482; Emma; f; 28; Miss. Choctaw; S; Dau; 479
483; Marshall; m; 26; Miss. Choctaw; S; Son; 480
484; Maggie; f; 21; Miss. Choctaw; S; Dau; 481
485; Lena; f; 18; Miss. Choctaw; S; Dau; 482
486; Bill; m; 15; Miss. Choctaw; S; Son; 483
487; Rainey; f; 11; Miss. Choctaw; S; Dau; 484

488; Moses; m; 31; Miss. Choctaw; M; Head; 485
489; Lottie; f; 23; Miss. Choctaw; M; Wife; 486
490; Mealie; f; 9/12; Miss. Choctaw; S; Dau

491; Thomas; m; 65; Miss. Choctaw; M; Head; 487
492; Melissa; f; 58; Miss. Choctaw; M; Wife; 488

493; Howard; m; 19; C; M; Head; 489
494; Lena; f; 17; Miss. Choctaw; M; Wife; 490

Census of the **Mississippi Choctaw** reservation of the **Choctaw Agency** jurisdiction, as of **April 1**, 19**31**, taken by **R. J. Enochs**, Superintendent.

KEY; Surname; Census Number; Given Name; Sex; Age at Last Birthday; Tribe; Degree of Blood; Marital Status; Relationship to Head of Family; Last Census Roll Number; At Jurisdiction Where Enrolled (Yes, unless given otherwise)

FARVE

495; Bennett; f; 38; Miss. Choctaw; S; Alone; 491

496; Paul; m; 43; Miss. Choctaw; M; Head; 492
497; Renia; f; 26; Miss. Choctaw; M; Wife; 493
498; Phillip, Jr; m; 7; Miss. Choctaw; S; Son; 494
499; Zula Mae; f; 5; Miss. Choctaw; S; Dau; 495
500; Estelle; f; 3; Miss. Choctaw; S; Dau; 496
501; Viola; f; 1; Miss. Choctaw; S; Dau; 497

502; Joseph S; m; 19; Miss. Choctaw; M; Head; 498
503; Rachel; f; 52; Miss. Choctaw; M; Wife; 499

504; Western; m; 41; Miss. Choctaw; Wd; Father; 500
505; Chester; m; 26; Miss. Choctaw; S; Son; 501
506; Josie; f; 23; Miss. Choctaw; S; Dau; 502
507; John; m; 23; Miss. Choctaw; S; Son; 503
508; Lillian; f; 20; Miss. Choctaw; S; Dau; 504
509; Ima; f; 15; Miss. Choctaw; S; Dau; 505
510; Hilda; f; 7; Miss. Choctaw; S; Dau; 506

511; Antwine; m; 54; Miss. Choctaw; M; Head; 507
512; Liseeda; f; 57; Miss. Choctaw; M; Wife; 508
513; Edna; f; 21; Miss. Choctaw; S; Dau; 509
514; Cecilia; f; 19; Miss. Choctaw; S; Dau; 510
515; Isileen; f; 18; Miss. Choctaw; S; Dau; 511
516; Earl; m; 13; Miss. Choctaw; S; Son; 512
517; Mamie; f; 11; Miss. Choctaw; S; Dau; 513
518; Corbrin; m; 8; Miss. Choctaw; S; Son; 514

519; Dave; m; 53; Miss. Choctaw; Wd; Head; 515
520; Lena; f; 31; Miss. Choctaw; S; Dau; 517
521; Sarah Alma; f; 20; Miss. Choctaw; S; Dau; 518

Census of the **Mississippi Choctaw** reservation of the **Choctaw Agency** jurisdiction, as of **April 1**, 19**31**, taken by **R. J. Enochs**, Superintendent.

KEY; Surname; Census Number; Given Name; Sex; Age at Last Birthday; Tribe; Degree of Blood; Marital Status; Relationship to Head of Family; Last Census Roll Number; At Jurisdiction Where Enrolled (Yes, unless given otherwise)

522; Georgia; f; 12; Miss. Choctaw; S; Dau; 519
523; John; m; 9; Miss. Choctaw; S; Son; 520

524; William; m; 30; Miss. Choctaw; M; Head; 516
525; Mary Lou; f; 14; Miss. Choctaw; M; Wife; 1206

526; Rosine H; m; 48; Miss. Choctaw; M; Head; 521
527; Winoa; f; 53; Miss. Choctaw; M; Wife; 522

528; Charles; m; 43; Miss. Choctaw; M; Head; 523
529; Edwina; f; 40; Miss. Choctaw; M; Wife; 524
530; Retha; f; 13; Miss. Choctaw; S; Dau; 525
531; Alvin; m; 11; Miss. Choctaw; S; Son; 526
532; Irvin; m; 9; Miss. Choctaw; S; Son; 527
533; Audrey; f; 6; Miss. Choctaw; S; Dau; 528
534; Vivian; f; 5; Miss. Choctaw; S; Dau; 529

535; Thomas; m; 49; Miss. Choctaw; M; Head; 530
536; Mary; f; 33; Miss. Choctaw; M; Wife; 531
537; Hazel; f; 13; Miss. Choctaw; S; Dau; 532
538; Robert; m; 12; Miss. Choctaw; S; Son; 533
539; Gertrude; f; 10; Miss. Choctaw; S; Dau; 534
540; Ruth; f; 7; Miss. Choctaw; S; Dau; 535

541; Sylvester; m; 43; Miss. Choctaw; S; Alone; 536

542; Joe Tole; m; 66; Miss. Choctaw; M; Head; 537
543; Lela; f; 63; Miss. Choctaw; M; Wife; 538
544; Dora; f; 38; Miss. Choctaw; S; Dau; 539
545; Victoria; f; 31; Miss. Choctaw; S; Dau; 540

546; Gilmore; m; 29; Miss. Choctaw; M; Head; 541
547; Gertrude; f; 27; Miss. Choctaw; M; Wife; 542

Census of the **Mississippi Choctaw** reservation of the **Choctaw Agency** jurisdiction, as of **April 1**, 19**31**, taken by **R. J. Enochs**, Superintendent.

KEY; Surname; Census Number; Given Name; Sex; Age at Last Birthday; Tribe; Degree of Blood; Marital Status; Relationship to Head of Family; Last Census Roll Number; At Jurisdiction Where Enrolled (Yes, unless given otherwise)

548; Joe; m; 25; Miss. Choctaw; M; Head; 543
549; Lillian; f; 22; Miss. Choctaw; M; Wife; 544;

550; Basie; m; 20; Miss. Choctaw; S; Alone; 545

551; Jessie; f; 19; Miss. Choctaw; S; Alone; 546

552; Corrine; m; 36; Miss. Choctaw; M; Head; 547
553; Viola; f; 34; Miss. Choctaw; M; Wife; 548
554; William; m; 15; Miss. Choctaw; S; Son; 549
555; Francis; m; 9; Miss. Choctaw; S; Son; 550
556; J. C; m; 7; Miss. Choctaw; S; Son; 551
557; Wilma; f; 5; Miss. Choctaw; S; Dau; 552

558; John Tole; m; 48; Miss. Choctaw; S; Alone; 553

559; Charles T; m; 47; Miss. Choctaw; M; Head; 554
560; Alfonsine; f; 33; Miss. Choctaw; M; Wife; 555

561; Emeline; f; 41; Miss. Choctaw; S; Alone; 556

562; Mary; f; 35; Miss. Choctaw; S; Alone; 557

563; Julia; f; 46; Miss. Choctaw; S; Alone; 558

564; R. C; m; 30; Miss. Choctaw; S; Alone; 559

565; Dennis; m; 43; Miss. Choctaw; S; Alone; 560

566; Western; m; 5 1; Miss. Choctaw; S; Alone; 561

567; Noah; m; 39; Miss. Choctaw; S; Alone; 562

568; Bennett; m; 37; Miss. Choctaw; S; Alone; 563

Census of the **Mississippi Choctaw** reservation of the **Choctaw Agency** jurisdiction, as of **April 1**, 19**31**, taken by **R. J. Enochs**, Superintendent.

KEY; Surname; Census Number; Given Name; Sex; Age at Last Birthday; Tribe; Degree of Blood; Marital Status; Relationship to Head of Family; Last Census Roll Number; At Jurisdiction Where Enrolled (Yes, unless given otherwise)

569; William; m; 33; Miss. Choctaw; S; Alone; 564

570; Seman; m; 65; Miss. Choctaw; Wd; Alone; 565

571; Elinor; f; 37; Miss. Choctaw; S; Alone; 566

572; Joe; m; 58; Miss. Choctaw; S; Alone; 567

573; Albert; m; 50; Miss. Choctaw; M; Head; 568
574; Iktial; f; 48; Miss. Choctaw; M; Wife; 569

575; Lucille; f; 28; Miss. Choctaw; S; Alone; 570

576; Ethel; f; 27; Miss. Choctaw; S; Alone; 571

577; Ida; f; 51; Miss. Choctaw; S; Alone; 572

578; Roselle; f; 55; Miss. Choctaw; S; Alone; 573

579; Amelia; f; 37; Miss. Choctaw; S; Alone; 574

580; Renrites; f; 33; Miss. Choctaw; S; Alone; 575

581; Bay Turner; m; 26; Miss. Choctaw; S; Alone; 576

582; Ceciline; m; 25; Miss. Choctaw; S; Alone; 577

583; Charles; m; 51; Miss. Choctaw; S; Alone; 578

FORBES

584; Wesley; m; 67; Miss. Choctaw; M; Head; 579
585; Sallie; f; 66; Miss. Choctaw; M; Wife; 580
586; Ella; f; 21; Miss. Choctaw; S; Dau; 581

Census of the **Mississippi Choctaw** reservation of the **Choctaw Agency** jurisdiction, as of **April 1**, 19**31**, taken by **R. J. Enochs**, Superintendent.

KEY; Surname; Census Number; Given Name; Sex; Age at Last Birthday; Tribe; Degree of Blood; Marital Status; Relationship to Head of Family; Last Census Roll Number; At Jurisdiction Where Enrolled (Yes, unless given otherwise)

587; Clint; m; 29; Miss. Choctaw; M; Head; 582
588; Josey; f; 30; Miss. Choctaw; M; Wife; 583
589; Ida Mae; f; 14; Miss. Choctaw; S; Dau; 584
590; Gaston; m; 9; Miss. Choctaw; S; Son; 585
591; Henry; m; 1; Miss. Choctaw; S; Son; 586

FRAZIER

592; Mollie; f; 56; Miss. Choctaw; Wd; Head; 587
593; Essie; f; 24; Miss. Choctaw; S; Dau; 588
594; John; m; 20; Miss. Choctaw; S; Son; 589

595; West; m; 23; Miss. Choctaw; M; Head; 590
596; Nannie; f; 22; Miss. Choctaw; M; Wife; 591
597; Marshall; m; 2; Miss. Choctaw; S; Son; 592

598; Forbes; m; 30; Miss. Choctaw; M; Head; 593
599; Iam; f; 26; Miss. Choctaw; M; Wife; 594
600; **Box**, Sam Davis; m; 7; Miss. Choctaw; S; Stepson; 595
601; Homer; m; 7; Miss. Choctaw; S; Son; 596

602; Will; m; 31; Miss. Choctaw; M; Head; 597
603; Lavena; f; 28; Miss. Choctaw; M; Wife; 598

604; Seale; m; 61; Miss. Choctaw; M; Head; 599
605; Eliza; f; 76; Miss. Choctaw; M; Wife; 600
606; Willie; f; 6; Miss. Choctaw; S; Grand-dau; 601

607; Jim; m; 25; Miss. Choctaw; M; Head; 602
608; Nannie; f; 27; Miss. Choctaw; M; Wife; 603
609; A. B; m; 4; Miss. Choctaw; S; Son; 604
610; Henry; m; 5; Miss. Choctaw; S; Son; 605
611; Nancy; f; 2; Miss. Choctaw; S; Dau; 606

Census of the Mississippi Choctaw reservation of the   Choctaw
 Agency   jurisdiction, as of   April 1   , 19 31 , taken
by R. J. Enochs , Superintendent.

KEY; Surname; Census Number; Given Name; Sex; Age at Last Birthday; Tribe; Degree of Blood; Marital Status; Relationship to Head of Family; Last Census Roll Number; At Jurisdiction Where Enrolled (Yes, unless given otherwise)

612; Ligman; m; 37; Miss. Choctaw; M; Head; 607
613; Sina; f; 22; Miss. Choctaw; M; Wife; 608
614; Edmon; m; 9; Miss. Choctaw; S; Son; 609
615; Sallie; f; 7; Miss. Choctaw; S; Dau; 610

616; Emma; f; 33; Miss. Choctaw; Wd; Head; 611
617; Susie; f; 15; Miss. Choctaw; S; Dau; 612
618; Simpson; m; 11; Miss. Choctaw; S; Dau; 613
619; Herman; m; 10; Miss. Choctaw; S; Son; 614
620; Frazier; m; 8; Miss. Choctaw; S; Son; 615
621; Velma; f; 6; Miss. Choctaw; S; Dau; 616

622; Henson; m; 63; Miss. Choctaw; M; Head; 617
623; Fenie; f; 61; Miss. Choctaw; M; Wife; 618
624; Lucy; f; 13; Miss. Choctaw; S; Dau; 619
625; Wade; m; 13; Miss. Choctaw; S; Nephew; 620
626; Jake; m; 9; Miss. Choctaw; S; Nephew; 621

GARDNER

627; Jim; m; 32; Miss. Choctaw; M; Head; 622
628; Celia; f; 27; Miss. Choctaw; M; Wife; 623
629; Arleta; f; 10; Miss. Choctaw; S; Dau; 624
630; Alton; m; 4; Miss. Choctaw; S; Son; 625

GIPSON

631; Bart; m; 55; Miss. Choctaw; M; Head; 626
632; Lucy; f; 51; Miss. Choctaw; M; Wife; 627
633; Homer; m; 18; Miss. Choctaw; S; Son; 629

634; Hensley; m; 20; Miss. Choctaw; M; Head; 630
635; Elizabeth; f; 20; Miss. Choctaw; M; Wife; 631

Census of the **Mississippi Choctaw** reservation of the **Choctaw Agency** jurisdiction, as of **April 1**, 19**31**, taken by **R. J. Enochs**, Superintendent.

KEY; Surname; Census Number; Given Name; Sex; Age at Last Birthday; Tribe; Degree of Blood; Marital Status; Relationship to Head of Family; Last Census Roll Number; At Jurisdiction Where Enrolled (Yes, unless given otherwise)

636; Andrew; m; 26; Miss. Choctaw; M; Head; 632
637; Esther; f; 18; Miss. Choctaw; M; Wife; 967

638; Gus; m; 22; Miss. Choctaw; S; Alone; 633

639; Nolie; m; 29; Miss. Choctaw; M; Head; 634
640; Frances; f; 31; Miss. Choctaw; M; Wife; 635
641; Houston; m; 6; Miss. Choctaw; S; Son; 636
642; Paul; m; 5; Miss. Choctaw; S; Son; 837
643; Annie; f; 2; Miss. Choctaw; S; Dau; 838

644; Steve; m; 67; Miss. Choctaw; M; Head; 839
645; Jennie; f; 63; Miss. Choctaw; M; Wife; 840
646; Ikey; f; 28; Miss. Choctaw; S; Dau; 643
647; Fannie; f; 23; Miss. Choctaw; S; Dau; 644
648; Annie; f; 22; Miss. Choctaw; S; Dau; 645
649; Willie; m; 13; Miss. Choctaw; S; Son; 642
650; Hugh; m; 5; Miss. Choctaw; S; Grand-son; 646
651; **(unknown)**, Aron; m; 4; Miss. Choctaw; S; Grand-son; 647

HALL

652; Bessie; f; 19; Miss. Choctaw; Wd; Head; 648
653; Henrietta; f; 3; Miss. Choctaw; S; 649
654; **Thomas**, Lula; f; 17; Miss. Choctaw; S; Sister; 650

655; Langford; m; 36; Miss. Choctaw; M; Head; 651
656; Lou; f; 26; Miss. Choctaw; M; Wife; 652
657; Travis; m; 8; Miss. Choctaw; S; Son; 653
658; Arlone; f; 7; Miss. Choctaw; S; Dau; 654
659; Frank; m; 5; Miss. Choctaw; S; Son; 655

HARPER

Census of the **Mississippi Choctaw** reservation of the **Choctaw Agency** jurisdiction, as of **April 1**, 19 **31**, taken by **R. J. Enochs**, Superintendent.

KEY; Surname; Census Number; Given Name; Sex; Age at Last Birthday; Tribe; Degree of Blood; Marital Status; Relationship to Head of Family; Last Census Roll Number; At Jurisdiction Where Enrolled (Yes, unless given otherwise)

660; Lena; f; 19; Miss. Choctaw; S; Alone; 656

HARRIS

661; Elsmore; f; 23; Miss. Choctaw; S; Alone; 657

HAWKINS

662; John; m; 71; Miss. Choctaw; M; Head; 658
663; Alice; f; 49; Miss. Choctaw; M; Wife; 659
664; **Shoemaker**, Mary; f; 20; Miss. Choctaw; S; Step-dau; 660
665; **Shoemaker**, Lester; f; 18; Miss. Choctaw; S; Step-dau; 661
666; **Lewis**, Mamie; f; 39; Miss. Choctaw; S; Sister-in-law; 662

HENRY

667; Albert; m; 53; Miss. Choctaw; M; Head; 663
668; Martha; f; 43; Miss. Choctaw; M; Wife; 664
669; Guiser; f; 27; Miss. Choctaw; S; Dau; 665
670; Beulah; f; 23; Miss. Choctaw; S; Dau; 667
671; Lige; m; 21; Miss. Choctaw; S; Son; 668
672; Melvin; m; 18; Miss. Choctaw; S; Son; 669
673; Nettie; f; 16; Miss. Choctaw; S; Dau; 670
674; Sis; f; 13; Miss. Choctaw; S; Dau; 671
675; Susie; f; 11; Miss. Choctaw; S; Dau; 672
676 R. D; m; 9; Miss. Choctaw; S; Son; 673
677; Ellen M; f; 2; Miss. Choctaw; S; Grand-dau; 666; Daughter of Guiser Henry

678; Jim; m; 28; Miss. Choctaw; M; Head; 674
679; Sallie; f; 26; Miss. Choctaw; M; Wife; 675
680; Frank; m; 4; Miss. Choctaw; S; Son; 676
681; Wicks; m; 2; Miss. Choctaw; S; Son; 677

Census of the **Mississippi Choctaw** reservation of the **Choctaw Agency** jurisdiction, as of **April 1**, 19**31**, taken by **R. J. Enochs**, Superintendent.

KEY; Surname; Census Number; Given Name; Sex; Age at Last Birthday; Tribe; Degree of Blood; Marital Status; Relationship to Head of Family; Last Census Roll Number; At Jurisdiction Where Enrolled (Yes, unless given otherwise)

682; Robert; m; 57; Miss. Choctaw; M; Head; 678
683; Nellie; f; 47; Miss. Choctaw; M; Wife; 679
684; Bob; m; 23; Miss. Choctaw; S; Son; 680
685; Mattie; f; 19; Miss. Choctaw; S; Dau; 681
686; Jasper; m; 14; Miss. Choctaw; S; Son; 682
687; Dolphus; m; 11; Miss. Choctaw; S; Son; 683

HICKMAN

688; Billy; m; 45; Miss. Choctaw; M; Head; 684
689; Rhodie; f; 47; Miss. Choctaw; M; Wife; 685
690; Sim; m; 19; Miss. Choctaw; S; Son; 687
691; Susan; f; 13; Miss. Choctaw; S; Dau; 688
692; Lula; f; 11; Miss. Choctaw; S; Dau; 689

693; Willie; m; 21; Miss. Choctaw; M; Head; 686
694; Lodie Mae; f; 23; Miss. Choctaw; M; Wife; 55

695; Ellis; m; 61; Miss. Choctaw; M; Head; 690
696; Susan; f; 55; Miss. Choctaw; M; Wife; 691
697; **Bell**, Burton; m; 11; Miss. Choctaw; S; Grand-son; 692
698; **Bell**, Henry; m; 9; Miss. Choctaw; S; Grand-son; 693

699; Johnkin; m; 31; Miss. Choctaw; M; Head; 694
700; Minnie; f; 26; Miss. Choctaw; M; Wife; 695

701; **Gipson**, Minnie; f; 18; Miss. Choctaw; S; Alone; 641

702; Enoch; m; 57; Miss. Choctaw; M; Head; 696
703; Malinda; f; 55; Miss. Choctaw; M; Wife; 697
704; Sallie; f; 21; Miss. Choctaw; S; Dau; 698
705; Sadie; f; 20; Miss. Choctaw; S; Dau; 699
706; Tubby; m; 18; Miss. Choctaw; S; Son; 700
707; Eliza Jane; f; 17; Miss. Choctaw; S; Dau; 701

Census of the **Mississippi Choctaw** reservation of the **Choctaw Agency** jurisdiction, as of **April 1**, 19 **31**, taken by **R. J. Enochs**, Superintendent.

KEY; Surname; Census Number; Given Name; Sex; Age at Last Birthday; Tribe; Degree of Blood; Marital Status; Relationship to Head of Family; Last Census Roll Number; At Jurisdiction Where Enrolled (Yes, unless given otherwise)

708; Mary Long; f; 15; Miss. Choctaw; S; Dau; 702
709; Annie; f; 10; Miss. Choctaw; S; Dau; 703
710; Wm. Penn; m; 9; Miss. Choctaw; S; Son; 704
711; Vardeman; m; 7; Miss. Choctaw; S; Son; 705
712; John; m; 6; Miss. Choctaw; S; Son; 706

713; Wallace; m; 25; Miss. Choctaw; M; Head; 707
714; Dona; f; 22; Miss. Choctaw; M; Wife; 708
715; Robinson; m; 5; Miss. Choctaw; S; Son; 709

716; Stennis; m; 27; Miss. Choctaw; M; Head; 710
717; Winnie; f; 26; Miss. Choctaw; M; Wife; 711
718; Eula; f; 4; Miss. Choctaw; S; Dau; 712
719; Snooks; m; 3; Miss. Choctaw; S; Son; 713

720; Mary; f; 75; Miss. Choctaw; Wd; Head; 714
721; **Charlie**, Beckie; f; 14; Miss. Choctaw; S; Grand-dau; 715

HUDSON

722; Celia; f; 24; Miss. Choctaw; S; Alone; 716

ISAAC

723; Jim; m; 36; Miss. Choctaw; M; Head; 717
724; Bessie; f; 30; Miss. Choctaw; M; Wife; 718
725; Steve; m; 76; Miss. Choctaw; Wd; Father; 719

726; Byrd; m; 35; Miss. Choctaw; M; Head; 720
727; Pauline; f; 19; Miss. Choctaw; M; Wife; 799
728; Odie Mae; f; 15; Miss. Choctaw; S; Dau; 721
729; Bernice; f; 13; Miss. Choctaw; S; Dau; 722
730; Catherine; f; 11; Miss. Choctaw; S; Dau; 723
731; Edwin; m; 4; Miss. Choctaw; S; Son; 724

Census of the **Mississippi Choctaw** reservation of the **Choctaw Agency** jurisdiction, as of **April 1**, 19**31**, taken by **R. J. Enochs**, Superintendent.

KEY; Surname; Census Number; Given Name; Sex; Age at Last Birthday; Tribe; Degree of Blood; Marital Status; Relationship to Head of Family; Last Census Roll Number; At Jurisdiction Where Enrolled (Yes, unless given otherwise)

732; **Hall**, Herbert H; m; 2; Miss. Choctaw; S; Son; 800

733; Hickman; m; 24; Miss. Choctaw; S; Alone; 725

734; Simon; m; 47; Miss. Choctaw; M; Head; 726
735; Nannie; f; 50; Miss. Choctaw; M; Wife; 727
736; Beaman; m; 18; Miss. Choctaw; S; Son; 728
737; Effi[sic]; f; 8; Miss. Choctaw; S; Dau; 729
738; Lillie Mae; f; 6; Miss. Choctaw; S; Grand-dau; 730

739; Hugh; m; 21; Miss. Choctaw; M; Head; 731
740; Celia; f; 22; Miss. Choctaw; M; Wife; 732
741; Veneda; f; 5/12; Miss. Choctaw; S; Dau

742; Isaac; m; 30; Miss. Choctaw; M; Head; 733
743; Maggie; f; 22; Miss. Choctaw; M; Wife; 734
744; Claudine; f; 9; Miss. Choctaw; S; Dau; 735
745; Wilbur; m; 7; Miss. Choctaw; S; Son; 736
746; Claud Preston; m; 3; Miss. Choctaw; S; Son; 737
747; Enochs; m; 2; Miss. Choctaw; S; Son; 738

748; Will; m; 33; Miss. Choctaw; M; Head; 739
749; Louisa; f; 32; Miss. Choctaw; M; Wife; 740
750; Annie; f; 13; Miss. Choctaw; S; Dau; 741
751; Cornelia; f; 4; Miss. Choctaw; S; Dau; 742

752; Wilson; m; 77; Miss. Choctaw; M; Head; 743
753; Martha; f; 64; Miss. Choctaw; M; Wife; 744
754; Jackson; m; 26; Miss. Choctaw; S; Son; 746
755; John Day; m; 17; Miss. Choctaw; S; Son; 745
756; **Sam**, Edna; f; 9; Miss. Choctaw; S; Orphan; 747

757; David; m; 24; Miss. Choctaw; M; Head; 748
758; Lesper; f; 23; Miss. Choctaw; M; Wife; 749

Census of the **Mississippi Choctaw** reservation of the **Choctaw Agency** jurisdiction, as of **April 1**, 19**31**, taken by **R. J. Enochs**, Superintendent.

KEY; Surname; Census Number; Given Name; Sex; Age at Last Birthday; Tribe; Degree of Blood; Marital Status; Relationship to Head of Family; Last Census Roll Number; At Jurisdiction Where Enrolled (Yes, unless given otherwise)

759; Joe Day; m; 4; Miss. Choctaw; S; Son; 750
760; Franklin; m; 2; Miss. Choctaw; S; Son; 751
761; Wansey; f; 1/12; Miss. Choctaw; S; Dau

762; Dixon; m; 79; Miss. Choctaw; M; Head; 752
763; Lou; f; 26; Miss. Choctaw; M; Wife; 753
764; Elsie; f; 13; Miss. Choctaw; S; Dau; 754
765; Rainey; f; 10; Miss. Choctaw; S; Dau; 755
766; Manda; f; 8; Miss. Choctaw; S; Dau; 756
767; Lester; f[sic]; 7; Miss. Choctaw; S; Dau; 757
768; **Billy**, Emma; f; 25; Miss. Choctaw; S; Sister-in-law; 758

ISOM

769; Willie; m; 17; Miss. Choctaw; S; Alone; 759
770; Isom; m; 31; Miss. Choctaw; S; Alone; 760

JACKSON

771; Betty; f; 55; Miss. Choctaw; Wd; Head; 761
772; Rosie; f; 19; Miss. Choctaw; S; Dau; 762
773; Nancie; f; 17; Miss. Choctaw; S; Dau; 763
774; Carlson; m; 11; Miss. Choctaw; S; Son; 764

775; Lena; f; 43; Miss. Choctaw; Wd; Head; 765
776; Gipson; m; 18; Miss. Choctaw; S; Son; 767
777; Ella; f; 17; Miss. Choctaw; S; Dau; 766
778; Floyd F; m; 16; Miss. Choctaw; S; Son; 768
779; Jackson; m; 13; Miss. Choctaw; S; Son; 769
780; Emmett; m; 11; Miss. Choctaw; S; Son; 770
781; Lucille; f; 10; Miss. Choctaw; S; Dau; 771

782; Tom; m; 43; Miss. Choctaw; Wd; Head; 772
783; Woodrow; m; 13; Miss. Choctaw; S; Son; 773

Census of the **Mississippi Choctaw** reservation of the **Choctaw Agency** jurisdiction, as of **April 1**, 19**31**, taken by **R. J. Enochs**, Superintendent.

KEY; Surname; Census Number; Given Name; Sex; Age at Last Birthday; Tribe; Degree of Blood; Marital Status; Relationship to Head of Family; Last Census Roll Number; At Jurisdiction Where Enrolled (Yes, unless given otherwise)

784; Eva; f; 12; Miss. Choctaw; S; Dau; 774

785; Sam; m; 47; Miss. Choctaw; M; Head; 775
786; Martha; f; 48; Miss. Choctaw; M; Wife; 776

787; Tubby; m; 21; Miss. Choctaw; M; Head; 777
788; Missie; f; 21; Miss. Choctaw; M; Wife; 778

789; Prentiss; m; 28; Miss. Choctaw; M; Head; 779
790; Mary; f; 28; Miss. Choctaw; M; Wife; 780

791; Mike; m; 30; Miss. Choctaw; S; Alone; 781

JEFFERSON

792; Braxton; m; 25; Miss. Choctaw; Wd; Head; 782
~~Addie; f; 21; Miss. Choctaw; S; Sister; 783~~
Reported under Addie Solomon

793; Amos; m; 24; Miss. Choctaw; M; Head; 784
794; Ida; f; 19; Miss. Choctaw; M; Wife; 785

795; Willis; m; 56; Miss. Choctaw; S; Head; 786
796; Elsie; f; 44; Miss. Choctaw; S; Sister; 787

797; Oscar; m; 26; Miss. Choctaw; M; Head; 788
798; Salina; f; 24; Miss. Choctaw; M; Wife; 789
799; Malcolm; m; 5; Miss. Choctaw; S; Son; 790

800; Otis; m; 28; Miss. Choctaw; M; Head; 791
801; Onie; f; 26; Miss. Choctaw; M; Wife; 792
802; Otto; m; 6; Miss. Choctaw; S; Son; 793
803; Andy; m; 5; Miss. Choctaw; S; Son; 794

Census of the **Mississippi Choctaw** reservation of the **Choctaw Agency** jurisdiction, as of **April 1**, 19**31**, taken by **R. J. Enochs**, Superintendent.

KEY; Surname; Census Number; Given Name; Sex; Age at Last Birthday; Tribe; Degree of Blood; Marital Status; Relationship to Head of Family; Last Census Roll Number; At Jurisdiction Where Enrolled (Yes, unless given otherwise)

JIM

804; George; m; 63; Miss. Choctaw; M; Head; 795
805; Eliza; f; 53; Miss. Choctaw; M; Wife; 796
806; Lee; m; 25; Miss. Choctaw; S; Son; 797
807; Sidney; m; 15; Miss. Choctaw; S; Son; 798
808; **Hall**, Pauline; f; 19; Miss. Choctaw; Wd; Niece; 799
809; **Hall**, Herbert H; m; 2; Miss. Choctaw; S; Grand-son; 800

810; Cooley; m; 61; Miss. Choctaw; M; Head; 801
811; Lorena; f; 33; Miss. Choctaw; M; Wife; 802
812; William; m; 10; Miss. Choctaw; S; Son; 803
813; Tom; m; 8; Miss. Choctaw; S; Son; 804

814; John; m; 25; Miss. Choctaw; M; Head; 805
815; Bessie; m; 22; Miss. Choctaw; M; Wife; 806
816; Susie Ann; f; 7/12; Miss. Choctaw; S; Dau

817; Henry; m; 46; Miss. Choctaw; M; Head; 807
818; Mollie; f; 59; Miss. Choctaw; M; Wife; 808

819; Harvey; m; 16; Miss. Choctaw; M; Head; 809
820; Mattie; f; 33; Miss. Choctaw; M; Wife; 810

821; Ben; m; 53; Miss. Choctaw; M; Head; 811
822; Dora; f; 41; Miss. Choctaw; M; Wife; 812
823; Annie Mae; f; 17; Miss. Choctaw; S; Dau; 813
824; Rena; f; 9; Miss. Choctaw; S; Dau; 814
825; Frank; m; 3; Miss. Choctaw; S; Grand-son; 815
826; Bobbie Sue; f; 2; Miss. Choctaw; S; Grand-son; 816

827; Logan; m; 83; Miss. Choctaw; Wd; Alone; 817

828; Amon; m; 54; Miss. Choctaw; M; Head; 818

Census of the **Mississippi Choctaw** reservation of the **Choctaw Agency** jurisdiction, as of **April 1**, 19**31**, taken by **R. J. Enochs**, Superintendent.

KEY; Surname; Census Number; Given Name; Sex; Age at Last Birthday; Tribe; Degree of Blood; Marital Status; Relationship to Head of Family; Last Census Roll Number; At Jurisdiction Where Enrolled (Yes, unless given otherwise)

829; Lucy; f; 46; Miss. Choctaw; M; Wife; 819
830; Opal; f; 11; Miss. Choctaw; S; Dau; 820
831; Carter; m; 2; Miss. Choctaw; S; Son; 821

832; Goodman; m; 66; Miss. Choctaw; M; Head; 823
833; Leona; f; 29; Miss. Choctaw; M; Wife; 824
834; Clifton; m; 10; Miss. Choctaw; S; Son; 825
835; Frank McKinley; m; 5; Miss. Choctaw; S; Son; 826
836; Claud Yates; m; 3; Miss. Choctaw; S; Son; 827
837; **Farmer**, Sallie; f; 76; Miss. Choctaw; Wd; Sister; 828

838; Albert; m; 24; Miss. Choctaw; M; Head; 829
839; Dora; f; 25; Miss. Choctaw; M; Wife; 830
840; Grace; f; 1; Miss. Choctaw; S; Dau; 831

841; Henry; m; 31; M; 30[sic]; Head; 832
842; Maggie; f; 37; Miss. Choctaw; M; Wife; 833

843; Victor; m; 30; Miss. Choctaw; M; Head; 834
844; Lena; f; 21; Miss. Choctaw; M; Wife; 835
845; Foy; m; 5; Miss. Choctaw; S; Son; 836
846; Egbert; m; 1; Miss. Choctaw; S; Son; 837

847; Winston; m; 21; Miss. Choctaw; S; Alone; 838

JIMMIE

848; Mary; f; 24; Miss. Choctaw; Wd; Head; 840
849; Ona C; f; 3; Miss. Choctaw; S; Dau; 841
850; Dolores; f; 1; Miss. Choctaw; S; Dau; 842
851; Frank M; m; 19; Miss. Choctaw; S; Bro; 843

852; Ike; m; 61; Miss. Choctaw; S; Alone; 844

Census of the **Mississippi Choctaw** reservation of the **Choctaw Agency** jurisdiction, as of **April 1**, 19 **31**, taken by **R. J. Enochs**, Superintendent.

KEY; Surname; Census Number; Given Name; Sex; Age at Last Birthday; Tribe; Degree of Blood; Marital Status; Relationship to Head of Family; Last Census Roll Number; At Jurisdiction Where Enrolled (Yes, unless given otherwise)

853; Mack; m; 25; Miss. Choctaw; S; Alone; 845

854; Will; m; 51; Miss. Choctaw; M; Head; 846
855; Hester; f; 49; Miss. Choctaw; M; Wife; 847
856; Homer; m; 22; Miss. Choctaw; S; Son; 848

JOE

857; Nicholas; m; 41; Miss. Choctaw; M; Head; 849
858; Ella; f; 36; Miss. Choctaw; M; Wife; 850
859; Austin; m; 17; Miss. Choctaw; S; Son; 851
860; Henry; m; 13; Miss. Choctaw; S; Son; 852
861; Widge; f; 10; Miss. Choctaw; S; Dau; 853
862; Bessie; f; 8; Miss. Choctaw; S; Dau;; 854
863; Billie Joe; m; 7; Miss. Choctaw; S; Son; 855
864; Mary; f; 1; Miss. Choctaw; S; Dau; 856
865; **Lewis**, Susie; f; 7; Miss. Choctaw; S; Step-dau; 857
866; **Lewis**, Elsie; f; 6; Miss. Choctaw; S; Step-dau; 858

867; Jasper; m; 43; Miss. Choctaw; M; Head; 859
868; Sallie; f; 38; Miss. Choctaw; M; Wife; 860
869; Lula; f; 18; Miss. Choctaw; S; Dau; 861
870; Houston; m; 13; Miss. Choctaw; S; Son; 862
871; Watkins; m; 9; Miss. Choctaw; S; Son; 863

872; Emily; f; 75; Miss. Choctaw; Wd; Alone; 864

873; John; m; 32; Miss. Choctaw; M; Head; 865
874; Emma; f; 31; Miss. Choctaw; M; Wife; 866
875; Bessie; f; 10; Miss. Choctaw; S; Dau; 867
876; Killie; f; 6; Miss. Choctaw; S; Dau; 868
877; Claud; f; 3; Miss. Choctaw; S; Son; 869

878; Langley; f; 83; Miss. Choctaw; Wd; Alone; 870

Census of the **Mississippi Choctaw** reservation of the **Choctaw Agency** jurisdiction, as of **April 1**, 19**31**, taken by **R. J. Enochs**, Superintendent.

KEY; Surname; Census Number; Given Name; Sex; Age at Last Birthday; Tribe; Degree of Blood; Marital Status; Relationship to Head of Family; Last Census Roll Number; At Jurisdiction Where Enrolled (Yes, unless given otherwise)

JOHN

879; Mike; m; 58; Miss. Choctaw; M; Head; 871
880; Lizzie; f; 73; Miss. Choctaw; M; Wife; 872
881; **Willis**, Dina; f; 17; Miss. Choctaw; S; Grand-dau; 873

882; Josh; m; 55; Miss. Choctaw; Wd; Alone; 874

883; Anderson; m; 54; Miss. Choctaw; M; Head; 875
884; Bettie; f; 42; Miss. Choctaw; M; Wife; 876
885; Sina; f; 19; Miss. Choctaw; S; Dau; 878
886; L. E; m; 16; Miss. Choctaw; S; Son; 879
887; Hubert; m; 15; Miss. Choctaw; S; Son; 880
888; Oden; m; 10; Miss. Choctaw; S; Son; 881
889; Wilson; m; 3; Miss. Choctaw; S; Son; 882

890; Bennett; m; 22; Miss. Choctaw; M; Head; 877
891; Lena Pearl; f; 16; Miss. Choctaw; M; Wife; 1573

892; Clint; m; 40; Miss. Choctaw; S; Alone; 883

893; Lue; m; 26; Miss. Choctaw; M; Head; 884
894; Leda; f; 18; Miss. Choctaw; M; Wife; 885
895; Macele; f; 7/12; Miss. Choctaw; S; Dau

896; Bob; m; 57; Miss. Choctaw; M; Head; 886
897; Onie; f; 46; Miss. Choctaw; M; Wife; 887
898; Oliver; m; 16; Miss. Choctaw; S; Son; 888
899; Otis; m; 14; Miss. Choctaw; S; Son; 889
900; Roby; m; 10; Miss. Choctaw; S; Son; 890
901; Rose; f; 8; Miss. Choctaw; S; Dau; 891

902; Jack; m; 57; Miss. Choctaw; M; Head; 892
903; Amanda; f; 36; Miss. Choctaw; M; Wife; 893

Census of the **Mississippi Choctaw** reservation of the **Choctaw Agency** jurisdiction, as of **April 1**, 19 **31**, taken by **R. J. Enochs**, Superintendent.

KEY; Surname; Census Number; Given Name; Sex; Age at Last Birthday; Tribe; Degree of Blood; Marital Status; Relationship to Head of Family; Last Census Roll Number; At Jurisdiction Where Enrolled (Yes, unless given otherwise)

904; Jefferson; m; 9; Miss. Choctaw; S; Son; 894
905; Mary; f; 7; Miss. Choctaw; S; Dau; 895
906; **Box**, Mamie; f; 9; Miss. Choctaw; S; Orphan; 1666

907; Betsie; f; 33; Miss. Choctaw; Wd; Head; 896
908; Belba; m; 14; Miss. Choctaw; S; Son; 897
909; Mable; f; 11; Miss. Choctaw; S; Dau; 898
910; Renie; f; 9; Miss. Choctaw; S; Dau; 899
911; Vardeman; m; 6; Miss. Choctaw; S; Son; 900
912; Smith; m; 4; Miss. Choctaw; s; Son; 901
913; Lisette H; f; 1; Miss. Choctaw; S; Dau; 902

JOHNSON

914; Quitman; m; 20; Miss. Choctaw; S; Alone; 903

915; Will; m; 59; Miss. Choctaw; M; Head; 904
916; Dixie; f; 37; Miss. Choctaw; M; Wife; 905
917; **Comby**, Venie; f; 15; Miss. Choctaw; S; Step-dau; 906
918; **Comby**, Gus; m; 6; Miss. Choctaw; S; Step-son; 907
919; Sallie; f; 76; Miss. Choctaw; Wd; Mother; 908

920; Afton; m; 27; Miss. Choctaw; M; Head; 909
921; Sevenia; f; 25; f; M; Wife; 910
922; Callie; f; 2; Miss. Choctaw; S; Dau; 911

923; Edgar; m; 32; Miss. Choctaw; M; Head; 912
924; Beatrice; f; 28; Miss. Choctaw; M; Wife; 913
925; Callie; f; 8; Miss. Choctaw; S; Dau; 914
926; Frances; f; 6; Miss. Choctaw; S; Dau; 915
927; Egbert; m; 4; Miss. Choctaw; S; Son; 916

928; Frank; m; 39; Miss. Choctaw; M; Head; 917
929; Lorine; f; 31; Miss. Choctaw; M; Wife; 918

Census of the **Mississippi Choctaw** reservation of the **Choctaw Agency** jurisdiction, as of **April 1**, 19**31**, taken by **R. J. Enochs**, Superintendent.

KEY; Surname; Census Number; Given Name; Sex; Age at Last Birthday; Tribe; Degree of Blood; Marital Status; Relationship to Head of Family; Last Census Roll Number; At Jurisdiction Where Enrolled (Yes, unless given otherwise)

930; Otha; m; 15; Miss. Choctaw; S; Son; 919
931; Athens; m; 13; Miss. Choctaw; S; Son; 920
932; Sadie; f; 11; Miss. Choctaw; S; Dau; 921
933; Bertha; f; 9; Miss. Choctaw; S; Dau; 922
934; Haven; m; 7; Miss. Choctaw; S; Son; 923
935; Sudan; f; 5; Miss. Choctaw; S; Dau; 924
936; Bena; f; 3; Miss. Choctaw; S; Dau; 925

JOSHUA

937; Jennie; f; 61; Miss. Choctaw; Wd; Head; 927
938; **John**, Callie; f; 20; Miss. Choctaw; S; Grand-dau; 928
939; **John**, Edison; m; 3; Miss. Choctaw; S; Grand-son; 929

KING

940; John W; m; 71; Miss. Choctaw; Wd; Head; 930
941; Mollie; f; 28; Miss. Choctaw; S; Dau; 931
942; Enos; m; 19; Miss. Choctaw; S; Son; 932
943; Varnam; m; 19; Miss. Choctaw; S; Son; 933
944; John Lee; m; 17; Miss. Choctaw; S; Great-nephew; 934
945; Lavenia; f; 12; Miss. Choctaw; S; Great-niece; 935

946; Clay I; m; 25; Miss. Choctaw; M; Head; 936
947; Alice; f; 29; Miss. Choctaw; M; Wife; 937

948; Betsie; f; 49; Miss. Choctaw; Wd; Head; 938
949; Christine; f; 21; Miss. Choctaw; S; Dau; 939
950; Jospeh[sic]; m; 14; Miss. Choctaw; S; Son; 940
951; Joe; m; 12; Miss. Choctaw; S; Son; 941
952; Barkum; m; 10; Miss. Choctaw; S; Son; 942

953; Banks; m; 26; Miss. Choctaw; M; Head; 943
954; Betsie; f; 35; Miss. Choctaw; M; Wife; 944

Census of the Mississippi Choctaw reservation of the Choctaw Agency jurisdiction, as of April 1 , 19 31 , taken by R. J. Enochs , Superintendent.

KEY; Surname; Census Number; Given Name; Sex; Age at Last Birthday; Tribe; Degree of Blood; Marital Status; Relationship to Head of Family; Last Census Roll Number; At Jurisdiction Where Enrolled (Yes, unless given otherwise)

LEBAN

955; Ben; m; 59; Miss. Choctaw; M; Head; 945
956; Lena; f; 58; Miss. Choctaw; M; Wife; 946
957; Mary; f; 30; Miss. Choctaw; S; Dau; 947

LEFLORE

958; John; m; 60; Miss. Choctaw; M; Head; 948
959; Emma; f; 51; Miss. Choctaw; M; Wife; 949
960; Richard Earl; m; 38; Miss. Choctaw; S; Son; 950
961; S. D; m; 25; Miss. Choctaw; S; Son; 951
962; Willie; f; 27; Miss. Choctaw; S; Dau; 952
963; Bertha Lee; f; 23; Miss. Choctaw; S; Dau; 953
964; John; m; 20; Miss. Choctaw; S; Son; 954
965; Lewis; m; 19; Miss. Choctaw; S; Son; 955

LEWIS

966; Jim; m; 63; Miss. Choctaw; M; Head; 956
967; Fannie; f; 41; Miss. Choctaw; M; Wife; 957

968; Adam; m; 26; Miss. Choctaw; M; Head; 960
969; Sillie; f; 25; Miss. Choctaw; M; Wife; 961
970; Nannie; f; 3; Miss. Choctaw; S; Dau; 962
971; Nammie; f; 1; Miss. Choctaw; S; Dau; 963
972; Tom; m; 5; Miss. Choctaw; S; Step-son; 964

973; Elon; m; 50; Miss. Choctaw; M; Head; 965
974; Lula; f; 53; Miss. Choctaw; M; Wife; 966
975; **Jefferson**, Nute; m; 15; Miss. Choctaw; S; Step-son; 968

976; Johnnie; m; 33; Miss. Choctaw; Wd; Head; 969
977; Marzine; f; 7; Miss. Choctaw; S; Dau; 970

Census of the **Mississippi Choctaw** reservation of the **Choctaw Agency** jurisdiction, as of **April 1**, 19**31**, taken by **R. J. Enochs**, Superintendent.

KEY; Surname; Census Number; Given Name; Sex; Age at Last Birthday; Tribe; Degree of Blood; Marital Status; Relationship to Head of Family; Last Census Roll Number; At Jurisdiction Where Enrolled (Yes, unless given otherwise)

978; Marshall; m; 56; Miss. Choctaw; M; Head; 971
979; Martha; f; 45; Miss. Choctaw; M; Wife; 972
980; Eliza; f; 16; Miss. Choctaw; S; Dau; 973
981; Belfa; f; 15; Miss. Choctaw; S; Dau; 974
982; Houston; m; 12; Miss. Choctaw; S; Son; 975
983; Lee; m; 10; Miss. Choctaw; S; Son; 976
984; Hodges; m; 4; Miss. Choctaw; S; Son; 978
985; Leon; m; 3; Miss. Choctaw; S; Son; 979
986; Lucille R; f; 1; Miss. Choctaw; S; Dau; 980
987; Betty; f; 7; Miss. Choctaw; S; Dau; 977

988; Joe; m; 57; Miss. Choctaw; Wd; Alone; 981

989; Reuben; m; 71; Miss. Choctaw; Wd; Head; 982
990; Amos; m; 18; Miss. Choctaw; S; Grand-son; 983

991; Lennis; m; 24; Miss. Choctaw; M; Head; 984
992; Ola; f; 19; Miss. Choctaw; M; Wife; 985
993; Nervie; f; 2; Miss. Choctaw; S; Dau; 986

994; Edd; m; 57; Miss. Choctaw; M; Head; 987
995; Edna; f; 49; Miss. Choctaw; M; Wife; 988
996; Hollis; m; 15; Miss. Choctaw; S; Son; 989

997; Albert; m; 37; Miss. Choctaw; M; Head; 990
998; Mollie; f; 34; Miss. Choctaw; M; Wife; 991
999; Indiana; f; 16; Miss. Choctaw; S; Dau; 992
1000; Bernice; f; 14; Miss. Choctaw; S; Dau; 993
1001; Eastland; m; 12; Miss. Choctaw; S; Son; 994
1002; Ivena; f; 10; Miss. Choctaw; S; Dau; 995

1003; Calvin; m; 51; Miss. Choctaw; Wd; Alone; 996

1004; Jim; m; 28; Miss. Choctaw; M; Head; 997

Census of the **Mississippi Choctaw** reservation of the **Choctaw Agency** jurisdiction, as of **April 1**, 19 **31**, taken by **R. J. Enochs**, Superintendent.

KEY; Surname; Census Number; Given Name; Sex; Age at Last Birthday; Tribe; Degree of Blood; Marital Status; Relationship to Head of Family; Last Census Roll Number; At Jurisdiction Where Enrolled (Yes, unless given otherwise)

1005; Jennie; f; 23; Miss. Choctaw; M; Wife; 998
1006; Jennie Lin; f; 2; Miss. Choctaw; S; Dau; 999

1007; Duffie; m; 35; Miss. Choctaw; M; Head; 1000
1008; Lilly; f; 51; Miss. Choctaw; M; Wife; 1001
1009; **Briscoe**, Jim; m; 16; Miss. Choctaw; S; Step-son; 1003
1010; **Briscoe**, Egbert; m; 8; Miss. Choctaw; S; Step-son; 1004
1011; **Farmer**, Henry; m; 20; Miss. Choctaw; S; Nephew; 1005
1012; **Wickson**, Ollie or Yates; m; 2; Miss. Choctaw; S; Nephew; 1006

MARTIN

1013; Willie; m; 41; Miss. Choctaw; M; Head; 1007
1014; Mary; f; 35; Miss. Choctaw; M; Wife; 1008
1015; Raymond; m; 11; Miss. Choctaw; S; Son; 1009
1016; Edmond J; m; 8; Miss. Choctaw; S; Son; 1010
1017; Phillip; m; 5; Miss. Choctaw; S; Son; 1011
1018; Annie Mae; f; 3; Miss. Choctaw; S; Dau; 1012
1019; Harry M; m; 1 mo; Miss. Choctaw; S; Son

1020; Ennis; m; 22; Miss. Choctaw; M; Head; 1013
1021; Nancy; f; 21; Miss. Choctaw; M; Wife; 1014
1022; Thomas; m; 6/12; Miss. Choctaw; S; Son
1023; **Alex**, Herbert F; m; 4; Miss. Choctaw; S; Step-son; 1015

McMILLEN

1024; Sorsby; m; 55; Miss. Choctaw; Wd; Head; 1016
1025; Mary; f; 17; Miss. Choctaw; S; Dau; 1017
1026; Emma; f; 16; Miss. Choctaw; S; Dau; 1018
1027; Clarence; m; 15; Miss. Choctaw; S; Son; 1019
1028; Bessie; f; 12; Miss. Choctaw; S; Dau; 1020
1029; Gipson; m; 7; Miss. Choctaw; S; Son; 1021
1030; Pauline; f; 3; Miss. Choctaw; S; Dau; 1022

Census of the **Mississippi Choctaw** reservation of the **Choctaw** **Agency** jurisdiction, as of **April 1**, 19**31**, taken by **R. J. Enochs**, Superintendent.

KEY; Surname; Census Number; Given Name; Sex; Age at Last Birthday; Tribe; Degree of Blood; Marital Status; Relationship to Head of Family; Last Census Roll Number; At Jurisdiction Where Enrolled (Yes, unless given otherwise)

1031; Lemmie; m; 21; Miss. Choctaw; M; Head; 1023
1032; Maggie. f; 22; Miss. Choctaw; M; Wife; 1024

1033; Cephus; m; 49; Miss. Choctaw; M; Head; 1025
1034; Mina; f; 37; Miss. Choctaw; M: Wife; 1026
1035; Anthony; m; 23; Miss. Choctaw; S; Son; 1027
1036; Mary; f; 18; Miss. Choctaw; S; Dau; 1028
1037; Willie; m; 15; Miss. Choctaw; S; Son; 1031
1038; Enochs; m; 3; Miss. Choctaw; S; Son; 1032
1039; **Billy**, Clemon; m; 17; Miss. Choctaw; S; Step-son; 1030

1040; Egbert; m; 30; Miss. Choctaw; M; Head; 1033
1041; Nola; f; 26; Miss. Choctaw; M; Wife; 1034
1042; A. J; m; 9; Miss. Choctaw; S; Son; 1035
1043; Odie Mae; f; 7; Miss. Choctaw; S; Dau; 1036
1044; John; m; 4; Miss. Choctaw; S; Son; 1037
1045; Mattie; f; 10/12; Miss. Choctaw; S; Dau

1046; Oscar; m; 37; Miss. Choctaw; M; Head; 1038
1047; Bennie; f; 32; Miss. Choctaw; M; Wife; 1039
1048; Arnold; m; 17; Miss. Choctaw; S; Son; 1040
1049; Leslie; f; 9; Miss. Choctaw; S; Dau; 1041
1050; Bert; m; 7; Miss. Choctaw; S; Son; 1042
1051; Frances; f; 5; Miss. Choctaw; S; Dau; 1043
1052; John; m; 2; Miss. Choctaw; S; Son; 1944

MINGO

1053; Rich; m; 26; Miss. Choctaw; M: Head; 1045
1054; Annie; f; 27; Miss. Choctaw; M; Wife; 1046
1055; Davidson; m; 8; Miss. Choctaw; S; Son; 1047
1056; Effie; f; 8; Miss. Choctaw; S; Dai; 1048

1057; John; m; 55; Miss. Choctaw; M; Head; 1049

Census of the **Mississippi Choctaw** reservation of the **Choctaw Agency** jurisdiction, as of **April 1**, 19**31**, taken by **R. J. Enochs**, Superintendent.

KEY; Surname; Census Number; Given Name; Sex; Age at Last Birthday; Tribe; Degree of Blood; Marital Status; Relationship to Head of Family; Last Census Roll Number; At Jurisdiction Where Enrolled (Yes, unless given otherwise)

1058; Hattie; f; 29; Miss. Choctaw; M; Wife; 1050
1059; Arch; m; 9; Miss. Choctaw; S; Son; 1051
1060; Odie; m; 6; Miss. Choctaw; S; Son; 1052
1061; Sister; f; 4; Miss. Choctaw; S; Dau; 1053
1062; Mary; f; 1; Miss. Choctaw; S; Dau; 1054

1063; Lilly; f; 53; Miss. Choctaw; Wd; Head; 1056
1064; Jim; m; 16; Miss. Choctaw; S; Son; 1057
1065; Olin; m; 13; Miss. Choctaw; S; Son; 1058
1066; Nettie; f; 10; Miss. Choctaw; S; Dau; 1059

1067; Oscar; m; 21; Miss. Choctaw; M; Head; 1060
1068; Linday; f; 26; Miss. Choctaw; M; Wife; 1061

MITCH

1069; Sarah; f; 47; Miss. Choctaw; Wd; Head; 1062
1070; Elea; m; 29; Miss. Choctaw; S; Son; 1063
1071; Divan; m; 27; Miss. Choctaw; S; Son; 1064
1072; Wilson; m; 25; Miss. Choctaw; S; Son; 1065
1073; Gilmore; m; 16; Miss. Choctaw; S; Son; 1066
1074; Annie; f; 11; Miss. Choctaw; S; Dau; 1067

MORRIS

1075; Rich; m; 24; Miss. Choctaw; M; Head; 1068
1076; Callie; f; 19; Miss. Choctaw; M; Wife; 1069
1077; Arwin; f; 4; Miss. Choctaw; S; Dau; 1070

1078; Julius; m; 29; Miss. Choctaw; M; Head; 1071
1079; Beauty; f; 26; Miss. Choctaw; M; Wife; 1072
1080; Eddie; f; 7; Miss. Choctaw; S; Dau; 1073
1081; Lena; f; 4; Miss. Choctaw; S; Dau; 1074
1082; Water[sic] Olin; m; 1; Miss. Choctaw; S; Son; 1075

Census of the **Mississippi Choctaw** reservation of the **Choctaw Agency** jurisdiction, as of **April 1**, 19 **31**, taken by **R. J. Enochs**, Superintendent.

KEY; Surname; Census Number; Given Name; Sex; Age at Last Birthday; Tribe; Degree of Blood; Marital Status; Relationship to Head of Family; Last Census Roll Number; At Jurisdiction Where Enrolled (Yes, unless given otherwise)

1083; Mosley; m; 65; Miss. Choctaw; M; Head; 1076
1084; Ida; f; 50; Miss. Choctaw; M; Wife; 1077
1085; Lilly; f; 31; Miss. Choctaw; S; Dau; 1078
1086; Sue; f; 29; Miss. Choctaw; Wd; Dau; 1079
1087; Wilson; m; 27; Miss. Choctaw; S; Son; 1080
1088; Joe; m; 10; Miss. Choctaw; S; Son; 1081
1089; **Wesley**, Rufus; m; 6; Miss. Choctaw; S; Grand-son; 1082

1090; Dempsey; m; 30; Miss. Choctaw; M; Head; 1083
1091; Janie; f; 29; Miss. Choctaw; M; Wife; 1084
1092; Ora; f; 10; Miss. Choctaw; S; Dau; 1085
1093; Vesney; m; 7; Miss. Choctaw; S; Son; 1086
1094; Davis; m; 5; Miss. Choctaw; S; Son; 1087
1095; Champs; m; 2; Miss. Choctaw; S; Son; 1088

1096; Sallie; f; 62; Miss. Choctaw; Wd; Head; 1089
1097; Seward; m; 30; Miss. Choctaw; S; Son; 1090

1098; Howard; m; 24; Miss. Choctaw; M; Head; 1091
1099; Bertie; f; 21; Miss. Choctaw; M; Wife; 1092
1100; Jimmie; m; 5; Miss. Choctaw; S; Son; 1093

1101; Huston; m; 25; Miss. Choctaw; M; Head; 1094
1102; Bertha; f; 23; Miss. Choctaw; M; Wife; 1095

1103; Boston; m; 28; Miss. Choctaw; M; Head; 1096
1104; Nola; f; 26; Miss. Choctaw; M; Wife; 1097

1105; Velma; f; 22; Miss. Choctaw; S; Alone; 1098

MOSES

1106; Alma; f; 20; Miss. Choctaw; S; Alone; 1099

Census of the **Mississippi Choctaw** reservation of the **Choctaw Agency** jurisdiction, as of **April 1**, 19**31**, taken by **R. J. Enochs**, Superintendent.

KEY; Surname; Census Number; Given Name; Sex; Age at Last Birthday; Tribe; Degree of Blood; Marital Status; Relationship to Head of Family; Last Census Roll Number; At Jurisdiction Where Enrolled (Yes, unless given otherwise)

1107; Allen; m; 25; Miss. Choctaw; M; Head; 1100
1108; Florence; f; 25; Miss. Choctaw; M; Wife; 1101

NICKEY

1109; Sam; m; 46; Miss. Choctaw; M; Head; 1102
1110; Malissie; f; 44; Miss. Choctaw; M; Wife; 1103
1111; Dora; f; 16; Miss. Choctaw; S; Dau; 1104
1112; Sherman; m; 9; Miss. Choctaw; S; Son; 1105
1113; Copeland; m; 3; Miss. Choctaw; S; Son; 1106

1114; Billy; m; 46; Miss. Choctaw; M; Head; 1107
1115; Fronie; f; 50; Miss. Choctaw; M; Wife; 1108
1116; Ode; f; 22; Miss. Choctaw; S; Dau; 1109
1117; Zelma; f; 19; Miss. Choctaw; S; Dau; 1110
1118; Hughie; m; 16; Miss. Choctaw; S; Son; 1111
1119; Zona; f; 14; Miss. Choctaw; S; Dau; 1112
1120; Cosette; m[sic]; 12; Miss. Choctaw; S; Dau; 1113
1121; Thomas; m; 8; Miss. Choctaw; S; Son; 1114

NOAH

1122; Elizabeth; f; 59; Miss. Choctaw; Wd; Head; 1115
1123; Celia; f; 31; Miss. Choctaw; S; Dau; 1116

1124; Lizzie; f; 41; Miss. Choctaw; Wd; Head; 1117
1125; Nancie; f; 15; Miss. Choctaw; S; Dau; 1118
1126; Annie; f; 12; Miss. Choctaw; S; Dau; 1119

NUBBY

1127; Billy; m; 71; Miss. Choctaw; M; Head; 1120
1128; Lilly; f; 51; Miss. Choctaw; M; Wife; 1121

Census of the **Mississippi Choctaw** reservation of the **Choctaw Agency** jurisdiction, as of **April 1**, 19**31**, taken by **R. J. Enochs**, Superintendent.

KEY; Surname; Census Number; Given Name; Sex; Age at Last Birthday; Tribe; Degree of Blood; Marital Status; Relationship to Head of Family; Last Census Roll Number; At Jurisdiction Where Enrolled (Yes, unless given otherwise)

PHILLIPS

1129; Riley; m; 35; Miss. Choctaw; Wd; Head; 1122
1130; Edmond; m; 4; Miss. Choctaw; S; Son; 1123
1131; Empsey; m; 2; Miss. Choctaw; S; Son; 1124

POLK

1132; Henry; m; 23; Miss. Choctaw; M; Head; 1125
1133; Susie; f; 29; Miss. Choctaw; M; Wife; 1126
1134; Eula; f; 2; Miss. Choctaw; S; Dau; 1127
1135; Hudson; m; 9/12; Miss. Choctaw; S; Son

1136; George; m; 69; Miss. Choctaw; Wd; Alone; 1128

1137; Josie; m; 50; Miss. Choctaw; M; Head; 1129
1138; Lennie; f; 51; Miss. Choctaw; M; Wife; 1130
1139; Ada; f; 13; Miss. Choctaw; S; Dau; 1131
1140; Frances; f; 13; Miss. Choctaw; S; Dau; 1132

1141; Tom; m; 53; Miss. Choctaw; Wd; Head; 1133
1142; Comelia; m; 21; Miss. Choctaw; S; Son; 1134
1143; Alma; f; 17; Miss. Choctaw; S; Dau; 1135
1144; Osborn; m; 15; Miss. Choctaw; S; Son; 1136

POULSON

1145; Allie; f; 58; Miss. Choctaw; S; Alone; 1137

1146; Frank; m; 31; Miss. Choctaw; M; Head; 1138
1147; Mary; f; 29; Miss. Choctaw; M; Wife; 1139

1148; Eddie M; m; 24; Miss. Choctaw; M; Head; 1140
1149; Cornelia; f; 27; Miss. Choctaw; M; Wife; 1141

Census of the __Mississippi Choctaw__ reservation of the ___Choctaw Agency___ jurisdiction, as of ___April 1___, 19_31_, taken by __R. J. Enochs__, Superintendent.

KEY; Surname; Census Number; Given Name; Sex; Age at Last Birthday; Tribe; Degree of Blood; Marital Status; Relationship to Head of Family; Last Census Roll Number; At Jurisdiction Where Enrolled (Yes, unless given otherwise)

1150; Julius; m; 24; Miss. Choctaw; S; Alone; 1142

1151; Johnnie; m; 22; Miss. Choctaw; S; Alone; 1143

1152; Charlie; m; 20; Miss. Choctaw; S; Alone; 1144

ROBINSON

1153; Thomas; m; 41; Miss. Choctaw; M; Head; 1145
1154; Syble; f; 36; Miss. Choctaw; M; Wife; 1146
1155; Jimmie; m; 17; Miss. Choctaw; S; Son; 1147
1156; Georgie; f; 15; Miss. Choctaw; S; Dau; 1148
1157; Sallie; f; 14; Miss. Choctaw; S; Dau; 1149
1158; Carl; m; 12; Miss. Choctaw; S; Son; 1150
1159; Mamie; f; 11; Miss. Choctaw; S; Dau; 1151
1160; Betsey; f; 9; Miss. Choctaw; S; Dau; 1152
1161; Homer; m; 7; Miss. Choctaw; S; Son; 1153
1162; Teach; m; 2; Miss. Choctaw; S; Son; 1154

1163; Belia; f; 24; Miss. Choctaw; Wd; Head; 1155
1164; Campbell; m; 4; Miss. Choctaw; S; So; 1156

RUTHERFORD

1165; Henrietta; f; 33; Miss. Choctaw; S; Alone; 1158

SAM

1166; Truman; m; 22; Miss. Choctaw; S; Alone; 1159

1167; Raymond; m; 50; Miss. Choctaw; S; Alone; 1160

1168; Oscar; m; 77; Miss. Choctaw; M; Head; 1161
1169; Mattie; f; 51; Miss. Choctaw; M; Wife; 1162

Census of the **Mississippi Choctaw** reservation of the **Choctaw Agency** jurisdiction, as of **April 1**, 19**31**, taken by **R. J. Enochs**, Superintendent.

KEY; Surname; Census Number; Given Name; Sex; Age at Last Birthday; Tribe; Degree of Blood; Marital Status; Relationship to Head of Family; Last Census Roll Number; At Jurisdiction Where Enrolled (Yes, unless given otherwise)

1170; Seer; f; 17; Miss. Choctaw; S; Grand-dau; 1163
1171; Lavada; f; 19; Miss. Choctaw; S; Grand-dau; 1164

1172; Jimpsey; m; 28; Miss. Choctaw; M; Head; 1165
1173; Lousiana[sic] Dan; f; 26; Miss. Choctaw; M; Wife; 822

1174; Walter; m; 41; Miss. Choctaw; Wd; Head; 1166
1175; Grace; f; 14; Miss. Choctaw; S; Dau; 1167
1176; Tom; m; 12; Miss. Choctaw; S; Son; 1168
1177; Edna; f; 9; Miss. Choctaw; S; Dau; omitted on roll, 1930
1178; Manzie; f; 7; Miss. Choctaw; S; Dau; 1169

1179; Fontain; m; 45; Miss. Choctaw; M; Head; 1170
1180; Emily; f; 41; Miss. Choctaw; M; Wife; 1171
1181; Leona; f; 9; Miss. Choctaw; S; Dau; 1172
1182; Ellis; m; 6; Miss. Choctaw; S; Son; 1173
1183; Fannie; f; 5; Miss. Choctaw; S; Dau; 1174
1184; Ella Ruth; f; 3; Miss. Choctaw; S; Dau; 1175
1185; Armond; m; 1; Miss. Choctaw; S; Son; 1176
1186; Beaman; m; 11; Miss. Choctaw; S; Nephew; 1177

1187; Willie; m; 32; Miss. Choctaw; M; Head; 1178
1188; Eva; f; 30; Miss. Choctaw; M; Wife; 1179
1189; Nettie; f; 10; Miss. Choctaw; S; Dau; 1180
1190; Abel; m; 9; Miss. Choctaw; S; Son; 1181
1191; Lonie; f; 7; Miss. Choctaw; S; Dau; 1182
1192; Grisaline; f; 1; Miss. Choctaw; S; Dau; 1183

SCOTT

1193; Marshall; m; 61; Miss. Choctaw; M; Head; 1184
1194; Lona; f; 26; Miss. Choctaw; M; Wife; 1185
1195; Rachel; f; 5; Miss. Choctaw; S; Dau; 1186

Census of the **Mississippi Choctaw** reservation of the **Choctaw Agency** jurisdiction, as of **April 1**, 19**31**, taken by **R. J. Enochs**, Superintendent.

KEY; Surname; Census Number; Given Name; Sex; Age at Last Birthday; Tribe; Degree of Blood; Marital Status; Relationship to Head of Family; Last Census Roll Number; At Jurisdiction Where Enrolled (Yes, unless given otherwise)

SHOEMAKER

1196; Alonzo; m; 43; Miss. Choctaw; M; Head; 1187
1197; Susan; f; 31; Miss. Choctaw; M; Wife; 1188
1198; Dempsey; m; 10; Miss. Choctaw; S; Son; 1189
1199; Layman; m; 8; Miss. Choctaw; S; Son; 1190
1200; Ruben; m; 5; Miss. Choctaw; S; Son; 1191
1201; Noleen; f; 2; Miss. Choctaw; S; Dau; 1192

1202; Buck; m; 46; Miss. Choctaw; M; Head; 1193
1203; Annie; f; 31; Miss. Choctaw; M; wife; 1194;
1204; Leona; f; 11; Miss. Choctaw; S; Dau; 1195
1205; Eliza; f; 9; Miss. Choctaw; S; Dau; 1196
1206; Martha; f; 7; Miss. Choctaw; S; Dau; 1197
1207; Daisy; f; 5; Miss. Choctaw; S; Dau; 1198
1208; Carrie Mae; f; 4; Miss. Choctaw; S; Dau; 1199
1209; Hubert; m; [?]; Miss. Choctaw; S; Son

SIMPSON

1210; John; m; 53; Miss. Choctaw; M; Head; 1200
1211; Sallie; f; 51; Miss. Choctaw; M; Wife; 1201
1212; Pauline; f; 15; Miss. Choctaw; S; Dau; 1202
1213; Celie; f; 13; Miss. Choctaw; S; Dau; 1203

SMITH

1214; George; m; 59; Miss. Choctaw; M; Head; 1204
1215; Mandy; f; 45; Miss. Choctaw; M; Wife; 1205
1216; **Farmer**, Lilly Kate; f; 11; Miss. Choctaw; S; Step-dau; 1207
1217; **Farmer**, Grace; f; 8; Miss. Choctaw; S; Step-dau; 1208

1218; Sebe; m; 41; Miss. Choctaw; M; Head; 1209
1219; Sinie; f; 40; Miss. Choctaw; M; Wife; 1210

Census of the **Mississippi Choctaw** reservation of the **Choctaw Agency** jurisdiction, as of **April 1**, 19**31**, taken by **R. J. Enochs**, Superintendent.

KEY; Surname; Census Number; Given Name; Sex; Age at Last Birthday; Tribe; Degree of Blood; Marital Status; Relationship to Head of Family; Last Census Roll Number; At Jurisdiction Where Enrolled (Yes, unless given otherwise)

1220; Sophie; f; 18; Miss. Choctaw; S; Dau; 1211
1221; Clemon; m; 12; Miss. Choctaw; S; Dan[sic]; 1212

1222; John Wesley; m; 56; Miss. Choctaw; M; Head; 1213
1223; Mary; f; 71; Miss. Choctaw; M; Wife; 1214

1224; Minnie; f; 36; Miss. Choctaw; Wd; Head; 1213
1225; Melton; m; 5; Miss. Choctaw; S; Son; 1216
1226; Elton; m; 3; Miss. Choctaw; S; Son; 1217
1227; **Stephens**, Phoeba; f; 11; Miss. Choctaw; S; Grand-dau; 1218

1228; Clay; m; 26; Miss. Choctaw; M; Head; 1219
1229; Mattie; f; 29; Miss. Choctaw; M; Wife; 1220

SOCKEY

1230; Irvin; m; 49; Miss. Choctaw; M; Head; 1221
1231; Lula; f; 36; Miss. Choctaw; M: Wife; 1222
1232; Benny; m; 23; Miss. Choctaw; S; Son; 1223
1233; Homer; m; 8; Miss. Choctaw; S; Son; 1224
1234; Ill; m; 3; Miss. Choctaw; S; Son; 1225

1235; Mike; m; 29; Miss. Choctaw; M; Head; 1226
1236; Nephus; f; 28; Miss. Choctaw; M; Wife; 1227
1237; Varelia; f; 9; Miss. Choctaw; S; Dau; 1228
1238; Odell; m; 7; Miss. Choctaw; S; Son; 1229
1239; Enochs; m; 4; Miss. Choctaw; S; Son; 1230

SOLOMON

1240; Willie; m; 47; Miss. Choctaw; Wd; Alone; 1232

1241; Marshall; m; 27; Miss. Choctaw; M; Head; 1233
1242; Addie; f; 22; Miss. Choctaw; M; Wife; 783

Census of the **Mississippi Choctaw** reservation of the **Choctaw Agency** jurisdiction, as of **April 1**, 19**31**, taken by **R. J. Enochs**, Superintendent.

KEY; Surname; Census Number; Given Name; Sex; Age at Last Birthday; Tribe; Degree of Blood; Marital Status; Relationship to Head of Family; Last Census Roll Number; At Jurisdiction Where Enrolled (Yes, unless given otherwise)

1243; Willie; m; 68; Miss. Choctaw; M; Head; 1234
1244; Winnie L; f; 26; Miss. Choctaw; M; Wife; 1235
1245; Mollie Lee; f; 2; Miss. Choctaw; S; Dau; 1236

1246; Raymond; m; 37; Miss. Choctaw; M: Head; 1237
1247; Bessie; f; 38; Miss. Choctaw; M; Wife; 1238
1248; Earnest; m; 15; Miss. Choctaw; S; Son; 1239
1249; Murphy; m; 12; Miss. Choctaw; S; Son; 1240
1250; Mollie; f; 9; Miss. Choctaw; S; Dau; 1241

STAR

1251; Lucy; f; 43; Miss. Choctaw; Wd; Alone; 1242

1252; Bill; m; 42; Miss. Choctaw; Wd; Head; 1243
1253; Summers; m; 15; Miss. Choctaw; S; Son; 1244
1254; Edna; f; 13; Miss. Choctaw; S; Dau; 1245
1255; Nannie; f; 10; Miss. Choctaw; S; Dau; 1246
1256; Mary; f; 8; Miss. Choctaw; S; Dau; 1247

STEPHENS

1257; Nathan; m; 28; Miss. Choctaw; M; Head; 1248
1258; Annie; f; 33; Miss. Choctaw; M; Wife; 1249
1259; Maxton; m; 6; Miss. Choctaw; S; Son; 1250
1260; Cutie Mae; f; 4; Miss. Choctaw; S; Dau; 1251
1261; Dorthy[sic] D; f; 3; Miss. Choctaw; S; Dau; 1252
1262; Bonnie B; f; 1; Miss. Choctaw; S; Dau; 1253

1263; Tom; m; 68; Miss. Choctaw; Wd; Head; 1254
1264; Silman; m; 36; Miss. Choctaw; S; Son; 1255
1265; Cornelia; f; 25; Miss. Choctaw; S; Dau; 1260
1266; Willie; m; 21; Miss. Choctaw; S; Son; 1259

Census of the **Mississippi Choctaw** reservation of the **Choctaw Agency** jurisdiction, as of **April 1**, 19 **31**, taken by **R. J. Enochs**, Superintendent.

KEY; Surname; Census Number; Given Name; Sex; Age at Last Birthday; Tribe; Degree of Blood; Marital Status; Relationship to Head of Family; Last Census Roll Number; At Jurisdiction Where Enrolled (Yes, unless given otherwise)

1267; Felix; m; 26; Miss. Choctaw; M; Head; 1256
1268; Martha; f; 23; Miss. Choctaw; M; Wife; 1257
1269; Martha Lee; f; 1; Miss. Choctaw; S; Dau; 1258

STEVE

1270; Murphy; m; 57; Miss. Choctaw; M; Head; 1261
1271; Patsy; f; 24; Miss. Choctaw; M; wife; 1262
1272; Helen; f; 4; Miss. Choctaw; S; Dau; 1263
1273; George; m; 1; Miss. Choctaw; S; Son; 1264
1274; Winston; m; 1; Miss. Choctaw; S; Son; 1265

1275; Josie; m; 29; Miss. Choctaw; M; Head; 1266
1276; Maggie; f; 22; Miss. Choctaw; M; Wife; 1267
1277; Ruby; f; 5; Miss. Choctaw; S; Dau; 1268
1278; Jane; f; 4; Miss. Choctaw; S; Dau; 1269

1279; Huston; m; 43; Miss. Choctaw; M; Head; 1270
1280; Lena; f; 39; Miss. Choctaw; M; Wife; 1271
1281; Ennis; m; 22; Miss. Choctaw; S; Son; 1272
1282; McKinley; m; 12; Miss. Choctaw; S; Son; 1273
1283; Yates; m; 8; Miss. Choctaw; S; Son; 1274
1284; Marabelle; f; 4; Miss. Choctaw; S; Dau; 1275

1285; Bobo; m; 24; Miss. Choctaw; M; Head; 1276
1286; Lucille; f; 19; Miss. Choctaw; M; Wife; 1277
1287; Maurice; f; 5; Miss. Choctaw; S; Dau; 1278
1288; Audrey; f; 3; Miss. Choctaw; S; Dau; 1279
1289; Vivian; f; 1; Miss. Choctaw; S; Dau; 1280

1290; Smith; m; 37; Miss. Choctaw; M; Head; 1281
1291; Winnie; f; 34; Miss. Choctaw; M; Wife; 1281
1292; Tonie; f; 11; Miss. Choctaw; S; Dau; 1283
1293; Pauline; f; 10; Miss. Choctaw; S; Dau; 1284

Census of the **Mississippi Choctaw** reservation of the **Choctaw Agency** jurisdiction, as of **April 1**, 19**31**, taken by **R. J. Enochs**, Superintendent.

KEY; Surname; Census Number; Given Name; Sex; Age at Last Birthday; Tribe; Degree of Blood; Marital Status; Relationship to Head of Family; Last Census Roll Number; At Jurisdiction Where Enrolled (Yes, unless given otherwise)

1294; Mollie; f; 6; Miss. Choctaw; S; Dau; 1285
1295; Aileen; f; 2; Miss. Choctaw; S; Dau; 1286

STOLIBY

1296; Missouri; f; 63; Miss. Choctaw; Wd; Head; 1287
1297; Tom; m; 28; Miss. Choctaw; S; Son; 1288
1298; Elum Ferum; m; 5; Miss. Choctaw; S; Grand-son; 1289

1299; John; m; 41; Miss. Choctaw; Wd; Head; 1290
1300; Nancy; f; 20; Miss. Choctaw; S; Dau; 1291
1301; Will Banks; m; 12; Miss. Choctaw; S; Son; 1292
1302; Otis; m; 10; Miss. Choctaw; S; Son; 1293
1303; Zona Miller; f; 6; Miss. Choctaw; S; Son; 1294

STRIBLING

1304; Malissie; f; 59; Miss. Choctaw; Wd; Alone; 1295

THOMAS

1305; Lewis; m; 47; Miss. Choctaw; M; Head; 1298
1306; Mamie; f; 44; Miss. Choctaw; M; Wife; 1299
1307; Newman; m; 12; Miss. Choctaw; S; Son; 1300
1308; Isaac; m; 8; Miss. Choctaw; S; Son; 1301
1309; Mina; f; 6; Miss. Choctaw; S; Dau; 1302

1310; George; m; 82; Miss. Choctaw; Wd; Alone; 1303

1311; Riley; m; 26; Miss. Choctaw; S; Alone; 1304

1312; Cleve; m; 28; Miss. Choctaw; M; Head; 1305
1313; Phoebe; f; 23; Miss. Choctaw; M; Wife; 1306

Census of the **Mississippi Choctaw** reservation of the **Choctaw Agency** jurisdiction, as of **April 1**, 19**31**, taken by **R. J. Enochs**, Superintendent.

KEY; Surname; Census Number; Given Name; Sex; Age at Last Birthday; Tribe; Degree of Blood; Marital Status; Relationship to Head of Family; Last Census Roll Number; At Jurisdiction Where Enrolled (Yes, unless given otherwise)

1314; Wilman; m; 31; Miss. Choctaw; M; Head; 1307
1315; Sallie; f; 30; Miss. Choctaw; M; Wife; 1308
1316; Woodrow; m; 12; Miss. Choctaw; S; Son; 1309
1317; Mollie; f; 10; Miss. Choctaw; S; Dau; 1310
1318; Golden; m; 8; Miss. Choctaw; S; Son; 1311
1319; Amos; m; 6; Miss. Choctaw; S; Son; 1312
1320; Single; m; 2; Miss. Choctaw; S; Son; 1313
1321; Linnie Helen; f; 6/12; Miss. Choctaw; S; Dau

1322; Lester; m; 22; Miss. Choctaw; M; Head; 1314
1323; Rosie; f; 20; Miss. Choctaw; M; Wife; 1315

1324; Rosie; f; 36; Miss. Choctaw; S; Alone; 1316

1325; Leona; f; 31; Miss. Choctaw; M; Wife *; 1317

1326; Evaline; f; 35; Miss. Choctaw; M; Wife *; 1318

* Leona and Evaline Thomas listed above are married to white men — no children.

THOMPSON

1327; Will; m; 27; Miss. Choctaw; M; Head; 1319
1328; Sina; f; 24; Miss. Choctaw; M; Wife; 1320
1329; Otis; m; 7; Miss. Choctaw; S; Son; 1321
1330; Claudine; f; 4; Miss. Choctaw; S; Dau; 1322
1331; Henry; m; 2; Miss. Choctaw; S; Son; 1323

1332; Cephus; m; 41; Miss. Choctaw; M: Head; 1324
1333; Amie; f; 26; Miss. Choctaw; M; Wife; 1325
1334; Dixon; m; 17; Miss. Choctaw; S; Son; 1326
1335; Farmer; m; 7; Miss. Choctaw; S; Son; 1327
1336; Alice; f; 6; Miss. Choctaw; S; Dau; 1328

Census of the **Mississippi Choctaw** reservation of the **Choctaw Agency** jurisdiction, as of **April 1**, 19**31**, taken by **R. J. Enochs**, Superintendent.

KEY; Surname; Census Number; Given Name; Sex; Age at Last Birthday; Tribe; Degree of Blood; Marital Status; Relationship to Head of Family; Last Census Roll Number; At Jurisdiction Where Enrolled (Yes, unless given otherwise)

1337; Annie; f; 3; Miss. Choctaw; S; Dau; 1329

1338; Malinda; f; 66; Miss. Choctaw; Wd; Head; 1330
1339; Beneva; f; 20; Miss. Choctaw; S; Dau; 1331

1340; Mose; m; 34; Miss. Choctaw; M; Head; 1332
1341; Jean; f; 35; Miss. Choctaw; M; Wife; 1333
1342; Jim; m; 11; Miss. Choctaw; S; Son; 1334
1343; Annie; f; 8; Miss. Choctaw; S; Dau; 1335
1344; Therman; m; 6; Miss. Choctaw; S; Son; 1336
1345; Steve; m; 4; Miss. Choctaw; S; Son; 1337

1346; John; m; 39; Miss. Choctaw; M; Head; 1338
1347; Lula; f; 37; Miss. Choctaw; M; Wife; 1339
1348; Moline; f; 10; Miss. Choctaw; S; Dau; 1340
1349; Onie; f; 9; Miss. Choctaw; S; Dau; 1341
1350; Tom; m; 4; Miss. Choctaw; S; Son; 1342

1351; Tommie; m; 32; Miss. Choctaw; M; Head; 1343
1352; Bonnie; f; 29; Miss. Choctaw; M; Wife; 1344
1353; Nathan; m; 6/12; Miss. Choctaw; S; Son

TUBBY

1354; Dan; m; 29; Miss. Choctaw; M; Head; 1345
1355; Lola; f; 35; Miss. Choctaw; M; Wife; 1346
1356; **Lewis**, Lum; m; 5; Miss. Choctaw; S; Step-son; 1347

1357; George; m; 23; Miss. Choctaw; M; Head; 1348
1358; Mary; f; 20; Miss. Choctaw; M; Wife; 1349
1359; Thomas; m; 2; Miss. Choctaw; S; Son; 1350
1360; Jennie; f; 13; Miss. Choctaw; S; Sister; 1351

1361; Lefus; m; 38; Miss. Choctaw; M; Head; 1352

Census of the **Mississippi Choctaw** reservation of the **Choctaw Agency** jurisdiction, as of **April 1**, 19**31**, taken by **R. J. Enochs**, Superintendent.

KEY; Surname; Census Number; Given Name; Sex; Age at Last Birthday; Tribe; Degree of Blood; Marital Status; Relationship to Head of Family; Last Census Roll Number; At Jurisdiction Where Enrolled (Yes, unless given otherwise)

1362; Frances; f; 31; Miss. Choctaw; M; Wife; 1353
1363; Ina; f; 9; Miss. Choctaw; S; Dau; 1354
1364; Irene; f; 7; Miss. Choctaw; S; Dau; 1355
1365; Leona; f; 4; Miss. Choctaw; S; Dau; 1356
1366; **Ben**, Rufus; m; 13; Miss. Choctaw; S; Step-son; 1357

1367; Sidney; m; 31; Miss. Choctaw; M; Head; 1358
1368; Kate; f; 30; Miss. Choctaw; M; Wife; 1359
1369; Rufus; m; 12; Miss. Choctaw; S; Son; 1360
1370; Phelia; f; 9; Miss. Choctaw; S; Dau; 1361
1371; Eva Kate; f; 6; Miss. Choctaw; S; Dau; 1362
1372; Edmon; m; 3; Miss. Choctaw; S; Son; 1363

1373; Annis; m; 52; Miss. Choctaw; M; Head; 1364
1374; Annie; f; 31; Miss. Choctaw; M; Wife; 1365

1375; Edgar; m; 31; Miss. Choctaw; M; Head; 1366
1376; Annie; f; 29; Miss. Choctaw; M; Wife; 1367
1377; Steve; m; 10; Miss. Choctaw; S; Son; 1368
1378; Willie; m; 9; Miss. Choctaw; S; Son; 1369
1379; Odie; m; 7; Miss. Choctaw; S; Soon; 1370
1380; Parline; f; 4; Miss. Choctaw; S; Dau; 1371

1381; Dick; m; 60; Miss. Choctaw; M; Head; 1372
1382; Eline; f; 51; Miss. Choctaw; M; Wife; 1373
1383; Jeff; m; 25; Miss. Choctaw; S; Nephew; 1374

1384; Allen; m; 75; Miss. Choctaw; M; Head; 3175[sic]
1385; Mary; f; 28; Miss. Choctaw; S; Dau; 1376
1386; Lilly; f; 26; Miss. Choctaw; S; Dau; 1377

1387; Pat; m; 37; Miss. Choctaw; M; Head; 1378
1388; Frances; f; 37; Miss. Choctaw; M: Wife; 1379
1389; Vernal; m; 19; Miss. Choctaw; S; Son; 1380

Census of the Mississippi Choctaw reservation of the Choctaw Agency jurisdiction, as of April 1, 19 31, taken by R. J. Enochs, Superintendent.

KEY; Surname; Census Number; Given Name; Sex; Age at Last Birthday; Tribe; Degree of Blood; Marital Status; Relationship to Head of Family; Last Census Roll Number; At Jurisdiction Where Enrolled (Yes, unless given otherwise)

1390; Earnest; m; 11; Miss. Choctaw; S; Son; 1381
1391; Loraine; f; 9; Miss. Choctaw; S; Dau; 1382
1392; Alice; f; 7; Miss. Choctaw; S; Dau; 1383
1393; Aileen; f; 4; Miss. Choctaw; S; Dau; 1384;

1394; Lysander; m; 43; Miss. Choctaw; M; Head; 1385
1395; Annie Mae; f; 22; Miss. Choctaw; M; Wife; 1386

1396; Moley; m; 28; Miss. Choctaw; M: Head; 1387;
1397; Sallie; f; 24; Miss. Choctaw; M; Wife; 1388

1398; Adam; m; 29; Miss. Choctaw; S; Alone; 1389

1399; Dewitt; m; 24; Miss. Choctaw; M; Head; 1390
1400; Katie; f; 25; Miss. Choctaw; M; Wife; 1391

1401; Rainey; f; 61; Miss. Choctaw; Wd; Head; 1392
1402; Lena; f; 31; Miss. Choctaw; S; Dau; 1393
1403; Mollie; f; 26; Miss. Choctaw; S; Dau; 1394
1404; Herbert; m; 23; Miss. Choctaw; S; Son; 1395

1405; Jimpson; m; 67; Miss. Choctaw; Wd; Alone; 1396

1406; Anderson; m; 31; Miss. Choctaw; M: Head; 1397
1407; Nancy; f; 21; Miss. Choctaw; M; Wife; 1398
1408; Jim; m; 7; Miss. Choctaw; S; Son; 1399
1409; Oscar; f; 5; Miss. Choctaw; S; Dau; 1400
1410; Buracy; f; 3; Miss. Choctaw; S; Dau; 1401
1411; Etoyle; f; 1; Miss. Choctaw; S; Dau; 1402

1412; Evan; m; 38; Miss. Choctaw; M: Head; 1403
1413; Jennie; f; 43; Miss. Choctaw; M; Wife; 1404
1414; Annie; f; 8; Miss. Choctaw; S; Dau; 1405

Census of the **Mississippi Choctaw** reservation of the **Choctaw Agency** jurisdiction, as of **April 1**, 19**31**, taken by **R. J. Enochs**, Superintendent.

KEY; Surname; Census Number; Given Name; Sex; Age at Last Birthday; Tribe; Degree of Blood; Marital Status; Relationship to Head of Family; Last Census Roll Number; At Jurisdiction Where Enrolled (Yes, unless given otherwise)

1415; Charlie; m; 35; Miss. Choctaw; M; Head; 1406
1416; Betsy; f; 30; Miss. Choctaw; M: Wife; 1407
1417; Alice; f; 8; Miss. Choctaw; S; Dau; 1408
1418; Jack; m; 6; Miss. Choctaw; S; Son; 1410
1419; J. C; m; 4; Miss. Choctaw; S; Son; 1411
1420; Colie; f; 2; Miss. Choctaw; S; Dau; 1412
1421; Kate; f; 10; Miss. Choctaw; S; Step-dau; 1409
1422; Ellis; m; 7; Miss. Choctaw; S; Orphan; 1413

1423; Henderson; m; 38; Miss. Choctaw; M; Head; 1414
1424; Maggie; f; 26; Miss. Choctaw; M; Wife; 1415
1425; Otis; f; 8; Miss. Choctaw; S; Dau; 1417
1426; W. C; m; 6; Miss. Choctaw; S; Son; 1418
1427; Gladys; f; 4; Miss. Choctaw; S; Dau; 1419
1428; Finis; m; 2; Miss. Choctaw; S; Son; 1420
1429; Martha Lee; f; 7/12; Miss. Choctaw; S; Dau

1430; Clemon; m; 56; Miss. Choctaw; M; Head; 1421
1431; Alice; f; 56; Miss. Choctaw; M; Wife; 1422
1432; **Bell**, Joe; m; 22; Miss. Choctaw; S; Step-son; 1423
1433; Lash; m; 5; Miss. Choctaw; S; Great-newphew[sic]; 1424
1434; Sarah; f; 4; Miss. Choctaw; S; Great-neice[sic]; 1425

1435; Jackson; m; 23; Miss. Choctaw; M; Head; 1426
1436; Mallissa; f; 24; Miss. Choctaw; M; Wife; 1427

1437; Nichols; m; 33; Miss. Choctaw; M; Head; 1428
1438; Esther; f; 28; Miss. Choctaw; M; Wife; 1429
1439; Sullivan; m; 9; Miss. Choctaw; S; Son; 1430
1440; Alice; f; 8; Miss. Choctaw; S; Dau; 1431
1441; Minnie; f; 6; Miss. Choctaw; S; Dau; 1432
1442; Catherine; f; 4; Miss. Choctaw; S; Dau; 1433

1443; Alice; f; 41; Miss. Choctaw; Wd; Head; 1434

Census of the **Mississippi Choctaw** reservation of the **Choctaw Agency** jurisdiction, as of **April 1**, 19**31**, taken by **R. J. Enochs**, Superintendent.

KEY; Surname; Census Number; Given Name; Sex; Age at Last Birthday; Tribe; Degree of Blood; Marital Status; Relationship to Head of Family; Last Census Roll Number; At Jurisdiction Where Enrolled (Yes, unless given otherwise)

1444; **Johnson**, Leo; m; 19; Miss. Choctaw; S; Son; 1435

1445; Tom; m; 22; Miss. Choctaw; M; Head; 1436
1446; Marceline; f; 24; Miss. Choctaw; M; wife; 1437
1447; Inis; m; 1; Miss. Choctaw; S; Son; 1438
1448; Joseph; m; 3; Miss. Choctaw; S; Step-son; 1439

1449; Anderson; m; 39; Miss. Choctaw; M; Head; 1440
1450; Louisiana; f; 41; Miss. Choctaw; M; Wife; 1441
1451; Hazel; f; 17; Miss. Choctaw; S; Dau; 1442
1452; Smith; m; 15; Miss. Choctaw; S; Son; 1443
1453; Icy; f; 13; Miss. Choctaw; S; Dau; 1444
1454; John; m; 11; Miss. Choctaw; S; Son; 1445

1455; Simpson; m; 71; Miss. Choctaw; M; Head; 1446
1456; Minnie; f; 38; Miss. Choctaw; M; Wife; 1447
1457; Ike; m; 19; Miss. Choctaw; S; Son; 1448
1458; Henry; m; 18; Miss. Choctaw; S; Son; 1449
1459; Eva; f; 17; Miss. Choctaw; S; Dau; 1450
1460; Lewis; m; 14; Miss. Choctaw; S; Son; 1451
1461; McKinley; m; 11; Miss. Choctaw; S; Son; 1452
1462; Hudson; m; 8; Miss. Choctaw; S; Son; 1453
1463; Sullivan; m; 7; Miss. Choctaw; S; Son; 1454
1464; Callie; f; 5; Miss. Choctaw; S; Dau; 1455
1465; Nellie; f; 4; Miss. Choctaw; S; Dau; 1456

TUCKALLOO

1466; Frances; f; 68; Miss. Choctaw; Wd; Head; 1457
1467; **Tubby**, Wesley; m; 12; Miss. Choctaw; S; Grand-son; 1458
1468; Mason; m; 17; Miss. Choctaw; S; Grand-son; 1459
1469; Enia; m; 7; Miss. Choctaw; S; Grand-son; 1460
1470; Alice; f; 6; Miss. Choctaw; S; Grand-dau; 1461
1471; Sarah; f; 5; Miss. Choctaw; S; Grand-dau; 1462

Census of the **Mississippi Choctaw** reservation of the **Choctaw Agency** jurisdiction, as of **April 1**, 19**31**, taken by **R. J. Enochs**, Superintendent.

KEY; Surname; Census Number; Given Name; Sex; Age at Last Birthday; Tribe; Degree of Blood; Marital Status; Relationship to Head of Family; Last Census Roll Number; At Jurisdiction Where Enrolled (Yes, unless given otherwise)

VAUGHN

1472; John; m; 66; Miss. Choctaw; Wd; Alone; 1463

1473; Greer; m; 56; Miss. Choctaw; M; Head; 1464
1474; Jane; f; 51; Miss. Choctaw; M; Wife; 1465
1475; Agnes; f; 5; Miss. Choctaw; S; Dau; 1466

1476; Cooksie; m; 66; Miss. Choctaw; M; Head; 1467
1477; Susan; f; 59; Miss. Choctaw; M; Wife; 1468
1478; Lena; f; 36; Miss. Choctaw; S; Dau; 1469
1479; Ludie; f; 24; Miss. Choctaw; S; Dau; 1470

1480; Silmon; m; 19; Miss. Choctaw; M; Head; 1471
1481; Seta; f; 15; Miss. Choctaw; M; Wife; 1472

1482; Howard; m; 29; Miss. Choctaw; M; Head; 1473
1483; Bessie; f; 29; Miss. Choctaw; M; Wife; 1474
1484; Clifton; m; 5; Miss. Choctaw; S; Son; 1475
1485; Mary Rose; f; 3; Miss. Choctaw; S; Dau; 1476

1486; John; m; 25; Miss. Choctaw; M; Head; 1477
1487; Mallisa; f; 38; Miss. Choctaw; M; Wife; 1478
1488; Mollie; f; 18; Miss. Choctaw; S; Step-dau; 1479
1489; Annie; f; 13; Miss. Choctaw; S; Step-dau; 1480

WAITER

1490; Gipson; m; 68; Miss. Choctaw; Wd; Alone; 1481

1491; Minnie; f; 55; Miss. Choctaw; Wd; Head; 1482
1492; Ruby; f; 21; Miss. Choctaw; S; Dau; 1483

1493; Lonnie; m; 26; Miss. Choctaw; M; Head; 1485

Census of the __Mississippi Choctaw__ reservation of the __Choctaw Agency__ jurisdiction, as of __April 1__, 19__31__, taken by __R. J. Enochs__, Superintendent.

KEY; Surname; Census Number; Given Name; Sex; Age at Last Birthday; Tribe; Degree of Blood; Marital Status; Relationship to Head of Family; Last Census Roll Number; At Jurisdiction Where Enrolled (Yes, unless given otherwise)

1494;   Sue; f; 21; Miss. Choctaw; M: Wife; 1486

WALLACE

1495;   Eunice; f; 41; Miss. Choctaw; Wd; Head; 1487
1496;   Susie; f; 18; Miss. Choctaw; S; Dau; 1488
1497;   Henry; m; 16; Miss. Choctaw; S; Son; 1489
1498;   Celia; f; 15; Miss. Choctaw; S; Dau; 1490
1499;   Austin; m; 4; Miss. Choctaw; S; Son; 1491

1500;   Rachel; f; 46; Miss. Choctaw; Wd; Head; 1492
1501;   Leona; f; 16; Miss. Choctaw; S; Dau; 1493

1502;   Columbus; m; 21; Miss. Choctaw; M; Head; 1494
1503;   Essie; f; 19; Miss. Choctaw; M; Wife; 1495

1504;   Stenot; m; 23; Miss. Choctaw; M; Head; 1496
1505;   Annie; f; 18; Miss. Choctaw; M; Wife; 1497
1506;   Alton; m; 11; Miss. Choctaw; S; Orphan; 1498

WARNER

1507;   Johnnie Lee; m; 19; Miss. Choctaw; S; Alone; 1500

WESLEY

1508;   Sidney; m; 66; Miss. Choctaw; Wd; Alone; 1501

1509;   Cameron; m; 41; Miss. Choctaw; M; Head; 1502
1510;   Julie; f; 27; Miss. Choctaw; M: Wife; 1503
1511;   Bennie; m; 14; Miss. Choctaw; S; Son; 1504
1512;   John; m; 6; Miss. Choctaw; S; Son; 1505
1513;   Willie B; m; #[sic]; Miss. Choctaw; S; Son; 1506

Census of the **Mississippi Choctaw** reservation of the **Choctaw Agency** jurisdiction, as of **April 1**, 19 **31**, taken by **R. J. Enochs**, Superintendent.

KEY; Surname; Census Number; Given Name; Sex; Age at Last Birthday; Tribe; Degree of Blood; Marital Status; Relationship to Head of Family; Last Census Roll Number; At Jurisdiction Where Enrolled (Yes, unless given otherwise)

WICKSON

1514; Jim; m; 23; Miss. Choctaw; M; Head; 1507
1515; Alma; f; 16; Miss. Choctaw; M; Wife; 1508

WILEY

1516; Lizza; f; 61; Miss. Choctaw; S; Alone; 1509

WILLIAMS

1517; Jonas; m; 56; Miss. Choctaw; M; Head; 1510
1518; Maggie; f; 46; Miss. Choctaw; M; Wife; 1511
1519; Tony; m; 22; Miss. Choctaw; S; Son; 1512

1520; Rufus; m; 25; Miss. Choctaw; M; Head; 1513
1521; Nellie; f; 30; Miss. Choctaw; M; Wife; 1514
1522; Evan; m; 9; Miss. Choctaw; S; Son; 1515
1523; Phillip; m; 8; Miss. Choctaw; S; Son; 1516
1524; Fillman; m; 4; Miss. Choctaw; S; Son; 1517
1525; Coy; m; 2; Miss. Choctaw; S; Son; 1518

1526; Jennie; f; 87; Miss. Choctaw; Wd; Head; 1519
1527; Fate; m; 42; Miss. Choctaw; S; Son; 1520

1528; Lewis; m; 54; Miss. Choctaw; M; Head; 1521
1529; Mamie; f; 32; Miss. Choctaw; M; Wife; 1522
1530; Mary Ann; f; 6; Miss. Choctaw; S; Dau; 1523
1531; Sarah; f; 2; Miss. Choctaw; S; Dau; 1524
1532; Carter; m; 5/12; Miss. Choctaw; S; Son

WILLIAMSON

1533; Mack; m; 56; Miss. Choctaw; M; Head; 1525

Census of the **Mississippi Choctaw** reservation of the **Choctaw Agency** jurisdiction, as of **April 1**, 19**31**, taken by **R. J. Enochs**, Superintendent.

KEY; Surname; Census Number; Given Name; Sex; Age at Last Birthday; Tribe; Degree of Blood; Marital Status; Relationship to Head of Family; Last Census Roll Number; At Jurisdiction Where Enrolled (Yes, unless given otherwise)

1534; Ida; f; 56; Miss. Choctaw; M; Wife; 1526
1535; Arnold; m; 12; Miss. Choctaw; S; Son; 1527
1536; **Lewis**, Marceline; f; 7; Miss. Choctaw; S; Grand-dau; 1528

1537; Bike; m; 39; Miss. Choctaw; M: Head; 1529
1538; Effie; f; 27; Miss. Choctaw; M: Wife; 1530
1539; Mary; f; 11; Miss. Choctaw; S; Dau; 1531
1540; Lallie; f; 9; Miss. Choctaw; S; Dau; 1532

WILLIS

1541; Bill; m; 35; Miss. Choctaw; M; Head; 1533
1542; Savenia; f; 29; Miss. Choctaw; M; Wife; 1534
1543; Claud Yates; m; 12; Miss. Choctaw; S; Son; 1535
1544; Elsie; f; 11; Miss. Choctaw; S; Dau; 1536
1545; William B; m; 8; Miss. Choctaw; S; Son; 1537

1546; Nath; m; 24; Miss. Choctaw; M; Head; 1539
1547; Ester; f; 28; Miss. Choctaw; M; Wife; 1540
1548; Silma; f; 3; Miss. Choctaw; S; Dau; 1541
1549; Joe; m; 1; Miss. Choctaw; S; Son; 1542

1550; Ike; m; 24; Miss. Choctaw; M; Head; 1543
1551; Ellen; f; 22; Miss. Choctaw; M Wife; 1544
1552; Adam; m; 5; Miss. Choctaw; S; Son; 1546
1553; Jasper; m; 2; Miss. Choctaw; S; Son; 1547

1554; Robert; m; 43; Miss. Choctaw; M; Head; 1548
1555; Celie; f; 30; Miss. Choctaw; M; Wife; 1549
1556; Mallie; f; 19; Miss. Choctaw; S; Dau; 1550

1557; **Ben**, Wilson; m; 22; Miss. Choctaw; S; Orphan; 1551

1558; Finis; m; 29; Miss. Choctaw; M; Head; 1552

Census of the **Mississippi Choctaw** reservation of the **Choctaw Agency** jurisdiction, as of **April 1**, 19**31**, taken by **R. J. Enochs**, Superintendent.

KEY; Surname; Census Number; Given Name; Sex; Age at Last Birthday; Tribe; Degree of Blood; Marital Status; Relationship to Head of Family; Last Census Roll Number; At Jurisdiction Where Enrolled (Yes, unless given otherwise)

1559;   Nora; f; 24; Miss. Choctaw; M; Wife; 1553
1560;   Onie; f; 6; Miss. Choctaw; S; Dau; 1554
1561;   Leona; f; 2; Miss. Choctaw; S; Dau; 1555

1562;   John; m; 25; Miss. Choctaw; M; Head; 1556
1563;   Susiana; f; 17; Miss. Choctaw; M; Wife; 1557

1564;   Johnson; m; 66; Miss. Choctaw; Wd; Alone; 1558

1565;   Gus; m; 58; Miss. Choctaw; M; Head; 1559
1566;   Rainey; f; 34; Miss. Choctaw; M; Wife; 1560
1567;   Hester; m; 4; Miss. Choctaw; S; Son; 1561
1568;   **Isaac**, Nannie; f; 13; Miss. Choctaw; S; Step-dau; 1562
1569;   **Isaac**, Eunice; f; 11; Miss. Choctaw; S; Step-dau; 1563
1570;   **Isaac**, Rosie; f; 7; Miss. Choctaw; S; Step-dau; 1564
1571;   **Isaac**, William; m; 18; Miss. Choctaw; S; Step-son; 1565

1572;   Ganblin[sic]; m; 31; Miss. Choctaw; M; Head; (a)1566
1573;   Ellen; f; 33; Miss. Choctaw; M; Wife; (b)1566
1574;   Mattie; f; 13; Miss. Choctaw; S; Dau; 1568
1575;   G. C; m; 10; Miss. Choctaw; S; Son; 1569
1576;   Eula; f; 8; Miss. Choctaw; S; Dau; 1570
1577;   Maurice; f; 7; Miss. Choctaw; S; Dau; 1571
1578;   Marabelle; f; 2; Miss. Choctaw; S; Dau; 1572

1579;   Ed; m; 60; Miss. Choctaw; M; Head; 1574
1580;   Panzie; f; 69; Miss. Choctaw; M; Wife; 1575

1581;   Joe; m; 62; Miss. Choctaw; M; Head; 1576
1582;   Adaline; f; 59; Miss. Choctaw; M; Wife; 1577
1583;   Nannie; f; 21; Miss. Choctaw; S; Grand-dau; 1578

1584;   Elias; m; 28; Miss. Choctaw; S; Alone; 1579

Census of the **Mississippi Choctaw** reservation of the **Choctaw Agency** jurisdiction, as of **April 1**, 19 **31**, taken by **R. J. Enochs**, Superintendent.

KEY; Surname; Census Number; Given Name; Sex; Age at Last Birthday; Tribe; Degree of Blood; Marital Status; Relationship to Head of Family; Last Census Roll Number; At Jurisdiction Where Enrolled (Yes, unless given otherwise)

1585; Jim; m; 53; Miss. Choctaw; M; Head; 1580
1586; Louisa; f; 51; Miss. Choctaw; M; Wife; 1581
1587; Tom; m; 29; Miss. Choctaw; S; Son; 1582
1588; Dennis; m; 27; Miss. Choctaw; S; Son; 1583
1589; Waggoner; m; 22; Miss. Choctaw; S; Son; 1584
1590; Deiley; f; 20; Miss. Choctaw; S; Dau; 1585
1591; Dora; f; 19; Miss. Choctaw; S; Dau; 1586
1592; Rosie; f; 17; Miss. Choctaw; S; Dau; 1587
1593; Smith; 16; Miss. Choctaw; S; Son; 1588
1594; Woodrow Wilson; m; 11; Miss. Choctaw; S; Grand-son; 1589

1595; Edmon; m; 23; Miss. Choctaw; M; Head; 1590
1596; Sallie; f; 18; Miss. Choctaw; M; Wife; 1591
1597; John; m; 2; Miss. Choctaw; S; Son; 1592

1598; Elea; m; 30; Miss. Choctaw; M; Head; 1593
1599; Otis; f; 24; Miss. Choctaw; M; Wife; 1594
1600; Vanola; f; 11; Miss. Choctaw; S; Dau; 1595
1601; Flora; f; 9; Miss. Choctaw; S; Dau; 1596
1602; Kittie; f; 8; Miss. Choctaw; S; Dau; 1597
1603; Bonnie; m; 6; Miss. Choctaw; S; Son; 1598

1604; Cohan; m; 33; Miss. Choctaw; M; Head; 1599
1605; Sis; f; 29; Miss. Choctaw; M; Wife; 1600
1606; Ancie; f; 13; Miss. Choctaw; S; Dau; 1601
1607; Una; f; 11; Miss. Choctaw; S; Dau; 1602
1608; Sallie; f; 8; Miss. Choctaw; S; Dau; 1603
1609; Harrison; m; 6; Miss. Choctaw; S; Son; 1604
1610; A. J; m; 3; Miss. Choctaw; S; Son; 1605

1611; Hugh; m; 48; Miss. Choctaw; M; Head; 1606
1612; Mollie; f; 45; Miss. Choctaw; M; Wife; 1607
1613; Thompson; m; 16; Miss. Choctaw; S; Son; 1608
1614; Clemon; m; 14; Miss. Choctaw; S; Son; 1609

Census of the **Mississippi Choctaw** reservation of the **Choctaw** **Agency** jurisdiction, as of **April 1**, 19**31**, taken by **R. J. Enochs**, Superintendent.

KEY; Surname; Census Number; Given Name; Sex; Age at Last Birthday; Tribe; Degree of Blood; Marital Status; Relationship to Head of Family; Last Census Roll Number; At Jurisdiction Where Enrolled (Yes, unless given otherwise)

1615; J. C; m; 10; Miss. Choctaw; S; Son; 1610
1616; Colline[sic]; m; 8; Miss. Choctaw; S; Son; 1611
1617; Lillie; f; 7; Miss. Choctaw; S; Dau; 1612
1618; Walter; m; 6; Miss. Choctaw; S; Son; 1613
1619; Lola; f; 5; Miss. Choctaw; S; Dau; 1614

1620; Spinks; m; 41; Miss. Choctaw; M; Head; 1615
1621; Susie; f; 32; Miss. Choctaw; M; Wife; 1616
1622; Wilson; m; 12; Miss. Choctaw; S; Son; 1617
1623; Flennie; f; 9; Miss. Choctaw; S; Dau; 1618

1624; Wesley M; m; 65; Miss. Choctaw; Wd; Head; 1619
1625; Meley; f; 7; Miss. Choctaw; S; Dau; 1620
1626; John Banks; m; 4; Miss. Choctaw; S; Son; 1621
1627; Leighton; m; 1; Miss. Choctaw; S; Son; 1622

1628; Salum; m; 26; Miss. Choctaw; S; Alone; 1623

WILSON

1629; John; m; 36; Miss. Choctaw; M; Head; 1624
1630; Eva; f; 28; Miss. Choctaw; M; Wife; 1625
1631; Silman; m; 12; Miss. Choctaw; S; Son; 1626
1632; Mollie; f; 10; Miss. Choctaw; S; Dau; 1627
1633; Sidney; m; 9; Miss. Choctaw; S; Son; 1628
1634; Leo; m; 6; Miss. Choctaw; S; Son; 1629
1635; Edna; f; 2; Miss. Choctaw; S; Dau; 1630
1636; Martha; f; 83; Miss. Choctaw; Wd; Mother; 1631

1637; Will; m; 43; Miss. Choctaw; M; Head; 1632
1638; Martha; f; 37; Miss. Choctaw; M; Wife; 1633
1639; Sammie; m; 10; Miss. Choctaw; S; Son; 1634
1640; Linnie; f; 9; Miss. Choctaw; S; Dau; 1635
1641; Louisana; f; 8; Miss. Choctaw; S; Dau; 1636

Census of the **Mississippi Choctaw** reservation of the **Choctaw Agency** jurisdiction, as of **April 1**, 19**31**, taken by **R. J. Enochs**, Superintendent.

KEY; Surname; Census Number; Given Name; Sex; Age at Last Birthday; Tribe; Degree of Blood; Marital Status; Relationship to Head of Family; Last Census Roll Number; At Jurisdiction Where Enrolled (Yes, unless given otherwise)

1642; R. L; m; 2; Miss. Choctaw; S; Son; 1637
1643; Jim; m; 1; Miss. Choctaw; S; Son; 1638

WISHORK

1644; Massey; m; 35; Miss. Choctaw; M; Head; 1639
1645; Alpha; f; 29; Miss. Choctaw; M; Wife; 1640
1646; Zelia; f; 10; Miss. Choctaw; S; Dau; 1641
1647; Evelyn; f; 9; Miss. Choctaw; S; Dau; 1642
1648; Nugar; m; 6; Miss. Choctaw; S; Son; 1643
1649; Lyn Presley; m; 2; Miss. Choctaw; S; Son; 1644

1650; Sampson; m; 67; Miss. Choctaw; Wd; Alone; 1645

YORK

1651; Ben; m; 40; Miss. Choctaw; M; Head; 1646
1652; Louella; f; 46; Miss. Choctaw; M; Wife; 1647
1653; Elsie; f; 15; Miss. Choctaw; S; Dau; 1648
1654; Hester; m; 9; Miss. Choctaw; S; Son; 1649

1655; Scott; m; 76; Miss. Choctaw; M; Head; 1650
1656; Celie; f; 81; Miss. Choctaw; M; Wife; 1651
1657; Berkley; m; 19; Miss. Choctaw; S; Grand-son; 1652

1658; Bennett; m; 41; Miss. Choctaw; M; Head; 1653
1659; Lacie; f; 23; Miss. Choctaw; M; Wife; 1654
1660; G. B; m; 5; Miss. Choctaw; S; Son; 1655
1661; Colie; f; 4; Miss. Choctaw; S; Dau; 1656

1662; Necie; f; 43; Miss. Choctaw; Wd; Head; 1657
1663; Emmet; m; 27; Miss. Choctaw; S; Son; 1658
1664; Baxter; m; 24; Miss. Choctaw; S; Son; 1659
1665; Addie; f; 22; Miss. Choctaw; S; Dau; 1660

Census of the **Mississippi Choctaw** reservation of the **Choctaw Agency** jurisdiction, as of **April 1**, 19**31**, taken by **R. J. Enochs**, Superintendent.

KEY; Surname; Census Number; Given Name; Sex; Age at Last Birthday; Tribe; Degree of Blood; Marital Status; Relationship to Head of Family; Last Census Roll Number; At Jurisdiction Where Enrolled (Yes, unless given otherwise)

1666; Gasler; m; 19; Miss. Choctaw; S; Son; 1661
1667; Eunice; f; 17; Miss. Choctaw; S; Dau; 1662
1668; Beaman; m; 14; Miss. Choctaw; S; Son; 1663

1669; **Box**, Eula; f; 8; Miss. Choctaw; S; Alone; 1665

Mississippi Choctaw Census

as of

April 1, 1932

taken by R. J. Enochs, Superintendent

Census of the **Mississippi Choctaw** reservation of the **Choctaw Agency** jurisdiction, as of **April 1**, 19**32**, taken by **R. J. Enochs**, Superintendent.

KEY; Surname; Census Number; Given Name; Sex; Age at Last Birthday; Tribe; Degree of Blood; Marital Status; Relationship to Head of Family; Last Census Roll Number; At Jurisdiction Where Enrolled (Yes/No); Ward (Yes/No, if given)

ALEX

1;   Cooper; m; 22; Miss. Choctaw; F; S; Head; 1; Yes; Yes

2;   Missie; f; 52; Miss. Choctaw; F; Wd; Head; 3; Yes; Yes
3;   Nelson; m; 9; Miss. Choctaw; F; S; Son; 4; Yes; Yes
4;   **Dixon**, Lonie; f; 18; Miss. Choctaw; F; S; Step-dau; 5; Yes; Yes

ALLEN

5;   Willis; m; 37; Miss. Choctaw; F; M; Head; 6; Yes; Yes
6;   Bessie; f; 37; Miss. Choctaw; F; M; Wife; 7; Yes; Yes
7;   Bob; m; 15; Miss. Choctaw; F; S; Son; 8; Yes; Yes
8;   Sulum; m; 11; Miss. Choctaw; F; S; Son; 9; Yes; Yes
9;   Maggie; f; 9; Miss. Choctaw; F; S; Dau; 10; Yes; Yes
10; Huston; m; 8; Miss. Choctaw; F; S; Son; 12; Yes; Yes
11; Nell; f; 7; Miss. Choctaw; F; S; Dau; 11; Yes; Yes
12; Willie; m; 4; Miss. Choctaw; F; S; Son; 13; Yes; Yes

13; Jim; m; 46; Miss. Choctaw; F; M; Head; 14; Yes; Yes
14; Manda; f; 48; Miss. Choctaw; F; M; Wife; 15; Yes; Yes
15; I. C.; m; 18; Miss. Choctaw; F; S; Son; 16; Yes
16; Annie Mae; f; 18; Miss. Choctaw; F; S; Dau; 17; Yes
17; J. C.; m; 17; Miss. Choctaw; F; S; Son; 18; Yes
18; R. G.; m; 16; Miss. Choctaw; F; S; Son; 19; Yes
19; Will; m; 9; Miss. Choctaw; F; S; Son; 20; Yes

20; Joseph; m; 39; Miss. Choctaw; F; S; Head; 21; Yes

21; Lacey; m[sic]; 38; Miss. Choctaw; F; S; Head; 22; Yes

AMOS

22;   Sebbie; f; 54; Miss. Choctaw; F; Wd; Head; 23; Yes

Census of the **Mississippi Choctaw** reservation of the **Choctaw Agency** jurisdiction, as of **April 1**, 19**32**, taken by **R. J. Enochs**, Superintendent.

KEY; Surname; Census Number; Given Name; Sex; Age at Last Birthday; Tribe; Degree of Blood; Marital Status; Relationship to Head of Family; Last Census Roll Number; At Jurisdiction Where Enrolled (Yes/No); Ward (Yes/No, if given)

23; Albert; m; 28; Miss. Choctaw; F; S; Head; 24; Yes

24; Griffin; m; 44; Miss. Choctaw; F; M; Head; 25; Yes
25; Sallie; f; 40; Miss. Choctaw; F; M; Wife; 26; Yes
26; Beauty; f; 22; Miss. Choctaw; F; S; Dau; 27; Yes
27; Julia; f; 20; Miss. Choctaw; F; S; Dau; 28; Yes
28; John; m; 18; Miss. Choctaw; F; S; Son; 29; Yes
29; Land; m; 16; Miss. Choctaw; F; S; Son; 30; Yes
30; Fulton; m; 11; Miss. Choctaw; F; S; Son; 31; Yes
31; Floyed; m; 11; Miss. Choctaw; F; S; Son; 32; Yes
32; Mose; m; 10; Miss. Choctaw; F; S; Son; 33; Yes

33; Lampkin; m; 54; Miss. Choctaw; F; M; Head; 34; Yes
34; Ann; f; 54; Miss. Choctaw; F; M; Wife; 35; Yes
35; Bonnie; f; 21; Miss. Choctaw; F; S; Dau; 36; Yes
36; Lonie; f; 15; Miss. Choctaw; F; S; Dau; 37; Yes
37; **Isom**, Mary; f; 5; Miss. Choctaw; F; S; Grand-dau; 38; Yes

ANDERSON

38; Bob; m; 47; Miss. Choctaw; F; M; Head; 39; Yes
39; Ella; f; 44; Miss. Choctaw; F; M; Wife; 40; Yes
40; A. J; m; 20; Miss. Choctaw; F; S; Son; 41; Yes
41; Chuty; f; 14; Miss. Choctaw; F; S; Dau; 42; Yes
42; Josephine; f; 10; Miss. Choctaw; F; S; Dau; 43; Yes
43; Sallie Mae; f; 7; Miss. Choctaw; F; S; Dau; 44; Yes
44; Burnice; f; 4; Miss. Choctaw; F; S; Dau; 45; Yes

45; John; m; 64; Miss. Choctaw; F; M; Head; 46; Yes
46; Sallie; f; 29; Miss. Choctaw; F; M; Wife; 47; Yes
47; J. C; m; 7; Miss. Choctaw; F; S; Son; 48; Yes

48; Mattie; f; 62; Miss. Choctaw; F; Wd; Head; 49; Yes
49; Ike; m; 30; Miss. Choctaw; F; S; Son; 50; Yes

Census of the **Mississippi Choctaw** reservation of the **Choctaw Agency** jurisdiction, as of **April 1**, 19**32**, taken by **R. J. Enochs**, Superintendent.

KEY; Surname; Census Number; Given Name; Sex; Age at Last Birthday; Tribe; Degree of Blood; Marital Status; Relationship to Head of Family; Last Census Roll Number; At Jurisdiction Where Enrolled (Yes/No); Ward (Yes/No, if given)

50; Vada; f; 26; Miss. Choctaw; F; S; Dau; 51; Yes

51; Evan; m; 28; Miss. Choctaw; F; M; Head; 52; Yes
52; Thelma; f; 16; Miss. Choctaw; F; M; Wife; 53; Yes

53; Roy; m; 36; Miss. Choctaw; F; M; Head; 54; Yes
54; Lonie; f; 32; Miss. Choctaw; F; M; Wife; 55; Yes
55; Frances B; f; 3; Miss. Choctaw; F; S; Dau; 56; Yes

56; Ollie; m; 46; Miss. Choctaw; F; M; Head; 57; Yes
57; Kate; f; 51; Miss. Choctaw; F; M; Wife; 58; Yes
58; Grace; f; 9; Miss. Choctaw; F; S; Dau; 59; Yes
59; Jennie; f; 20; Miss. Choctaw; F; S; Step-dau; 60; Yes

60; Oliver; m; 46; Miss. Choctaw; F; M; Head; 61; Yes
61; Sallie; f; 39; Miss. Choctaw; F; M; Wife; 62; Yes
62; Hinton; m; 18; Miss. Choctaw; F; S; Son; 63; Yes
63; Lonie; f; 17; Miss. Choctaw; F; S; Dau; 64; Yes
64; Phillip; m; 13; Miss. Choctaw; F; S; Son; 65; Yes
65; Houston; m; 11; Miss. Choctaw; F; S; Son; 66; Yes
66; Lucille; f; 9; Miss. Choctaw; F; S; Dau; 67; Yes

67; Abel; m; 26; Miss. Choctaw; F; M; Head; 68; Yes
68; Nancy; f; 46; Miss. Choctaw; F; M; Wife; 69; Yes
69; **Farmer**, Allie; f; 16; Miss. Choctaw; F; S; Step-dau; 70; Yes
70; **Farmer**, Ella Mae; f; 10; Miss. Choctaw; F; S; Step-dau; 71; Yes
71; **Farmer**, Annie Mae; f; 8; Miss. Choctaw; F; S; Step-dau; 72; Yes

BELL

72; Hugh; m; 52; Miss. Choctaw; F; Wd; Head; 73; Yes
73; Viola; f; 20; Miss. Choctaw; F; S; Dau; 74; Yes
74; Mamie; f; 6; Miss. Choctaw; F; S; Dau; 75; Yes

Census of the **Mississippi Choctaw** reservation of the **Choctaw Agency** jurisdiction, as of **April 1**, 19**32**, taken by **R. J. Enochs**, Superintendent.

KEY; Surname; Census Number; Given Name; Sex; Age at Last Birthday; Tribe; Degree of Blood; Marital Status; Relationship to Head of Family; Last Census Roll Number; At Jurisdiction Where Enrolled (Yes/No); Ward (Yes/No, if given)

75; John; m; 41; Miss. Choctaw; F; M; Head; 76; Yes
76; Lillian; f; 42; Miss. Choctaw; F; M; Wife; 77; Yes
77; Hattie; f; 11; Miss. Choctaw; F; S; Dau; 78; Yes
78; Eva; f; 7; Miss. Choctaw; F; S; Dau; 79; Yes
79; Ola; f; 5; Miss. Choctaw; F; S; Dau; 80; Yes

80; Sallie; f; 42; Miss. Choctaw; F; Wd; Head; 81; Yes
81; Emma; f; 20; Miss. Choctaw; F; S; Dau; 82; Yes
82; Effie; f; 13; Miss. Choctaw; F; S; Dau; 83; Yes

83; Junus; m; 35; Miss. Choctaw; F; M; Head; 84; Yes
84; Winnie; f; 30; Miss. Choctaw; F; M; Wife; 85; Yes
85; Ronie; f; 15; Miss. Choctaw; F; S; Dau; 86; Yes
86; Woods; m; 12; Miss. Choctaw; F; S; Son; 87; Yes
87; Minnie; f; 10; Miss. Choctaw; F; S; Dau; 88; Yes
88; Edmond; m; 7; Miss. Choctaw; F; S; Son; 89; Yes
89; George; m; 5; Miss. Choctaw; F; S; Son; 90; Yes

90; Evans; m; 30; Miss. Choctaw; F; M; Head; 91; Yes
91; Willie; f; 20; Miss. Choctaw; F; M; Wife; 92; Yes
92; Homer; m; 5; Miss. Choctaw; F; S; Son; 93; Yes
93; Nancy L; f; 3; Miss. Choctaw; F; S; Dau; 94; Yes

94; Mack; m; 27; Miss. Choctaw; F; M; Head; 95; Yes
95; Lin; f; 18; Miss. Choctaw; F; M; Wife; 96; Yes
96; James; m; 4; Miss. Choctaw; F; S; Son; 97; Yes
97; Herbert H; 8 da; Miss. Choctaw; F; S; Son; Yes

98; Thompson; m; 34; Miss. Choctaw; F; M; Head; 98; Yes
99; Ellen; f; 34; Miss. Choctaw; F; M; Wife; 99; Yes
100; Frank K; m; 18; Miss. Choctaw; F; S; Son; 100; Yes

101; Nicholas; m; 32; Miss. Choctaw; F; M; Head; 101; Yes
102; Cleddie; f; 19; Miss. Choctaw; F; M; Wife; 102; Yes

Census of the **Mississippi Choctaw** reservation of the **Choctaw Agency** jurisdiction, as of **April 1**, 19**32**, taken by **R. J. Enochs**, Superintendent.

KEY; Surname; Census Number; Given Name; Sex; Age at Last Birthday; Tribe; Degree of Blood; Marital Status; Relationship to Head of Family; Last Census Roll Number; At Jurisdiction Where Enrolled (Yes/No); Ward (Yes/No, if given)

103; Rubie; f; 2; Miss. Choctaw; F; S; Dau; 103; Yes
104; Bonnie K; f; 11/12; Miss. Choctaw; F; S; Dau; Yes

105; Gibson; m; 19; Miss. Choctaw; F; M; Head; 776; Yes
106; Lucy; f; 19; Miss. Choctaw; F; M; Wife; 370; Yes
107; Gibson, Jr; m; 25 da; Miss. Choctaw; F; S; Son; Yes

108; Amon; m; 30; Miss. Choctaw; F; M; Head; 104; Yes
109; Alice; f; 29; Miss. Choctaw; F; M; Wife; 105; Yes

110; Jim; m; 62; Miss. Choctaw; F; S; Alone; 106; Yes

111; Joe; m; 40; Miss. Choctaw; F; M; Head; 107; Yes
112; Susie; f; 32; Miss. Choctaw; F; M; Wife; 108; Yes
113; Tom; m; 12; Miss. Choctaw; F; S; Son; 109; Yes
114; Bill; m; 8; Miss. Choctaw; F; S; Son; 110; Yes
115; Henry; m; 6; Miss. Choctaw; F; S; Son; 111; Yes
116; Polly Ann; f; 4; Miss. Choctaw; F; S; Dau; 112; Yes
117; Sallie; f; 55; Miss. Choctaw; F; Wd; Mother-in-law; 113; Yes

118; Boston; m; 47; Miss. Choctaw; F; M; Head; 114; Yes
119; Lela; f; 32; Miss. Choctaw; F; M; Wife; 115; Yes
120; Sophia; f; 24; Miss. Choctaw; F; S; Dau; 116; Yes
121; Ola; f; 22; Miss. Choctaw; F; S; Dau; 117; Yes
122; Effie; f; 20; Miss. Choctaw; F; S; Dau; 118; Yes
123; John; m; 10; Miss. Choctaw; F; S; Son; 119; Yes
124; Emma; f; 8; Miss. Choctaw; F; S; Dau; 120; Yes
125; Emmet; m; 7; Miss. Choctaw; F; S; Son; 121; Yes
126; Marshall; m; 2; Miss. Choctaw; F; S; Grand-son; 122; Yes

127; Cornelius; m; 74; Miss. Choctaw; F; Wd; Head; 123; Yes
128; John; m; 25; Miss. Choctaw; F; S; Son; 124; Yes

129; Jim; m; 70; Miss. Choctaw; F; S; Alone; 125; Yes

Census of the **Mississippi Choctaw** reservation of the **Choctaw Agency** jurisdiction, as of **April 1**, 19**32**, taken by **R. J. Enochs**, Superintendent.

KEY; Surname; Census Number; Given Name; Sex; Age at Last Birthday; Tribe; Degree of Blood; Marital Status; Relationship to Head of Family; Last Census Roll Number; At Jurisdiction Where Enrolled (Yes/No); Ward (Yes/No, if given)

130; Lish; m; 42; Miss. Choctaw; F; M; Head; 126; Yes
131; Martha; f; 37; Miss. Choctaw; F; M; Wife; 127; Yes
132; Willie; m; 17; Miss. Choctaw; F; S; Son; 128; Yes
133; Houston; m; 12; Miss. Choctaw; F; S; Son; 129; Yes
134; Minnie; f; 11; Miss. Choctaw; F; S; Dau; 130; Yes
135; Less C; m; 9; Miss. Choctaw; F; S; Son; 131; Yes
136; Gene D; m; 7; Miss. Choctaw; F; S; Dau; 132; Yes
137; Jay; m; 5; Miss. Choctaw; F; S; Son; 133; Yes
138; Gaston; m; 23; Miss. Choctaw; F; S; Bro; 134; Yes

139; Bob; m; 22; Miss. Choctaw; F; M; Head; 135; Yes
140; Geneva; m; 21; Miss. Choctaw; F; M; Wife; 136; Yes
141; Sadie; f; 2; Miss. Choctaw; F; S; Dau; 137; Yes
142; Naomi Ruth; f; 6/12; Miss. Choctaw; F; S; Dau; Yes

143; Lish; m; 51; Miss. Choctaw; F; M; Head; 138; Yes
144; Maggie; f; 51; Miss. Choctaw; F; M; Wife; 139; Yes
145; Minnie; f; 24; Miss. Choctaw; F; S; Dau; 140; Yes
146; Lula; f; 16; Miss. Choctaw; F; S; Dau; 141; Yes
147; Tom; m; 26; Miss. Choctaw; F; S; Son; 142; Yes
148; Bob; m; 22; Miss. Choctaw; F; S; Son; 143; Yes
149; Basin; m; 7; Miss. Choctaw; F; S; Son; 144; Yes

BEN

150; Olin; m; 32; Miss. Choctaw; F; M; Head; 145; Yes
151; Nega; f; 25; Miss. Choctaw; F; M; Wife; 146; Yes
152; Nannie Mae; f; 8; Miss. Choctaw; F; S; Dau; 147; Yes
153; Annie Laura; f; 6; Miss. Choctaw; F; S; Dau; 148; Yes
154; Mattie Lou; f; 4; Miss. Choctaw; F; S; Dau; 149; Yes
155; **Isaac**, Lessie; f; 19; Miss. Choctaw; F; S; Sister-in-law; 150; Yes
156; **Isaac**, Coline; f; 13; Miss. Choctaw; F; S; Sister-in-law; 151; Yes

157; Wyatt; m; 64; Miss. Choctaw; F; M; Head; 152; Yes

Census of the **Mississippi Choctaw** reservation of the **Choctaw Agency** jurisdiction, as of **April 1**, 19 **32**, taken by **R. J. Enochs**, Superintendent.

KEY; Surname; Census Number; Given Name; Sex; Age at Last Birthday; Tribe; Degree of Blood; Marital Status; Relationship to Head of Family; Last Census Roll Number; At Jurisdiction Where Enrolled (Yes/No); Ward (Yes/No, if given)

158;   Ellen; f; 60; Miss. Choctaw; F; M; Wife; 153

159;   Lula; f; 48; Miss. Choctaw; F; Wd; Head; 154
160;   Jimpson; m; 26; Miss. Choctaw; F; S; Son; 155
161;   Otha; m; 18; Miss. Choctaw; F; S; Son; 156
162;   Wilson; m; 15; Miss. Choctaw; F; S; Son; 157

163;   Tom; m; 37; Miss. Choctaw; F; M; Head; 158
164;   Gladys; f; 26; Miss. Choctaw; F; M; Wife; 159
165;   Fannie Lou; f; 7; Miss. Choctaw; F; S; Dau; 160
166;   Hubert; m; 5; Miss. Choctaw; F; S; Son; 161
167;   Henry Ford; m; 3; Miss. Choctaw; F; S; Son; 162; Yes

168;   Charlie; m; 33; Miss. Choctaw; F; M; Head; 163; Yes
169;   Emeline; f; 25; Miss. Choctaw; F; M; Wife; 164; Yes
170;   Opal Grace; f; 6/12; Miss. Choctaw; F; S; Dau; Yes

171;   Jim; m; 56; Miss. Choctaw; F; Wd; Alone; 165; Yes

172;   Monroe; m; 21; Miss. Choctaw; F; M; Head; 166; Yes
173;   Lillie May; f; 21; Miss. Choctaw; F; M; Wife; 167; Yes

BILLY

174;   Lum; m; 47; Miss. Choctaw; F; M; Head; 168; Yes
175;   Minnie; f; 49; Miss. Choctaw; F; M; Wife; 169; Yes
176;   **Charles**, James; m; 34; Miss. Choctaw; F; S; Brother-in-law; 170; Yes

177;   Tom; m; 21; Miss. Choctaw; F; M; Head; 171; Yes
178;   Sallie; f; 22; Miss. Choctaw; F; M; Wife; 172; Yes
179;   Robert; m; 4; Miss. Choctaw; F; S; Son; 173; Yes
180;   James; m; 1; Miss. Choctaw; F; S; Son; 174; Yes

Census of the **Mississippi Choctaw** reservation of the **Choctaw Agency** jurisdiction, as of **April 1**, 19**32**, taken by **R. J. Enochs**, Superintendent.

KEY; Surname; Census Number; Given Name; Sex; Age at Last Birthday; Tribe; Degree of Blood; Marital Status; Relationship to Head of Family; Last Census Roll Number; At Jurisdiction Where Enrolled (Yes/No); Ward (Yes/No, if given)

181; Will; m; 55; Miss. Choctaw; F; S; Alone; 175; Yes

182; Williston; m; 38; Miss. Choctaw; F; M; Head; 176; Yes
183; Jessie; f; 28; Miss. Choctaw; F; M; Wife; 177; Yes
184; Melton; m; 11; Miss. Choctaw; F; S; Son; 178; Yes
185; Beaman; m; 8; Miss. Choctaw; F; S; Son; 179; Yes
186; Maurice; m; 6; Miss. Choctaw; F; S; Son; 180; Yes
187; Horace; m; 5; Miss. Choctaw; F; S; Son; 181; Yes
188; Betty Jean; f; 1; Miss. Choctaw; F; S; Dau; 182; Yes

189; Nicy; f; 72; Miss. Choctaw; F; Wd; Head; 183; Yes
190; Leona; f; 32; Miss. Choctaw; F; S; Dau; 184; Yes
191; Ike; m; 22; Miss. Choctaw; F; S; Son; 186; Yes
192; Earl; f; 6; Miss. Choctaw; F; S; Grand-dau; 185; Yes

193; Augustan; m; 22; Miss. Choctaw; F; M; Head; 187; Yes
194; Lorene; f; 22; Miss. Choctaw; F; M; Wife; 188; Yes
195; Cicero L; m; 9/12; Miss. Choctaw; F; S; Son; Yes

196; Johnson; m; 66; Miss. Choctaw; F; M; Head; 189; Yes
197; Belaria; f; 51; Miss. Choctaw; F; M; Wife; 190; Yes
198; Gipson; m; 21; Miss. Choctaw; F; S; Son; 191; Yes
199; Ike; m; 20; Miss. Choctaw; F; S; Son; 192; Yes
200; Maude; f; 19; Miss. Choctaw; F; S; Dau; 193; Yes
201; Wilson; m; 15; Miss. Choctaw; F; S; Son; 194; Yes
202; Greer; m; 13; Miss. Choctaw; F; S; Son; 195; Yes
203; Frank; m; 8; Miss. Choctaw; F; S; Son; 196; Yes
204; Phillip; m; 2; Miss. Choctaw; F; S; Grand-son; 197; Yes

205; Lewis; m; 27; Miss. Choctaw; F; M; Head; 198; Yes
206; Zelma; f; 27; Miss. Choctaw; F; M; Wife; 199; Yes
207; Clennie; f; 12; Miss. Choctaw; F; S; Step-dau; 200; Yes
208; Mamie; f; 10; Miss. Choctaw; F; S; Step-dau; 201; Yes
209; Frank; m; 6; Miss. Choctaw; F; S; Son; 202; Yes

Census of the **Mississippi Choctaw** reservation of the **Choctaw Agency** jurisdiction, as of **April 1**, 19**32**, taken by **R. J. Enochs**, Superintendent.

KEY; Surname; Census Number; Given Name; Sex; Age at Last Birthday; Tribe; Degree of Blood; Marital Status; Relationship to Head of Family; Last Census Roll Number; At Jurisdiction Where Enrolled (Yes/No); Ward (Yes/No, if given)

210; Annie; f; 3; Miss. Choctaw; F; S; Dau; 203; Yes

211; Will; m; 44; Miss. Choctaw; F; M; Head; 204; Yes
212; Alice; f; 42; Miss. Choctaw; F; M; Wife; 205; Yes
213; William; m; 17; Miss. Choctaw; F; S; Son; 206; Yes
214; Lee; m; 16; Miss. Choctaw; F; S; Son; 207; Yes
215; Rose; f; 13; Miss. Choctaw; F; S; Dau; 208; Yes
216; Irene; f; 10; Miss. Choctaw; F; S; Dau; 209; Yes
217; Joe; m; 9; Miss. Choctaw; F; S; Son; 210; Yes
218; Will, Jr; m; 5; Miss. Choctaw; F; S; Son; 211; Yes
219; Marchie; f; 4; Miss. Choctaw; F; S; Dau; 212; Yes
220; Charlie; m; 2; Miss. Choctaw; F; S; Son; 213; Yes

221; Jordan; m; 47; Miss. Choctaw; F; M; Head; 214; Yes
222; Lilly; f; 29; Miss. Choctaw; F; M; Wife; 215; Yes
223; Sallie Mae; f; 14; Miss. Choctaw; F; S; Dau; 216; Yes
224; Nellie; f; 11; Miss. Choctaw; F; S; Dau; 217; Yes
225; Jim; m; 6; Miss. Choctaw; F; S; Son; 218; Yes
226; Mary Lou; f; 4; Miss. Choctaw; F; S; Dau; 219; Yes
227; Paul; m; 1; Miss. Choctaw; F; S; Son; 220; Yes

228; Richard; m; 21; Miss. Choctaw; F; M; Head; 221; Yes
229; Eva; f; 17; Miss. Choctaw; F; M; Wife; 222; Yes
230; Duley; f; 3/12; Miss. Choctaw; F; S; Dau; Yes

231; Wade; m; 53; Miss. Choctaw; F; M; Head; 223; Yes
232; Lina; f; 35; Miss. Choctaw; F; M; Wife; 224; Yes
233; **McMillen**, Mary; f; 12; Miss. Choctaw; F; S; Step-dau; 225; Yes

BOB

234; Simon; m; 62; Miss. Choctaw; F; S; Head; 226; Yes

Census of the **Mississippi Choctaw** reservation of the **Choctaw Agency** jurisdiction, as of **April 1**, 19**32**, taken by **R. J. Enochs**, Superintendent.

KEY; Surname; Census Number; Given Name; Sex; Age at Last Birthday; Tribe; Degree of Blood; Marital Status; Relationship to Head of Family; Last Census Roll Number; At Jurisdiction Where Enrolled (Yes/No); Ward (Yes/No, if given)

BOX

235; Illiman; m; 26; Miss. Choctaw; F; M; Head; 227; Yes
236; Rosie; f; 20; Miss. Choctaw; F; M; Wife; 228; Yes

237; Lillie; f; 44; Miss. Choctaw; F; Wd; Head; 229; Yes
238; Ollie T; m; 17; Miss. Choctaw; F; S; Son; 230; Yes
239; Bathie; f; 9; Miss. Choctaw; F; S; Dau; 231; Yes
240; Bethy; f; 7; Miss. Choctaw; F; S; Dau; 232; Yes
241; **Joe**, Emly; f; 72; Miss. Choctaw; F; Wd; Mother; 233; Yes

242; Ola; f; 17; Miss. Choctaw; F; S; Orphan; 234; Yes
243; Eula; f; 9; Miss. Choctaw; F; S; Orphan; 1669; Yes

BOYD

244; Archie; m; 69; Miss. Choctaw; F; Wd; Alone; 235; Yes

BRISCOE

245; Tom; m; 31; Miss. Choctaw; F; M; Head; 237; Yes
246; Lucy; m; 49; Miss. Choctaw; F; M; Wife; 238; Yes
247; **Polk**, Francis; m; 22; Miss. Choctaw; F; S; Nephew; 239; Yes

248; Stephens; m; 23; Miss. Choctaw; F; M; Head; 240; Yes
249; Maggie; f; 24; Miss. Choctaw; F; M; Wife; 241; Yes
250; J. Claud; m; 1/12; Miss. Choctaw; F; S; Son; Yes

BULL

251; Pink; m; 54; Miss. Choctaw; F; Wd; Alone; 242; Yes

252; George; m; 58; Miss. Choctaw; F; M; Head; 244; Yes
253; Sissy; f; 50; Miss. Choctaw; F; M; Wife; 245; Yes

Census of the **Mississippi Choctaw** reservation of the **Choctaw Agency** jurisdiction, as of **April 1**, 19**32**, taken by **R. J. Enochs**, Superintendent.

KEY; Surname; Census Number; Given Name; Sex; Age at Last Birthday; Tribe; Degree of Blood; Marital Status; Relationship to Head of Family; Last Census Roll Number; At Jurisdiction Where Enrolled (Yes/No); Ward (Yes/No, if given)

254; Foreman; m; 29; Miss. Choctaw; F; M; Head; 246; Yes
255; Sarah; f; 28; Miss. Choctaw; F; M; Wife; 247; Yes

CAMPBELL

256; Wiley; m; 31; Miss. Choctaw; F; Wd; Alone; 248; Yes

CATES

257; Susan; f; 54; Miss. Choctaw; F; Wd; Head; 249; Yes
258; Enis; m; 27; Miss. Choctaw; F; S; Son; 250; Yes
259; Essie; f; 24; Miss. Choctaw; F; S; Dau; 251; Yes
260; John; m; 20; Miss. Choctaw; F; S; Son; 252; Yes
261; Lonie; f; 19; Miss. Choctaw; F; S; Dau; 253; Yes
262; Molpus; m; 18; Miss. Choctaw; F; S; Son; 254; Yes
263; Iona; f; 14; Miss. Choctaw; F; S; Dau; 255; Yes
264; John; m; 4; Miss. Choctaw; F; S; Grand-son; 256; Yes

265; Oscar; m; 22; Miss. Choctaw; F; S; Alone; 257; Yes

266; Alice; f; 27[sic]; Miss. Choctaw; F; Wd; Head; 258; Yes
267; Dock; m; 30; Miss. Choctaw; F; S; Son; 259; Yes
268; Dee; m; 24; Miss. Choctaw; F; S; Son; 260; Yes

269; Ned; m; 34; Miss. Choctaw; F; M; Head; 261; Yes
270; Janie; f; 30; Miss. Choctaw; F; M; Wife; 262; Yes
271; Susan Mabel; f; 15; Miss. Choctaw; F; S; Dau; 263; Yes
272; Emma; f; 15; Miss. Choctaw; F; S; Dau; 264; Yes
273; Tubby; m; 14; Miss. Choctaw; F; S; Son; 265; Yes
274; Henry M; f; 12; Miss. Choctaw; F; S; Son; 266; Yes
275; Willie F; m; 9; Miss. Choctaw; F; S; Son; 267; Yes
276; Nannie; f; 7; Miss. Choctaw; F; S; Dau; 268; Yes
277; Julia; f; 6; Miss. Choctaw; F; S; Dau; 269; Yes

Census of the **Mississippi Choctaw** reservation of the **Choctaw Agency** jurisdiction, as of **April 1**, 19**32**, taken by **R. J. Enochs**, Superintendent.

KEY: Surname; Census Number; Given Name; Sex; Age at Last Birthday; Tribe; Degree of Blood; Marital Status; Relationship to Head of Family; Last Census Roll Number; At Jurisdiction Where Enrolled (Yes/No); Ward (Yes/No, if given)

CHAPMAN

278; Will; m; 45; Miss. Choctaw; F; M; Head; 270; Yes
279; Bettie; f; 48; Miss. Choctaw; F; M; Wife; 271; Yes
280; Asa; m; 14; Miss. Choctaw; F; S; Son; 272; Yes
281; Ralston; m; 13; Miss. Choctaw; F; S; Son; 273; Yes
282; Hattie; f; 9; Miss. Choctaw; F; S; Dau; 274; Yes
283; Ronie; f; 8; Miss. Choctaw; F; S; Dau; 275; Yes
284; Lilly; f; 7; Miss. Choctaw; F; S; Dau; 276; Yes
285; Raymond; m; 6; Miss. Choctaw; F; S; Son; 277; Yes
286; Cris; m; 5; Miss. Choctaw; F; S; Son; 278; Yes
287; Minnie; f; 4; Miss. Choctaw; F; S; Dau; 279; Yes

CHARLIE

288; Onie; f; 46; Miss. Choctaw; F; Wd; Head; 280; Yes
289; Beaman; m; 17; Miss. Choctaw; F; S; Son; 281; Yes
290; Juanita; f; 12; Miss. Choctaw; F; S; Dau; 282; Yes
291; Charlie C; m; 10; Miss. Choctaw; F; S; Son; 283; Yes

292; William; m; 81; Miss. Choctaw; F; M; Head; 284; Yes
293; Fannie; m; 67; Miss. Choctaw; F; M; Wife; 285; Yes

294; John; m; 38; Miss. Choctaw; F; M; Head; 286; Yes
295; Mary; f; 30; Miss. Choctaw; F; M; Wife; 287; Yes
296; Elsie; f; 13; Miss. Choctaw; F; S; Dau; 288; Yes

CHICKAWAY

297; Sim; m; 34; Miss. Choctaw; F; M; Head; 289; Yes
298; Maggie; f; 31; Miss. Choctaw; F; M; Wife; 290; Yes
299; Clemon; m; 13; Miss. Choctaw; F; S; Son; 291; Yes
300; Nellie; f; 11; Miss. Choctaw; F; S; Dau; 292; Yes
301; Agnes; f; 9; Miss. Choctaw; F; S; Dau; 293; Yes

Census of the **Mississippi Choctaw** reservation of the **Choctaw Agency** jurisdiction, as of **April 1**, 19**32**, taken by **R. J. Enochs**, Superintendent.

KEY; Surname; Census Number; Given Name; Sex; Age at Last Birthday; Tribe; Degree of Blood; Marital Status; Relationship to Head of Family; Last Census Roll Number; At Jurisdiction Where Enrolled (Yes/No); Ward (Yes/No, if given)

302; Albert; m; 6; Miss. Choctaw; F; S; Son; 294; Yes
303; Maggie Kate; f; 4; Miss. Choctaw; F; S; Dau; 295; Yes
304; Mary; f; 11/12; Miss. Choctaw; F; S; Dau; Yes
305; Isabell; f; 70; Miss. Choctaw; F; Wd; Mother; 296; Yes
306; Ola; f; 25; Miss. Choctaw; F; S; Sister; 297; Yes

307; Jim; m; 29; Miss. Choctaw; F; M; Head; 298; Yes
308; Eunice; f; 26; Miss. Choctaw; F; M; Wife; 299; Yes
309; John Hester; m; 4; Miss. Choctaw; F; S; Son; 300; Yes
310; Henry; m; 1; Miss. Choctaw; F; S; Son; 301; Yes
311; **Grant**, Rosie Lee; f; 10; Miss. Choctaw; F; S; Step-dau; 302; Yes

312; Kelly; m; 39; Miss. Choctaw; F; M; Head; 303; Yes
313; Lilla; f; 30; Miss. Choctaw; F; M; Wife; 304; Yes
314; Mikel; m; 9; Miss. Choctaw; F; S; Son; 305; Yes
315; Anna; f; 7; Miss. Choctaw; F; S; Dau; 306; Yes
316; Jane; f; 5; Miss. Choctaw; F; S; Dau; 307; Yes

317; Rufus; m; 30; Miss. Choctaw; F; M; Head; 308; Yes
318; Bessie; f; 27; Miss. Choctaw; F; M; Wife; 309; Yes
319; Ross C; m; 4; Miss. Choctaw; F; S; Son; 310; Yes
320; Elizabeth; f; 2; Miss. Choctaw; F; S; Dau; 311; Yes

CHITTO

321; Joe; m; 32; Miss. Choctaw; F; M; Head; 312; Yes
322; Callie; f; 32; Miss. Choctaw; F; M; Wife; 313; Yes
323; Leo Clifton; m; 4; Miss. Choctaw; F; S; Son; 314; Yes

324; Pat; m; 55; Miss. Choctaw; F; Wd; Head; 315; Yes
325; Henrietta; f; 17; Miss. Choctaw; F; S; Dau; 316; Yes
326; Jefferson; m; 15; Miss. Choctaw; F; S; Son; 317; Yes
327; Erma; f; 10; Miss. Choctaw; F; S; Dau; 318; Yes
328; Isom; m; 8; Miss. Choctaw; F; S; Son; 319; Yes

Census of the **Mississippi Choctaw** reservation of the **Choctaw Agency** jurisdiction, as of **April 1**, 19**32**, taken by **R. J. Enochs**, Superintendent.

KEY; Surname; Census Number; Given Name; Sex; Age at Last Birthday; Tribe; Degree of Blood; Marital Status; Relationship to Head of Family; Last Census Roll Number; At Jurisdiction Where Enrolled (Yes/No); Ward (Yes/No, if given)

329; John; m; 42; Miss. Choctaw; F; M; Head; 320; Yes
330; Sallie; f; 41; Miss. Choctaw; F; M; Wife; 321; Yes
331; Minnie; f; 3-21; Miss. Choctaw; F; S; Dau; 322; Yes
332; Hattie; f; 14; Miss. Choctaw; F; S; Dau; 323; Yes
333; Allie Nora; f; 12; Miss. Choctaw; F; S; Dau; 324; Yes
334; Ella; f; 10; Miss. Choctaw; F; S; Dau; 325; Yes
335; Lum Billy; m; 6; Miss. Choctaw; F; S; Son; 326; Yes

336; Laura; f; 64; Miss. Choctaw; F; Wd; Head; 327; Yes
337; Alyne; f; 22; Miss. Choctaw; F; S; Dau; 328; Yes

CLEMONS

338; Phillip; m; 37; Miss. Choctaw; F; S; Alone; 329; Yes

CLEMONS or COWED

339; Jim; m; 27; Miss. Choctaw; F; M; Head; 331; Yes
340; Bessie; f; 25; Miss. Choctaw; F; M; Wife; 332; Yes
341; Margie; f; 4; Miss. Choctaw; F; S; Dau; 333; Yes
342; Lewisman; m; 2; Miss. Choctaw; F; S; Son; 334; Yes

CLARK

343; Stella; f; 37; Miss. Choctaw; F; S; Alone; 335; Yes

CLEMONS

344; Jeff; m; 35; Miss. Choctaw; F; M; Head; 336; Yes
345; Cora; f; 31; Miss. Choctaw; F; M; Wife; 337; Yes
346; Mattie; f; 10; Miss. Choctaw; F; S; Dau; 338; Yes
347; Ethel; f; 9; Miss. Choctaw; F; S; Dau; 339; Yes
348; Letha; f; 7; Miss. Choctaw; F; S; Dau; 340; Yes
349; John; m; 6; Miss. Choctaw; F; S; Son; 341; Yes

Census of the **Mississippi Choctaw** reservation of the **Choctaw Agency** jurisdiction, as of **April 1**, 19**32**, taken by **R. J. Enochs**, Superintendent.

KEY; Surname; Census Number; Given Name; Sex; Age at Last Birthday; Tribe; Degree of Blood; Marital Status; Relationship to Head of Family; Last Census Roll Number; At Jurisdiction Where Enrolled (Yes/No); Ward (Yes/No, if given)

350;   Rena Mae; f; 4; Miss. Choctaw; F; S; Dau; 342; Yes

351;   Munch; m; 49; Miss. Choctaw; F; M; Head; 343; Yes
352;   Nellie; f; 42; Miss. Choctaw; F; M; Wife; 344; Yes
353;   Ruth; f; 14; Miss. Choctaw; F; S; Dau; 345; Yes
354;   Bathia; f; 13; Miss. Choctaw; F; S; Dau; 346; Yes
355;   Mollie; f; 11; Miss. Choctaw; F; S; Dau; 347; Yes

COMBY

356;   Alma; f; 40; Miss. Choctaw; F; Wd; Head; 348; Yes
357;   **McMillian**, Jimmie; m; 21; Miss. Choctaw; F; S; Son; 349; Yes
358;   **McMillian**, Jimpson; m; 19; Miss. Choctaw; F; S; Son; 350; Yes
359;   **McMillian**, Ella; f; 17; Miss. Choctaw; F; S; Dau; 351; Yes
360;   **McMillian**, Jordan; m; 2; Miss. Choctaw; F; S; Grand-son; 352; Yes

361;   Arbin; m; 44; Miss. Choctaw; F; Wd; Head; 353; Yes
362;   Gilbert; m; 20; Miss. Choctaw; F; S; Son; 354; Yes
363;   Rosella; f; 12; Miss. Choctaw; F; S; Dau; 355; Yes
364;   Maudell; f; 9; Miss. Choctaw; F; S; Dau; 356; Yes

365;   Semour[sic]; m; 31; Miss. Choctaw; F; M; Head; 357; Yes
366;   Edna; f; 26; Miss. Choctaw; F; M; Wife; 358; Yes
367;   W. C; m; 10; Miss. Choctaw; F; S; Son; 359; Yes
368;   B. C; m; 8; Miss. Choctaw; F; S; Son; 360; Yes
369;   Leroy; m; 6; Miss. Choctaw; F; S; Son; 361; Yes

370;   Allie; f; 27; Miss. Choctaw; F; Wd; Head; 362; Yes
371;   Jonas; m; 8; Miss. Choctaw; F; S; Son; 363; Yes
372;   Irene; f; 6; Miss. Choctaw; F; S; Dau; 364; Yes
373;   Joyce Ann; f; 4; Miss. Choctaw; F; S; Dau; 365; Yes
374;   R. L; m; 2; Miss. Choctaw; F; S; Son; 366; Yes
375;   **Chitto**, Mary; f; 33; Miss. Choctaw; F; S; Sister; 367; Yes

Census of the **Mississippi Choctaw** reservation of the **Choctaw Agency** jurisdiction, as of **April 1**, 19_32_, taken by **R. J. Enochs**, Superintendent.

KEY; Surname; Census Number; Given Name; Sex; Age at Last Birthday; Tribe; Degree of Blood; Marital Status; Relationship to Head of Family; Last Census Roll Number; At Jurisdiction Where Enrolled (Yes/No); Ward (Yes/No, if given)

376; Ben; m; 70; Miss. Choctaw; F; Wd; Alone; 375; Yes

377; Olmon; m; 54; Miss. Choctaw; F; M; Head; 376; Yes
378; Laura; f; 51; Miss. Choctaw; F; M; Wife; 377; Yes

COOPER

379; Dixon; m; 31; Miss. Choctaw; F; M; Head; 378; Yes
380; Leana; f; 24; Miss. Choctaw; F; M; Wife; 379; Yes

381; Gaston; m; 46; Miss. Choctaw; F; M; Head; 380; Yes
382; Ada; f; 48; Miss. Choctaw; F; M; Wife; 381; Yes
383; Odell; f; 19; Miss. Choctaw; F; S; Dau; 382; Yes
384; Fannie; f; 14; Miss. Choctaw; F; S; Dau; 383; Yes
385; Hubert; m; 11; Miss. Choctaw; F; S; Son; 384; Yes
386; Christine; f; 8; Miss. Choctaw; F; S; Dau; 385; Yes
387; Alma; f; 5; Miss. Choctaw; F; S; Dau; 386; Yes

COTTON

388; John; m; 22; Miss. Choctaw; F; S; Alone; 387; Yes

389; George; m; 32; Miss. Choctaw; F; M; Head; 388; Yes
390; Ellen; f; 31; Miss. Choctaw; F; M; Wife; 389; Yes
391; Minnie; f; 6; Miss. Choctaw; F; S; Dau; 390; Yes
392; **Crenshaw**, Amos; m; 20; Miss. Choctaw; F; S; Orphan; 391; Yes
393; **Crenshaw**, Austin; m; 16; Miss. Choctaw; F; S; Orphan; 392; Yes

DAN

394; Lela; f; 24; Miss. Choctaw; F; Wd; Head; 394; Yes
395; Irene; f; 6; Miss. Choctaw; F; S; Dau; 395; Yes
396; Albert B; m; 2; Miss. Choctaw; F; S; Son; 396; Yes

Census of the __Mississippi Choctaw__ reservation of the ___Choctaw Agency___ jurisdiction, as of ____April 1____, 19_32_, taken by __R. J. Enochs__, Superintendent.

KEY; Surname; Census Number; Given Name; Sex; Age at Last Birthday; Tribe; Degree of Blood; Marital Status; Relationship to Head of Family; Last Census Roll Number; At Jurisdiction Where Enrolled (Yes/No); Ward (Yes/No, if given)

397; Williston; m; 35; Miss. Choctaw; F; M; Head; 397; Yes
398; Dinah; f; 20; Miss. Choctaw; F; M; Wife; 398; Yes
399; Rose Ida; f; 10; Miss. Choctaw; F; S; Dau; 399; Yes

DANSBY

400; Jacob; m; 60; Miss. Choctaw; F; M; Head; 400; Yes
401; Jennie; f; 47; Miss. Choctaw; F; M; Wife; 401; Yes
402; **Tubby**, R. B; m; 25; Miss. Choctaw; F; S; Brother-in-law; 402; Yes
403; **Tubby**, Jim; m; 59; Miss. Choctaw; F; S; Brother-in-law; 403; Yes

DAVIS

404; Culberson; m; 70; Miss. Choctaw; F; M; Head; 404; Yes
405; Leona; f; 56; Miss. Choctaw; F; M; Wife; 405; Yes
406; Hobbie; m; 26; Miss. Choctaw; F; S; Son; 406; Yes

407; Will; m; 58; Miss. Choctaw; F; M; Head; 407; Yes
408; Mattie; f; 30; Miss. Choctaw; F; M; Wife; 408; Yes
409; Annie; f; 13; Miss. Choctaw; F; S; Dau; 409; Yes
410; John; m; 11; Miss. Choctaw; F; S; Son; 410; Yes
411; Mary; f; 4; Miss. Choctaw; F; S; Dau; 411; Yes
412; Mack; m; 3; Miss. Choctaw; F; S; Son; 412; Yes
413; Lewis; m; 1; Miss. Choctaw; F; S; Son; 413; Yes

414; Sidney; m; 44; Miss. Choctaw; F; Wd; Head; 414; Yes
415; Elamer; f; 23; Miss. Choctaw; F; S; Dau; 415; Yes
416; Mabel; f; 20; Miss. Choctaw; F; S; Dau; 416; Yes
417; Anna; f; 12; Miss. Choctaw; F; S; Dau; 417; Yes
418; Johnnie; m; 10; Miss. Choctaw; F; S; Son; 418; Yes

419; Malissie; f; 62; Miss. Choctaw; F; Wd; Head; 419; Yes

Census of the **Mississippi Choctaw** reservation of the **Choctaw Agency** jurisdiction, as of **April 1**, 19 **32**, taken by **R. J. Enochs**, Superintendent.

KEY; Surname; Census Number; Given Name; Sex; Age at Last Birthday; Tribe; Degree of Blood; Marital Status; Relationship to Head of Family; Last Census Roll Number; At Jurisdiction Where Enrolled (Yes/No); Ward (Yes/No, if given)

420; Alice; f; 35; Miss. Choctaw; F; S; Dau; 420; Yes
421; Bessie; f; 22; Miss. Choctaw; F; S; Dau; 421; Yes
422; Sina; f; 20; Miss. Choctaw; F; S; Grand-dau; 422; Yes
423; Ada Francis; f; 12; Miss. Choctaw; F; S; Grand-dau; 423; Yes
424; Mary; f; 17; Miss. Choctaw; F; S; Grand-dau; 424; Yes

425; Tom; m; 32; Miss. Choctaw; F; Wd; Head; 425; Yes
426; Millie; f; 12; Miss. Choctaw; F; S; Dau; 427; Yes
427; Henderson; m; 10; Miss. Choctaw; F; S; Son; 428; Yes

DENSON

428; Lilly; f; 44; Miss. Choctaw; F; Wd; Head; 429; Yes
429; Hendrix; m; 15; Miss. Choctaw; F; S; Son; 430; Yes
430; Emma; f; 12; Miss. Choctaw; F; S; Dau; 431; Yes
431; Charley; m; 9; Miss. Choctaw; F; S; Son; 432; Yes
432; David; m; 7; Miss. Choctaw; F; S; Son; 433; Yes
433; **Farmer**, Eula Mae; f; 9/12; Miss. Choctaw; F; S; Grand-dau; Yes

434; Pete; m; 44; Miss. Choctaw; F; M; Head; 434; Yes
435; Rosie; f; 31; Miss. Choctaw; F; M; Wife; 435; Yes
436; Mary; f; 16; Miss. Choctaw; F; S; Dau; 436; Yes
437; Jeffie; f; 14; Miss. Choctaw; F; S; Dau; 437; Yes
438; Edna; f; 9; Miss. Choctaw; F; S; Dau; 438; Yes
439; Nancy; f; 3; Miss. Choctaw; F; S; Dau; 439; Yes
440; Jennie E; f; 9 da; Miss. Choctaw; F; S; Dau; 4[sic]; Yes

441; Willie; m; 24; Miss. Choctaw; F; M; Head; 440; Yes
442; Beauty; f; 20; Miss. Choctaw; F; M; Wife; 441; Yes

443; Ezell; m; 20; Miss. Choctaw; F; M; Head; 444; Yes
444; Beauty; f; 20; Miss. Choctaw; F; M; Wife; 445; Yes
445; Ruth; f; 1; Miss. Choctaw; F; S; Dau; 446; Yes

Census of the **Mississippi Choctaw** reservation of the **Choctaw Agency** jurisdiction, as of **April 1**, 19 **32**, taken by **R. J. Enochs**, Superintendent.

KEY; Surname; Census Number; Given Name; Sex; Age at Last Birthday; Tribe; Degree of Blood; Marital Status; Relationship to Head of Family; Last Census Roll Number; At Jurisdiction Where Enrolled (Yes/No); Ward (Yes/No, if given)

DIXON

446; Nannie; f; 52; Miss. Choctaw; F; Wd; Head; 447; Yes
446; **Sam**, Charlie; m; 17; Miss. Choctaw; F; S; Nephew; 448; Yes

448; Jim; m; 31; Miss. Choctaw; F; M; Head; 449; Yes
449; Sarah; f; 29; Miss. Choctaw; F; M; Wife; 450; Yes
450; Marie; f; 9; Miss. Choctaw; F; S; Dau; 451; Yes
451; Imogene; f; 6; Miss. Choctaw; F; S; Dau; 452; Yes
452; Ellen; f; 4; Miss. Choctaw; F; S; Dau; 453; Yes
453; Mable C; f; 1; Miss. Choctaw; F; S; Dau; 454; Yes

454; Jess; m; 54; Miss. Choctaw; F; M; Head; 455; Yes
455; Callie; f; 62; Miss. Choctaw; F; M; Wife; 456; Yes
456; Scott; m; 21; Miss. Choctaw; F; S; Son; 457; Yes
457; Young; m; 15; Miss. Choctaw; F; S; Son; 458; Yes
458; Lilly; f; 12; Miss. Choctaw; F; S; Dau; 459; Yes
459; **Thompson**, Mary Jane; f; 82; Miss. Choctaw; F; Wd; Mother-in-law; 460; Yes

460; Horace; m; 26; Miss. Choctaw; F; M; Head; 461; Yes
461; Esther; f; 25; Miss. Choctaw; F; M; Wife; 462; Yes
462; Calonia; f; 5; Miss. Choctaw; F; S; Dau; 463; Yes

463; Edmond; m; 24; Miss. Choctaw; F; M; Head; 464; Yes
464; Julia; f; 23; Miss. Choctaw; F; M; Wife; 465; Yes
465; Addie Mae; f; 2; Miss. Choctaw; F; S; Dau; 466; Yes

466; Wilson; m; 73; Miss. Choctaw; F; M; Head; 467; Yes
467; Hope; f; 46; Miss. Choctaw; F; M; Wife; 468; Yes

468; Kanis; m; 40; Miss. Choctaw; F; Wd; Head; 469; Yes
469; Esby; f; 21; Miss. Choctaw; F; S; Dau; 470; Yes
470; Lonie; f; 18; Miss. Choctaw; F; S; Dau; 471; Yes

Census of the __Mississippi Choctaw__ reservation of the __Choctaw Agency__ jurisdiction, as of __April 1__, 19__32__, taken by __R. J. Enochs__, Superintendent.

KEY; Surname; Census Number; Given Name; Sex; Age at Last Birthday; Tribe; Degree of Blood; Marital Status; Relationship to Head of Family; Last Census Roll Number; At Jurisdiction Where Enrolled (Yes/No); Ward (Yes/No, if given)

471; Jim; m; 27; Miss. Choctaw; F; S; Son; 472; Yes
472; Wade; m; 17; Miss. Choctaw; F; S; Son; 473; Yes

EVANS

473; John; m; 57; Miss. Choctaw; F; Wd; Head; 474; Yes
474; **Wickson**, Kelly; m; 7; Miss. Choctaw; F; S; Grand-son; 475; Yes

FARMER

475; Silmon; m; 58; Miss. Choctaw; F; Wd; Head; 476; Yes
476; Henry; m; 20; Miss. Choctaw; F; S; Son; 477; Yes
477; Bennie; f; 14; Miss. Choctaw; F; S; Dau; 478; Yes
478; Corine; f; 11; Miss. Choctaw; F; S; Dau; 479; Yes

479; Ishman; m; 87; Miss. Choctaw; F; M; Head; 480; Yes
480; Sweeter; f; 59; Miss. Choctaw; F; M; Wife; 481; Yes
481; Emma; f; 29; Miss. Choctaw; F; S; Dau; 482; Yes
482; Marshall; m; 27; Miss. Choctaw; F; S; Son; 483; Yes
483; Maggie; f; 22; Miss. Choctaw; F; S; Dau; 484; Yes
484; Lena; f; 19; Miss. Choctaw; F; S; Dau; 485; Yes
485; Bill; m; 16; Miss. Choctaw; F; S; Son; 486; Yes
486; Rainey; f; 12; Miss. Choctaw; F; S; Dau; 487; Yes

487; Moses; m; 32; Miss. Choctaw; F; M; Head; 488; Yes
488; Lottie; f; 24; Miss. Choctaw; F; M; Wife; 489; Yes
489; Mealie; f; 1; Miss. Choctaw; F; S; Dau; 490; Yes

490; Thomas; m; 66; Miss. Choctaw; F; M; Head; 491; Yes
491; Melissa; f; 59; Miss. Choctaw; F; M; Wife; 492; Yes
492; Howard; m; 20; Miss. Choctaw; F; Wd; Son; 493; Yes

FARVE

Census of the **Mississippi Choctaw** reservation of the **Choctaw** **Agency** jurisdiction, as of **April 1**, 19**32**, taken by **R. J. Enochs**, Superintendent.

KEY; Surname; Census Number; Given Name; Sex; Age at Last Birthday; Tribe; Degree of Blood; Marital Status; Relationship to Head of Family; Last Census Roll Number; At Jurisdiction Where Enrolled (Yes/No); Ward (Yes/No, if given)

493; Bennett; m; 39; Miss. Choctaw; F; S; Alone; 495; Yes

494; Paul; m; 44; Miss. Choctaw; F; M; Head; 496; Yes
495; Renia; f; 27; Miss. Choctaw; F; M; Wife; 497; Yes
496; Phillip, Jr; m; 8; Miss. Choctaw; F; S; Son; 498; Yes
497; Eula Mae; f; 6; Miss. Choctaw; F; S; Dau; 499; Yes
498; Estelle; f; 4; Miss. Choctaw; F; S; Dau; 500; Yes
499; Viola; f; 2; Miss. Choctaw; F; S; Dau; 501; Yes

500; Joseph S; m; 20; Miss. Choctaw; F; M; Head; 502; Yes
501; Rachel; f; 53; Miss. Choctaw; F; M; Wife; 503; Yes

502; Western; m; 42; Miss. Choctaw; F; Wd; Head; 504; Yes
503; Chester; m; 27; Miss. Choctaw; F; S; Son; 505; Yes
504; Josie; f; 24; Miss. Choctaw; F; S; Dau; 506; Yes
505; John; m; 24; Miss. Choctaw; F; S; Dau; 507; Yes
506; Lillian; f; 21; Miss. Choctaw; F; S; Dau; 508; Yes
507; Ima; f; 16; Miss. Choctaw; F; S; Dau; 509; Yes
508; Hilda; f; 8; Miss. Choctaw; F; S; Dau; 510; Yes

509; Antwine; m; 55; Miss. Choctaw; F; M; Head; 511; Yes
510; Liseeda; f; 58; Miss. Choctaw; F; M; Wife; 512; Yes
511; Edna; f; 22; Miss. Choctaw; F; S; Dau; 513; Yes
512; Cecilia; f; 20; Miss. Choctaw; F; S; Dau; 514; Yes
513; Isileen; f; 19; Miss. Choctaw; F; S; Dau; 515; Yes
514; Earl; m; 14; Miss. Choctaw; F; S; Son; 516; Yes
515; Mammie; f; 12; Miss. Choctaw; F; S; Dau; 517; Yes
516; Corbrin; m; 9; Miss. Choctaw; F; S; Son; 518; Yes

517; Dave; m; 54; Miss. Choctaw; F; Wd; Head; 519; Yes
518; Lena; f; 32; Miss. Choctaw; F; S; Dau; 520; Yes
519; Sarah Alma; f; 21; Miss. Choctaw; F; S; Dau; 521; Yes
520; Georgia; f; 13; Miss. Choctaw; F; S; Dau; 522; Yes
521; John; m; 10; Miss. Choctaw; F; S; Son; 523; Yes; Yes

Census of the **Mississippi Choctaw** reservation of the **Choctaw Agency** jurisdiction, as of **April 1**, 19**32**, taken by **R. J. Enochs**, Superintendent.

KEY; Surname; Census Number; Given Name; Sex; Age at Last Birthday; Tribe; Degree of Blood; Marital Status; Relationship to Head of Family; Last Census Roll Number; At Jurisdiction Where Enrolled (Yes/No); Ward (Yes/No, if given)

522; William; m; 31; Miss. Choctaw; F; M; Head; 524; Yes
523; Mary Lou; f; 15; Miss. Choctaw; F; M; Wife; 525; Yes

524; Rosine H; m; 49; Miss. Choctaw; F; M; Head; 526; Yes
525; Winoa; f; 54; Miss. Choctaw; F; M; Wife; 527; Yes

526; Charles; m; 44; Miss. Choctaw; F; M; Head; 528; Yes
517; Edwina; f; 41; Miss. Choctaw; F; M; Wife; 529; Yes
528; Retha; f; 14; Miss. Choctaw; F; S; Dau; 530; Yes
529; Alvin; m; 12; Miss. Choctaw; F; S; Son; 531; Yes
530; Irvin; m; 10; Miss. Choctaw; F; S; Son; 532; Yes
531; Audrey; f; 7; Miss. Choctaw; F; S; Dau; 533; Yes
532; Vivian; f; 6; Miss. Choctaw; F; S; Dau; 534; Yes

533; Thomas; m; 50; Miss. Choctaw; F; M; Head; 535; Yes
534; Mary; f; 34; Miss. Choctaw; F; M; Wife; 536; Yes
535; Hazel; f; 14; Miss. Choctaw; F; S; Dau; 537; Yes
536; Robert; m; 13; Miss. Choctaw; F; S; Son; 538; Yes
537; Gertrude; f; 11; Miss. Choctaw; F; S; Dau; 539; Yes
538; Ruth; f; 8; Miss. Choctaw; F; S; Dau; 540; Yes

539; Sylvester; m; 44; Miss. Choctaw; F; S; Alone; 541; Yes

540; Joe Tole; m; 67; Miss. Choctaw; F; M; Head; 542; Yes
541; Lola; f; 64; Miss. Choctaw; F; M; Wife; 543; Yes
542; Dora; f; 39; Miss. Choctaw; F; S; Dau; 544; Yes
543; Victoria; f; 32; Miss. Choctaw; F; S; Dau; 545; Yes

544; Gilmore; m; 30; Miss. Choctaw; F; M; Head; 546; Yes
545; Gertrude; f; 28; Miss. Choctaw; F; M; Wife; 547; Yes

546; Joe; m; 26; Miss. Choctaw; F; M; Head; 548; Yes
547; Lillian; f; 23; Miss. Choctaw; F; M; Wife; 549; Yes

Census of the **Mississippi Choctaw** reservation of the **Choctaw Agency** jurisdiction, as of **April 1**, 19**32**, taken by **R. J. Enochs**, Superintendent.

KEY; Surname; Census Number; Given Name; Sex; Age at Last Birthday; Tribe; Degree of Blood; Marital Status; Relationship to Head of Family; Last Census Roll Number; At Jurisdiction Where Enrolled (Yes/No); Ward (Yes/No, if given)

548; Basie; m; 21; Miss. Choctaw; F; S; Alone; 550; Yes

549; Jessie; f; 20; Miss. Choctaw; F; S; Alone; 551; Yes

550; Corrin; m; 37; Miss. Choctaw; F; M; Head; 552; Yes
551; Viola; f; 35; Miss. Choctaw; F; M; Wife; 553; Yes
552; William; m; 16; Miss. Choctaw; F; S; Son; 554; Yes
553; Francis; m; 10; Miss. Choctaw; F; S; Son; 555; Yes
554; J. C; m; 8; Miss. Choctaw; F; S; Son; 556; Yes
555; Wilma; f; 6; Miss. Choctaw; F; S; Dau; 557; Yes

556; John Tole; m; 49; Miss. Choctaw; F; S; Alone; 558; Yes

557; Charles T; m; 48; Miss. Choctaw; F; M; Head; 559; Yes
558; Alfonsine; f; 34; Miss. Choctaw; F; M; Wife; 560; Yes

559; Emeline; f; 42; Miss. Choctaw; F; S; Alone; 561; Yes

560; Mary; f; 36; Miss. Choctaw; F; S; Alone; 562; Yes

561; Julia; f; 47; Miss. Choctaw; F; S; Alone; 563; Yes

562; R.C; m; 31; Miss. Choctaw; F; S; Alone; 564; Yes

563; Dennis; m; 44; Miss. Choctaw; F; S; Alone; 565; Yes

564; Western; m; 52; Miss. Choctaw; F; S; Alone; 566; Yes

565; Noah; m; 40; Miss. Choctaw; F; S; Alone; 567; Yes

566; Bennett; m; 38; Miss. Choctaw; F; S; Alone; 568; Yes

567; William; m; 34; Miss. Choctaw; F; S; Alone; 569; Yes

Census of the **Mississippi Choctaw** reservation of the **Choctaw Agency** jurisdiction, as of **April 1**, 19**32**, taken by **R. J. Enochs**, Superintendent.

KEY; Surname; Census Number; Given Name; Sex; Age at Last Birthday; Tribe; Degree of Blood; Marital Status; Relationship to Head of Family; Last Census Roll Number; At Jurisdiction Where Enrolled (Yes/No); Ward (Yes/No, if given)

568; Seman; m; 66; Miss. Choctaw; F; S; Alone; 570; Yes

569; Elinor; f; 38; Miss. Choctaw; F; S; Alone; 571; Yes

570; Joe; m; 59; Miss. Choctaw; F; S; Alone; 572; Yes

571; Albert; m; 51; Miss. Choctaw; F; M; Head; 573; Yes
572; Iktial; f; 49; Miss. Choctaw; F; M; Wife; 574; Yes

573; Lucille; f; 29; Miss. Choctaw; F; S; Alone; 575; Yes

574; Ethel; f; 28; Miss. Choctaw; F; S; Alone; 576; Yes

575; Ia[sic]; f; 52; Miss. Choctaw; F; S; Alone; 577; Yes

576; Roselle; f; 56; Miss. Choctaw; F; S; Alone; 578; Yes

577; Amelia; f; 38; Miss. Choctaw; F; S; Alone; 579; Yes

578; Henrietta; f; 34; Miss. Choctaw; F; S; Alone; 580; Yes

579; Bay Turner; m; 27; Miss. Choctaw; F; S; Alone; 581; Yes

580; Ceciline; m; 26; Miss. Choctaw; F; S; Alone; 582; Yes

581; Charles; m; 52; Miss. Choctaw; F; S; Alone; 583; Yes

FORBES

582; Wesley; m; 68; Miss. Choctaw; F; M; Head; 584; Yes
583; Sallie; f; 67; Miss. Choctaw; F; M; Wife; 585; Yes
584; Ella; f; 21; Miss. Choctaw; F; S; Dau; 586; Yes

585; Clint; m; 30; Miss. Choctaw; F; M; Head; 587; Yes

Census of the **Mississippi Choctaw** reservation of the **Choctaw Agency** jurisdiction, as of **April 1**, 19 **32**, taken by **R. J. Enochs**, Superintendent.

KEY; Surname; Census Number; Given Name; Sex; Age at Last Birthday; Tribe; Degree of Blood; Marital Status; Relationship to Head of Family; Last Census Roll Number; At Jurisdiction Where Enrolled (Yes/No); Ward (Yes/No, if given)

586; Josey; f; 31; Miss. Choctaw; F; M; Wife; 588; Yes
587; Ida Mae; f; 15; Miss. Choctaw; F; S; Dau; 589; Yes
588; Gaston; m; 10; Miss. Choctaw; F; S; Dau; 590; Yes
589; Henry; m; 2; Miss. Choctaw; F; S; Son; 591; Yes

FRAZIER

590; Mollie; f; 57; Miss. Choctaw; F; Wd; Head; 592; Yes
591; Essie; f; 25; Miss. Choctaw; F; S; Dau; 593; Yes
592; John; m; 21; Miss. Choctaw; F; S; Son; 594; Yes

593; West; m; 24; Miss. Choctaw; F; M; Head; 595; Yes
594; Nannie; f; 23; Miss. Choctaw; F; M; Wife; 596; Yes
595; Marshall; m; 3; Miss. Choctaw; F; S; Son; 597; Yes

596; Forbes; m; 31; Miss. Choctaw; F; M; Head; 598; Yes
597; Iam; f; 27; Miss. Choctaw; F; M; Wife; 599; Yes
598; Homer; m; 8; Miss. Choctaw; F; S; Son; 601; Yes
599; **Box**, Sam Davis; m; 8; Miss. Choctaw; F; S; Step-son; 600; Yes

600; Will; m; 32; Miss. Choctaw; F; M; Head; 602; Yes
601; Lavena; f; 29; Miss. Choctaw; F; M; Wife; 603; Yes

602; Seale; m; 62; Miss. Choctaw; F; M; Head; 604; Yes
603; Eliza; f; 77; Miss. Choctaw; F; M; Wife; 605; Yes
604; Willie; f; 7; Miss. Choctaw; F; S; Grand-dau; 606; Yes

605; Jim; m; 26; Miss. Choctaw; F; M; Head; 607; Yes
606; Nannie; f; 28; Miss. Choctaw; F; M; Wife; 608; Yes
607; A.B; m; 5; Miss. Choctaw; F; S; Son; 609; Yes
608; Henry; m; 6; Miss. Choctaw; F; S; Son; 610; Yes
609; Nancy; f; 3; Miss. Choctaw; F; S; Dau; 611; Yes

610; Ligman; m; 38; Miss. Choctaw; F; M; Head; 612; Yes

Census of the __Mississippi Choctaw__ reservation of the __Choctaw Agency__ jurisdiction, as of __April 1__, 19__32__, taken by __R. J. Enochs__, Superintendent.

KEY; Surname; Census Number; Given Name; Sex; Age at Last Birthday; Tribe; Degree of Blood; Marital Status; Relationship to Head of Family; Last Census Roll Number; At Jurisdiction Where Enrolled (Yes/No); Ward (Yes/No, if given)

611; Sina; f; 23; Miss. Choctaw; F; M; Wife; 613; Yes
612; Edmond; m; 10; Miss. Choctaw; F; S; Son; 614; Yes
613; Sallie; f; 8; Miss. Choctaw; F; S; Dau; 615; Yes

614; Emma; f; 34; Miss. Choctaw; F; Wd; Head; 616; Yes
615; Susie; f; 16; Miss. Choctaw; F; S; Dau; 617; Yes
616; Simpson; f; 12; Miss. Choctaw; F; S; Dau; 618; Yes
617; Herman; m; 11; Miss. Choctaw; F; S; Son; 619; Yes
618; Frazier; m; 9; Miss. Choctaw; F; S; Son; 620; Yes
619; Velma; f; 7; Miss. Choctaw; F; S; Dau; 621; Yes

620; Henson; m; 64; Miss. Choctaw; F; M; Head; 622; Yes
621; Fenie; f; 62; Miss. Choctaw; F; M; Wife; 623; Yes
622; Lucy; f; 14; Miss. Choctaw; F; S; Dau; 624; Yes
623; Wade; m; 14; Miss. Choctaw; F; S; Son; 625; Yes
624; Jake; m; 10; Miss. Choctaw; F; S; Son; 626; Yes

GARDNER

625; Jim; m; 33; Miss. Choctaw; F; M; Head; 627; Yes
626; Celia; f; 28; Miss. Choctaw; F; M; Wife; 628; Yes
627; Arleta; f; 11; Miss. Choctaw; F; S; Dau; 629; Yes
628; Alton; m; 5; Miss. Choctaw; F; S; Son; 630; Yes

GIPSON

629; Bart; m; 56; Miss. Choctaw; F; M; Head; 631; Yes
630; Lucy; f; 52; Miss. Choctaw; F; M; Wife; 632; Yes
631; Homer; m; 19; Miss. Choctaw; F; S; Son; 633; Yes

632; Hensley; m; 21; Miss. Choctaw; F; M; Head; 634; Yes
633; Elizabeth; f; 21; Miss. Choctaw; F; M; Wife; 635; Yes
634; Henrietta; f; 7/12; Miss. Choctaw; F; S; Dau; Yes

Census of the **Mississippi Choctaw** reservation of the **Choctaw Agency** jurisdiction, as of **April 1**, 19**32**, taken by **R. J. Enochs**, Superintendent.

KEY; Surname; Census Number; Given Name; Sex; Age at Last Birthday; Tribe; Degree of Blood; Marital Status; Relationship to Head of Family; Last Census Roll Number; At Jurisdiction Where Enrolled (Yes/No); Ward (Yes/No, if given)

635; Andrew; m; 27; Miss. Choctaw; F; M; Head; 636; Yes
636; Esther; f; 19; Miss. Choctaw; F; M; Wife; 637; Yes

637; Gus; m; 23; Miss. Choctaw; F; S; Alone; 638; Yes

638; Nolie; m; 30; Miss. Choctaw; F; M; Head; 639; Yes
639; Frances; f; 32; Miss. Choctaw; F; M; Wife; 640; Yes
640; Houston; m; 7; Miss. Choctaw; F; S; Son; 641; Yes
641; Paul; m; 6; Miss. Choctaw; F; S; Son; 642; Yes
642; Annie; f; 3; Miss. Choctaw; F; S; Dau; 643; Yes

643; Steve; m; 68; Miss. Choctaw; F; M; Head; 644; Yes
644; Jennie; f; 64; Miss. Choctaw; F; M; Wife; 645; Yes
645; Ikey; f; 29; Miss. Choctaw; F; S; Dau; 646; Yes
646; Fannie; f; 24; Miss. Choctaw; F; S; Dau; 647; Yes
647; Annie; f; 23; Miss. Choctaw; F; S; Dau; 648; Yes
648; Willie; m; 14; Miss. Choctaw; F; S; Son; 649; Yes
649; Hugh; m; 6; Miss. Choctaw; F; S; Grand-son; 650; Yes
650; Aron; m; 5; Miss. Choctaw; F; S; Grand-son; 651; Yes

HALL

651; Bessie; f; 20; Miss. Choctaw; F; Wd; Head; 652; Yes
652; Henrietta; f; 4; Miss. Choctaw; F; S; Dau; 653; Yes
653; **Thomas**, Lula; f; 18; Miss. Choctaw; F; S; Sister; 654; Yes

654; Langford; m; 37; Miss. Choctaw; F; M; Head; 655; Yes
655; Lou; f; 27; Miss. Choctaw; F; M; Wife; 656; Yes
656; Travis; m; 9; Miss. Choctaw; F; S; Son; 657; Yes
657; Arlone; f; 8; Miss. Choctaw; F; S; Dau; 658; Yes
658; Frank; m; 6; Miss. Choctaw; F; S; Son; 659; Yes
659; Francis; m; 3/12; Miss. Choctaw; F; S; Son ; Yes

Census of the __Mississippi Choctaw__ reservation of the __Choctaw Agency__ jurisdiction, as of __April 1__, 19__32__, taken by __R. J. Enochs__, Superintendent.

KEY; Surname; Census Number; Given Name; Sex; Age at Last Birthday; Tribe; Degree of Blood; Marital Status; Relationship to Head of Family; Last Census Roll Number; At Jurisdiction Where Enrolled (Yes/No); Ward (Yes/No, if given)

HARPER

660; Lena; f; 20; Miss. Choctaw; F; S; Alone; 660; Yes

HARRIS

661; Elsmore; f; 24; Miss. Choctaw; F; S; Alone; 661; Yes

HAWKINS

662; John; m; 72; Miss. Choctaw; F; M; Head; 662; Yes
663; Alice; f; 50; Miss. Choctaw; F; M; Wife; 663; Yes
664; **Shoemaker**, Mary; f; 21; Miss. Choctaw; F; S; Step-dau; 664; Yes

HENRY

665; Albert; m; 54; Miss. Choctaw; F; M; Head; 667; Yes
666; Martha; f; 44; Miss. Choctaw; F; M; Wife; 668; Yes
667; Guiser; f; 28; Miss. Choctaw; F; S; Dau; 669; Yes
668; Beulah; f; 24; Miss. Choctaw; F; S; Dau; 670; Yes
669; Lige; m; 22; Miss. Choctaw; F; S; Son; 671; Yes
670; Melvin; m; 19; Miss. Choctaw; F; S; Son; 672; Yes
671; Nettie; f; 17; Miss. Choctaw; F; S; Dau; 673; Yes
672; Sis; f; 14; Miss. Choctaw; F; S; Dau; 674; Yes
673; Susie; f; 12; Miss. Choctaw; F; S; Dau; 675; Yes
674; R. D; m; 10; Miss. Choctaw; F; S; Son; 676; Yes
675; Ellen M; f; 3; Miss. Choctaw; F; S; Grand-dau; 677; Yes
       Daughter of Guiser Henry

676; Jim; m; 29; Miss. Choctaw; F; M; Head; 678; Yes
677; Sallie; f; 27; Miss. Choctaw; F; M; Wife; 679; Yes
678; Frank; m; 5; Miss. Choctaw; F; S; Son; 680; Yes
679; Wicks; m; 3; Miss. Choctaw; F; S; Son; 681; Yes

Census of the **Mississippi Choctaw** reservation of the **Choctaw Agency** jurisdiction, as of **April 1**, 19**32**, taken by **R. J. Enochs**, Superintendent.

KEY; Surname; Census Number; Given Name; Sex; Age at Last Birthday; Tribe; Degree of Blood; Marital Status; Relationship to Head of Family; Last Census Roll Number; At Jurisdiction Where Enrolled (Yes/No); Ward (Yes/No, if given)

680; Robert; m; 58; Miss. Choctaw; F; M; Head; 682; Yes
681; Nellie; f; 48; Miss. Choctaw; F; M; Wife; 683; Yes
682; Bob; m; 24; Miss. Choctaw; F; S; Son; 684; Yes
683; Mattie; f; 20; Miss. Choctaw; F; S; Dau; 685; Yes
684; Jasper; m; 15; Miss. Choctaw; F; S; Son; 686; Yes
685; Dolphus; m; 12; Miss. Choctaw; F; S; Son; 687; Yes

HICKMAN

686; Billy; m; 46; Miss. Choctaw; F; M; Head; 688; Yes
687; Rhodie; f; 48; Miss. Choctaw; F; M; Wife; 689; Yes
688; Sim; m; 20; Miss. Choctaw; F; S; Son; 690; Yes
689; Susan; f; 14; Miss. Choctaw; F; S; Dau; 691; Yes
690; Lula; f; 12; Miss. Choctaw; F; S; Dau; 692; Yes

691; Willie; m; 22; Miss. Choctaw; F; M; Head; 693; Yes
692; Lodie Mae; f; 24; Miss. Choctaw; F; M; Wife; 694; Yes

693; Ellis; m; 62; Miss. Choctaw; F; M; Head; 695; Yes
694; Susan; f; 56; Miss. Choctaw; F; M; Wife; 696; Yes
695; **Bell**, Burton; m; 12; Miss. Choctaw; F; S; Grand-son; 697; Yes
696; **Bell**, Henry; m; 10; Miss. Choctaw; F; S; Grand-son; 698; Yes

697; Johnkin; m; 32; Miss. Choctaw; F; M; Head; 699; Yes
698; Minnie; f; 27; Miss. Choctaw; F; M; Wife; 701; Yes

699; Enoch; m; 58; Miss. Choctaw; F; M; Head; 702; Yes
700; Malinda; f; 56; Miss. Choctaw; F; M; Wife; 703; Yes
701; Sallie; f; 22; Miss. Choctaw; F; S; Dau; 704; Yes
702; Sadie; f; 21; Miss. Choctaw; F; S; Dau; 705; Yes
703; Tubby; m; 19; Miss. Choctaw; F; S; Son; 706; Yes
704; Eliza Jane; f; 18; Miss. Choctaw; F; S; Dau; 707; Yes
705; Mary Long; f; 16; Miss. Choctaw; F; S; Dau; 708; Yes
706; Annie; m; 11; Miss. Choctaw; F; S; Dau; 709; Yes

Census of the **Mississippi Choctaw** reservation of the **Choctaw Agency** jurisdiction, as of **April 1**, 19**32**, taken by **R. J. Enochs**, Superintendent.

KEY; Surname; Census Number; Given Name; Sex; Age at Last Birthday; Tribe; Degree of Blood; Marital Status; Relationship to Head of Family; Last Census Roll Number; At Jurisdiction Where Enrolled (Yes/No); Ward (Yes/No, if given)

707; Wm. Penn; m; 10; Miss. Choctaw; F; S; Son; 710; Yes
708; Vardeman; m; 8; Miss. Choctaw; F; S; Son; 711; Yes
709; John; m; 7; Miss. Choctaw; F; S; Son; 712; Yes

710; Wallace; m; 26; Miss. Choctaw; F; M; Head; 713; Yes
711; Dona; f; 23; Miss. Choctaw; F; M; Wife; 714; Yes
712; Robinson; m; 6; Miss. Choctaw; F; S; Son; 715; Yes

713; Stennis; m; 28; Miss. Choctaw; F; M; Head; 716; Yes
714; Winnie; f; 27; Miss. Choctaw; F; M; Wife; 717; Yes
715; Eula; f; 5; Miss. Choctaw; F; S; Dau; 718; Yes
716; Snooks; m; 4; Miss. Choctaw; F; S; Son; 719; Yes

717; Mary; f; 76; Miss. Choctaw; F; Wd; Head; 720; Yes
718; **Charlie**, Beckie; f; 15; Miss. Choctaw; F; S; Grand-dau; 721; Yes

HUDSON

719; Celia; f; 25; Miss. Choctaw; F; S; Alone; 722; Yes

ISAAC

720; Jim; m; 37; Miss. Choctaw; F; M; Head; 723; Yes
721; Bessie; f; 31; Miss. Choctaw; F; M; Wife; 724; Yes
722; Steve; m; 77; Miss. Choctaw; F; Wd; Father; 725; Yes

723; Byrd; m; 36; Miss. Choctaw; F; M; Head; 726; Yes
724; Pauline; f; 20; Miss. Choctaw; F; M; Wife; 727; Yes
725; Odie Mae; f; 16; Miss. Choctaw; F; S; Dau; 728; Yes
726; Bernice; f; 14; Miss. Choctaw; F; S; Dau; 729; Yes
727; Catherine; f; 12; Miss. Choctaw; F; S; Dau; 730; Yes
728; Edwin; m; 5; Miss. Choctaw; F; S; Son; 731; Yes
729; Jess A; m; 22 da; Miss. Choctaw; F; S; Son; ; Yes
730; **Hall**, Herbert H; m; 3; Miss. Choctaw; F; S; Step-son; 732; Yes

Census of the **Mississippi Choctaw** reservation of the **Choctaw Agency** jurisdiction, as of **April 1**, 19**32**, taken by **R. J. Enochs**, Superintendent.

KEY; Surname; Census Number; Given Name; Sex; Age at Last Birthday; Tribe; Degree of Blood; Marital Status; Relationship to Head of Family; Last Census Roll Number; At Jurisdiction Where Enrolled (Yes/No); Ward (Yes/No, if given)

731; Hickman; m; 25; Miss. Choctaw; F; S; Alone; 733; Yes

732; Simon; m; 48; Miss. Choctaw; F; M; Head; 734; Yes
733; Nannie; f; 51; Miss. Choctaw; F; M; Wife; 735; Yes
734; Effie; f; 9; Miss. Choctaw; F; S; Dau; 737; Yes
735; Lillie Mae; f; 7; Miss. Choctaw; F; S; Grand-dau; 738; Yes

736; Hugh; m; 22; Miss. Choctaw; F; M; Head; 739; Yes
737; Celia; f; 23; Miss. Choctaw; F; M; Wife; 740; Yes
738; Beneda; f; 1; Miss. Choctaw; F; S; Dau; 741; Yes

739; Isaac; m; 31; Miss. Choctaw; F; M; Head; 742; Yes
740; Magge; f; 23; Miss. Choctaw; F; M; Wife; 743; Yes
741; Claudine; f; 10; Miss. Choctaw; F; S; Dau; 744; Yes
742; Wilbur; m; 8; Miss. Choctaw; F; S; Son; 745; Yes
743; Claud P; m; 4; Miss. Choctaw; F; S; Son; 746; Yes
744; Enochs; m; 3; Miss. Choctaw; F; S; Son; 747; Yes

745; Will; m; 34; Miss. Choctaw; F; M; Head; 748; Yes
746; Louisa; f; 33; Miss. Choctaw; F; M; Wife; 749; Yes
747; Annie; f; 14; Miss. Choctaw; F; S; Dau; 750; Yes
748; Cornelia; f; 5; Miss. Choctaw; F; S; Dau; 751; Yes

749; Wilson; m; 78; Miss. Choctaw; F; M; Head; 752; Yes
750; Martha; f; 65; Miss. Choctaw; F; M; Wife; 753; Yes
751; Jackson; m; 27; Miss. Choctaw; F; S; Son; 754; Yes
752; John Day; m; 19; Miss. Choctaw; F; S; Son; 755; Yes
753; **Sam**, Edna; f; 10; Miss. Choctaw; F; S; Orphan; 756; Yes

754; David; m; 25; Miss. Choctaw; F; M; Head; 757; Yes
755; Lesper; f; 24; Miss. Choctaw; F; M; Wife; 758; Yes
756; Joe Day; m; 5; Miss. Choctaw; F; S; Son; 759; Yes
757; Franklin; m; 3; Miss. Choctaw; F; S; Son; 760; Yes
758; Wansey; f; 1; Miss. Choctaw; F; S; Dau; 761; Yes

Census of the **Mississippi Choctaw** reservation of the **Choctaw Agency** jurisdiction, as of **April 1**, 19**32**, taken by **R. J. Enochs**, Superintendent.

KEY; Surname; Census Number; Given Name; Sex; Age at Last Birthday; Tribe; Degree of Blood; Marital Status; Relationship to Head of Family; Last Census Roll Number; At Jurisdiction Where Enrolled (Yes/No); Ward (Yes/No, if given)

759; Dixon; m; 80; Miss. Choctaw; F; M; Head; 762; Yes
760; Lou; f; 27; Miss. Choctaw; F; M; Wife; 763; Yes
761; Elsie; f; 14; Miss. Choctaw; F; S; Dau; 764; Yes
762; Rainey; f; 11; Miss. Choctaw; F; S; Dau; 765; Yes
763; Manda; f; 9; Miss. Choctaw; F; S; Dau; 766; Yes
764; Lester; f; 8; Miss. Choctaw; F; S; Dau; 767; Yes
765; **Billy**, Emma; f; 26; Miss. Choctaw; F; S; Sister-in-law; 768; Yes

ISOM

766; Willie; m; 18; Miss. Choctaw; F; S; Alone; 769; Yes

767; Isom; m; 32; Miss. Choctaw; F; S; Alone; 770; Yes

JACKSON

768; Betty; f; 56; Miss. Choctaw; F; Wd; Head; 771; Yes
769; Rose; f; 20; Miss. Choctaw; F; S; Dau; 772; Yes
770; Nancie; f; 18; Miss. Choctaw; F; S; Dau; 773; Yes
771; Carlson; m; 12; Miss. Choctaw; F; S; Son; 774; Yes

772; Lena; f; 44; Miss. Choctaw; F; Wd; Head; 775; Yes
773; Ella; f; 18; Miss. Choctaw; F; S; Dau; 777; Yes
774; Floyd F; m; 17; Miss. Choctaw; F; S; Son; 778; Yes
775; Jackson; m; 14; Miss. Choctaw; F; S; Son; 779; Yes
776; Emmett; m; 12; Miss. Choctaw; F; S; Son; 780; Yes
777; Lucille; f; 11; Miss. Choctaw; F; S; Dau; 781; Yes

778; Tom; m; 44; Miss. Choctaw; F; M; Head; 782; Yes
779; Mamie; f; 40; Miss. Choctaw; F; M; Wife; 666; Yes
780; Woodrow; m; 13; Miss. Choctaw; F; S; Son; 783; Yes
781; Eva; f; 12; Miss. Choctaw; F; S; Dau; 784; Yes

782; Sam; m; 48; Miss. Choctaw; F; M; Head; 785; Yes

Census of the **Mississippi Choctaw** reservation of the **Choctaw Agency** jurisdiction, as of **April 1**, 19**32**, taken by **R. J. Enochs**, Superintendent.

KEY; Surname; Census Number; Given Name; Sex; Age at Last Birthday; Tribe; Degree of Blood; Marital Status; Relationship to Head of Family; Last Census Roll Number; At Jurisdiction Where Enrolled (Yes/No); Ward (Yes/No, if given)

783; Martha; f; 49; Miss. Choctaw; F; M; Wife; 786; Yes

784; Tubby; m; 22; Miss. Choctaw; F; M; Head; 787; Yes
785; Missie; f; 22; Miss. Choctaw; F; M; Wife; 788; Yes

786; Prentiss; m; 29; Miss. Choctaw; F; M; Head; 789; Yes
787; Mary; f; 29; Miss. Choctaw; F; M; Wife; 790; Yes

788; Mike; m; 31; Miss. Choctaw; F; S; Alone; 791; Yes

JEFFERSON

789; Braxton; m; 26; Miss. Choctaw; F; Wd; Head; 792; Yes

790; Amos; m; 25; Miss. Choctaw; F; M; Head; 793; Yes
791; Ida; f; 20; Miss. Choctaw; F; M; Wife; 794; Yes
797; Leon; m; 7/12; Miss. Choctaw; F; S; Son; Yes

792; Willis; m; 57; Miss. Choctaw; F; S; Alone; 795; Yes
793; Elsie; f; 45; Miss. Choctaw; F; S; Sister; 796; Yes

794; Oscar; m; 27; Miss. Choctaw; F; M; Head; 797; Yes
795; Saline; f; 25; Miss. Choctaw; F; M; Wife; 798; Yes
796; Malcolm; m; 6; Miss. Choctaw; F; S; Son; 799; Yes
797; Leon; m; 7/12; Miss. Choctaw; F; S; Son; Yes

798; Otis; m; 29; Miss. Choctaw; F; M; Head; 800; Yes
799; Onie; f; 27; Miss. Choctaw; F; M; Wife; 801; Yes
800; Otoo; m; 7; Miss. Choctaw; F; S; Son; 802; Yes
801; Andy; m; 6; Miss. Choctaw; F; S; Son; 803; Yes

JIM

802; George; m; 64; Miss. Choctaw; F; M; Head; 804; Yes

Census of the **Mississippi Choctaw** reservation of the **Choctaw Agency** jurisdiction, as of **April 1**, 19 **32**, taken by **R. J. Enochs**, Superintendent.

KEY; Surname; Census Number; Given Name; Sex; Age at Last Birthday; Tribe; Degree of Blood; Marital Status; Relationship to Head of Family; Last Census Roll Number; At Jurisdiction Where Enrolled (Yes/No); Ward (Yes/No, if given)

803; Eliza; f; 54; Miss. Choctaw; F; M; Wife; 805; Yes
804; Lee; m; 26; Miss. Choctaw; F; S; Son; 806; Yes
805; Sidney; m; 16; Miss. Choctaw; F; S; Son; 807; Yes

806; Cooley; m; 62; Miss. Choctaw; F; M; Head; 810; Yes
807; Lorena; f; 34; Miss. Choctaw; F; M; Wife; 811; Yes
808; William; m; 11; Miss. Choctaw; F; S; Son; 812; Yes
809; Tom; m; 9; Miss. Choctaw; F; S; Son; 813; Yes

810; John; m; 26; Miss. Choctaw; F; M; Head; 814; Yes
811; Bessie; f; 23; Miss. Choctaw; F; M; Wife; 815; Yes
812; Susie Ann; f; 1; Miss. Choctaw; F; S; Dau; 816; Yes

813; Henry; m; 47; Miss. Choctaw; F; M; Head; 817; Yes
814; Mollie; f; 60; Miss. Choctaw; F; M; Wife; 818; Yes

815; Harvey; m; 17; Miss. Choctaw; F; M; Head; 819; Yes
816; Mattie; f; 34; Miss. Choctaw; F; M; Wife; 820; Yes

817; Ben; m; 54; Miss. Choctaw; F; M; Head; 821; Yes
818; Dora; f; 42; Miss. Choctaw; F; M; Wife; 822; Yes
819; Annie Mae; f; 18; Miss. Choctaw; F; S; Dau; 823; Yes
820; Rena; f; 10; Miss. Choctaw; F; S; Dau; 824; Yes
821; Frank; m; 4; Miss. Choctaw; F; S; Grand-son; 825; Yes
822; Bobbie Sue; f; 3; Miss. Choctaw; F; S; Grand-dau; 826; Yes
823; Christine; f; 8/12; Miss. Choctaw; F; S; Dau; Yes

824; Logan; m; 84; Miss. Choctaw; F; Wd; Alone; 827; Yes

825; Amon; m; 55; Miss. Choctaw; F; M; Head; 828; Yes
826; Lucy; f; 47; Miss. Choctaw; F; M; Wife; 829; Yes
827; Opal; f; 12; Miss. Choctaw; F; S; Dau; 830; Yes
828; Carter; m; 3; Miss. Choctaw; F; S; Son; 831; Yes
829; Wm. Murrary[sic]; m; 2 da; Miss. Choctaw; F; S; Son; Yes

Census of the **Mississippi Choctaw** reservation of the **Choctaw Agency** jurisdiction, as of **April 1**, 19**32**, taken by **R. J. Enochs**, Superintendent.

KEY; Surname; Census Number; Given Name; Sex; Age at Last Birthday; Tribe; Degree of Blood; Marital Status; Relationship to Head of Family; Last Census Roll Number; At Jurisdiction Where Enrolled (Yes/No); Ward (Yes/No, if given)

830; Goodman; m; 67; Miss. Choctaw; F; M; Head; 832; Yes
831; Leona; f; 30; Miss. Choctaw; F; M; Wife; 833; Yes
832; Frank McKinley; m; 6; Miss. Choctaw; F; S; Son; 835; Yes
833; Claud Yates; m; 4; Miss. Choctaw; F; S; Son; 836; Yes
834; **Farmer**, Sallie; f; 77; Miss. Choctaw; F; Wd; Sister; 837; Yes

835; Albert; m; 25; Miss. Choctaw; F; M; Head; 838; Yes
836; Dora; f; 25; Miss. Choctaw; F; M; Wife; 839; Yes
837; Grace; f; 2; Miss. Choctaw; F; S; Dau; 840; Yes

838; Henry; m; 32; Miss. Choctaw; F; M; Head; 841; Yes
839; Maggie; f; 28; Miss. Choctaw; F; M; Wife; 842; Yes

840; Victor; m; 31; Miss. Choctaw; F; M; Head; 843; Yes
841; Lena; f; 22; Miss. Choctaw; F; M; Wife; 844; Yes
842; Foy; m; 6; Miss. Choctaw; F; S; Son; 845; Yes
843; Egbert; m; 2; Miss. Choctaw; F; S; Son; 846; Yes

844; Winston; m; 22; Miss. Choctaw; F; S; Alone; 847; Yes

JIMMIE

845; Mary; f; 25; Miss. Choctaw; F; Wd; Head; 848; Yes
846; Ona C; f; 4; Miss. Choctaw; F; S; Dau; 849; Yes
847; Delores; f; 2; Miss. Choctaw; F; S; Dau; 850; Yes

848; Frank M; m; 20; Miss. Choctaw; F; S; Alone; 851; Yes

849; Ike; m; 62; Miss. Choctaw; F; S; Alone; 852; Yes

850; Will; m; 52; Miss. Choctaw; F; M; Head; 854; Yes
851; Hester; f; 50; Miss. Choctaw; F; M; Wife; 855; Yes
852; Mack; m; 26; Miss. Choctaw; F; S; Son; 853; Yes
853; Homer; m; 23; Miss. Choctaw; F; S; Son; 856; Yes

Census of the **Mississippi Choctaw** reservation of the **Choctaw Agency** jurisdiction, as of **April 1**, 19**32**, taken by **R. J. Enochs**, Superintendent.

KEY; Surname; Census Number; Given Name; Sex; Age at Last Birthday; Tribe; Degree of Blood; Marital Status; Relationship to Head of Family; Last Census Roll Number; At Jurisdiction Where Enrolled (Yes/No); Ward (Yes/No, if given)

JOE

854; Nicholas; m; 42; Miss. Choctaw; F; M; Head; 857; Yes
855; Ella; f; 37; Miss. Choctaw; F; M; Wife; 858; Yes
856; Austin; m; 18; Miss. Choctaw; F; S; Son; 859; Yes
857; Henry; m; 14; Miss. Choctaw; F; S; Son; 860; Yes
858; Widge; f; 11; Miss. Choctaw; F; S; Dau; 861; Yes
859; Bessie; f; 9; Miss. Choctaw; F; S; Dau; 862; Yes
860; Billie Joe; m; 8; Miss. Choctaw; F; S; Son; 863; Yes
861; Mary; f; 2; Miss. Choctaw; F; S; Dau; 864; Yes
862; **Lewis**, Susie; f; 8; Miss. Choctaw; F; S; Step-dau; 865; Yes
863; **Lewis**, Elsie; f; 7; Miss. Choctaw; F; S; Step-dau; 866; Yes

864; Jasper; m; 44; Miss. Choctaw; F; M; Head; 867; Yes
865; Sallie; f; 39; Miss. Choctaw; F; M; Wife; 868; Yes
866; Lula; f; 19; Miss. Choctaw; F; S; Dau; 869; Yes
867; Houston; m; 14; Miss. Choctaw; F; S; Son; 870; Yes
868; Watkins; m; 10; Miss. Choctaw; F; S; Son; 871; Yes

869; Emily; f; 76; Miss. Choctaw; F; Wd; Alone; 872; Yes

870; John; m; 33; Miss. Choctaw; F; M; Head; 873; Yes
871; Emma; f; 32; Miss. Choctaw; F; M; Wife; 874; Yes
872; Bessie; f; 11; Miss. Choctaw; F; S; Dau; 875; Yes
873; Killie; f; 7; Miss. Choctaw; F; S; Dau; 876; Yes
874; Claud; m; 4; Miss. Choctaw; F; S; Son; 877; Yes

875; Langley; m; 84; Miss. Choctaw; F; Wd; Alone; 878; Yes

JOHN

876; Mike; m; 59; Miss. Choctaw; F; M; Head; 879; Yes
877; Lizzie; f; 74; Miss. Choctaw; F; M; Wife; 880; Yes
879; **Willis**, Dina; f; 18; Miss. Choctaw; F; S; Grand-dau; 881; Yes

Census of the **Mississippi Choctaw** reservation of the **Choctaw Agency** jurisdiction, as of **April 1**, 19 **32** , taken by **R. J. Enochs** , Superintendent.

KEY; Surname; Census Number; Given Name; Sex; Age at Last Birthday; Tribe; Degree of Blood; Marital Status; Relationship to Head of Family; Last Census Roll Number; At Jurisdiction Where Enrolled (Yes/No); Ward (Yes/No, if given)

878; **Denson**, Joe; m; 78; Miss. Choctaw; F; Wd; Alone; 442; Yes

880; Josh; m; 56; Miss. Choctaw; F; Wd; Alone; 882; Yes

881; Anderson; m; 55; Miss. Choctaw; F; M; Head; 883; Yes
882; Bettie; f; 43; Miss. Choctaw; F; M; Wife; 884; Yes
883; L. E; f; 17; Miss. Choctaw; F; S; Dau; 886; Yes
884; Hubert; m; 14; Miss. Choctaw; F; S; Son; 887; Yes
885; Oden; m; 11; Miss. Choctaw; F; S; Son; 888; Yes
886; Wilson; m; 4; Miss. Choctaw; F; S; Son; 889; Yes

887; Bennett; m; 23; Miss. Choctaw; F; M; Head; 890; Yes
888; Lena Pearl; f; 17; Miss. Choctaw; F; M; Wife; 891; Yes
889; Egbert; m; 11/12; Miss. Choctaw; F; S; Son; Yes

890; Clint; m; 41; Miss. Choctaw; F; S; Alone; 892; Yes

891; Ira; m; 27; Miss. Choctaw; F; M; Head; 893; Yes
892; Leda; f; 19; Miss. Choctaw; F; M; Wife; 894; Yes
893; Mercy Lee; f; 2; Miss. Choctaw; F; S; Dau; 895; Yes

894; Bob; m; 58; Miss. Choctaw; F; M; Head; 896; Yes
895; Onie; f; 47; Miss. Choctaw; F; M; Wife; 897; Yes
896; Oliver; m; 17; Miss. Choctaw; F; S; Son; 898; Yes
897; Otis; m; 15; Miss. Choctaw; F; S; Son; 899; Yes
898; Roby; m; 11; Miss. Choctaw; F; S; Son; 900; Yes
899; Rose; f; 9; Miss. Choctaw; F; S; Dau; 901; Yes

900; Jack; m; 58; Miss. Choctaw; F; M; Head; 902; Yes
901; Amanda; f; 37; Miss. Choctaw; F; M; Wife; 903; Yes
902; Jefferson; m; 10; Miss. Choctaw; F; S; Son; 904; Yes
903; Mary f; 8; Miss. Choctaw; F; S; Dau; 905; Yes
904; **Box**, Mamie; f; 10; Miss. Choctaw; F; S; Orphan; 906; Yes

Census of the **Mississippi Choctaw** reservation of the **Choctaw Agency** jurisdiction, as of **April 1**, 19**32**, taken by **R. J. Enochs**, Superintendent.

KEY; Surname; Census Number; Given Name; Sex; Age at Last Birthday; Tribe; Degree of Blood; Marital Status; Relationship to Head of Family; Last Census Roll Number; At Jurisdiction Where Enrolled (Yes/No); Ward (Yes/No, if given)

905; Betsie; f; 34; Miss. Choctaw; F; Wd; Head; 907; Yes
906; Bilbo; m; 15; Miss. Choctaw; F; S; Son; 908; Yes
907; Mable; f; 12; Miss. Choctaw; F; S; Dau; 909; Yes
908; Renie; f; 10; Miss. Choctaw; F; S; Dau; 910; Yes
909; Varderman; m; 7; Miss. Choctaw; F; S; Son; 911; Yes
910; Smith; m; 5; Miss. Choctaw; F; S; Son; 912; Yes
911; Lisette H; f; 2; Miss. Choctaw; F; S; Dau; 913; Yes

JOHNSON

912; Whitman; m; 21; Miss. Choctaw; F; S; Alone; 914; Yes

913; Will; m; 60; Miss. Choctaw; F; M; Head; 915; Yes
914; Dixie; f; 38; Miss. Choctaw; F; M; Wife; 916; Yes
915; **Comby**, Venie; f; 16; Miss. Choctaw; F; S; Step-dau; 917; Yes
916; **Comby**, Gus; m; 7; Miss. Choctaw; F; S; Step-son; 918; Yes
917; Sallie; f; 77; Miss. Choctaw; F; Wd; Mother; 919; Yes

918; Afton; m; 28; Miss. Choctaw; F; M; Head; 920; Yes
919; Sevenia; f; 26; Miss. Choctaw; F; M; Wife; 921; Yes
920; Callie; f; 3; Miss. Choctaw; F; S; Dau; 922; Yes

921; Edgar; m; 33; Miss. Choctaw; F; M; Head; 923; Yes
922; Beatrice; f; 29; Miss. Choctaw; F; M; Wife; 924; Yes
923; Callie; f; 9; Miss. Choctaw; F; S; Dau; 925; Yes
924; Frances; f; 7; Miss. Choctaw; F; S; Dau; 926; Yes
925; Egbert; m; 5; Miss. Choctaw; F; S; Son; 927; Yes
926; Phelia; f; 9/12; Miss. Choctaw; F; S; Dau; Yes

927; Frank; m; 40; Miss. Choctaw; F; M; Head; 928; Yes
928; Lorine; f; 32; Miss. Choctaw; F; M; Wife; 929; Yes
929; Otho; m; 16; Miss. Choctaw; F; S; Son; 930; Yes
930; Athens; m; 14; Miss. Choctaw; F; S; Son; 931; Yes
931; Sadie; f; 12; Miss. Choctaw; F; S; Dau; 932; Yes

Census of the **Mississippi Choctaw** reservation of the **Choctaw Agency** jurisdiction, as of **April 1**, 19**32**, taken by **R. J. Enochs**, Superintendent.

KEY; Surname; Census Number; Given Name; Sex; Age at Last Birthday; Tribe; Degree of Blood; Marital Status; Relationship to Head of Family; Last Census Roll Number; At Jurisdiction Where Enrolled (Yes/No); Ward (Yes/No, if given)

932; Bertha; f; 10; Miss. Choctaw; F; S; Dau; 933; Yes
933; Haven; m; 8; Miss. Choctaw; F; S; Son; 934; Yes
934; Sudan; f; 6; Miss. Choctaw; F; S; Dau; 935; Yes
935; Bena; f; 4; Miss. Choctaw; F; S; Dau; 936; Yes
936; Marvin; m; 11/12; Miss. Choctaw; F; S; Son; Yes

JOSHUA

937; Jennie; f; 62; Miss. Choctaw; F; Wd; Head; 937; Yes
938; **John**, Callie; f; 21; Miss. Choctaw; F; S; Grand-dau; 938; Yes
939; **John**, Edison; m; 4; Miss. Choctaw; F; S; Grand-son; 939; Yes

KING

940; John W; m; 72; Miss. Choctaw; F; Wd; Head; 940; Yes
941; Mollie; f; 29; Miss. Choctaw; F; S; Dau; 941; Yes
942; Enos; m; 20; Miss. Choctaw; F; S; Son; 942; Yes
943; Varman; m; 20; Miss. Choctaw; F; S; Son; 943; Yes
944; John Lee; m; 18; Miss. Choctaw; F; S; Great-nephew; 944; Yes
945; Lavenia; f; 13; Miss. Choctaw; F; S; Great-niece; 945; Yes

946; Clay I; m; 26; Miss. Choctaw; F; M; Head; 946; Yes
947; Alice; f; 30; Miss. Choctaw; F; M; Wife; 947; Yes

948; Betsie; f; 50; Miss. Choctaw; F; Wd; Head; 948; Yes
949; Christine; f; 22; Miss. Choctaw; F; S; Dau; 949; Yes
950; Joseph; m; 15; Miss. Choctaw; F; S; Son; 950; Yes
951; Joe; m; 13; Miss. Choctaw; F; S; Son; 951; Yes
952; Barkum; m; 11; Miss. Choctaw; F; S; Son; 952; Yes

953; Banks; m; 27; Miss. Choctaw; F; M; Head; 953; Yes
954; Betsie; f; 36; Miss. Choctaw; F; M; Wife; 954; Yes

Census of the **Mississippi Choctaw** reservation of the **Choctaw Agency** jurisdiction, as of **April 1**, 19 **32**, taken by **R. J. Enochs**, Superintendent.

KEY; Surname; Census Number; Given Name; Sex; Age at Last Birthday; Tribe; Degree of Blood; Marital Status; Relationship to Head of Family; Last Census Roll Number; At Jurisdiction Where Enrolled (Yes/No); Ward (Yes/No, if given)

LEBAN

955; Ben; m; 60; Miss. Choctaw; F; M; Head; 955; Yes
956; Lena; f; 59; Miss. Choctaw; F; M; Wife; 956; Yes
957; Mary; f; 31; Miss. Choctaw; F; S; Dau; 957; Yes

LEFLORE

958; John; m; 61; Miss. Choctaw; F; M; Head; 958; Yes
959; Emma; f; 52; Miss. Choctaw; F; M; Wife; 959; Yes
960; Richard E; m; 39; Miss. Choctaw; F; S; Son; 960; Yes
961; S. D; m; 26; Miss. Choctaw; F; S; Son; 961; Yes
962; Willie; f; 28; Miss. Choctaw; F; S; Dau; 962; Yes
963; Bertha Lee; f; 24; Miss. Choctaw; F; S; Dau; 963; Yes
964; John; m; 21; Miss. Choctaw; F; S; Son; 964; Yes
965; Lewis; m; 20; Miss. Choctaw; F; S; Son; 965; Yes

LEWIS

966; Jim; m; 64; Miss. Choctaw; F; M; Head; 966; Yes
967; Fannie; f; 42; Miss. Choctaw; F; M; Wife; 967; Yes

968; Adam; m; 27; Miss. Choctaw; F; M; Head; 968; Yes
969; Sillie; f; 26; Miss. Choctaw; F; M; Wife; 969; Yes
970; Nannie; f; 4; Miss. Choctaw; F; S; Dau; 970; Yes
971; Mammie; f; 2; Miss. Choctaw; F; S; Dau; 971; Yes
972; Tom; m; 6; Miss. Choctaw; F; S; Step-son; 972; Yes

973; Elon; m; 51; Miss. Choctaw; F; M; Head; 973; Yes
974; Lula; f; 54; Miss. Choctaw; F; M; Wife; 974; Yes
975; **Jefferson**, Nute; m; 16; Miss. Choctaw; F; S; Step-son; 975; Yes

976; Johnnie; m; 34; Miss. Choctaw; F; Wd; Head; 976; Yes
977; Marzine; f; 8; Miss. Choctaw; F; S; Dau; 977; Yes

Census of the **Mississippi Choctaw** reservation of the **Choctaw** **Agency** jurisdiction, as of **April 1**, 19 **32**, taken by **R. J. Enochs**, Superintendent.

KEY; Surname; Census Number; Given Name; Sex; Age at Last Birthday; Tribe; Degree of Blood; Marital Status; Relationship to Head of Family; Last Census Roll Number; At Jurisdiction Where Enrolled (Yes/No); Ward (Yes/No, if given)

978; Marshall; m; 57; Miss. Choctaw; F; M; Head; 978; Yes
979; Martha; f; 46; Miss. Choctaw; F; M; Wife; 979; Yes
980; Eliza; f; 17; Miss. Choctaw; F; S; Dau; 980; Yes
981; Belfa; f; 16; Miss. Choctaw; F; S; Dau; 981; Yes
982; Houston; m; 13; Miss. Choctaw; F; S; Son; 982; Yes
983; Lee; m; 11; Miss. Choctaw; F; S; Son; 983; Yes
984; Esther; f; 8; Miss. Choctaw; F; S; Dau; 987; Yes
985; Hodges; m; 5; Miss. Choctaw; F; S; Son; 984; Yes
986; Leon; m; 4; Miss. Choctaw; F; S; Son; 985; Yes
987; Lucille R; f; 2; Miss. Choctaw; F; S; Dau; 986; Yes
988; Prentiss; m; 8/12; Miss. Choctaw; F; S; Son; Yes

989; Joe; m; 58; Miss. Choctaw; F; Wd; Alone; 988; Yes

990; Lennie; m; 25; Miss. Choctaw; F; M; Head; 991; Yes
991; Ola; f; 20; Miss. Choctaw; F; M; Wife; 992; Yes
992; Nervie; f; 3; Miss. Choctaw; F; S; Dau; 993; Yes

993; Edd; m; 58; Miss. Choctaw; F; M; Head; 994; Yes
994; Edna; f; 50; Miss. Choctaw; F; M; Wife; 995; Yes
995; Hollis; m; 16; Miss. Choctaw; F; S; Son; 996; Yes

996; Reuben; m; 72; Miss. Choctaw; F; Wd; Head; 989; Yes
997; Amos; m; 19; Miss. Choctaw; F; S; Grand-son; 990; Yes

998; Albert; m; 38; Miss. Choctaw; F; M; Head; 997; Yes
999; Mollie; f; 35; Miss. Choctaw; F; M; Wife; 998; Yes
1000; Bernice; f; 15; Miss. Choctaw; F; S; Dau; 1000; Yes
1001; Eastland; m; 13; Miss. Choctaw; F; S; Son; 1001; Yes
1002; Ivena; f; 11; Miss. Choctaw; F; S; Dau; 1002; Yes

1003; Calvin; m; 52; Miss. Choctaw; F; Wd; Alone; 1003; Yes

1004; Jim; m; 29; Miss. Choctaw; F; M; Head; 1004; Yes

Census of the **Mississippi Choctaw** reservation of the **Choctaw Agency** jurisdiction, as of **April 1**, 19**32**, taken by **R. J. Enochs**, Superintendent.

KEY; Surname; Census Number; Given Name; Sex; Age at Last Birthday; Tribe; Degree of Blood; Marital Status; Relationship to Head of Family; Last Census Roll Number; At Jurisdiction Where Enrolled (Yes/No); Ward (Yes/No, if given)

1005; Jennie; f; 24; Miss. Choctaw; F; M; Wife; 1005; Yes
1006; Jennie Lin; f; 3; Miss. Choctaw; F; S; Dau; 1006; Yes
1007; Willie; m; 7/12; Miss. Choctaw; F; S; Son; Yes

1008; Duffie; m; 36; Miss. Choctaw; F; M; Head; 1007; Yes
1009; Lilly; f; 52; Miss. Choctaw; F; M; Wife; 1008; Yes
1010; **Briscoe**, Jim; m; 17; Miss. Choctaw; F; S; Step-son; 1009; Yes
1011; **Briscoe**, Egbert; m; 9; Miss. Choctaw; F; S; Step-son; 1010; Yes
1012; **Farmer**, Henry; m; 21; Miss. Choctaw; F; S; Nephew; 1011; Yes
1013; **Wickson**, Yates or Ollie; m; 3; Miss. Choctaw; F; S; Nephew; 1012; Yes

MARTIN

1014; Willie; m; 42; Miss. Choctaw; F; M; Head; 1013; Yes
1015; Mary; f; 36; Miss. Choctaw; F; M; Wife; 1014; Yes
1016; Raymond; m; 12; Miss. Choctaw; F; S; Son; 1015; Yes
1017; Edmond J; m; 9; Miss. Choctaw; F; S; Son; 1016; Yes
1018; Phillip; m; 6; Miss. Choctaw; F; S; Son; 1017; Yes
1019; Annie Mae; f; 4; Miss. Choctaw; F; S; Dau; 1018; Yes
1020; Harry M; m; 1; Miss. Choctaw; F; S; Son; 1019; Yes

1021; Ennis; m; 23; Miss. Choctaw; F; M; Head; 1020; Yes
1022; Nancy; f; 22; Miss. Choctaw; F; M; Wife; 1021; Yes
1023; Thomas; m; 2; Miss. Choctaw; F; S; Son; 1022; Yes
1024; **Alex**, Herbert F; m; 5; Miss. Choctaw; F; S; Step-son; 1023; Yes

McMILLEN

1025; Sorsby; m; 56; Miss. Choctaw; F; Wd; Head; 1024; Yes
1026; Mary; f; 18; Miss. Choctaw; F; S; Dau; 1025; Yes
1027; Emma; f; 17; Miss. Choctaw; F; S; Dau; 1026; Yes
1028; Clarence; m; 16; Miss. Choctaw; F; S; Son; 1027; Yes
1029; Bessie; f; 13; Miss. Choctaw; F; S; Dau; 1028; Yes

Census of the **Mississippi Choctaw** reservation of the **Choctaw Agency** jurisdiction, as of **April 1**, 19**32**, taken by **R. J. Enochs**, Superintendent.

KEY; Surname; Census Number; Given Name; Sex; Age at Last Birthday; Tribe; Degree of Blood; Marital Status; Relationship to Head of Family; Last Census Roll Number; At Jurisdiction Where Enrolled (Yes/No); Ward (Yes/No, if given)

1030; Gipson; m; 8; Miss. Choctaw; F; S; Son; 1029; Yes
1031; Pauline; f; 4; Miss. Choctaw; F; S; Dau; 1030; Yes

1032; Lemmie; m; 22; Miss. Choctaw; F; M; Head; 1031; Yes
1033; Maggie; f; 23; Miss. Choctaw; F; M; Wife; 1032; Yes

1034; Cephus; m; 50; Miss. Choctaw; F; M; Head; 1033; Yes
1035; Mina; f; 38; Miss. Choctaw; F; M; Wife; 1034; Yes
1036; Anthony; m; 24; Miss. Choctaw; F; S; Son; 1035; Yes
1037; Mary; f; 19; Miss. Choctaw; F; S; Dau; 1036; Yes
1038; Willie; m; 16; Miss. Choctaw; F; S; Son; 1037; Yes
1039; Enochs; m; 4; Miss. Choctaw; F; S; Son; 1038; Yes
1040; Lurline; f; 8/12; Miss. Choctaw; F; S; Dau; Yes
1041; **Billy**, Clemon; m; 18; Miss. Choctaw; F; S; Step-son; 1039; Yes

1042; Nola; f; 27; Miss. Choctaw; F; Wd; Head; 1041; Yes
1043; A. J; m; 10; Miss. Choctaw; F; S; Son; 1042; Yes
1044; Odie Mae; f; 8; Miss. Choctaw; F; S; Dau; 1043; Yes
1045; John; m; 5; Miss. Choctaw; F; S; Son; 1044; Yes
1046; Mattie; f; 1; Miss. Choctaw; F; S; Dau; 1045; Yes

1047; Oscar; m; 38; Miss. Choctaw; F; M; Head; 1046; Yes
1048; Bennie; f; 33; Miss. Choctaw; F; M; Wife; 1047; Yes
1049; Arnold; m; 18; Miss. Choctaw; F; S; Son; 1048; Yes
1050; Leslie; f; 10; Miss. Choctaw; F; S; Dau; 1049; Yes
1051; Bert; m; 8; Miss. Choctaw; F; S; Son; 1050; Yes
1052; Frances; f; 6; Miss. Choctaw; F; S; Dau; 1051; Yes
1053; John; m; 3; Miss. Choctaw; F; S; Son; 1052; Yes
1054; Jean; f; 11/12; Miss. Choctaw; F; S; Dau; Yes

MINGO

1055; Rich; m; 27; Miss. Choctaw; F; M; Head; 1053; Yes
1056; Annie; f; 27; Miss. Choctaw; F; M; Wife; 1054; Yes

Census of the **Mississippi Choctaw** reservation of the **Choctaw Agency** jurisdiction, as of **April 1**, 19**32**, taken by **R. J. Enochs**, Superintendent.

KEY; Surname; Census Number; Given Name; Sex; Age at Last Birthday; Tribe; Degree of Blood; Marital Status; Relationship to Head of Family; Last Census Roll Number; At Jurisdiction Where Enrolled (Yes/No); Ward (Yes/No, if given)

1057; Davidson; m; 9; Miss. Choctaw; F; S; Son; 1055; Yes
1058; Effie; f; 8; Miss. Choctaw; F; S; Dau; 1056; Yes

1059; John; m; 56; Miss. Choctaw; F; M; Head; 1057; Yes
1060; Hattie; f; 30; Miss. Choctaw; F; M; Wife; 1058; Yes
1061; Arch; m; 10; Miss. Choctaw; F; S; Son; 1059; Yes
1062; Odis; m; 7; Miss. Choctaw; F; S; Son; 1060; Yes
1063; Sister; f; 5; Miss. Choctaw; F; S; Dau; 1061; Yes
1064; Mary; f; 2; Miss. Choctaw; F; S; Dau; 1062; Yes

1065; Lilly; f; 54; Miss. Choctaw; F; Wd; Head; 1063; Yes
1066; Jim; m; 17; Miss. Choctaw; F; S; Son; 1064; Yes
1067; Olin; m; 14; Miss. Choctaw; F; S; Son; 1065; Yes
1068; Nettie; f; 11; Miss. Choctaw; F; S; Dau; 1066; Yes

1069; Oscar; m; 22; Miss. Choctaw; F; M; Head; 1067; Yes
1070; Linday; f; 27; Miss. Choctaw; F; M; Wife; 1068; Yes

MITCH

1071; Sarah; f; 48; Miss. Choctaw; F; Wd; Head; 1069; Yes
1072; Elea; m; 30; Miss. Choctaw; F; S; Son; 1070; Yes
1073; Divan; m; 28; Miss. Choctaw; F; S; Son; 1071; Yes
1074; Wilson; m; 26; Miss. Choctaw; F; S; Son; 1072; Yes
1075; Gilmore; m; 17; Miss. Choctaw; F; S; Son; 1073; Yes
1076; Annie; f; 13; Miss. Choctaw; F; S; Dau; 1074; Yes

MORRIS

1077; Julius; m; 30; Miss. Choctaw; F; M; Head; 1078; Yes
1078; Beauty; f; 27; Miss. Choctaw; F; M; Wife; 1079; Yes
1079; Eddie; f; 8; Miss. Choctaw; F; S; Dau; 1080; Yes
1080; Lena; f; 5; Miss. Choctaw; F; S; Dau; 1081; Yes
1081; Water Olin; m; 2; Miss. Choctaw; F; S; Son; 1082; Yes

Census of the **Mississippi Choctaw** reservation of the **Choctaw Agency** jurisdiction, as of **April 1**, 19 **32**, taken by **R. J. Enochs**, Superintendent.

KEY; Surname; Census Number; Given Name; Sex; Age at Last Birthday; Tribe; Degree of Blood; Marital Status; Relationship to Head of Family; Last Census Roll Number; At Jurisdiction Where Enrolled (Yes/No); Ward (Yes/No, if given)

1082; Mosley; m; 66; Miss. Choctaw; F; M; Head; 1083; Yes
1083; Ida; f; 51; Miss. Choctaw; F; M; Wife; 1084; Yes
1084; Lilly; f; 32; Miss. Choctaw; F; S; Dau; 1085; Yes
1085; Sue; f; 30; Miss. Choctaw; F; Wd; Dau; 1086; Yes
1086; Wilson; m; 28; Miss. Choctaw; F; S; Son; 1087; Yes
1087; Joe; m; 11; Miss. Choctaw; F; S; Grand-son; 1088; Yes
1088; **Wesley**, Rufus; m; 7; Miss. Choctaw; F; S; Grand-son; 1089; Yes

1089; Dempsey; m; 31; Miss. Choctaw; F; M; Head; 1090; Yes
1090; Janie; f; 30; Miss. Choctaw; F; M; Wife; 1091; Yes
1091; Ora; f; 11; Miss. Choctaw; F; S; Dau; 1092; Yes
1092; Vesney; m; 8; Miss. Choctaw; F; S; Son; 1093; Yes
1093; Davis; m; 6; Miss. Choctaw; F; S; Son; 1094; Yes
1094; Champs; m; 3; Miss. Choctaw; F; S; Son; 1095; Yes

1095; Sallie; f; 63; Miss. Choctaw; F; Wd; Head; 1096; Yes
1096; Seward; m; 31; Miss. Choctaw; F; S; Son; 1097; Yes

1097; Howard; m; 25; Miss. Choctaw; F; M; Head; 1098; Yes
1098; Bertie; f; 22; Miss. Choctaw; F; M; Wife; 1099; Yes
1099; Jimmie; m; 6; Miss. Choctaw; F; S; Son; 1100; Yes

1100; Huston; m; 26; Miss. Choctaw; F; M; Head; 1101; Yes
1101; Bertha; f; 24; Miss. Choctaw; F; M; Wife; 1102; Yes

1102; Boston; m; 29; Miss. Choctaw; F; M; Head; 1103; Yes
1103; Nola; f; 27; Miss. Choctaw; F; M; Wife; 1104; Yes

1104; Velma; f; 23; Miss. Choctaw; F; S; Alone; 1105; Yes

MOSES

1105; Alma; f; 21; Miss. Choctaw; F; S; Alone; 1106; Yes

Census of the **Mississippi Choctaw** reservation of the **Choctaw Agency** jurisdiction, as of **April 1**, 19 **32**, taken by **R. J. Enochs**, Superintendent.

KEY; Surname; Census Number; Given Name; Sex; Age at Last Birthday; Tribe; Degree of Blood; Marital Status; Relationship to Head of Family; Last Census Roll Number; At Jurisdiction Where Enrolled (Yes/No); Ward (Yes/No, if given)

1106; Allen; m; 26; Miss. Choctaw; F; M; Head; 1107; Yes
1107; Florence; f; 26; Miss. Choctaw; F; M; Wife; 1108; Yes

NICKEY

1108; Sam; m; 47; Miss. Choctaw; F; M; Head; 1109; Yes
1109; Malissie; f; 45; Miss. Choctaw; F; M; Wife; 1110; Yes
1110; Dora; f; 17; Miss. Choctaw; F; S; Dau; 1111; Yes
1111; Sherman; m; 10; Miss. Choctaw; F; S; Son; 1112; Yes
1112; Copeland; m; 4; Miss. Choctaw; F; S; Son; 1113; Yes

1113; Billy; m; 47; Miss. Choctaw; F; M; Head; 1114; Yes
1114; Fronie; f; 51; Miss. Choctaw; F; M; Wife; 1115; Yes
1115; Ode; f; 23; Miss. Choctaw; F; S; Dau; 1116; Yes
1116; Zelma; f; 20; Miss. Choctaw; F; S; Dau; 1117; Yes
1117; Hughie; m; 17; Miss. Choctaw; F; S; Son; 1118; Yes
1118; Jona; f; 15; Miss. Choctaw; F; S; Dau; 1119; Yes
1119; Cozette; f; 13; Miss. Choctaw; F; S; Dau; 1120; Yes
1120; Thomas; m; 9; Miss. Choctaw; F; S; Son; 1121; Yes

NOAH

1121; Elizabeth; f; 60; Miss. Choctaw; F; Wd; Head; 1122; Yes
1122; Celia; f; 32; Miss. Choctaw; F; S; Dau; 1123; Yes

1123; Lizzie; f; 42; Miss. Choctaw; F; Wd; Head; 1124; Yes
1124; Nancie; f; 16; Miss. Choctaw; F; S; Dau; 1125; Yes
1125; Annie; f; 13; Miss. Choctaw; F; S; Dau; 1126; Yes

NUBBY

1126; Billy; m; 72; Miss. Choctaw; F; M; Head; 1127; Yes
1127; Lilly; f; 52; Miss. Choctaw; F; M; Wife; 1128; Yes

Census of the **Mississippi Choctaw** reservation of the **Choctaw Agency** jurisdiction, as of **April 1**, 19**32**, taken by **R. J. Enochs**, Superintendent.

KEY; Surname; Census Number; Given Name; Sex; Age at Last Birthday; Tribe; Degree of Blood; Marital Status; Relationship to Head of Family; Last Census Roll Number; At Jurisdiction Where Enrolled (Yes/No); Ward (Yes/No, if given)

PHILLIPS

1128; Riley; m; 25; Miss. Choctaw; F; M; Head; 1129; Yes
1129; ~~Mary~~ Lester; f; ~~21~~ 19; Miss. Choctaw; F; M; Wife; 664; Yes
1130; Edmond; m; 5; Miss. Choctaw; F; S; Son; 1130; Yes
1131; Empsey; m; 3; Miss. Choctaw; F; S; Son; 1131; Yes

POLK

1132; Henry; m; 24; Miss. Choctaw; F; M; Head; 1132; Yes
1133; Susie; f; 30; Miss. Choctaw; F; M; Wife; 1133; Yes
1134; Sula; f; 3; Miss. Choctaw; F; S; Dau; 1134; Yes
1135; Hudson; m; 1; Miss. Choctaw; F; S; Son; 1135; Yes

1136; George; m; 70; Miss. Choctaw; F; Wd; Alone; 1136; Yes

1137; Josie; m; 51; Miss. Choctaw; F; M; Head; 1137; Yes
1138; Lennie; f; 52; Miss. Choctaw; F; M; Wife; 1138; Yes
1139; Ada; f; 14; Miss. Choctaw; F; S; Dau; 1139; Yes
1140; Frances; f; 14; Miss. Choctaw; F; S; Dau; 1140; Yes

1141; Tom; m; 54; Miss. Choctaw; F; Wd; Head; 1141; Yes
1142; Comelia; m; 22; Miss. Choctaw; F; S; Son; 1142; Yes
1143; Alma; f; 18; Miss. Choctaw; F; S; Dau; 1143; Yes
1144; Osborn; m; 16; Miss. Choctaw; F; S; Son; 1144; Yes

POULSON

1145; Allie; f; 59; Miss. Choctaw; F; S; Alone; 1145; Yes

1146; Frank; f; 32; Miss. Choctaw; F; M; Head; 1146; Yes
1147; Mary; f; 30; Miss. Choctaw; F; M; Wife; 1147; Yes

1148; Eddie M; m; 25; Miss. Choctaw; F; M; Head; 1148; Yes

Census of the **Mississippi Choctaw** reservation of the **Choctaw Agency** jurisdiction, as of **April 1**, 19**32**, taken by **R. J. Enochs**, Superintendent.

KEY; Surname; Census Number; Given Name; Sex; Age at Last Birthday; Tribe; Degree of Blood; Marital Status; Relationship to Head of Family; Last Census Roll Number; At Jurisdiction Where Enrolled (Yes/No); Ward (Yes/No, if given)

1149; Cornelia; f; 28; Miss. Choctaw; F; M; Wife; 1149; Yes

1150; Julius; m; 25; Miss. Choctaw; F; S; Alone; 1150; Yes

1151; Johnnie; m; 23; Miss. Choctaw; F; S; Alone; 1151; Yes

1152; Charlie; m; 20; Miss. Choctaw; F; S; Alone; 1152; Yes

ROBINSON

1153; Thomas; m; 42; Miss. Choctaw; F; M; Head; 1153; Yes
1154; Syble; f; 37; Miss. Choctaw; F; M; Wife; 1154; Yes
1155; Jimmie; m; 18; Miss. Choctaw; F; S; Son; 1155; Yes
1156; Georgie; f; 16; Miss. Choctaw; F; S; Dau; 1156; Yes
1157; Sallie; f; 15; Miss. Choctaw; F; S; Dau; 1157; Yes
1158; Carl; m; 13; Miss. Choctaw; F; S; Son; 1158; Yes
1159; Mamie; f; 12; Miss. Choctaw; F; S; Dau; 1159; Yes
1160; Betsey; f; 10; Miss. Choctaw; F; S; Dau; 1160; Yes
1161; Homer; m; 8; Miss. Choctaw; F; S; Son; 1161; Yes
1162; Teach; m; 3; Miss. Choctaw; F; S; Son; 1162; Yes

1163; Belia; f; 25; Miss. Choctaw; F; Wd; Head; 1163; Yes
1164; Campbell; m; 5; Miss. Choctaw; F; S; Son; 1164; Yes

RUTHERFORD

1165; Henrietta; f; 34; Miss. Choctaw; F; S; Alone; 1165; Yes

SAM

1166; Truman; m; 23; Miss. Choctaw; F; M; Head; 1166; Yes
1167; Sina; f; 20; Miss. Choctaw; F; M; Wife; 885; Yes

1168; Raymond; m; 51; Miss. Choctaw; F; S; Alone; 1167; Yes

Census of the **Mississippi Choctaw** reservation of the **Choctaw Agency** jurisdiction, as of **April 1**, 19**32**, taken by **R. J. Enochs**, Superintendent.

KEY; Surname; Census Number; Given Name; Sex; Age at Last Birthday; Tribe; Degree of Blood; Marital Status; Relationship to Head of Family; Last Census Roll Number; At Jurisdiction Where Enrolled (Yes/No); Ward (Yes/No, if given)

1169; Oscar; m; 78; Miss. Choctaw; F; M; Head; 1168; Yes
1170; Mattie; f; 52; Miss. Choctaw; F; M; Wife; 1169; Yes
1171; Seer; f; 18; Miss. Choctaw; F; S; Grand-dau; 1170; Yes
1172; Lavada; f; 20; Miss. Choctaw; F; S; Grand-dau; 1171; Yes

1173; Jimpsey; m; 29; Miss. Choctaw; F; M; Head; 1172; Yes
1174; Lousiana[sic]; f; 27; Miss. Choctaw; F; M; Wife; 1173; Yes

1175; Walter; m; 42; Miss. Choctaw; F; Wd; Head; 1174; Yes
1176; Grace; f; 15; Miss. Choctaw; F; S; Dau; 1175; Yes
1177; Tom; m; 13; Miss. Choctaw; F; S; Son; 1176; Yes
1178; Edna; f; 10; Miss. Choctaw; F; S; Dau; 1177; Yes
1179; Manzie; f; 8; Miss. Choctaw; F; S; Dau; 1178; Yes

1180; Fontaine; m; 46; Miss. Choctaw; F; M; Head; 1179; Yes
1181; Emily; f; 42; Miss. Choctaw; F; M; Wife; 1180; Yes
1182; Leona; f; 10; Miss. Choctaw; F; S; Dau; 1181; Yes
1183; Ellis; m; 7; Miss. Choctaw; F; S; Son; 1182; Yes
1184; Fannie; f; 6; Miss. Choctaw; F; S; Dau; 1183; Yes
1185; Ella Ruth; f; 4; Miss. Choctaw; F; S; Dau; 1184; Yes
1186; Armond; m; 2; Miss. Choctaw; F; S; Son; 1185; Yes
1187; Beaman; m; 12; Miss. Choctaw; F; S; Nephew; 1186; Yes

1188; Willie; m; 33; Miss. Choctaw; F; M; Head; 1187; Yes
1189; Eva; f; 31; Miss. Choctaw; F; M; Wife; 1188; Yes
1190; Nettie; f; 11; Miss. Choctaw; F; S; Dau; 1189; Yes
1191; Abel; m; 10; Miss. Choctaw; F; S; Son; 1190; Yes
1192; Lonie; f; 8; Miss. Choctaw; F; S; Dau; 1191; Yes
1193; Grisaline; f; 2; Miss. Choctaw; F; S; Dau; 1192; Yes

SCOTT

1194; Marshall; m; 62; Miss. Choctaw; F; M; Head; 1193; Yes
1195; Lonie; f; 27; Miss. Choctaw; F; M; Wife; 1194; Yes

Census of the __Mississippi Choctaw__ reservation of the __Choctaw Agency__ jurisdiction, as of __April 1__, 19__32__, taken by __R. J. Enochs__, Superintendent.

KEY; Surname; Census Number; Given Name; Sex; Age at Last Birthday; Tribe; Degree of Blood; Marital Status; Relationship to Head of Family; Last Census Roll Number; At Jurisdiction Where Enrolled (Yes/No); Ward (Yes/No, if given)

1196; Rachel; f; 6; Miss. Choctaw; F; S; Dau; 1195; Yes

SHOEMAKER

1197; Alonzo; m; 44; Miss. Choctaw; F; M; Head; 1196; Yes
1198; Susan; f; 32; Miss. Choctaw; F; M; Wife; 1197; Yes
1199; Dempsey; m; 11; Miss. Choctaw; F; S; Son; 1198; Yes
1200; Layman; m; 9; Miss. Choctaw; F; S; Son; 1199; Yes
1201; Ruben; m; 6; Miss. Choctaw; F; S; Son; 1200; Yes
1202; Noleen; f; 3; Miss. Choctaw; F; S; Dau; 1201; Yes

1203; Buck; m; 47; Miss. Choctaw; F; M; Head; 1202; Yes
1204; Annie; f; 32; Miss. Choctaw; F; M; Wife; 1203; Yes
1205; Leona; f; 12; Miss. Choctaw; F; S; Dau; 1204; Yes
1206; Eliza; f; 10; Miss. Choctaw; F; S; Dau; 1205; Yes
1207; Martha; f; 8; Miss. Choctaw; F; S; Dau; 1206; Yes
1208; Daisy; f; 6; Miss. Choctaw; F; S; Dau; 1207; Yes
1209; Carrie Mae; f; 5; Miss. Choctaw; F; S; Dau; 1208; Yes
1210; Hubert; m; 1; Miss. Choctaw; F; S; Son; 1209; Yes

SIMPSON

1211; John; m; 54; Miss. Choctaw; F; M; Head; 1210; Yes
1212; Sallie; f; 52; Miss. Choctaw; F; M; Wife; 1211; Yes
1213; Pauline; f; 16; Miss. Choctaw; F; S; Dau; 1212; Yes
1214; Celie; f; 14; Miss. Choctaw; F; S; Son; 1213; Yes

SMITH

1215; George; m; 60; Miss. Choctaw; F; M; Head; 1214; Yes
1216; Mandy; f; 46; Miss. Choctaw; F; M; Wife; 1215; Yes
1217; **Farmer**, Lilly Kate; f; 12; Miss. Choctaw; F; S; Step-dau; 1216; Yes
1218; **Farmer**, Grace; f; 9; Miss. Choctaw; F; S; Step-dau; 1217; Yes

Census of the **Mississippi Choctaw** reservation of the **Choctaw Agency** jurisdiction, as of **April 1**, 19 **32**, taken by **R. J. Enochs**, Superintendent.

KEY; Surname; Census Number; Given Name; Sex; Age at Last Birthday; Tribe; Degree of Blood; Marital Status; Relationship to Head of Family; Last Census Roll Number; At Jurisdiction Where Enrolled (Yes/No); Ward (Yes/No, if given)

1219; Sebe; m; 42; Miss. Choctaw; F; M; Head; 1218; Yes
1220; Sinie; f; 41; Miss. Choctaw; F; M; Wife; 1219; Yes
1221; Sophie; f; 19; Miss. Choctaw; F; S; Dau; 1220; Yes
1222; Clemon; m; 13; Miss. Choctaw; F; S; Son; 1221; Yes

1223; John W; m; 57; Miss. Choctaw; F; M; Head; 1222; Yes
1224; Mary; f; 72; Miss. Choctaw; F; M; Wife; 1223; Yes

1225; Minnie; f; 37; Miss. Choctaw; F; Wd; Head; 1224; Yes
1226; Melton; m; 6; Miss. Choctaw; F; S; Son; 1225; Yes
1227; Elton; m; 4; Miss. Choctaw; F; S; Son; 1226; Yes
1228; **Stephens**, Phoebe; f; 12; Miss. Choctaw; F; S; Niece; 1227; Yes

1229; Clay; m; 27; Miss. Choctaw; F; M; Head; 1228; Yes
1230; Mattie; f; 30; Miss. Choctaw; F; M; Wife; 1229; Yes

SOCKEY

1231; Irvin; m; 50; Miss. Choctaw; F; M; Head; 1230; Yes
1232; Lula; f; 37; Miss. Choctaw; F; M; Wife; 1231; Yes
1233; Benny; m; 24; Miss. Choctaw; F; S; Son; 1232; Yes
1234; Homer; m; 9; Miss. Choctaw; F; S; Son; 1233; Yes
1235; Ill; m; 4; Miss. Choctaw; F; S; Son; 1234; Yes

1236; Mike; m; 30; Miss. Choctaw; F; M; Head; 1235; Yes
1237; Nephus; f; 29; Miss. Choctaw; F; M; Wife; 1236; Yes
1238; Varelia; f; 10; Miss. Choctaw; F; S; Dau; 1237; Yes
1239; Odell; m; 8; Miss. Choctaw; F; S; Son; 1238; Yes
1240; Enochs; m; 5; Miss. Choctaw; F; S; Son; 1239; Yes

SOLOMON

1241; Willie; m; 48; Miss. Choctaw; F; Wd; Alone; 1240; Yes

Census of the **Mississippi Choctaw** reservation of the **Choctaw Agency** jurisdiction, as of **April 1**, 19**32**, taken by **R. J. Enochs**, Superintendent.

KEY; Surname; Census Number; Given Name; Sex; Age at Last Birthday; Tribe; Degree of Blood; Marital Status; Relationship to Head of Family; Last Census Roll Number; At Jurisdiction Where Enrolled (Yes/No); Ward (Yes/No, if given)

1242; Marshall; m; 28; Miss. Choctaw; F; M; Head; 1241; Yes
1243; Addie; f; 23; Miss. Choctaw; F; M; Wife; 1242; Yes

1244; Willie; m; 69; Miss. Choctaw; F; M; Head; 1243; Yes
1245; Winnie L; f; 27; Miss. Choctaw; F; M; Wife; 1244; Yes
1246; Mollie Lee; f; 3; Miss. Choctaw; F; S; Dau; 1245; Yes

1247; Raymond; m; 38; Miss. Choctaw; F; M; Head; 1246; Yes
1248; Bessie; f; 38; Miss. Choctaw; F; M; Wife; 1247; Yes
1249; Earnest; m; 16; Miss. Choctaw; F; S; Son; 1248; Yes
1250; Murphy; m; 13; Miss. Choctaw; F; S; Son; 1249; Yes
1251; Mollie; f; 10; Miss. Choctaw; F; S; Dau; 1250; Yes

STAR

1252; Lucy; f; 44; Miss. Choctaw; F; Wd; Alone; 1251; Yes

1253; Bill; m; 43; Miss. Choctaw; F; Wd; Head; 1252; Yes
1254; Summers; m; 16; Miss. Choctaw; F; S; Son; 1253; Yes
1255; Edna; f; 14; Miss. Choctaw; F; S; Dau; 1254; Yes
1256; Nannie; f; 10; Miss. Choctaw; F; S; Dau; 1255; Yes
1257; Mary; f; 9; Miss. Choctaw; F; S; Dau; 1256; Yes

STEPHENS

1258; Nathan; m; 29; Miss. Choctaw; F; M; Head; 1257; Yes
1259; Annie; f; 34; Miss. Choctaw; F; M; Wife; 1258; Yes
1260; Maxton; m; 7; Miss. Choctaw; F; S; Son; 1259; Yes
1261; Cutie Mae; f; 5; Miss. Choctaw; F; S; Dau; 1260; Yes
1262; Dorthy D; f; 4; Miss. Choctaw; F; S; Dau; 1261; Yes
1263; Bonnie B; f; 2; Miss. Choctaw; F; S; Dau; 1262; Yes

1264; Tom; m; 69; Miss. Choctaw; F; Wd; Head; 1263; Yes
1265; Silman; m; 37; Miss. Choctaw; F; S; Son; 1264; Yes

Census of the **Mississippi Choctaw** reservation of the **Choctaw Agency** jurisdiction, as of **April 1**, 19**32**, taken by **R. J. Enochs**, Superintendent.

KEY; Surname; Census Number; Given Name; Sex; Age at Last Birthday; Tribe; Degree of Blood; Marital Status; Relationship to Head of Family; Last Census Roll Number; At Jurisdiction Where Enrolled (Yes/No); Ward (Yes/No, if given)

1266; Cornelia; f; 26; Miss. Choctaw; F; S; Dau; 1265; Yes
1267; Willie; m; 22; Miss. Choctaw; F; S; Son; 1266; Yes

1268; Felix; m; 27; Miss. Choctaw; F; M; Head; 1267; Yes
1269; Martha; f; 24; Miss. Choctaw; F; M; Wife; 1268; Yes
1270; Martha Lee; f; 2; Miss. Choctaw; F; S; Dau; 1269; Yes
1271; Mary Francis; f; 8/12; Miss. Choctaw; F; S; Dau; Yes

STEVE

1272; Murphy; m; 58; Miss. Choctaw; F; M; Head; 1270; Yes
1273; Patsy; f; 25; Miss. Choctaw; F; M; Wife; 1271; Yes
1274; Helen; f; 5; Miss. Choctaw; F; S; Dau; 1272; Yes
1275; Winston; m; 2; Miss. Choctaw; F; S; Son; 1274; Yes

1276; Josie; m; 30; Miss. Choctaw; F; M; Head; 1275; Yes
1277; Maggie; f; 23; Miss. Choctaw; F; M; Wife; 1276; Yes
1278; Ruby; f; 6; Miss. Choctaw; F; S; Dau; 1277; Yes
1279; Jane; f; 5; Miss. Choctaw; F; S; Dau; 1278; Yes

1280; Houston; m; 44; Miss. Choctaw; F; M; Head; 1279; Yes
1281; Lena; f; 40; Miss. Choctaw; F; M; Wife; 1280; Yes
1282; McKinley; m; 13; Miss. Choctaw; F; S; Son; 1282; Yes
1283; Yates; m; 9; Miss. Choctaw; F; S; Son; 1283; Yes
1284; Marabelle; f; 5; Miss. Choctaw; F; S; Dau; 1284; Yes

1285; Ennis; m; 23; Miss. Choctaw; F; M; Head; 1281; Yes
1286; Callie; f; 20; Miss. Choctaw; F; M; Wife; 1076; Yes
1287; **Morris**, Arwin; f; 5; Miss. Choctaw; F; S; Step-dau; 1077; Yes
1288; Bobo; m; 25; Miss. Choctaw; F; M; Head; 1285; Yes
1289; Lucille; f; 20; Miss. Choctaw; F; M; Wife; 1286; Yes
1290; Maurice; f; 6; Miss. Choctaw; F; S; Dau; 1287; Yes
1291; Aubrey; f; 4; Miss. Choctaw; F; S; Dau; 1288; Yes
1292; Vivian; f; 2; Miss. Choctaw; F; S; Dau; 1289; Yes

Census of the **Mississippi Choctaw** reservation of the **Choctaw Agency** jurisdiction, as of **April 1**, 19__32_, taken by **R. J. Enochs**, Superintendent.

KEY; Surname; Census Number; Given Name; Sex; Age at Last Birthday; Tribe; Degree of Blood; Marital Status; Relationship to Head of Family; Last Census Roll Number; At Jurisdiction Where Enrolled (Yes/No); Ward (Yes/No, if given)

1293; Margurite[sic]; f; 11/12; Miss. Choctaw; F; S; Dau; 1[sic] ; Yes

1294; Smith; m; 38; Miss. Choctaw; F; M; Head; 1290; Yes
1295; Winnie; f; 356; Miss. Choctaw; F; M; Wife; 1291; Yes
1296; Tonie; f; 12; Miss. Choctaw; F; S; Dau; 1292; Yes
1297; Pauline; f; 11; Miss. Choctaw; F; S; Dau; 1293; Yes
1298; Mollie; f; 7; Miss. Choctaw; F; S; Dau; 1294; Yes
1299; Aileen; f; 3; Miss. Choctaw; F; S; Dau; 1295; Yes
1300; Rebecca; f; 1; Miss. Choctaw; F; S; Dau; Yes

STOLIBY

1301; Missouri; f; 64; Miss. Choctaw; F; Wd; Head; 1296; Yes
1302; Tom; m; 29; Miss. Choctaw; F; S; Son; 1297; Yes
1303; Elum Ferum; m; 6; Miss. Choctaw; F; S; Grand-son; 1298; Yes

1304; John; m; 42; Miss. Choctaw; F; Wd; Head; 1299; Yes
1305; Nancy; f; 21; Miss. Choctaw; F; S; Dau; 1300; Yes
1306; Will Banks; m; 13; Miss. Choctaw; F; S; Son; 1301; Yes
1307; Otis; m; 11; Miss. Choctaw; F; S; Son; 1302; Yes
1308; Zona Miller; f; 7; Miss. Choctaw; F; S; Dau; 1303; Yes

STRIBLING

1309; Malissie; f; 60; Miss. Choctaw; F; Wd; Alone; 1304; Yes

THOMAS

1310; Lewis; m; 48; Miss. Choctaw; F; M; Alone; 1305; Yes
1311; Mamie; f; 45; Miss. Choctaw; F; M; Wife; 1306; Yes
1312; Newman; m; 13; Miss. Choctaw; F; S; Son; 1307; Yes
1313; Isaac; m; 9; Miss. Choctaw; F; S; Son; 1308; Yes
1314; Mina; f; 7; Miss. Choctaw; F; S; Dau; 1309; Yes

Census of the **Mississippi Choctaw** reservation of the **Choctaw Agency** jurisdiction, as of **April 1**, 19_32_, taken by **R. J. Enochs**, Superintendent.

KEY; Surname; Census Number; Given Name; Sex; Age at Last Birthday; Tribe; Degree of Blood; Marital Status; Relationship to Head of Family; Last Census Roll Number; At Jurisdiction Where Enrolled (Yes/No); Ward (Yes/No, if given)

1315; George; m; 83; Miss. Choctaw; F; Wd; Alone; 1310; Yes

1316; Riley; m; 27; Miss. Choctaw; F; S; Alone; 1311; Yes

1317; Cleve; m; 29; Miss. Choctaw; F; M; Head; 1312; Yes
1318; Phoebe; f; 24; Miss. Choctaw; F; M; Wife; 1313; Yes

1319; Wilman; m; 32; Miss. Choctaw; F; M; Head; 1314; Yes
1320; Sallie; f; 31; Miss. Choctaw; F; M; Wife; 1315; Yes
1321; Woodrow; m; 13; Miss. Choctaw; F; S; Son; 1316; Yes
1322; Mollie; f; 11; Miss. Choctaw; F; S; Dau; 1317; Yes
1323; Golden; m; 9; Miss. Choctaw; F; S; Son; 1318; Yes
1324; Amos; m; 7; Miss. Choctaw; F; S; Son; 1319; Yes
1325; Single; m; 3; Miss. Choctaw; F; S; Son; 1320; Yes
1326; Linnie Helen; f; 1; Miss. Choctaw; F; S; Dau; 1321; Yes

1327; Lester; m; 23; Miss. Choctaw; F; M; Head; 1322; Yes
1328; Rosie; f; 21; Miss. Choctaw; F; M; Wife; 1323; Yes

1329; Rosie; f; 37; Miss. Choctaw; F; S; Alone; 1324; Yes

1330; *Leona; f; 32; Miss. Choctaw; F; M; Wife*; 1325; Yes

1331; *Evaline; f; 36; Miss. Choctaw; F; M; Wife*; 1326; Yes

* Leona and Evaline Thomas listed above are married to white men — no children.

THOMPSON

1332; Will; m; 28; Miss. Choctaw; F; M; Head; 1327; Yes
1333; Sina; f; 25; Miss. Choctaw; F; M; Wife; 1328; Yes
1334; Otis; m; 8; Miss. Choctaw; F; S; Son; 1329; Yes
1335; Claudine; f; 5; Miss. Choctaw; F; S; Dau; 1330; Yes

Census of the **Mississippi Choctaw** reservation of the **Choctaw Agency** jurisdiction, as of **April 1**, 19**32**, taken by **R. J. Enochs**, Superintendent.

KEY; Surname; Census Number; Given Name; Sex; Age at Last Birthday; Tribe; Degree of Blood; Marital Status; Relationship to Head of Family; Last Census Roll Number; At Jurisdiction Where Enrolled (Yes/No); Ward (Yes/No, if given)

1336; Henry; m; 3; Miss. Choctaw; F; S; Son; 1331; Yes
1337; Oneva; f; 1; Miss. Choctaw; F; S; Dau; Yes

1338; Cephus; m; 42; Miss. Choctaw; F; M; Head; 1332; Yes
1339; Amie; f; 27; Miss. Choctaw; F; M; Wife; 1333; Yes
1340; Dixon; m; 18; Miss. Choctaw; F; S; Son; 1334; Yes
1341; Farmer; m; 8; Miss. Choctaw; F; S; Son; 1335; Yes
1342; Alice; f; 7; Miss. Choctaw; F; S; Dau; 1336; Yes
1343; Annie; f; 4; Miss. Choctaw; F; S; Dau; 1337; Yes

1344; Malinda; f; 67; Miss. Choctaw; F; Wd; Head; 1338; Yes
1345; Beneva; f; 21; Miss. Choctaw; F; S; Dau; 1339; Yes

1346; Mose; m; 35; Miss. Choctaw; F; M; Head; 1340; Yes
1347; Jean; f; 36; Miss. Choctaw; F; M; Wife; 1341; Yes
1348 Jim; m; 12; Miss. Choctaw; F; S; Son; 1342; Yes
1349; Annie; f; 9; Miss. Choctaw; F; S; Dau; 1343; Yes
1350; Therman; m; 6; Miss. Choctaw; F; S; Son; 1344; Yes
1351; Steve; m; 5; Miss. Choctaw; F; S; Son; 1345; Yes

1352; John; m; 40; Miss. Choctaw; F; M; Head; 1346; Yes
1353; Lula; f; 38; Miss. Choctaw; F; M; Wife; 1347; Yes
1354; ~~Moline~~ Maurine; f; 11; Miss. Choctaw; F; S; Dau; 1348; Yes
1355; Onie; f; 10; Miss. Choctaw; F; S; Dau; 1349; Yes
1356; Tom; m; 5; Miss. Choctaw; F; S; Son; 1350; Yes

1357; Tommie; m; 33; Miss. Choctaw; F; M; Head; 1351; Yes
1358; Bonnie; f; 30; Miss. Choctaw; F; M; Wife; 1352; Yes
1359; Nathan; m; 1; Miss. Choctaw; F; S; Son; 1353; Yes

TUBBY

1360; Dan; m; 30; Miss. Choctaw; F; M; Head; 1354; Yes
1361; Lola; f; 336; Miss. Choctaw; F; M; Wife; 1355; Yes

Census of the **Mississippi Choctaw** reservation of the **Choctaw Agency** jurisdiction, as of **April 1**, 19**32**, taken by **R. J. Enochs**, Superintendent.

KEY; Surname; Census Number; Given Name; Sex; Age at Last Birthday; Tribe; Degree of Blood; Marital Status; Relationship to Head of Family; Last Census Roll Number; At Jurisdiction Where Enrolled (Yes/No); Ward (Yes/No, if given)

1362; **Lewis**, Lum; m; 6; Miss. Choctaw; F; S; Step-son; 1356; Yes

1363; George; m; 24; Miss. Choctaw; F; M; Head; 1357; Yes
1364; Mary; f; 21; Miss. Choctaw; F; M; Wife; 1358; Yes
1365; Thomas; m; 3; Miss. Choctaw; F; S; Son; 1359; Yes
1366; Jennie; f; 14; Miss. Choctaw; F; S; Sister; 1360; Yes

1367; Lefus; m; 39; Miss. Choctaw; F; M; Head; 1361; Yes
1368; Frances; f; 32; Miss. Choctaw; F; M; Wife; 1362; Yes
1369; Ina; f; 10; Miss. Choctaw; F; S; Dau; 1363; Yes
1370; Irene; f; 8; Miss. Choctaw; F; S; Dau; 1364; Yes
1371; Leona; f; 5; Miss. Choctaw; F; S; Dau; 1365; Yes
1372; **Ben**, Rufus; m; 14; Miss. Choctaw; F; S; Step-son; 1366; Yes
1373; Robert; m; 4/12; Miss. Choctaw; F; S; Son; Yes

1374; Sidney; m; 32; Miss. Choctaw; F; M; Head; 1367; Yes
1375; Kate; f; 31; Miss. Choctaw; F; M; Wife; 1368; Yes
1376; Rufus; m; 13; Miss. Choctaw; F; S; Son; 1369; Yes
1377; Phelia; f; 10; Miss. Choctaw; F; S; Dau; 1370; Yes
1378; Eva Kate; f; 7; Miss. Choctaw; F; S; Dau; 1371; Yes
1379; Edmond; m; 4; Miss. Choctaw; F; S; Son; 1372; Yes

1380; Annis; m; 53; Miss. Choctaw; F; M; Head; 1373; Yes
1381; Annie; f; 32; Miss. Choctaw; F; M; Wife; 1374; Yes

1382; Edgar; m; 32; Miss. Choctaw; F; M; Head; 1375; Yes
1383; Annie; f; 30; Miss. Choctaw; F; M; Wife; 1376; Yes
1384; Steve; m; 11; Miss. Choctaw; F; S; Son; 1377; Yes
1385; Willie; m; 10; Miss. Choctaw; F; S; Son; 1378; Yes
1386; Odie; m; 8; Miss. Choctaw; F; S; Son; 1379; Yes
1387; Parline; f; 5; Miss. Choctaw; F; S; Dau; 1380; Yes

1388; Dick; m; 61; Miss. Choctaw; F; M; Head; 1381; Yes
1389; Eline; f; 52; Miss. Choctaw; F; M; Wife; 1382; Yes

Census of the **Mississippi Choctaw** reservation of the **Choctaw Agency** jurisdiction, as of **April 1**, 19**32**, taken by **R. J. Enochs**, Superintendent.

KEY; Surname; Census Number; Given Name; Sex; Age at Last Birthday; Tribe; Degree of Blood; Marital Status; Relationship to Head of Family; Last Census Roll Number; At Jurisdiction Where Enrolled (Yes/No); Ward (Yes/No, if given)

1390; Jeff; m; 26; Miss. Choctaw; F; S; Nephew; 1383; Yes

1391; Allen; m; 76; Miss. Choctaw; F; Wd; Head; 1384; Yes
1392; Mary; f; 29; Miss. Choctaw; F; S; Dau; 1385; Yes
1393; Lilly; f; 27; Miss. Choctaw; F; S; Dau; 1386; Yes

1394; Pat; m; 38; Miss. Choctaw; F; M; Head; 1387; Yes
1395; Frances; f; 38; Miss. Choctaw; F; M; Wife; 1388; Yes
1396; Vernal; m; 20; Miss. Choctaw; F; S; Son; 1389; Yes
1397; Earnest; m; 12; Miss. Choctaw; F; S; Son; 1390; Yes
1398; Loraine; f; 10; Miss. Choctaw; F; S; Dau; 1391; Yes
1399; Alice; f; 8; Miss. Choctaw; F; S; Dau; 1392; Yes
1400; Aileen; f; 5; Miss. Choctaw; F; S; Dau; 1393; Yes

1401; Lysander; m; 44; Miss. Choctaw; F; M; Head; 1394; Yes
1402; Annie Mae; f; 23; Miss. Choctaw; F; M; Wife; 1395; Yes

1403; Moley; m; 29; Miss. Choctaw; F; M; Head; 1396; Yes
1404; Salie; f; 25; Miss. Choctaw; F; M; Wife; 1397; Yes

1405; Adam; m; 30; Miss. Choctaw; F; S; Alone; 1398; Yes

1406; Dewitt; m; 25; Miss. Choctaw; F; M; Head; 1399; Yes
1407; Katie; f; 26; Miss. Choctaw; F; M; Wife; 1400; Yes

1408; Rainey; f; 62; Miss. Choctaw; F; Wd; Head; 1401; Yes
1409; Lena; f; 32; Miss. Choctaw; F; S; Dau; 1402; Yes
1410; Mollie; f; 27; Miss. Choctaw; F; S; Dau; 1403; Yes
1411; Herbert; m; 24; Miss. Choctaw; F; S; Son; 1404; Yes

1412; Jimpson; m; 68; Miss. Choctaw; F; Wd; Alone; 1405; Yes

1413; Anderson; m; 32; Miss. Choctaw; F; M; Head; 1406; Yes
1414; Nancy; f; 22; Miss. Choctaw; F; M; Wife; 1407; Yes

Census of the **Mississippi Choctaw** reservation of the **Choctaw Agency** jurisdiction, as of **April 1**, 19**32**, taken by **R. J. Enochs**, Superintendent.

KEY; Surname; Census Number; Given Name; Sex; Age at Last Birthday; Tribe; Degree of Blood; Marital Status; Relationship to Head of Family; Last Census Roll Number; At Jurisdiction Where Enrolled (Yes/No); Ward (Yes/No, if given)

1415; Jim; m; 8; Miss. Choctaw; F; S; Son; 1408; Yes
1416; Oscar; f; 6; Miss. Choctaw; F; S; Dau; 1409; Yes
1417; Buracy; f; 4; Miss. Choctaw; F; S; Dau; 1410; Yes
1418; Etolye; f; 2; Miss. Choctaw; F; S; Dau; 1411; Yes

1419; Evan; m; 39; Miss. Choctaw; F; M; Head; 1412; Yes
1420; Jennie; f; 44; Miss. Choctaw; F; M; Wife; 1413; Yes
1421; Annie; f; 9; Miss. Choctaw; F; S; Dau; 1414; Yes

1422; Charlie; m; 36; Miss. Choctaw; F; M; Head; 1415; Yes
1423; Betsy; f; 31; Miss. Choctaw; F; M; Wife; 1416; Yes
1424; Alice; f; 9; Miss. Choctaw; F; S; Dau; 1417; Yes
1425; Jack; m; 7; Miss. Choctaw; F; S; Son; 1418; Yes
1426; J. C; m; 5; Miss. Choctaw; F; S; Son; 1419; Yes
1427; Colie; f; 3; Miss. Choctaw; F; S; Dau; 1420; Yes
1428; Bessie; f; 2/12; Miss. Choctaw; F; S; Dau; Yes
1429; Kate; f; 11; Miss. Choctaw; F; S; Step-dau; 1421; Yes
1430; Ellis; m; 8; Miss. Choctaw; F; S; Orphan; 1422; Yes

1431; Henderson; m; 39; Miss. Choctaw; F; M; Head; 1423; Yes
1432; Maggie; f; 27; Miss. Choctaw; F; M; Wife; 1424; Yes
1433; Otis; f; 9; Miss. Choctaw; F; S; Dau; 1425; Yes
1434; W. C; m; 7; Miss. Choctaw; F; S; Son; 1426; Yes
1435; Gladys; f; 5; Miss. Choctaw; F; S; Dau; 1427; Yes
1436; Finis; m; 3; Miss. Choctaw; F; S; Son; 1428; Yes
1437; Martha Lee; f; 1; Miss. Choctaw; F; S; Dau; 1429; Yes

1438; Clemon; m; 57; Miss. Choctaw; F; M; Head; 1430; Yes
1439; Alice; f; 57; Miss. Choctaw; F; M; Wife; 1431; Yes
1440; **Bell**, Joe; m; 23; Miss. Choctaw; F; S; Step-son; 1432; Yes
1441; Lash; m; 6; Miss. Choctaw; F; S; Great-nephew; 1433; Yes
1442; Sarah; f; 5; Miss. Choctaw; F; S; Great-niece; 1434; Yes

1443; Jackson; m; 24; Miss. Choctaw; F; M; Head; 1435; Yes

Census of the **Mississippi Choctaw** reservation of the **Choctaw Agency** jurisdiction, as of **April 1**, 19**32**, taken by **R. J. Enochs**, Superintendent.

KEY; Surname; Census Number; Given Name; Sex; Age at Last Birthday; Tribe; Degree of Blood; Marital Status; Relationship to Head of Family; Last Census Roll Number; At Jurisdiction Where Enrolled (Yes/No); Ward (Yes/No, if given)

1444; Malissa; f; 25; Miss. Choctaw; F; M; Wife; 1436; Yes

1445; Nichols; m; 34; Miss. Choctaw; F; M; Head; 1437; Yes
1446; Esther; f; 29; Miss. Choctaw; F; M; Wife; 1438; Yes
1447; Sullivan; m; 10; Miss. Choctaw; F; S; Son; 1439; Yes
1448; Alice; f; 9; Miss. Choctaw; F; S; Dau; 1440; Yes
1449; Minnie; f; 7; Miss. Choctaw; F; S; Dau; 1441; Yes
1450; Catherine; f; 5; Miss. Choctaw; F; S; Dau; 1442; Yes

1451; Alice; f; 42; Miss. Choctaw; F; Wd; Head; 1443; Yes
1452; **Johnson**, Lee; m; 20; Miss. Choctaw; F; S; Son; 1444; Yes

1453; Tom; m; 23; Miss. Choctaw; F; M; Head; 1445; Yes
1454; Marceline; f; 25; Miss. Choctaw; F; M; Wife; 1446; Yes
1455; Inis; m; 2; Miss. Choctaw; F; S; Son; 1447; Yes
1456; Joseph; m; 4; Miss. Choctaw; F; S; Step-son; 1448; Yes

1457; Anderson; m; 40; Miss. Choctaw; F; M; Head; 1449; Yes
1458; Louisiana; f; 42; Miss. Choctaw; F; M; Wife; 1450; Yes
1459; Hazel; f; 18; Miss. Choctaw; F; S; Dau; 1451; Yes
1460; Smith; m; 16; Miss. Choctaw; F; S; Son; 1452; Yes
1461; Icy; f; 14; Miss. Choctaw; F; S; Dau; 1453; Yes
1462; John; m; 12; Miss. Choctaw; F; S; Son; 1454; Yes

1463; Simpson; m; 72; Miss. Choctaw; F; M; Head; 1455; Yes
1464; Minnie; f; 39; Miss. Choctaw; F; M; Wife; 1456; Yes
1465; Ike; m; 20; Miss. Choctaw; F; S; Son; 1457; Yes
1466; Henry; m; 19; Miss. Choctaw; F; S; Son; 1458; Yes
1467; Eva; f; 18; Miss. Choctaw; F; S; Dau; 1459; Yes
1468; Lewis; m; 15; Miss. Choctaw; F; S; Son; 1460; Yes
1469; McKinley; m; 12; Miss. Choctaw; F; S; Son; 1461; Yes
1470; Hudson; m; 9; Miss. Choctaw; F; S; Son; 1462; Yes
1471; Sullivan; m; 8; Miss. Choctaw; F; S; Son; 1463; Yes
1472; Callie; f; 6; Miss. Choctaw; F; S; Dau; 1464; Yes

Census of the **Mississippi Choctaw** reservation of the **Choctaw Agency** jurisdiction, as of **April 1**, 19**32**, taken by **R. J. Enochs**, Superintendent.

KEY; Surname; Census Number; Given Name; Sex; Age at Last Birthday; Tribe; Degree of Blood; Marital Status; Relationship to Head of Family; Last Census Roll Number; At Jurisdiction Where Enrolled (Yes/No); Ward (Yes/No, if given)

1473; Nellie; f; 5; Miss. Choctaw; F; S; Dau; 1465; Yes

TUCKALLOO

1474; Frances; f; 69; Miss. Choctaw; F; Wd; Head; 1466; Yes
1475; **Tubby**, Wesley; m; 13; Miss. Choctaw; F; S; Grand-son; 1467; Yes
1476; Mason; m; 18; Miss. Choctaw; F; S; Grand-son; 1468; Yes
1477; Enia; m; 8; Miss. Choctaw; F; S; Grand-son; 1469; Yes
1478; Alice; f; 7; Miss. Choctaw; F; S; Grand-dau; 1470; Yes
1479; Sarah; f; 6; Miss. Choctaw; F; S; Grand-dau; 1471; Yes

VAUGHN

1480; John; m; 67; Miss. Choctaw; F; Wd; Alone; 1472; Yes

1481; Greet; m; 57; Miss. Choctaw; F; M; Head; 1473; Yes
1482; Jane; f; 52; Miss. Choctaw; F; M; Wife; 1474; Yes
1483; Agnes; f; 6; Miss. Choctaw; F; S; Dau; 1475; Yes

1484; Cooksie; m; 67; Miss. Choctaw; F; M; Head; 1476; Yes
1485; Susan; f; 60; Miss. Choctaw; F; M; Wife; 1477; Yes
1486; Lena; f; 37; Miss. Choctaw; F; S; Dau; 1478; Yes
1487; Ludie; f; 25; Miss. Choctaw; F; S; Dau; 1479; Yes

1488; Silmon; m; 20; Miss. Choctaw; F; M; Head; 1480; Yes
1489; Seta; f; 16; Miss. Choctaw; F; M; Wife; 1481; Yes

1490; Howard; m; 30; Miss. Choctaw; F; M; Head; 1482; Yes
1491; Bessie; f; 30; Miss. Choctaw; F; M; Wife; 1483; Yes
1492; Clifton; m; 6; Miss. Choctaw; F; S; Son; 1484; Yes
1493; Mary Rose; f; 4; Miss. Choctaw; F; S; Dau; 1485; Yes

1494; John; m; 26; Miss. Choctaw; F; M; Head; 1486; Yes

Census of the **Mississippi Choctaw** reservation of the **Choctaw Agency** jurisdiction, as of **April 1**, 19**32**, taken by **R. J. Enochs**, Superintendent.

KEY; Surname; Census Number; Given Name; Sex; Age at Last Birthday; Tribe; Degree of Blood; Marital Status; Relationship to Head of Family; Last Census Roll Number; At Jurisdiction Where Enrolled (Yes/No); Ward (Yes/No, if given)

1495; Mallisa; f; 39; Miss. Choctaw; F; M; Wife; 1487; Yes
1496; Mollie; f; 19; Miss. Choctaw; F; S; Step-dau; 1488; Yes
1497; Annie; f; 14; Miss. Choctaw; F; S; Step-dau; 1489; Yes

WAITER

1498; Gipson; m; 69; Miss. Choctaw; F; Wd; Alone; 1490; Yes

1499; Minnie; f; 56; Miss. Choctaw; F; Wd; Alone; 1491; Yes

1500; Lonnie; m; 27; Miss. Choctaw; F; M; Head; 1493; Yes
1501; Sue; f; 22; Miss. Choctaw; F; M; Wife; 1494; Yes
1502; Cora Mae; f; 9/12; Miss. Choctaw; F; S; Dau

WALLACE

1503; Comby; m; 60; Miss. Choctaw; F; M; Head; 368; Yes
1504; Betty; f; 56; Miss. Choctaw; F; M; Wife; 369; Yes
1505; Emma; f; 17; Miss. Choctaw; F; S; Dau; 371; Yes
1506; Maggie; f; 15; Miss. Choctaw; F; S; Dau; 372; Yes
1507; Tom; m; 11; Miss. Choctaw; F; S; Son; 373; Yes
1508; Fulton; m; 8; Miss. Choctaw; F; S; Son; 374; Yes

1509; Eunice; f; 42; Miss. Choctaw; F; Wd; Head; 1495; Yes
1510; Susie; f; 19; Miss. Choctaw; F; S; Dau; 1496; Yes
1511; Henry; m; 17; Miss. Choctaw; F; S; Son; 1497; Yes
1512; Celia; f; 16; Miss. Choctaw; F; S; Dau; 1498; Yes
1513; Austin; m; 5; Miss. Choctaw; F; S; Son; 1499; Yes

1514; Rachel; f; 47; Miss. Choctaw; F; Wd; Alone; 1500; Yes
1515; Leona; f; 17; Miss. Choctaw; F; S; Dau; 1501; Yes

1516; Columbus; m; 22; Miss. Choctaw; F; M; Head; 1502; Yes
1517; Essie; f; 20; Miss. Choctaw; F; M; Wife; 1503; Yes

Census of the **Mississippi Choctaw** reservation of the **Choctaw Agency** jurisdiction, as of **April 1**, 19 **32**, taken by **R. J. Enochs**, Superintendent.

KEY; Surname; Census Number; Given Name; Sex; Age at Last Birthday; Tribe; Degree of Blood; Marital Status; Relationship to Head of Family; Last Census Roll Number; At Jurisdiction Where Enrolled (Yes/No); Ward (Yes/No, if given)

1518; Stenot; m; 24; Miss. Choctaw; F; M; Head; 1504; Yes
1519; Annie; f; 19; Miss. Choctaw; F; M; Wife; 1505; Yes
1520; Alton; m; 12; Miss. Choctaw; F; S; Orphan; 1506; Yes

WARNER

1521; Johnnie Lee; m; 20; Miss. Choctaw; F; S; Alone; 1507; Yes

WESLEY

1522; Sidney; m; 67; Miss. Choctaw; F; Wd; Alone; 1508; Yes

1523; Cameron; m; 42; Miss. Choctaw; F; M; Head; 1509; Yes
1524; Julie; f; 28; Miss. Choctaw; F; M; Wife; 1510; Yes
1525; Bennie; m; 15; Miss. Choctaw; F; S; Son; 1511; Yes
1526; John; m; 7; Miss. Choctaw; F; S; Son; 1512; Yes
1527; Willie B; m; f; Miss. Choctaw; F; S; Son; 1513; Yes

WICKSON

1528; Jim; m; 24; Miss. Choctaw; F; M; Head; 1514; Yes
1529; Alma; f; 17; Miss. Choctaw; F; M; Wife; 1515; Yes

WILEY

1530; Lizzie; f; 62; Miss. Choctaw; F; S; Alone; 1516; Yes

WILLIAMS

1531; Jonas; m; 57; Miss. Choctaw; F; M; Head; 1517; Yes
1532; Maggie; f; 47; Miss. Choctaw; F; M; Wife; 1518; Yes
1533; Tony; m; 23; Miss. Choctaw; F; S; Son; 1519; Yes

1534; Rufus; m; 26; Miss. Choctaw; F; M; Head; 1520; Yes

Census of the **Mississippi Choctaw** reservation of the **Choctaw Agency** jurisdiction, as of **April 1**, 19**32**, taken by **R. J. Enochs**, Superintendent.

KEY; Surname; Census Number; Given Name; Sex; Age at Last Birthday; Tribe; Degree of Blood; Marital Status; Relationship to Head of Family; Last Census Roll Number; At Jurisdiction Where Enrolled (Yes/No); Ward (Yes/No, if given)

1535; Nellie; f; 31; Miss. Choctaw; F; M; Wife; 1521; Yes
1536; Evan; m; 10; Miss. Choctaw; F; S; Son; 1522; Yes
1537; Phillip; m; 9; Miss. Choctaw; F; S; Son; 1523; Yes
1538; Fillman; m; 5; Miss. Choctaw; F; S; Son; 1524; Yes
1539; Coy; m; 3; Miss. Choctaw; F; S; Son; 1525; Yes

1540; Jennie; f; 88; Miss. Choctaw; F; Wd; Head; 1526; Yes
1541; Fate; m; 43; Miss. Choctaw; F; S; Son; 1527; Yes

1542; Lewis; m; 55; Miss. Choctaw; F; M; Head; 1528; Yes
1543; Mamie; f; 33; Miss. Choctaw; F; M; Wife; 1529; Yes
1544; Mary Ann; f; 7; Miss. Choctaw; F; S; Dau; 1530; Yes
1545; Sarah; f; 3; Miss. Choctaw; F; S; Dau; 1531; Yes
1546; Carter; m; 1; Miss. Choctaw; F; S; Son; 1532; Yes

WILLIAMSON

1547; Mack; m; 57; Miss. Choctaw; F; M; Head; 1533; Yes
1548; Ida; f; 57; Miss. Choctaw; F; M; Wife; 1534; Yes
1549; Arnold; m; 13; Miss. Choctaw; F; S; Son; 1535; Yes
1550; **Lewis**, Marceline; f; 8; Miss. Choctaw; F; S; Grand-dau; 1536; Yes

1551; Bike; m; 40; Miss. Choctaw; F; M; Head; 1537; Yes
1552; Effie; f; 28; Miss. Choctaw; F; M; Wife; 1538; Yes
1553; Mary; f; 12; Miss. Choctaw; F; S; Dau; 1539; Yes
1554; Lallis; f; 10; Miss. Choctaw; F; S; Dau; 1540; Yes

WILLIS

1555; Bill; m; 36; Miss. Choctaw; F; M; Head; 1541; Yes
1556; Savenie; f; 30; Miss. Choctaw; F; M; Wife; 1542; Yes
1557; Claud Y; m; 13; Miss. Choctaw; F; S; Son; 1543; Yes
1558; Elsie; f; 12; Miss. Choctaw; F; S; Dau; 1544; Yes

Census of the **Mississippi Choctaw** reservation of the **Choctaw Agency** jurisdiction, as of **April 1**, 19**32**, taken by **R. J. Enochs**, Superintendent.

KEY; Surname; Census Number; Given Name; Sex; Age at Last Birthday; Tribe; Degree of Blood; Marital Status; Relationship to Head of Family; Last Census Roll Number; At Jurisdiction Where Enrolled (Yes/No); Ward (Yes/No, if given)

1559;   William B; m; 9; Miss. Choctaw; F; S; Son; 1545; Yes

1560;   Nath; m; 25; Miss. Choctaw; F; M; Head; 1546; Yes
1561;   Esther; f; 29; Miss. Choctaw; F; M; Wife; 1547; Yes
1562;   Silma; f; 4; Miss. Choctaw; F; S; Dau; 1548; Yes
1563;   Joe; m; 2; Miss. Choctaw; F; S; Son; 1549; Yes

1564;   Ike; m; 25; Miss. Choctaw; F; M; Head; 1550; Yes
1565;   Ellen; f; 23; Miss. Choctaw; F; M; Wife; 1551; Yes
1566;   Adam; m; 6; Miss. Choctaw; F; S; Son; 1552; Yes
1567;   Jasper; m; 3; Miss. Choctaw; F; S; Son; 1553; Yes

1568;   Robert; m; 44; Miss. Choctaw; F; M; Head; 1554; Yes
1569;   Celie; f; 31; Miss. Choctaw; F; M; Wife; 1555; Yes
1570;   Mollie; f; 20; Miss. Choctaw; F; S; Dau; 1556; Yes
1571;   **Ben**, Wilson; m; 12; Miss. Choctaw; F; S; Orphan; 1557; Yes

1572;   Finis; m; 30; Miss. Choctaw; F; M; Head; 1558; Yes
1573;   Nora; f; 25; Miss. Choctaw; F; M; Wife; 1559; Yes
1574;   Leona; f 3; Miss. Choctaw; F; S; Dau; 1560; Yes
1575;   Sarah; f; 9/12; Miss. Choctaw; F; S; Dau; Yes

1576;   John; m; 26; Miss. Choctaw; F; M; Head; 1562; Yes
1577;   Susiana; f; 18; Miss. Choctaw; F; M; Wife; 1563; Yes

1578;   Johnson; m; 67; Miss. Choctaw; F; Wd; Alone; 1564; Yes

1579;   Gus; m; 59; Miss. Choctaw; F; M; Head; 1565; Yes
1580;   Rainey; f; 35; Miss. Choctaw; F; M; Wife; 1566; Yes
1581;   Hester; m; 5; Miss. Choctaw; F; S; Son; 1567; Yes
1582;   Lester; m; 1; Miss. Choctaw; F; S; Son ; Yes
1583;   **Isaac**, Nannie; f; 14; Miss. Choctaw; F; S; Step-dau; 1568; Yes
1584;   **Isaac**, Eunice; f; 12; Miss. Choctaw; F; S; Step-dau; 1569; Yes
1585;   **Isaac**, Rose; f; 8; Miss. Choctaw; F; S; Step-dau; 1570; Yes

Census of the **Mississippi Choctaw** reservation of the **Choctaw Agency** jurisdiction, as of **April 1**, 19**32**, taken by **R. J. Enochs**, Superintendent.

KEY: Surname; Census Number; Given Name; Sex; Age at Last Birthday; Tribe; Degree of Blood; Marital Status; Relationship to Head of Family; Last Census Roll Number; At Jurisdiction Where Enrolled (Yes/No); Ward (Yes/No, if given)

1586; **Isaac**, William; m; 19; Miss. Choctaw; F; S; Step-son; 1571; Yes

1587; Gamblin; m; 32; Miss. Choctaw; F; M; Head; 1572; Yes
1588; Ellen; f; 34; Miss. Choctaw; F; M; Wife; 1573; Yes
1589; Mattie; f; 14; Miss. Choctaw; F; S; Dau; 1574; Yes
1590; G. C; m; 11; Miss. Choctaw; F; S; Son; 1575; Yes
1591; Eula; f; 9; Miss. Choctaw; F; S; Dau; 1576; Yes
1592; Maruice[sic]; f; 8; Miss. Choctaw; F; S; Dau; 1577; Yes
1593; Marabelle; f; 3; Miss. Choctaw; F; S; Dau; 1578; Yes
1594; Earl; m; 11/12; Miss. Choctaw; F; S; Son; Yes

1595; Ed; m; 61; Miss. Choctaw; F; M; Head; 1579; Yes
1596; Panzie; f; 60; Miss. Choctaw; F; M; Wife; 1580; Yes

1597; Joe; m; 63; Miss. Choctaw; F; M; Head; 1581; Yes
1598; Adaline; f; 60; Miss. Choctaw; F; M; Wife; 1582; Yes
1599; Nannie; f; 22; Miss. Choctaw; F; S; Grand-dau; 1583; Yes

1600; Eliss; m; 29; Miss. Choctaw; F; S; Alone; 1584; Yes

1601; Jim; m; 54; Miss. Choctaw; F; M; Head; 1585; Yes
1602; Louisa; f; 52; Miss. Choctaw; F; M; Wife; 1686[sic]; Yes
1603; Tom; m; 30; Miss. Choctaw; F; S; Son; 1687[sic]; Yes
1604; Dennis; m; 28; Miss. Choctaw; F; S; Son; 1688[sic]; Yes
1605; Waggoner; m; 23; Miss. Choctaw; F; S; Son; 1689[sic]; Yes
1606; Dailey; f; 21; Miss. Choctaw; F; S; Dau; 1590; Yes
1607; Dora; f; 20; Miss. Choctaw; F; S; Dau; 1591; Yes
1608; Rosie; f; 18; Miss. Choctaw; F; S; Dau; 1592; Yes
1609; Smith; m; 17; Miss. Choctaw; F; S; Son; 1593; Yes
1610; Woodrow Wilson; m; 12; Miss. Choctaw; F; S; Son; 1594; Yes

1611; Edmond; m; 24; Miss. Choctaw; F; M; Head; 1595; Yes
1612; Sallie; f; 19; Miss. Choctaw; F; M; Wife; 1596; Yes
1613; John; m; 3; Miss. Choctaw; F; S; Son; 1597; Yes

Census of the **Mississippi Choctaw** reservation of the **Choctaw Agency** jurisdiction, as of **April 1**, 19**32**, taken by **R. J. Enochs**, Superintendent.

KEY; Surname; Census Number; Given Name; Sex; Age at Last Birthday; Tribe; Degree of Blood; Marital Status; Relationship to Head of Family; Last Census Roll Number; At Jurisdiction Where Enrolled (Yes/No); Ward (Yes/No, if given)

1614; Hayward; m; 11/12; Miss. Choctaw; F; S; Son; Yes

1615; Elie; m; 31; Miss. Choctaw; F; M; Head; 1598; Yes
1616; Otis; f; 25; Miss. Choctaw; F; M; Wife; 1599; Yes
1617; Vanola; f; 12; Miss. Choctaw; F; S; Dau; 1600; Yes
1618; Flora; f; 10; Miss. Choctaw; F; S; Dau; 1601; Yes
1619; Kittie; f; 9; Miss. Choctaw; F; S; Dau; 1602; Yes
1620; Bonnie; m; 7; Miss. Choctaw; F; S; Son; 1603; Yes

1621; Cohan; m; 34; Miss. Choctaw; F; M; Head; 1604; Yes
1622; Sis; f; 30; Miss. Choctaw; F; M; Wife; 1605; Yes
1623; Ancie; f; 14; Miss. Choctaw; F; S; Dau; 1606; Yes
1624; Una; f; 12; Miss. Choctaw; F; S; Dau; 1607; Yes
1625; Sallie; f; 9; Miss. Choctaw; F; S; Dau; 1608; Yes
1626; Harrison; m; 7; Miss. Choctaw; F; S; Son; 1609; Yes
1627; A. J; m; 4; Miss. Choctaw; F; S; Son; 1610; Yes

1628; Hugh; m; 49; Miss. Choctaw; F; M; Head; 1611; Yes
1629; Mollie; f; 46; Miss. Choctaw; F; M; Wife; 1612; Yes
1630; Thompson; m; 17; Miss. Choctaw; F; S; Son; 1613; Yes
1631; Clemon; m; 15; Miss. Choctaw; F; S; Son; 1614; Yes
1632; J. C; m; 11; Miss. Choctaw; F; S; Son; 1615; Yes
1633; Collins; m; 9; Miss. Choctaw; F; S; Son; 1616; Yes
1634; Lillie; f; 8; Miss. Choctaw; F; S; Dau; 1617; Yes
1635; Walter; m; 7; Miss. Choctaw; F; S; Son; 1618; Yes
1636; Lola; f; 6; Miss. Choctaw; F; S; Dau; 1619; Yes

1637; Spinks; m; 42; Miss. Choctaw; F; M; Head; 1620; Yes
1638; Susie; f; 33; Miss. Choctaw; F; M; Wife; 1621; Yes
1639; Wilson; m; 13; Miss. Choctaw; F; S; Son; 1622; Yes
1640; Flennie; f; 10; Miss. Choctaw; F; S; Dau; 1623; Yes

1641; Wesley M; m; 66; Miss. Choctaw; F; Wd; Head; 1624; Yes
1642; Meley; f; 8; Miss. Choctaw; F; S; Dau; 1625; Yes

Census of the **Mississippi Choctaw** reservation of the **Choctaw Agency** jurisdiction, as of **April 1**, 19**32**, taken by **R. J. Enochs**, Superintendent.

KEY; Surname; Census Number; Given Name; Sex; Age at Last Birthday; Tribe; Degree of Blood; Marital Status; Relationship to Head of Family; Last Census Roll Number; At Jurisdiction Where Enrolled (Yes/No); Ward (Yes/No, if given)

1643; John Banks; m; 5; Miss. Choctaw; F; S; Son; 1626; Yes
1644; Leighton; m; 2; Miss. Choctaw; F; S; Son; 1627; Yes

1645; Salum; m; 27; Miss. Choctaw; F; S; Alone; 1628; Yes

WILSON

1646; John; m; 37; Miss. Choctaw; F; M; Head; 1629; Yes
1646; Eva; f; 29; Miss. Choctaw; F; M; Wife; 1630; Yes
1647; Silman; m; 13; Miss. Choctaw; F; S; Son; 1631; Yes
1648; Mollie; f; 11; Miss. Choctaw; F; S; Dau; 1632; Yes
1649; Sidney; m; 10; Miss. Choctaw; F; S; Son; 1633; Yes
1650; Leo; m; 7; Miss. Choctaw; F; S; Son; 1634; Yes
1651; Edna; f; 3; Miss. Choctaw; F; S; Dau; 1635; Yes
1652; Martha; f; 84; Miss. Choctaw; F; Wd; Mother; 1636; Yes

1653; Will; m; 44; Miss. Choctaw; F; M; Head; 1637; Yes
1654; Martha; f; 38; Miss. Choctaw; F; M; Wife; 1638; Yes
1655; Sammie; m; 11; Miss. Choctaw; F; S; Son; 1639; Yes
1656; Linnie; f; 10; Miss. Choctaw; F; S; Dau; 1640; Yes
1657; Louisana; f; 9; Miss. Choctaw; F; S; Dau; 1641; Yes
1658; R. L; m; 3; Miss. Choctaw; F; S; Son; 1642; Yes
1659; Jim; m; 2; Miss. Choctaw; F; S; Son; 1643; Yes

WISHORK

1660; Massey; m; 36; Miss. Choctaw; F; M; Head; 1644; Yes
1661; Alpha; f; 30; Miss. Choctaw; F; M; Wife; 1645; Yes
1662; Zelia; f; 11; Miss. Choctaw; F; S; Dau; 1646; Yes
1663; Evelyn; f; 10; Miss. Choctaw; F; S; Dau; 1647; Yes
1664; Nugar; m; 7; Miss. Choctaw; F; S; Son; 1648; Yes
1665; Lyn Presley; m; 3; Miss. Choctaw; F; S; Son; 1649; Yes
1666; Sampson; m; 68; Miss. Choctaw; F; Wd; Father; 1650; Yes

Census of the **Mississippi Choctaw** reservation of the **Choctaw Agency** jurisdiction, as of **April 1**, 19 **32**, taken by **R. J. Enochs**, Superintendent.

KEY; Surname; Census Number; Given Name; Sex; Age at Last Birthday; Tribe; Degree of Blood; Marital Status; Relationship to Head of Family; Last Census Roll Number; At Jurisdiction Where Enrolled (Yes/No); Ward (Yes/No, if given)

YORK

1667; Ben; m; 41; Miss. Choctaw; F; M; Head; 1651; Yes
1668; Louella; f; 47; Miss. Choctaw; F; M; Wife; 1652; Yes
1669; Elsie; f; 16; Miss. Choctaw; F; S; Dau; 1653; Yes
1670; Hester; m; 10; Miss. Choctaw; F; S; Son; 1654; Yes

1671; Scott; m; 77; Miss. Choctaw; F; M; Head; 1655; Yes
1672; Celie; f; 82; Miss. Choctaw; F; M; Wife; 1656; Yes
1673; Berkley; m; 20; Miss. Choctaw; F; S; Grand-son; 1657; Yes

1674; Bennett; m; 42; Miss. Choctaw; F; M; Head; 1658; Yes
1675; Lacie; f; 24; Miss. Choctaw; F; M; Wife; 1659; Yes
1676; G. B; m; 6; Miss. Choctaw; F; S; Son; 1660; Yes
1677; Colie; f; 5; Miss. Choctaw; F; S; Dau; 1661; Yes

1678; Necie; f; 44; Miss. Choctaw; F; Wd; Head; 1662; Yes
1679; Baxter; m; 25; Miss. Choctaw; F; S; Son; 1664; Yes
1680; Addie; f; 23; Miss. Choctaw; F; S; Dau; 1665; Yes
1681; Gasler; m; 20; Miss. Choctaw; F; S; Son; 1666; Yes
1682; Eunice; f; 18; Miss. Choctaw; F; S; Dau; 1667; Yes
1683; Beaman; m; 15; Miss. Choctaw; F; S; Son; 1668; Yes

1684; Emmett; m; 28; Miss. Choctaw; F; M; Head; 1663; Yes
1685; Indiana; f; 17; Miss. Choctaw; F; M; Wife; 999; Yes

1686; **Denson**, Winston; m; 18; Miss. Choctaw; F; S; Alone; 443; Yes

Mississippi Choctaw Census
Supplement No. I - -
Added Or Dropped From Census Roll
For Other Causes Than Births & Deaths.

taken by R. J. Enochs, Superintendent

Census of the __Mississippi Choctaw__ reservation of the ____Choctaw__
___Agency_____ jurisdiction, as of_____, 19__, taken by
___R. J. Enochs__, Superintendent.

KEY: Census Number; Surname, Given Name; Sex; Age at Last Birthday; Tribe; Degree of Blood; Marital Status; Relationship to Head of Family; At Jurisdiction Where Enrolled (Yes/No)

Supplement No. I - -
Added or Dropped From Census Roll
For Causes Other Than Births & Deaths.

PREVIOUSLY OMITTED ON CENSUS ROLL, 1930.

1931
1177;   **Sam**, Edna; f; 9; Miss. Choctaw; F; S; Daughter; Yes

DUPLICATED ON 1931 CENSUS ROLL

808;   **Hall**, Pauline; f; 19; Miss. Choctaw; F; S Wd; Niece; 799
809;   **Hall**, Herbert H; m; 2; Miss. Choctaw; F; S; Grand-son; 800

NUMBERS WITHOUT NAMES ON 1931 CENSUS ROLL

700
330

[NOTE: The above two numbers without names for the entries on the 1931 Census are wrongly stated. After checking the census, No. 330 is Sam Tubby, Orphan, page 147 and No. 700 is Minnie Hickman, Wife, page 162.]

BIRTHS -

July 1, 1924 to March 31, 1932

Choctaw Indian Agency, Mississippi.

State ____ Mississippi ____ Reservation _____ Agency
or jurisdiction __ Choctaw Indian Agency ____ Office of Indian Affairs

Key: Census Roll Number (if given); Surname, Given Name; Date of Birth (Year-Month-Day); Live Births (Yes, unless otherwise given); Still Births (blank unless otherwise given); Sex; Tribe; Ward (Yes/No); Degree of Blood (Father; Mother; Child); At Jurisdiction Where Enrolled (Yes/No); (If no – Where)

Births Occurring Between July 1, 1924 and June 30, 1925 to Parents Enrolled at Jurisdiction

Anderson, J. C; 1924-Oct-15; Male; Miss. Choctaw; Yes; Full; Full; Full; Yes

Billy, Frank; 1924-Oct-?; Male; Miss. Choctaw; Yes; Full; Full; Full; Yes

Ben, Anna Laura; 1925-Mar-9; Female; Miss. Choctaw; Yes; Full; Full; Full; Yes

Chitto, Isom; 1924-Dec-15; Male; Miss. Choctaw; Yes; Full; Full; Full; Yes

Farmer, Annie Mae; 1925-June-20; Female; Miss. Choctaw; Yes; Full; Full; Full; Yes

Hall, Ilone; 1924-Apr-16; Female; Miss. Choctaw; Yes; Full; Full; Full; Yes

Isaac, Rosa; 1924-Sept-4; Female; Miss. Choctaw; Yes; Full; Full; Full; Yes

John, Vardaman; 1924-Oct-23; Male; Miss. Choctaw; Yes; Full; Full; Full; Yes

McMillan, Josie; 1924-July-5; Female; Miss. Choctaw; Yes; Full; Full; Full; Yes

Polk, Augustine; 1925-June-1; Male; Miss. Choctaw; Yes; Full; Full; Full; Yes

Thomas, Peter; 1924-Oct-?; Male; Miss. Choctaw; Yes; Full; Full; Full; Yes

Thomas, Mina; 1925-June-?; Female; Miss. Choctaw; Yes; Full; Full; Full; Yes

Thompson, Alis[sic]; 1924-Sept-5; Male; Miss. Choctaw; Yes; Full; Full; Full; Yes

Tubby, Sullivan; 1924-Oct-28; Male; Miss. Choctaw; Yes; Full; Full; Full; Yes

Tubby, Odis; 1925-Apr-7; Male; Miss. Choctaw; Yes; Full; Full; Full; Yes

Tubby, W. C; 1925-May-16; Male; Miss. Choctaw; Yes; Full; Full; Full; Yes

State ___Mississippi___ Reservation _____ Agency
or jurisdiction__Choctaw Indian Agency___ Office of Indian Affairs

Key: Census Roll Number (if given); Surname, Given Name; Date of Birth (Year-Month-Day); Live Births (Yes, unless otherwise given); Still Births (blank unless otherwise given); Sex; Tribe; Ward (Yes/No); Degree of Blood (Father; Mother; Child); At Jurisdiction Where Enrolled (Yes/No); (If no – Where)

Williams, Mary Ann; 1924-Aug-16; Female; Miss. Choctaw; Yes; Full; Full; Full; Yes

Wickson, Kelley; 1924-Aug-26; Male; Miss. Choctaw; Yes; Full; Full; Full; Yes

Willis, Maurice; 1924-Nov-5; Female[sic]; Miss. Choctaw; Yes; Full; Full; Full; Yes

Wilson, Peter; 1925-Apr-21; Male; Miss. Choctaw; Yes; Full; Full; Full; Yes

Wilson, Paul; 1925-Apr-21; Male; Miss. Choctaw; Yes; Full; Full; Full; Yes

Willis, Boy; 1925-June-27; Male; Miss. Choctaw; Yes; Full; Full; Full; Yes

Wishork, Nuga; 1925-Apr-12; F; Miss. Choctaw; Yes; Full; Full; Full; Yes

York, J. B; 1925-May-31; M; Miss. Choctaw; Yes; Full; Full; Full; Yes

Births Occurring Between July 1, 1925 and June 30, 1926 to Parents Enrolled at Jurisdiction

Alex, Henry; 1925-Dec-28; M; Miss. Choctaw; Yes; Full; Full; Full; Yes

Anderson, Sallie Mae; 1925-Sept-1; F; Miss. Choctaw; Yes; Full; Full; Full; Yes

Billy, James; 1926-Feb-2; M; Miss. Choctaw; Yes; Full; Full; Full; Yes

Billy, Joseph; 1926-Jan-20; M; Miss. Choctaw; Yes; Full; Full; Full; Yes

Ben, Hubert; 1926-Jan-?; M; Miss. Choctaw; Yes; Full; Full; Full; Yes

Chapman, Raymond; 1925-Oct-1; M; Miss. Choctaw; Yes; Full; Full; Full; Yes

Chapman, Lilly; 1925-Oct-15; F; Miss. Choctaw; Yes; Full; Full; Full; Yes

Chickaway, Albert; 1925-Dec-7; M; Miss. Choctaw; Yes; Full; Full; Full; Yes

Chickaway, Anna; 1925-Aug-26; F; Miss. Choctaw; Yes; Full; Full; Full; Yes

Comby, Le Roy; 1926-Mar-8; M; Miss. Choctaw; Yes; Full; Full; Full; Yes

State ____Mississippi____ Reservation _____ Agency
or jurisdiction__Choctaw Indian Agency____ Office of Indian Affairs

Key: Census Roll Number (if given); Surname, Given Name; Date of Birth (Year-Month-Day); Live Births (Yes, unless otherwise given); Still Births (blank unless otherwise given); Sex; Tribe; Ward (Yes/No); Degree of Blood (Father; Mother; Child); At Jurisdiction Where Enrolled (Yes/No); (If no – Where)

Comby, Irene; 1925-Oct-10; F; Miss. Choctaw; Yes; Full; Full; Full; Yes
Farve, Zula Mae; 1925-Aug-18; F; Miss. Choctaw; Yes; Full; Full; Full; Yes
Hall, Frank; 1926-Apr-12; M; Miss. Choctaw; Yes; Full; Full; Full; Yes
Jefferson, Otto; 1925-Nov-16; M; Miss. Choctaw; Yes; Full; Full; Full; Yes
Jim, McKinley; 1925-July-11; M; Miss. Choctaw; Yes; Full; Full; Full; Yes
Lewis, Horace; 1925-Aug-10; M; Miss. Choctaw; Yes; Full; Full; Full; Yes
Martin, Phillip; 1926-Mar-26; M; Miss. Choctaw; Yes; Full; Full; Full; Yes
Mingo, Sarah; 1926-Jun-14; F; Miss. Choctaw; Yes; Full; Full; Full; Yes
McMillan, Mary; 1925-July-1; F; Miss. Choctaw; Yes; Full; Full; Full; Yes
Sam, Fannie; 1925-Oct-5; F; Miss. Choctaw; Yes; Full; Full; Full; Yes
Steve, Maurice; 1925-July-31; M; Miss. Choctaw; Yes; Full; Full; Full; Yes
Steve, Mary; 1925-Sept-17; F; Miss. Choctaw; Yes; Full; Full; Full; Yes
Steve, Mollie; 1925-Nov-18; F; Miss. Choctaw; Yes; Full; Full; Full; Yes
Shumaker, John; 1925-Nov-3; M; Miss. Choctaw; Yes; Full; Full; Full; Yes
Shumaker, Reuben; 1925-Nov-3; M; Miss. Choctaw; Yes; Full; Full; Full; Yes
Thomas, Amos; 1925-Oct-15; M; Miss. Choctaw; Yes; Full; Full; Full; Yes
Willis, Boniface; 1925-Aug-27; M; Miss. Choctaw; Yes; Full; Full; Full; Yes

Births Occurring Between July 1, 1926 and June 30, 1927 to Parents Enrolled at Jurisdiction

Bell, Homer; 1926-Oct-14; M; Miss. Choctaw; Yes; Full; Full; Full; Yes

State ____Mississippi____ Reservation _____ Agency
or jurisdiction__Choctaw Indian Agency____ Office of Indian Affairs

Key: Census Roll Number (if given); Surname, Given Name; Date of Birth (Year-Month-Day); Live Births (Yes, unless otherwise given); Still Births (blank unless otherwise given); Sex; Tribe; Ward (Yes/No); Degree of Blood (Father; Mother; Child); At Jurisdiction Where Enrolled (Yes/No); (If no – Where)

Billy, Maurice; 1927-Apr-23; M; Miss. Choctaw; Yes; Full; Full; Full; Yes

Davis, Harry; 1927-Mar-10; M; Miss. Choctaw; Yes; Full; Full; Full; Yes

Davis, Mary; 1926-Sept-25; F; Miss. Choctaw; Yes; Full; Full; Full; Yes

Dixon, Imogene; 1926-Sept-2; F; Miss. Choctaw; Yes; Full; Full; Full; Yes

Henry, Frank; 1927-May-10; M; Miss. Choctaw; Yes; Full; Full; Full; Yes

Isaac, Edwin; 1927-Feb-3; M; Miss. Choctaw; Yes; Full; Full; Full; Yes

Jefferson, Malcolm; 1926-Aug-16; M; Miss. Choctaw; Yes; Full; Full; Full; Yes

Morris, Irene; 1927-Jan-3; F; Miss. Choctaw; Yes; Full; Full; Full; Yes

Morris, Prentiss; 1926-Aug-10; M; Miss. Choctaw; Yes; Full; Full; Full; Yes

McMillan, John; 1926-Nov-28; M; Miss. Choctaw; Yes; Full; Full; Full; Yes

McMillan, Frances; 1926-Aug-12; F; Miss. Choctaw; Yes; Full; Full; Full; Yes

McMillan, Ettie; 1926-July-4; F; Miss. Choctaw; Yes; Full; Full; Full; Yes

Smith, Melton; 1926-Oct-5; M; Miss. Choctaw; Yes; Full; Full; Full; Yes

Steve, Minnie; 1926-Aug-28; F; Miss. Choctaw; Yes; Full; Full; Full; Yes

Thompson, Claudine; 1927-Feb-17; F; Miss. Choctaw; Yes; Full; Full; Full; Yes

Tubby, Pauline; 1926-Aug-14; F; Miss. Choctaw; Yes; Full; Full; Full; Yes

Births Occurring Between July 1, 1927 and June 30, 1928 to Parents Enrolled at Jurisdiction

20; **Alex**, Hubert; 1928-Mar-25; m; Miss. Choctaw; Yes; Full; Full; Full; Yes

47; **Anderson**, Nelson; 1927-Oct-29; m; Miss. Choctaw; Yes; Full; Full; Full; Yes

State ___Mississippi___ Reservation _____ Agency
or jurisdiction__Choctaw Indian Agency___ Office of Indian Affairs

Key: Census Roll Number (if given); Surname, Given Name; Date of Birth (Year-Month-Day); Live Births (Yes, unless otherwise given); Still Births (blank unless otherwise given); Sex; Tribe; Ward (Yes/No); Degree of Blood (Father; Mother; Child); At Jurisdiction Where Enrolled (Yes/No); (If no – Where)

17; **Allen**, Willie; 1927-Aug-16; m; Miss. Choctaw; Yes; Full; Full; Full; Yes

150; **Ben**, Mattie Lou; 1928-Apr-5; f; Miss. Choctaw; Yes; Full; Full; Full; Yes

170; **Billy**, Mary Lee; 1928-Apr-?; f; Miss. Choctaw; Yes; Full; Full; Full; Yes

102; **Bell**, James Cook; 1928-Apr-24; m; Miss. Choctaw; Yes; Full; Full; Full; Yes

Billy, William; 1927-Aug-15; m; Miss. Choctaw; Yes; Full; Full; Full; Yes

196; **Billy**, Horace; 1927-Aug-13; m; Miss. Choctaw; Yes; Full; Full; Full; Yes

273; **Chickaway**, Ross; 1928-Apr-11; m; Miss. Choctaw; Yes; Full; Full; Full; Yes

276; **Chickaway**, John; 1927-Dec-5; m; Miss. Choctaw; Yes; Full; Full; Full; Yes

291; **Chitto**, Leo; 1928-Mar-8; m; Miss. Choctaw; Yes; Full; Full; Full; Yes

314; **Clemons**, Hester; 1927-Dec-12; m; Miss. Choctaw; Yes; Full; Full; Full; Yes

311; **Clemons**, Rena Mae; 1928-Jan-15; f; Miss. Choctaw; Yes; Full; Full; Full; Yes

330; **Comby**, Joyce Ann; 1928-Jan; 17; f; Miss. Choctaw; Yes; Full; Full; Full; Yes

416; **Dixon**, Ellen; 1927-Aug-27; f; Miss. Choctaw; Yes; Full; Full; Full; Yes

459; **Farve**, Estelle; 1927-Sept-18; f; Miss. Choctaw; Yes; Full; Full; Full; Yes

566; **Frazier**, Velma; 1928-Jan-24; f; Miss. Choctaw; Yes; Full; Full; Full; Yes

574; **Frazier**, A. B; 1927-Nov-3; m; Miss. Choctaw; Yes; Full; Full; Full; Yes

586; **Gipson**, Aaron; 1927-Dec-16; m; Miss. Choctaw; Yes; Full; Full; Full; Yes

State __Mississippi__ Reservation _____ Agency
or jurisdiction __Choctaw Indian Agency__ Office of Indian Affairs

Key: Census Roll Number (if given); Surname, Given Name; Date of Birth (Year-Month-Day); Live Births (Yes, unless otherwise given); Still Births (blank unless otherwise given); Sex; Tribe; Ward (Yes/No); Degree of Blood (Father; Mother; Child); At Jurisdiction Where Enrolled (Yes/No); (If no – Where)

645; **Hickman**, Mary Ellen; 1928-May-1; f; Miss. Choctaw; Yes; Full; Full; Full; Yes
694; **Isaac**, Claude Preston; 1928-June -20; m; Miss. Choctaw; Yes; Full; Full; Full; Yes
686; **Isaac**, Joe Day; 1927-July-7; m; Miss. Choctaw; Yes; Full; Full; Full; Yes
770; **Jimmie**, Onie; 1928-Mar-1; f; Miss. Choctaw; Yes; Full; Full; Full; Yes
750; **Jim**, Faye; 1927-Aug-14; m[sic]; Miss. Choctaw; Yes; Full; Full; Full; Yes
830; **Johnson**, Callie; 1928-June-15; f; Miss. Choctaw; Yes; Full; Full; Full; Yes
878; **Johnson**, Rena; 1928-May-27; f; Miss. Choctaw; Yes; Full; Full; Full; Yes
940; **McMillan**, Pauline; 1928-June-26; f; Miss. Choctaw; Yes; Full; Full; Full; Yes
931; **McMillan**, Enochs; 1927-Oct-8; m; Miss. Choctaw; Yes; Full; Full; Full; Yes
995; **Nickey**, Copeland; 1928-Apr-1; m; Miss. Choctaw; Yes; Full; Full; Full; Yes
1136; **Steve**, Helen; 1927-Oct-8; f; Miss. Choctaw; Yes; Full; Full; Full; Yes
1150; **Steve**, Audrey; 1927-July-3; f; Miss. Choctaw; Yes; Full; Full; Full; Yes
Sam, Ella Ruth; 1927-Sept-10; f; Miss. Choctaw; Yes; Full; Full; Full; Yes
Stephens, Bobby; 1928-Feb-3; f; Miss. Choctaw; Yes; Full; Full; Full; Yes
1204; **Thompson**, Steve; 1927-Nov-26; m; Miss. Choctaw; Yes; Full; Full; Full; Yes
1246; **Tubby**, Leona; 1927-Aug-28; f; Miss. Choctaw; Yes; Full; Full; Full; Yes
1351; **Wallace**, Houston; 1927-Nov-1; m; Miss. Choctaw; Yes; Full; Full; Full; Yes

State ___Mississippi___ Reservation _____ Agency
or jurisdiction__Choctaw Indian Agency____ Office of Indian Affairs

Key: Census Roll Number (if given); Surname, Given Name; Date of Birth (Year-Month-Day); Live Births (Yes, unless otherwise given); Still Births (blank unless otherwise given); Sex; Tribe; Ward (Yes/No); Degree of Blood (Father; Mother; Child); At Jurisdiction Where Enrolled (Yes/No); (If no – Where)

1464; **Willis,** John B; 1927-Sept-2; m; Miss. Choctaw; Yes; Full; Full; Full; Yes

Births Occurring Between July 1, 1928 and June 30, 1929 to Parents Enrolled at Jurisdiction

134; **Ben,** Henry Ford; 1929-May-9; m; Miss. Choctaw; Yes; Full; Full; Full; Yes

Bell, Jennie; 1928-Nov-24; f; Miss. Choctaw; Yes; Full; Full; Full; Yes

Comby, R. L; 1929-Feb-26; m; Miss. Choctaw; Yes; Full; Full; Full; Yes

282; **Chickaway,** Maggie; 1928-Sept-4; f; Miss. Choctaw; Yes; Full; Full; Full; Yes

367; **Davis,** William; #[sic]-Sept-24; m; Miss. Choctaw; Yes; Full; Full; Full; Yes

Hall, Herbert; 1929-Mar-4; m; Miss. Choctaw; Yes; Full; Full; Full; Yes

630; **Henry,** Wicks John; 1929-Feb-14; m; Miss. Choctaw; Yes; Full; Full; Full; Yes

626; **Henry,** Ellen; 1928-Aug-17; f; Miss. Choctaw; Yes; Full; Full; Full; Yes

678; **Isaac,** Franklin; 1929-May-11; m; Miss. Choctaw; Yes; Full; Full; Full; Yes

692; **Isaac,** Enochs; 1929-May-15; m; Miss. Choctaw; Yes; Full; Full; Full; Yes

944; **Jim,** Bobbie Sue; 1928-Dec-31; f; Miss. Choctaw; Yes; Full; Full; Full; Yes

800; **John,** Lisette; 1929-June-29; f; Miss. Choctaw; Yes; Full; Full; Full; Yes

751; **Jim,** Carter; 1928-Sept-27; m; Miss. Choctaw; Yes; Full; Full; Full; Yes

Jim, Claud Yates; 1928-Aug-18; m; Miss. Choctaw; Yes; Full; Full; Full; Yes

State _____Mississippi_____ Reservation _____ Agency
or jurisdiction __Choctaw Indian Agency____ Office of Indian Affairs

Key: Census Roll Number (if given); Surname, Given Name; Date of Birth (Year-Month-Day); Live Births (Yes, unless otherwise given); Still Births (blank unless otherwise given); Sex; Tribe; Ward (Yes/No); Degree of Blood (Father; Mother; Child); At Jurisdiction Where Enrolled (Yes/No); (If no – Where)

718; **Jefferson**, Otho; 1928-?-?; m; Miss. Choctaw; Yes; Full; Full; Full; Yes

880; **Lewis**, Jennie Lin; 1928-Sept-1; f; Miss. Choctaw; Yes; Full; Full; Full; Yes

920; **McMillan**, John; 1928-Sept-25; m; Miss. Choctaw; Yes; Full; Full; Full; Yes

912; **Martin**, Annie Mae; 1928-July-26; f; Miss. Choctaw; Yes; Full; Full; Full; Yes

1016; **Polk**, Zula; 1928-June-7; f; Miss. Choctaw; Yes; Full; Full; Full; Yes

1011; **Phillips**, M. C; 1928-July-30; m; Miss. Choctaw; Yes; Full; Full; Full; Yes

Solomon, Mollie Lee; 1929-Feb-19; f; Miss. Choctaw; Yes; Full; Full; Full; Yes

1145; **Steve**, Vivian; 1929-May-11; f; Miss. Choctaw; Yes; Full; Full; Full; Yes

1151; **Steve**, Earleen; 1928-Nov-23; f; Miss. Choctaw; Yes; Full; Full; Full; Yes

Sam, Bertha; 1928-Apr-6; f; Miss. Choctaw; Yes; Full; Full; Full; Yes

1222; **Tubby**, Katie; 1929-Feb-6; f; Miss. Choctaw; Yes; Full; Full; Full; Yes

Thompson, Henry; 1928-Dec-22; m; Miss. Choctaw; Yes; Full; Full; Full; Yes

Thompson, Annie; 1928-July-19; f; Miss. Choctaw; Yes; Full; Full; Full; Yes

Tubby, Sallie Mae; 1928-Nov-26; f; Miss. Choctaw; Yes; Full; Full; Full; Yes

1426; **Willis**, Mary Bell; 1929-Jan-23; f; Miss. Choctaw; Yes; Full; Full; Full; Yes

1419; **Willis**, John; 1929-Mar-8; m; Miss. Choctaw; Yes; Full; Full; Full; Yes

1453; **Willis**, Lucy; 1928-Setp[sic]-19; f; Miss. Choctaw; Yes; Full; Full; Full; Yes

State ____Mississippi____ Reservation _____ Agency
or jurisdiction__Choctaw Indian Agency____ Office of Indian Affairs

Key: Census Roll Number (if given); Surname, Given Name; Date of Birth (Year-Month-Day); Live Births (Yes, unless otherwise given); Still Births (blank unless otherwise given); Sex; Tribe; Ward (Yes/No); Degree of Blood (Father; Mother; Child); At Jurisdiction Where Enrolled (Yes/No); (If no – Where)

1492; **Wickson**, Yates; 1928-July-24; m; Miss. Choctaw; Yes; Full; Full; Full; Yes

Births Occurring Between July 1, 1929 and June 30, 1930 to Parents Enrolled at Jurisdiction

13; **Allen**, B. C; 1929-Sept-15; m; Miss. Choctaw; Yes; Full; Full; Full; Yes

120; **Bell**, Marshall; 1929-Nov-9; m; Miss. Choctaw; Yes; Full; Full; Full; Yes

180; **Billy,** Phillip; 1929-Oct-15; m; Miss. Choctaw; Yes; Full; Full; Full; Yes

195; **Billy**, Charles; 1930-Feb-10; m; Miss. Choctaw; Yes; Full; Full; Full; Yes

112; **Bell**, Ruby; 1930-Jan-6; f; Miss. Choctaw; Yes; Full; Full; Full; Yes

135; **Bell**, Sudie; 1929-Oct-?; f; Miss. Choctaw; Yes; Full; Full; Full; Yes

288; **Billy**, Jim; 1930-Jan-?; m; Miss. Choctaw; Yes; Full; Full; Full; Yes

289; **Chitto**, Linnie; 1929-July-11; f; Miss. Choctaw; Yes; Full; Full; Full; Yes

288[sic]; **Chitto**, Lucy; 1929-July-11; f; Miss. Choctaw; Yes; Full; Full; Full; Yes

284; **Chickaway**, Elizabeth; 1930-Mar-11; f; Miss. Choctaw; Yes; Full; Full; Full; Yes

306; **Cowed**, Lewisman; 1929-Nov-1; m; Miss. Choctaw; Yes; Full; Full; Full; Yes

364; **Dan**, Albert; 1929-Dec-15; m; Miss. Choctaw; Yes; Full; Full; Full; Yes

Dixon. Ruby Ruth; 1929-Oct-19; f; Miss. Choctaw; Yes; Full; Full; Full; Yes

498; **Farve**, Viola; 1929-Nov-4; f; Miss. Choctaw; Yes; Full; Full; Full; Yes

State ____ Mississippi ____ Reservation _____ Agency
or jurisdiction __ Choctaw Indian Agency ____ Office of Indian Affairs

Key: Census Roll Number (if given); Surname, Given Name; Date of Birth (Year-Month-Day); Live Births (Yes, unless otherwise given); Still Births (blank unless otherwise given); Sex; Tribe; Ward (Yes/No); Degree of Blood (Father; Mother; Child); At Jurisdiction Where Enrolled (Yes/No); (If no – Where)

534; **Forbes**, Henry; 1929-Dec-5; m; Miss. Choctaw; Yes; Full; Full; Full; Yes

655; **Hickman**, George; 1930-April-25; m; Miss. Choctaw; Yes; Full; Full; Full; Yes

Hall, Henrietta; 1929-Aug-30; f; Miss. Choctaw; Yes; Full; Full; Full; Yes

768; **Jimmie**, Delores; 1929-Oct-3; f; Miss. Choctaw; Yes; Full; Full; Full; Yes

762; **Jim**, Grace; 1929-Oct-13; f; Miss. Choctaw; Yes; Full; Full; Full; Yes

Jim, Egbert; 1929-Aug-15; m; Miss. Choctaw; Yes; Full; Full; Full; Yes

782; **Joe**, Mary; 1929-Dec-10; f; Miss. Choctaw; Yes; Full; Full; Full; Yes

859; **Lewis**, Nannie; 1930-Feb-4; f; Miss. Choctaw; Yes; Full; Full; Full; Yes

Lewis, Lucille; 1929-Sept-16; f; Miss. Choctaw; Yes; Full; Full; Full; Yes

949; **Mingo**, Mary; 1929-Sept-17; f; Miss. Choctaw; Yes; Full; Full; Full; Yes

964; **Morris**, Walter Olin; 1929-Nov-1; m; Miss. Choctaw; Yes; Full; Full; Full; Yes

977; **Morris**, Champ; 1930-June-10; m; Miss. Choctaw; Yes; Full; Full; Full; Yes

324; **McMillan**, Jordon; 1930-Feb-10; m; Miss. Choctaw; Yes; Full; Full; Full; Yes

1135; **Polk**, Hudson; 1930-June-1; m; Miss. Choctaw; Yes; Full; Full; Full; Yes

1118; **Sockey**, Arnold; 1929-Nov-4; m; Miss. Choctaw; Yes; Full; Full; Full; Yes

1148; **Stephens**, Bonnie; 1929-Dec-27; f; Miss. Choctaw; Yes; Full; Full; Full; Yes

1071; **Sam**, Grisiline; 1929-Nov-30; f; Miss. Choctaw; Yes; Full; Full; Full; Yes

State _____ Mississippi _____ Reservation _____ Agency
or jurisdiction__Choctaw Indian Agency____ Office of Indian Affairs

Key: Census Roll Number (if given); Surname, Given Name; Date of Birth (Year-Month-Day); Live Births (Yes, unless otherwise given); Still Births (blank unless otherwise given); Sex; Tribe; Ward (Yes/No); Degree of Blood (Father; Mother; Child); At Jurisdiction Where Enrolled (Yes/No); (If no – Where)

      Stephens, Martha Lee; 1929-July-17; f; Miss. Choctaw; Yes; Full; Full; Full; Yes

1064; **Sam**, Armand; 1930-Feb-2; m; Miss. Choctaw; Yes; Full; Full; Full; Yes

1159; **Steve**, Winston; 1930-Mar-20; m; Miss. Choctaw; Yes; Full; Full; Full; Yes

1158; **Steve**, George; 1930-Mar-20; m; Miss. Choctaw; Yes; Full; Full; Full; Yes

490; **Farmer**, Mealie   [No other information given]

1289; **Tubby**, Etoyle; 1930-Mar-1; m; Miss. Choctaw; Yes; Full; Full; Full; Yes

1408; **Willis**, Joe; 1929-July-10; m; Miss. Choctaw; Yes; Full; Full; Full; Yes

1489; **Willis**, Leighton; 1929-Oct-1; m; Miss. Choctaw; Yes; Full; Full; Full; Yes

1503; **Wilson**, Jim; 1930-Mar-1; m; Miss. Choctaw; Yes; Full; Full; Full; Yes

Births Occurring Between April 1, 1930 and March 31, 1931 to Parents Enrolled at Jurisdiction

174; **Billy**, Jim; 1931-Jan-?; m; Miss. Choctaw; Yes; Full; Full; Full; Yes

182; **Billy**, Betty Jean; 1930-Nov-12; f; Miss. Choctaw; Yes; Full; Full; Full; Yes

220; **Billy**, Paul; 1930-July-11; m; Miss. Choctaw; Yes; Full; Full; Full; Yes

301; **Chickaway**, Henry; 1930-Dec-29; m; Miss. Choctaw; Yes; Full; Full; Full; Yes

413; **Davis**, Lewis; 1930-Oct-2; m; Miss. Choctaw; Yes; Full; Full; Full; Yes

446; **Denson**, Ruth; 1930-Nov-22; f; Miss. Choctaw; Yes; Full; Full; Full; Yes

State __Mississippi____ Reservation _____ Agency
or jurisdiction__Choctaw Indian Agency____ Office of Indian Affairs

Key: Census Roll Number (if given); Surname, Given Name; Date of Birth (Year-Month-Day); Live Births (Yes, unless otherwise given); Still Births (blank unless otherwise given); Sex; Tribe; Ward (Yes/No); Degree of Blood (Father; Mother; Child); At Jurisdiction Where Enrolled (Yes/No); (If no – Where)

   Decow or **Clemons**, Mable C; 1930-Sep-12; f; Miss. Choctaw; Yes; Full; Full; Full; Yes

490; **Farmer**, Mealie; 1930-June-18; f; Miss. Choctaw; Yes; Full; Full; Full; Yes

   Hickman, George L; 1930-Apr-25; m; Miss. Choctaw; Yes; Full; Full; Full; Yes

741; **Isaac**, Venada; 1930-Nov-11; f; Miss. Choctaw; Yes; Full; Full; Full; Yes

761; **Isaac**, Wansey; 1931-Mar-22; f; Miss. Choctaw; Yes; Full; Full; Full; Yes

816; **Jim**, Susie Anna; 1930-Oct-9; f; Miss. Choctaw; Yes; Full; Full; Full; Yes

895; **John**, Macele; 1930-Aug-?; f; Miss. Choctaw; Yes; Full; Full; Full; Yes

1022; **Martin**, Thomas; 1930-Oct-14; m; Miss. Choctaw; Yes; Full; Full; Full; Yes

1019; **Martin**, Harry M; 1931-Mar-6; m; Miss. Choctaw; Yes; Full; Full; Full; Yes

1046; **McMillan**, Mattie; 1930-July-21; f; Miss. Choctaw; Yes; Full; Full; Full; Yes

   Morris, Chester; 1930-June-10; m; Miss. Choctaw; Yes; Full; Full; Full; Yes

1135; **Polk**, Hudson; 1930-June-1; m; Miss. Choctaw; Yes; Full; Full; Full; Yes

1321; **Thomas**, Linnie Helen; 1930-Oct-8; f; Miss. Choctaw; Yes; Full; Full; Full; Yes

1353; **Thompson**, Nathan; 1930-Oct-6; m; Miss. Choctaw; Yes; Full; Full; Full; Yes

1429; **Tubby**, Martha Lee; 1930-Aug-31; f; Miss. Choctaw; Yes; Full; Full; Full; Yes

1532; **Williams**, Carter; 1930-Nov-8; m; Miss. Choctaw; Yes; Full; Full; Full; Yes

490; **Farmer,** Mealie; 1930-June-18; f; Miss. Choctaw; Yes; Full; Full; Full; Yes

State _____Mississippi_____ Reservation _____ Agency
or jurisdiction__Choctaw Indian Agency____ Office of Indian Affairs

Key: Census Roll Number (if given); Surname, Given Name; Date of Birth (Year-Month-Day); Live Births (Yes, unless otherwise given); Still Births (blank unless otherwise given); Sex; Tribe; Ward (Yes/No); Degree of Blood (Father; Mother; Child); At Jurisdiction Where Enrolled (Yes/No); (If no – Where)

Births Occurring Between April 1, 1931 and March 31, 1932 to Parents Enrolled at Jurisdiction

142; **Bell**, Naomi Ruth; 1931-Oct-9; f; Miss. Choctaw; Yes; Yes; F; F; F; Yes

107; **Bell**, Gibson, Jr; 1932-March-5; m; Miss. Choctaw; Yes; Yes; F; F; F; Yes

97; **Bell**, Herbert Hoover; 1932-March-22; m; Miss. Choctaw; Yes; F; F; F; Yes

104; **Bell**, Bonnie Kate; 1931-May-1; f; Miss. Choctaw; Yes; F; F; F; Yes

170; **Ben**, Grace Opal; 1931-Oct-2; f; Miss. Choctaw; Yes; F; F; F; Yes

195; **Billy**, Cicero L; 1931-June-29; m; Miss. Choctaw; Yes; F; F; F; Yes

230; **Billy**, Duley; 1931-Dec-2; m; Miss. Choctaw; Yes; F; F; F; Yes

250; **Briscoe**, John Claud Yates; 1932-Feb-14; m; Miss. Choctaw; Yes; F; F; F; Yes

304; **Chickaway**, Mary; 1931-Apr-30; f; Miss. Choctaw; Yes; F; F; F; Yes

440; **Denson**, Jennie E; 1932-Mar-22; f; Miss. Choctaw; Yes; F; F; F; Yes

433; **Farmer**, Eula Mae; 1931-Aug-20; f; Miss. Choctaw; Yes; F; F; F; Yes

636; **Gipson**, Henrietta; 1931-Aug-13; f; Miss. Choctaw; Yes; F; F; F; Yes

659; **Hall**, Francis; 1931-Dec-12; m; Miss. Choctaw; Yes; F; F; F; Yes

729; **Isaac**, Jesse Andrew; 1932-Mar-8; m; Miss. Choctaw; Yes; F; F; F; Yes

823; **Jim**, Christine; 1931-Jul-21; f; Miss. Choctaw; Yes; F; F; F; Yes

State ___Mississippi___ Reservation _____ Agency
or jurisdiction___Choctaw Indian Agency____ Office of Indian Affairs

Key: Census Roll Number (if given); Surname, Given Name; Date of Birth (Year-Month-Day); Live Births (Yes, unless otherwise given); Still Births (blank unless otherwise given); Sex; Tribe; Ward (Yes/No); Degree of Blood (Father; Mother; Child); At Jurisdiction Where Enrolled (Yes/No); (If no – Where)

  829; **Jim**, Wm Murray; 1932-Mar-28; m; Miss. Choctaw; Yes; F; F; F; Yes

      Jim, Betty Lou; 1931-June-7; f; Miss. Choctaw; Yes; F; F; F; Yes

  797; **Jefferson**, Leon; 1931-Aug-23; m; Miss. Choctaw; Yes; F; F; F; Yes

  889; **John**, Egbert; 1931-May-4; m; Miss. Choctaw; Yes; F; F; F; Yes

  936; **Johnson**, Marvin; 1931-May-5; m; Miss. Choctaw; Yes; F; F; F; Yes

  926; **Johnson**, Phelia; 1931-June-14; f; Miss. Choctaw; Yes; F; F; F; Yes

1007; **Lewis**, Willie; 1931-Aug-26; m; Miss. Choctaw; Yes; F; F; F; Yes

  988; **Lewis**, Printess; 1931-Jul-29; m; Miss. Choctaw; Yes; F; F; F; Yes

      McMillan, James; 1931-May-3; m; Miss. Choctaw; Yes; F; F; F; Yes

1040; **McMillan**, Lurline; 1931-Aug-6; f; Miss. Choctaw; Yes; F; F; F; Yes

1054; **McMillan**, Jean; 1931-May-3; f; Miss. Choctaw; Yes; F; F; F; Yes

1300; **Steve**, Rebecca; 1931-Apr-21; f; Miss. Choctaw; Yes; F; F; F; Yes

1293; **Steve**, Marguarite; 1931-May-19; f; Miss. Choctaw; Yes; F; F; F; Yes

1271; **Stephens**, Mary Francis; 1931-Aug-19; f; Miss. Choctaw; Yes; F; F; F; Yes

1337; **Thompson**, Oneva; 1931-Apr-1; f; Miss. Choctaw; Yes; F; F; F; Yes

1373; **Tubby**, Robert; 1931-Dec-4; m; Miss. Choctaw; Yes; F; F; F; Yes

1428; **Tubby**, Bessie; 1932-Feb-3; f; Miss. Choctaw; Yes; F; F; F; Yes

1614; **Willis**, Hayward; 1931-Apr-24; m; Miss. Choctaw; Yes; F; F; F; Yes

1502; **Waiter**, Cora Mae; 1931-Jul-2; f; Miss. Choctaw; Yes; F; F; F; Yes

1594; **Willis**, Earl; 1931-Apr-24; m; Miss. Choctaw; Yes; F; F; F; Yes

State ____Mississippi____ Reservation _____ Agency
or jurisdiction___Choctaw Indian Agency____ Office of Indian Affairs

Key: Census Roll Number (if given); Surname, Given Name; Date of Birth (Year-Month-Day); Live Births (Yes, unless otherwise given); Still Births (blank unless otherwise given); Sex; Tribe; Ward (Yes/No); Degree of Blood (Father; Mother; Child); At Jurisdiction Where Enrolled (Yes/No); (If no – Where)

1575; **Willis**, Sarah; 1931-Aug-29; f; Miss. Choctaw; Yes; F; F; F; Yes

RECAPITULATION OF BIRTHS COVERING
THE ABOVE PERIOD
Males - - - -   15
Females - - - - - 19

Births as of April 1, 1931

Key: Census Roll Number; Surname, Given Name; Sex; Age; Tribe; Degree of Blood; Marital Status; Relationship to Head of Family; At Jurisdiction Where Enrolled (Yes/No)

- 174; **Billy**, Jim; m; 3/12; Miss. Choctaw; F; S; Son; Yes
- 182; **Billy**, Betty Jean; f; 3/12; Miss. Choctaw; F; S; Dau; Yes
- 220; **Billy**, Paul; m; 9/12; Miss. Choctaw; F; S; Son; Yes
- 301; **Chickaway**, Henry; m; 3/12; Miss. Choctaw; F; S; Son; Yes
- 413; **Davis**, Lewis; m; 6/12; Miss. Choctaw; F; S; Son; Yes
- 446; **Denson**, Ruth; f; 4/12; Miss. Choctaw; F; S; Daughter; Yes; Yes
- 454; **Dixon**, Mable C; f; 7/12; Miss. Choctaw; F; S; Daughter; Yes; Yes
- 490; **Farmer**, Mealie; f; 9/12; Miss. Choctaw; F; S; Daughter; Yes; Yes
- 741; **Isaac**, Veneda; f; 5/12; Miss. Choctaw; F; S; Daughter; Yes
- 761; **Isaac**, Wansey; f; 1/12; Miss. Choctaw; F; S; Daughter; Yes
- 816; **Jim**, Susie Ann; f; 7/12; Miss. Choctaw; F; S; Daughter; Yes
- 895; **John**, Macele; f; 8/12; Miss. Choctaw; F; S; Daughter; Yes
- 1022; **Martin**, Thomas; m; 8/12; Miss. Choctaw; F; S; Son; Yes
- 1019; **Martin**, Harry M; m; 1/12; Miss. Choctaw; F; S; Son; Yes
- 1045; **McMillen**, Mattie; f; 10/12; Miss. Choctaw; F; S; Daughter; Yes
- 1135; **Polk**, Hudson; Yes; m; 9/12; Miss. Choctaw; F; S; Son; Yes
- 1209; **Shoemaker**, Hubert; m; 6/12; Miss. Choctaw; F; S; Son; Yes
- 1321; **Thomas**, Linnie Helen; f; 6/12; Miss. Choctaw; F; S; Daughter; Yes
- 1353; **Thompson**, Nathan; m; 6/12; Miss. Choctaw; F; S; Son; Yes
- 1429; **Tubby**, Martha Lee; f; 7/12; Miss. Choctaw; F; S; Daughter; Yes
- 1532; **Williams**, Carter; m; 5/12; Miss. Choctaw; F; S; Son; Yes

DEATHS -

July 1, 1924 to March 31, 1932

Choctaw Indian Agency, Mississippi.

State _____Mississippi_____ Reservation _____ Agency
or jurisdiction___Choctaw Indian Agency_____ Office of Indian Affairs

Key: Year and Number Last Census Roll (if given); Surname, Given Name; Date of Death (Year-Month-Day); Age at Death; Sex; Tribe; Ward (Yes/No); Degree of Blood; Cause of Death (if given); At Jurisdiction Where Enrolled (Yes/No); (If no – Where)

Deaths Occurring Between July 1, 1924 and June 30, 1925 of Indians Enrolled at Jurisdiction

Alex, Celie; 1924-Oct-30; 60; f; Miss. Choctaw; Yes; Full; Pneumonia; Yes

Chitto, Nora; 1925-May-2; 30; f; Miss. Choctaw; Yes; Full; Nephritis; Yes

Comby, Gus; 1925-Jan-5; 35; m; Miss. Choctaw; Yes; Full; Pulmonary T.B.; Yes

Farmer, Tom; 1925-Apr-7; 70; m; Miss. Choctaw; Yes; Full; Pulmonary T.B.; Yes

Isaac, Watson; 1925-June-23; m; Miss. Choctaw; Yes; Full; Appendicitis; Yes

Jim, Emily; 1925-Feb-18; f; Miss. Choctaw; Yes; Full; Accidental Gun Shot; Yes

Jackson, Summer; 1925-Feb-19; 37; m[sic]; Miss. Choctaw; Yes; Full; Pneumonia; Yes

McMillan, Fannie; 1925-Feb-4; 5; f; Miss. Choctaw; Yes; Full; Pneumonia; Yes

Polk, Mary Gabriel; 1925-Jan-19; 1; f; Miss. Choctaw; Yes; Full; Pneumonia; Yes

Stribling, Budd; 1925-June-21; 45; m; Miss. Choctaw; Yes; Full; Gun Shot Wound, Homicide; Yes

Stoliby, Solomon; 1925-April-12; 65; f[sic]; Miss. Choctaw; Yes; Full; Brights Disease; Yes

York, Wilbur; 1924-July-6; 1; m; Miss. Choctaw; Yes; Full; Malaria; Yes

Deaths Occurring Between July 1, 1925 and June 30, 1926 of Indians Enrolled at Jurisdiction

Billy, Betty; 1926-Mar-10; 44; f; Miss. Choctaw; Yes; Full; Influenza; Yes

Farmer, Isom; 1925-Dec-25; 28; m; Miss. Choctaw; Yes; Full; Gun Shot Wound, Homicide; Yes

State _____ Mississippi _____ Reservation _____ Agency
or jurisdiction __ Choctaw Indian Agency _____ Office of Indian Affairs

Key: Year and Number Last Census Roll (if given); Surname, Given Name; Date of Death (Year-Month-Day); Age at Death; Sex; Tribe; Ward (Yes/No); Degree of Blood; Cause of Death (if given); At Jurisdiction Where Enrolled (Yes/No); (If no – Where)

Jim, Mina; 1925-July-18; 30; f; Miss. Choctaw; Yes; Full; Puerperal Eclampsia; Yes

Lewis, Louise; 1926-June-30; 26; f; Miss. Choctaw; Yes; Full; Puerperal Eclampsia; Yes

McMillan, Mary; 1925-Sept-7; 1/6; f; Miss. Choctaw; Yes; Full; Dysentery; Yes

Polk, Augustine; 1925-De-10; 1/2; m; Miss. Choctaw; Yes; Full; Influenza; Yes

Star, Minnie; 1926-Mar-19; 30; f; Miss. Choctaw; Yes; Full; Pulmonary T.B.; Yes

Wesley, Leon; 1925-July-16; 18; m; Miss. Choctaw; Yes; Full; Pulmonary T.B.; Yes

Wesley, Johnson; 1925-July-18; 80; m; Miss. Choctaw; Yes; Full; Heart Failure; Yes

Hickman, Willis; 1925-July-17; 50; m; Miss. Choctaw; Yes; Full; Gun Shot Wound, Homicide; Yes

Wilson, Alonzo; 1925-Oct-22; 3; m; Miss. Choctaw; Yes; Full; Locked Bowels; Yes

Wilson, Paul; 1926-Jan-12; 2/3; m; Miss. Choctaw; Yes; Full; Bronchitis; Yes

Wilson, Peter; 1925-Dec-31; 2/3; m; Miss. Choctaw; Yes; Full; Pneumonia; Yes

Deaths Occurring Between July 1, 1926 and June 30, 1927 of Indians Enrolled at Jurisdiction

Alex, Henry; 1926-Oct-27; 5/6; m; Miss. Choctaw; Yes; Full; Pneumonia; Yes

Davis, Harry; 1927-Mar-21; 2 das; m; Miss. Choctaw; Yes; Full; Umbilical Infection; Yes

Isom, Molly; 1926-Nov-14; 60; f; Miss. Choctaw; Yes; Full; Influenza; Yes

McMillan, Ettie; 1926-Nov-14; 60; f; Miss. Choctaw; Yes; Full; Pulmonary T.B.; Yes

State ___Mississippi___ Reservation _____ Agency
or jurisdiction___Choctaw Indian Agency___ Office of Indian Affairs

Key: Year and Number Last Census Roll (if given); Surname, Given Name; Date of Death (Year-Month-Day); Age at Death; Sex; Tribe; Ward (Yes/No); Degree of Blood; Cause of Death (if given); At Jurisdiction Where Enrolled (Yes/No); (If no – Where)

Polk, Winston; 1927-Feb-12; 60; m; Miss. Choctaw; Yes; Full; Pneumonia; Yes

Stoliby, Sarah; 1927-June-10; 44; f; Miss. Choctaw; Yes; Full; T.B. Meningitis; Yes

Wishark[sic], Frank; 1927-April-4; 3; m; Miss. Choctaw; Yes; Full; Bronchitis; Yes

Deaths Occurring Between July 1, 1927 and June 30, 1928 of Indians Enrolled at Jurisdiction

Ben, Lillian; 1927-Dec-30; 17; f; Miss. Choctaw; Yes; Full; Pulmonary T.B.; Yes

Bell, Olis; 1928-Feb-21; 5; m; Miss. Choctaw; Yes; Full; Burns caused from open fireplace; Yes

Denson, Millie; 1928-May-14; 58; f; Miss. Choctaw; Yes; Full; Pulmonary T.B.; Yes

Isaac, Eleyann; 1928-June-22; 24; f; Miss. Choctaw; Yes; Full; Puerperal Eclopsia[sic]; Yes

Isaac, Ella; 1928-Jan-13; 26; f; Miss. Choctaw; Yes; Full; Dilation of Heart; Yes

Lewis, Henry; 1928-Mar-31; 4; m; Miss. Choctaw; Yes; Full; Pulmonary T.B.; Yes

McMillan, William; 1927-Dec-25; 12; m; Miss. Choctaw; Yes; Full; Hookworm; Yes

Waiter, Ada Bell; 1928-May-11; 23; f; Miss. Choctaw; Yes; Full; Pneumonia; Yes

Deaths Occurring Between July 1, 1928 and June 30, 1929 of Indians Enrolled at Jurisdiction

1928; 18; **Alex**, George; 1928-Dec-22; 23; m; Miss. Choctaw; Yes; Full; Pulmonary T.B.; Yes

1928; 42; **Anderson**, H. B; 1928-Aug-2; 19; m; Miss. Choctaw; Yes; Full; Pneumonia; Yes

State _____ Mississippi _____ Reservation _____ Agency
or jurisdiction __ Choctaw Indian Agency_____ Office of Indian Affairs

Key: Year and Number Last Census Roll (if given); Surname, Given Name; Date of Death (Year-Month-Day); Age at Death; Sex; Tribe; Ward (Yes/No); Degree of Blood; Cause of Death (if given); At Jurisdiction Where Enrolled (Yes/No); (If no – Where)

1928; 87; **Barney**, Thompson; 1929-Jan-29; 19; m; Miss. Choctaw; Yes; Full; Pneumonia; Yes

1928; 110; **Bell**, Chester; 1928-Oct-20; 5; m; Miss. Choctaw; Yes; Full; Diphtheria; Yes

1928; 346; **Cooper**, Allie; 1929-Jan-22; 12; f; Miss. Choctaw; Yes; Full; Pneumonia; Yes

1928; 345; **Cooper**, Arthur; 1929-Jan-9; 16; m; Miss. Choctaw; Yes; Full; Pneumonia; Yes

1928; **Comby**, Jennie; 1928-July-29; 80; f; Miss. Choctaw; Yes; Full; Mitral Leak; Yes

1928; 378; **Davis**, Jim; 1928-Aug-2; 69; m; Miss. Choctaw; Yes; Full; Nephritis; Yes

1928; 449; **Farmer**, John; 1928-Dec-25; 64; m; Miss. Choctaw; Yes; Full; Alcoholism; Yes

1928; 706; **Jackson**, Alex; 1928-July-15; 22; m; Miss. Choctaw; Yes; Full; Influenza; Yes

1928; **Jim**, Agnes; 1928-Sept-27; 78; f; Miss. Choctaw; Yes; Full; Acute Indigestion; Yes

1928; 807; **John**, Ruby; 1929-Mar-25; 13; f; Miss. Choctaw; Yes; Full; Pneumonia; Yes

1928; 750; **Jim**, Mary; 1929-Jan-9; 20; f; Miss. Choctaw; Yes; Full; Influenza; Yes

1928; 735; **Jim**, Billy; 1929-Feb-26; 70; m; Miss. Choctaw; Yes; Full; Senile Atrophy; Yes

1928; 748; **Jefferson**, Liza; 1929-Apr-18; 18; f; Miss. Choctaw; Yes; Full; Puerperal Eclampsia; Yes

1928; 839; **Jackson**, King; 1929-Apr-20; 45; m; Miss. Choctaw; Yes; Full; Auto accident; Yes

1928; 846; **King**, Jimmie; 1928-July-22; 28; m; Miss. Choctaw; Yes; Full; Syphillis[sic]; Yes

1928; 867; **Lewis**, John; 1929-Mar-22; 75; m; Miss. Choctaw; Yes; Full; Pneumonia; Yes

1928; 961; **Mitch**, Arch; 1929-Jan-23; 49; m; Miss. Choctaw; Yes; Full; Alcoholism; Yes

State _____ Mississippi _____ Reservation _____ Agency
or jurisdiction__ Choctaw Indian Agency ____ Office of Indian Affairs

Key: Year and Number Last Census Roll (if given); Surname, Given Name; Date of Death (Year-Month-Day); Age at Death; Sex; Tribe; Ward (Yes/No); Degree of Blood; Cause of Death (if given); At Jurisdiction Where Enrolled (Yes/No); (If no – Where).

1928;1004; **Noah**, Tom; 1938[sic]-Dec-25; 60; m; Miss. Choctaw; Yes; Full; Accidental Drowning; Yes

1928; 1010; **Phillips**, Beulah; 1929-June-17; 21; f; Miss. Choctaw; Yes; Full; Acute Appendicitis; Yes

1928; 1011; **Phillips**, Louisa; 1929-June-18; 105; f; Miss. Choctaw; Yes; Full; Intussuseption[sic]; Yes

1928; 1013; **Polk**, Mary; 1929-Marc-16; 50; f; Miss. Choctaw; Yes; Full; Pneumonia; Yes

1928; 1040; **Robinson**, Willis; 1929-Jan-16; 14; m; Miss. Choctaw; Yes; Full; Influenza; Yes

1928; 1056; **Sam**, Houston; 1928-Oct-20; 38; m; Miss. Choctaw; Yes; Full; Chronic Nephritis; Yes

1928; 1125; **Stephens**, Betsy; 1929-June-16; 104; f; Miss. Choctaw; Yes; Full; Old Age; Yes

1928; **Tubby**, Sallie Mae; 1928-Dec-30; 1/12; f; Miss. Choctaw; Yes; Full; Pneumonia; Yes

1928; 1304; **Tubby**, T. B; 1929-May-19; 24; m; Miss. Choctaw; Yes; Full; Pulmonary T.B; Yes

1928; **Tubby**, Sim; 1928-Dec-28; 70; m; Miss. Choctaw; Yes; Full; Hepatic Abscess; Yes

1928; 1232; **Tubby**, Maud; 1928-Dec-2; 21; f; Miss. Choctaw; Yes; Full; Pulmonary T.B; Yes

1928; 1347; **Wallace**, Lewis; 1929-Jan-30; 55; m; Miss. Choctaw; Yes; Full; Influenza; Yes

1928; 1424; **Willis**, Emmett; 1928-Aug-25; 17; m; Miss. Choctaw; Yes; Full; Pulmonary T.B; Yes

1928; 1373; **Williams**, Elsie; 1929-May-15; 14; f; Miss. Choctaw; Yes; Full; Typhoid; Yes

1928; 1457; **Willis**, Dixon; 1929-Jan-9; 95; m; Miss. Choctaw; Yes; Full; Influenza; Yes

Wickson, Lola; 1928-July-24; 25; f; Miss. Choctaw; Yes; Full; Peritonis[sic]; Yes

Deaths Occurring Between July 1, 1929 and June 30, 1930 of Indians Enrolled at Jurisdiction

State   Mississippi   Reservation _____ Agency
or jurisdiction   Choctaw Indian Agency   Office of Indian Affairs

Key: Year and Number Last Census Roll (if given); Surname, Given Name; Date of Death (Year-Month-Day); Age at Death; Sex; Tribe; Ward (Yes/No); Degree of Blood; Cause of Death (if given); At Jurisdiction Where Enrolled (Yes/No); (If no – Where)

1929; 63; **Anderson**, Phoebe; 1930-Mar-13; 50; f; Miss. Choctaw; Yes; Full; Atrophy of Liver; Yes

1929; 100; **Bell**, Nash; 1930-Apr-15; 60; m; Miss. Choctaw; Yes; Full; Cholecystitis; Yes

1929; 255; **Charley**, Johnson; 1929-Aug-28; 67; m; Miss. Choctaw; Yes; Full; Typhoid; Yes

1929; 388; **Denson**, Lula; 1929-Aug-22; 11; f; Miss. Choctaw; Yes; Full; Pulmonary T.B; Yes

1929; 367; **Davis**, William; 1929-Sept-29; 1; m; Miss. Choctaw; Yes; Full; Colitis; Yes

1929; 413; **Dixon**, Phillip; 1930-Apr-6; 52; m; Miss. Choctaw; Yes; Full; Ulcer of Stomach; Yes

1929; 389; **Denson**, John; 1930-Mar-20; 27; m; Miss. Choctaw; Yes; Full; Acute Appendicitis; Yes

1929; 512; **Farve**, Charles; 1929-Sept-10; 42; m; Miss. Choctaw; Yes; Full; Pneumonia; Yes

1929; 555; **Frazier**, Corrine; 1929-Aug-28; 9; f; d Miss. Choctaw; Yes; Full; Colitis; Yes

1929; 556; **Frazier**, Ellis; 1929-Oct-30; 60; m; Miss. Choctaw; Yes; Full; Pneumonia; Yes

1929; 544; **Frazier**, Eckle; 1929-Dec-26; 54; m; Miss. Choctaw; Yes; Full; Burns (probably from open fire); Yes

1929; 604; **Hall**, Henry; 1929-Aug-25; 21; m; Miss. Choctaw; Yes; Full; Pulmonary T.B; Yes

1929; 597; **Hall**, George; 1929-Sept-6; 22; m; Miss. Choctaw; Yes; Full; Shot accidentally; Yes

1929; 656; **Hickman**, Sam; 1929-Dec-14; 10; m; Miss. Choctaw; Yes; Full; Pneumonia; Yes

1929; 794; **John**, Empsey; 1929-Sept-1; 43; m; Miss. Choctaw; Yes; Full; Gun shot (Homicide); Yes

1929; 718; **Jefferson**, Otho; 1929-July-17; 1; m; Miss. Choctaw; Yes; Full; Pneumonia; Yes

1929; 936; **McMillan**, Annie; 1929-Nov-18; 36; f; Miss. Choctaw; Yes; Full; Cancer of Stomach; Yes

State ____Mississippi____ Reservation _____ Agency
or jurisdiction__Choctaw Indian Agency____ Office of Indian Affairs

Key: Year and Number Last Census Roll (if given); Surname, Given Name; Date of Death (Year-Month-Day); Age at Death; Sex; Tribe; Ward (Yes/No); Degree of Blood; Cause of Death (if given); At Jurisdiction Where Enrolled (Yes/No); (If no – Where)

1928; 1165; **Stribling**, Warder; 1929-Dec-19; 19; f; Miss. Choctaw; Yes; Full; Pulmonary T.B; Yes

1928; 1108; **Solomon**, Bicey; 1929-Nov-13; 56; f; Miss. Choctaw; Yes; Full; Pulmonary T.B; Yes

1929; 1115; **Star**, Dave; 1929-Oct-19; 38; m; Miss. Choctaw; Yes; Full; Gun Shot (Suicide)

1929; 1087; **Smith**, Robert; 1929-Sept-27; 36; m; Miss. Choctaw; Yes; Full; Pneumonia; Yes

1929; 1235; **Tubby**, Henson; 1929-Sept-3; 24; m; Miss. Choctaw; Yes; Full; Pneumonia; Yes

1929; 1238; **Tubby**, Helen; 1929-Nov-3; 51; f; Miss. Choctaw; Yes; Full; Pneumonia; Yes

1929; 1260; **Tubby**, Eliza; 1929-Sept-27; 84; f; Miss. Choctaw; Yes; Full; Cerebral Hemorrhage; Yes

1929; 1228; **Tubby**, Caroline; 1929-Dec-5; 97; f; Miss. Choctaw; Yes; Full; Burns (from open fire); Yes

1929; 1372; **Wilson**, Joseph; 1929-Sept-1; 15; m; Miss. Choctaw; Yes; Full; Pneumonia; Yes

Deaths Occurring Between April 1, 1930 and March 31, 1931 of Indians Enrolled at Jurisdiction

1930; 13; **Allen**, B. C; 1930-Dec-16; 3/4; m; Miss. Choctaw; Yes; Full; Pneumonia; Yes

Ben, Thompson; 1931-Feb-8; 17; m; Miss. Choctaw; Yes; Full; Pulmonary T.B; Yes

1930; 226; **Campbell**, Alice; 1931-Mar-18; 27; f; Miss. Choctaw; Yes; Full; Pulmonary T.B; Yes

1930; 289; **Chitto**, Linnie; 1930-Oct-22; 1 1/4; f; Miss. Choctaw; Yes; Full; Dysentery; Yes

1930; 288; **Chitto**, Lucy; 1930-Oct-22; 1 1/4; f; Miss. Choctaw; Yes; Full; Dysentery; Yes

1930; 300; **Chitto**, Tom; 1930-July-12; 80; m; Miss. Choctaw; Yes; Full; Pneumonia; Yes

State _____Mississippi_____ Reservation _____ Agency
or jurisdiction__Choctaw Indian Agency_____ Office of Indian Affairs

Key: Year and Number Last Census Roll (if given); Surname, Given Name; Date of Death (Year-Month-Day); Age at Death; Sex; Tribe; Ward (Yes/No); Degree of Blood; Cause of Death (if given); At Jurisdiction Where Enrolled (Yes/No); (If no – Where)

1930; 334; **Comby**, William; 1930-June-2; 34; m; Miss. Choctaw; Yes; Full; Auto Accident; Yes

1930; 399; **Denson**, Floyd; 1930-Oct-1; 7; m; Miss. Choctaw; Yes; Full; Diphtheria; Yes

1930; 765; **Jimmie**, Melton; 1931-Jan-11; 28; m; Miss. Choctaw; Yes; Full; Meningitis, Tonsilitis[sic]; Yes

1930; 950; **Mingo**, Horace; 1930-Aug-10; 48; m; Miss. Choctaw; Yes; Full; Gun shot (Homicide); Yes

1930; 834; **Sam**, Joshua; 1930-Dec-12; 75; m; Miss. Choctaw; Yes; Full; Chronic Bronchitis; Yes

1930; 1118; **Sockey**, Arnold; 1931-Feb-28; 1 1/3; m; Miss. Choctaw; Yes; Full; Pneumonia; Yes

1930; 1191; **Stribling**, Vardamon; 1930-May-16; 28; m; Miss. Choctaw; Yes; Full; Pulmonary T.B; Yes

1930; 1192; **Stribling**, Marion; 1930-June-11; 24; m; Miss. Choctaw; Yes; Full; Pulmonary T.B; Yes

1930; 1398; **Warren**, Ellen; 1930-Oct-9; 90; f; Miss. Choctaw; Yes; Full; Mitral Regurgation[sic]; Yes

1930; 1404; **Willis**, Lucy; 1930-June-4; 1 2/3; f; Miss. Choctaw; Yes; Full; Dysentery; Yes

1930; 1445; **Willis**, Adeline; 1930-June-26; 60; f; Miss. Choctaw; Yes; Full; Nephritis; Yes

Deaths Occurring Between April 1, 1931 and March 31, 1932 of Indians Enrolled at Jurisdiction

1931; 2; **Alex**, Lee; 1932-Jan-19; 45; m; Miss. Choctaw; Yes; Full; Heart disease; Yes

1931; 236; **Boyd**, Elizabeth; 1931-Oct-10; 71; f; Miss. Choctaw; Yes; Full; Heart disease; Yes

1931; 243; **Bull**, Emma; 1932-Feb-12; 55; f; Miss. Choctaw; Yes; Full; Heart disease; Yes

1931; 393; **Dan**, S. D; 1931-Apr-4; 26; m; Miss. Choctaw; Yes; Full; Pulmo. tuberculosis; Yes

State _____ Mississippi _____ Reservation _____ Agency
or jurisdiction __ Choctaw Indian Agency _____ Office of Indian Affairs

Key: Year and Number Last Census Roll (if given); Surname, Given Name; Date of Death (Year-Month-Day); Age at Death; Sex; Tribe; Ward (Yes/No); Degree of Blood; Cause of Death (if given); At Jurisdiction Where Enrolled (Yes/No); (If no – Where)

1931; 426; **Davis**, Cilian; 1931-Apr-4; 30; f; Miss. Choctaw; Yes; Full; F[sic] tuberculosis; Yes

1931; 494; **Farmer**, Lena; 1931-Aug-20; 17; f; Miss. Choctaw; Yes; Full; Eclampsia; Yes

1931; 736; **Isaac,** Beaman; 1931-May-18; 18; m; Miss. Choctaw; Yes; Full; Pulmo. tuberculosis; Yes

1931; 834; **Jim**, Clifton; 1931-May-22; 10; m; Miss. Choctaw; Yes; Full; Acute nephritis; Yes

Jim, Betty Lou; 1931-Sept-21; 3/12; f; Miss. Choctaw; Yes; Full; Diarrhea; Yes

1931; 1075; **Morris**, Rich; 1931-Dec-3; 24; m; Miss. Choctaw; Yes; Full; Pulmo. tuberculosis; Yes

McMillan, Gene; 1931-June-8; 1/12; f; Miss. Choctaw; Yes; Full; Gastro Enteritis; Yes

1931; 1040; **McMillan**, Egbert; 1931-April-5; 30; m; Miss. Choctaw; Yes; Full; Pulmo. tuberculosis; Yes

1931; 1273; **Steve**, George; 1931-Oct-4; 1; m; Miss. Choctaw; Yes; Full; Diarrhea; Yes

1931; 1492; **Waiter**, Ruby; 1931-Nov-28; 21; f; Miss. Choctaw; Yes; Full; Pulmo. tuberculosis; Yes

1931; 1560; **Willis**, Onie; 1931-Sept-3; 6; f; Miss. Choctaw; Yes; Full; Pneumonia; Yes

RECAPITULATION OF DEATHS COVERING THE ABOVE PERIOD.
    Females 6
    Males   7
    Total - - 13

Deaths as of April 1, 1931

Key: Census Number; Surname, Given Name; Sex; Age at Last Birthday; Tribe; Degree of Blood; Marital Status; Relationship to Head of Family; At Jurisdiction Where Enrolled (Yes/No)

- 14; **Allen**, B. C; m; 7/12; Miss. Choctaw; F; S; Son; Yes
- 50; **Anderson**; Fronie Mae; f; 2; Miss. Choctaw; F; S; Daughter; Yes
- 169; **Ben**, Thompson; m; 11; Miss. Choctaw; F; S; Son; Yes
- 246; **Campbell**, Alice; f; 29; Miss. Choctaw; F; M; Wife; Yes
- 312; **Chitto**, Lucy D; f; 9/12; Miss. Choctaw; F; S; Daughter; Yes
- 312; **Chitto**, Linnie Mc; f; 9/12; Miss. Choctaw; F; S; Daughter; Yes
- 326; **Chitto**, Tom; m; 70; Miss. Choctaw; F; M; Head; Yes
- 347; **Clemons**, Sleeper; m; Miss. Choctaw; F; S; Son; Yes
- 362; **Comby**, William; m; 34; Miss. Choctaw; F; M; Head; Yes
- 438, **Denson**, Floyd; m; 3; Miss. Choctaw; F; S; Son; Yes
- 839; **Jimmie**, Melton; m; 26; Miss. Choctaw; F; M; Head; Yes
- 926; **Joshua**, Sam; m; 80; Miss. Choctaw; F; M; Head; Yes
- 1055; **Mingo**, Horace; m; 48; Miss. Choctaw; F; M; Head; Yes
- 1231; **Sockey**, Arnold; m; 5/12; Miss. Choctaw; F; S; Son; Yes
- 1296; **Stribling**, Varderman; m; 28; Miss. Choctaw; F; S; Son; Yes
- 1297; **Stribling**, Marvin; m; 24; Miss. Choctaw; F; S; Son; Yes
- 1499; **Warner**, Ellen; f; 90; Miss. Choctaw; F; Wd; Head; Yes
- 1538; **Willis**, Lucy; f; 2; Miss. Choctaw; F; S; Daughter; Yes
- 1157; **Robinson**, Mary; f; 82; Miss. Choctaw; F; Wd; Head; Yes

Limited Index

ALEX
  Celie 305
  George...307
  Henry....................................288,306
  Herbert F 108,180,252
  Hubert...290
  Lee...312
ALLEN
  B C 295,311,313
  Willie..291
ANDERSON
  Fronie Mae 313
  H B...307
  J C 287
  Nelson...290
  Phoebe 310
  Sallie Mae 288
BARNEY, Thompson.................308
BELL
  Bonnie Kate..................................299
  Burton 95,167,239
  Chester 308
  Ella...31
  Gibson, Jr.......................................299
  Henry 95,167,239
  Herbert Hoover 299
  Homer...289
  Horace...291
  James Cook...................................291
  Jennie 293
  Joe..269
  Marshall...295
  Naomi Ruth.................................299
  Nash 310
  Olis 307
  Ruby...295
  Sudie 295
BEN
  Anna Laura 287
  Grace Opal 299
  Henry Ford..................................293
  Hubert...288
  Lillian...307
  Mattie Lou 291
  Rufus 122,195,267
  Thompson 311,313
  Wilson 130,202,275
BENN
  Aline 12
  Wilson 61,64
BILLY
  Betty 305
  Betty Jean 297,302
  Charles 295
  Cicero L 299
  Clemon................40,108,181,253
  Duley 299
  Egbert..38
  Emma 97,170,242
  Frank..287
  James 288
  Jim...............................295,297,302
  Joseph...288
  Mary Lee 291
  Maurice 290
  Paul.......................................297,302
  Phillip 295
BOX
  Eula......................................135,207
  Mamie......................135,176,247
  Ola 135
  Sam Davis 163,235
BOYD, Elizabeth 312
BRISCOE
  Egbert 107,180,252
  Jim..............................107,180,252
  John Claud Yates....................299
  Stephens 107
BULL, Emma 312
CAMPBELL
  Alice....................................311,313
  Ginnie 69
CHAPMAN
  Lilly..288
  Raymond......................................288
CHARLES
  James 217
  Jim..73,145
CHARLEY
  Beckey 28

Limited Index

Johnson..................................310
CHARLIE, Beckie...........96,168,240
CHICKAWAY
   Albert....................................288
   Anna.....................................288
   Elizabeth..............................295
   Henry............................297,302
   John......................................291
   Maggie.................................293
   Mary.....................................299
   Ross......................................291
CHITTO
   Isom......................................287
   Leo..291
   Linnie............................295,311
   Linnie Mc.............................313
   Lucy...............................295,311
   Lucy D..................................313
   Mary.........................81,153,225
   Nora......................................305
   Tom................................311,313
CLEMONS
   Hester...................................291
   Mable C................................298
   Rena Mae.............................291
   Sleeper.................................313
COMBY
   Gus......................103,176,248,305
   Guss..36
   Irene.....................................289
   Jennie...................................308
   Joyce Ann............................291
   Le Roy..................................288
   R L..293
   Vena..36
   Venie.........................103,176,248
   William...........................312,313
COOPER
   Allie......................................308
   Arthur..................................308
COWED, Lewisman......................295
CRENSHAW
   Amos..............................154,226
   Austin.............................154,226
DAN

   Albert....................................295
   Louisana..............................100
   S D..312
DAVIS
   Cilian....................................313
   Harry.............................290,306
   Jim..308
   Lewis.............................297,302
   Mary.....................................290
   William..........................293,310
DECOW, Mable C......................298
DENSON
   Floyd..............................312,313
   Jennie E................................299
   Joe..247
   John......................................310
   Lula......................................310
   Millie....................................307
   Ruth...............................297,302
   Winston................................279
DIXON
   Ellen.....................................291
   Imogene...............................290
   Lonie........................67,139,211
   Mable C................................302
   Phillip..................................310
   Ruby Ruth............................295
FARMER
   Allie.........................69,141,213
   Annie Mae.........69,141,213,287
   Ella Mae..................69,141,213
   Eula Mae........................228,299
   Grace.......................116,188,260
   Henry......................107,180,252
   Isom......................................305
   John......................................308
   Lena.....................................313
   Lilly Kate................116,188,260
   Mary Lou.............................116
   Mealie......................297,298,302
   Sallie........................100,173,245
   Tom......................................305
FARVE
   Charles.................................310
   Estelle..................................291

Limited Index

Viola 295
Zula Mae 289
FORBES, Henry 296
FOX, Sam Davis 91
FRAZIER
   A B 291
   Corrine 310
   Eckle 310
   Ellie 310
   Velma 291
GIPSON
   Aaron 291
   Henrietta 299
   Minnie 167
GRANT, Rosie Lee 13,78,150,223
HALL
   Francis 299
   Frank 289
   George 310
   Henrietta 296
   Henry 310
   Herbert 293
   Herbert H 99,169,172,240,271
   Herbert Hoover 64
   Ilone 287
   Pauline 99,172,271
HENRY
   Ellen 280
   Frank 290
   Wicks John 293
HICKMAN
   George 296,298
   Mary Ellen 292
   Minnie 271
   Sam 310
   Willis 306
ISAAC
   Beaman 313
   Claude Preston 292
   Coline 8,72,144,216
   Edwin 290
   Eleyann 307
   Ella 307
   Enochs 293
   Eunice 62,131,203,275

Franklin 293
Hickman 64
Isom 62
Jesse Andrew 299
Joe Day 292
Lessie 8,72,144,216
Malton 62
Nannie 62,131,203,275
Rosa 287
Rose 275
Rosie 62,131,203
Tom 62
Veneda 298,302
Wansey 298,302
Watson 305
William 203,276
Wilson 62,131
ISOM
   Mary 68,140,212
   Molly 306
JACKSON
   Alex 308
   King 308
   Sallie 71
   Summer 305
JEFFERSON
   Addie 117
   Esther 106
   Leon 300
   Liza 308
   Malcolm 290
   Nute 106,178,250
   Otho 294,310
   Otto 289
JIM
   Agnes 308
   Betty Lou 300,313
   Billy 308
   Bobbie Sue 293
   Carter 293
   Christine 299
   Claud Yates 293
   Clifton 313
   Egbert 296
   Emily 305

Limited Index

Faye 292
Grace 296
Mary 308
McKinley 289
Mina 306
Susie Ann 302
Susie Anna 298
Wm Murray 300
JIMMIE
   Delores 296
   Melton 312,313
   Onie 292
JOE
   Emly 75,147,220
   Mary 296
JOHN
   Callie 104,177,249
   Edison 104,177,249
   Egbert 300
   Empsey 310
   Lisetta 293
   Macele 298,302
   Ruby 308
   Vardaman 287
JOHNSON
   Callie 292
   Lee 125,270
   Leo 198
   Marvin 300
   Phelia 300
   Rena 292
JOSHUA, Sam 313
KING, Jimmie 308
KINGS, Mollie 104
LEWIS
   Elsie 101,174,246
   Henry 307
   Horace 289
   Jinnie Lin 294
   John 308
   Louise 306
   Lucille 296
   Lum 122,194
   Mamie 94,166
   Marceline 130,202,274

Nannie 296
Printess 300
Susie 101,174,246
Willie 300
MARTIN
   Annie Mae 294
   Harry M 298,302
   Phillip 289
   Thomas 298,302
MCMILLAN
   Annie 310
   Egbert 313
   Enochs 292
   Ettie 290,306
   Fannie 305
   Frances 290
   Gene 313
   James 300
   Jean 300
   John 290,294
   Jordon 296
   Josie 287
   Lurline 300
   Mary 289,306
   Mattie 298
   Pauline 292
   William 307
MCMILLEN
   Mary 232
   Mattie 302
MCMILLIAN
   Ella 81,153,225
   Jimmie 81,153,225
   Jimpson 81,225
   Jordan 81,153,225
   Mary 75,147
MINGO
   Horace 312,313
   Mary 296
   Sarah 289
MITCH, Arch 308
MORRIS
   Champ 296
   Chester 298
   Irene 290

Limited Index

Prentiss 290
Rich 313
Walter Olin 296
MOSES, Alma 64
NICKEY, Copeland 292
NOAH, Tom 309
PHILLIPS
   Beulah 309
   Louisa 309
   M C 294
POLK
   Augustine 287,306
   Frances 76
   Francis 148,220
   Hudson 296,298,302
   Mary 309
   Mary Gabriel 305
   Winston 307
   Zula 294
ROBINSON
   Mary 313
   Willis 309
SAM
   Armand 297
   Bertha 294
   Charlie 85,157,229
   Edna 64,97,169,241,271
   Ella Ruth 292
   Fannie 289
   Grisiline 296
   Houston 309
   Joshua 312
SHOEMAKER
   Hubert 302
   Lesta 27
   Lester 94,166
   Mary 27,166,238
SHUMAKER
   John 289
   Reuben 289
SMITH
   Melton 290
   Robert 311
SOCKEY, Arnold 296,312,313
SOLOMON
   Bicey 311
   Mollie Lee 294
STAR
   Dave 311
   Minnie 306
STEPHENS
   Betsy 309
   Bobby 292
   Bonnie 296
   Martha Lee 297
   Mary Francis 300
   Phoeba 116,189
   Phoebe 261
STEVE
   Audrey 292
   Earleen 294
   George 297,313
   Helen 292
   Marguarite 300
   Mary 289
   Maurice 289
   Minnie 290
   Mollie 289
   Rebecca 300
   Vivian 294
   Winston 297
STOLIBY
   Sarah 307
   Solomon 305
STRIBLING
   Budd 305
   Marion 312
   Marvin 313
   Vardamon 312
   Varderman 313
   Warder 311
THOMAS
   Amos 289
   Linnie Helen 298,302
   Lula 93,165,237
   Mina 287
   Peter 287
THOMPSON
   Alis 287
   Annie 294

Limited Index

Claudine 290
Henry 294
Mary Jane 85,157,229
Nathan 298,302
Oneva 300
Steve 292
TUBBY
   Bessie 300
   Caroline 311
   Eliza 311
   Etoyle 297
   Helen 311
   Henson 311
   Jim 83,155,227
   Katie 294
   Leona 292
   Martha Lee 298,302
   Maud 309
   Odis 287
   Pauline 290
   R B 83,155,227
   Robert 300
   Sallie Mae 63,294,309
   Sam 152,271
   Sim 309
   Sullivan 287
   T B 309
   W C 287
   Wesley 126,198,271
   West 11
UNKNOWN, Aron 93,165
VAUGHN, John 76
WAITER
   Ada Bell 307
   Cora Mae 300
   Ruby 313
WALLACE
   Houston 292
   Lewis 309
WARNER, Ellen 313
WARREN, Ellen 312
WESLEY
   Johnson 306
   Leon 306
   Rufus 110,183,255

WICKSON
   Kelley 288
   Kelly 85,158,230
   Lola 309
   Ollie 107,180,252
   Yates 107,180,252,295
WILLIAMS
   Carter 298,302
   Elsie 309
   Mary Ann 288
WILLIS
   Adeline 312
   Boniface 289
   Boy 288
   Clennie 74,146
   Dina 102,175,246
   Dixon 309
   Earl 300
   Emmett 309
   Hayward 300
   Joe 297
   John 294
   John B 293
   Leighton 297
   Lucy 294,312,313
   Mamie 74,146
   Mary Bell 294
   Maurice 288
   Onie 313
   Sarah 301
WILSON
   Alonzo 306
   Jim 297
   Joseph 311
   Paul 288,306
   Peter 288,306
   Selma 64
WISHARK, Frank 307
WISHORK, Nuga 288
YORK
   J B 288
   Lena Pearl 131
   Wilbur 305

www.ingramcontent.com/pod-product-compliance
Lightning Source LLC
Chambersburg PA
CBHW020239030426
42336CB00010B/544